Critical Schooling

Francisco J. Villegas · Janelle Brady
Editors

Critical Schooling

Transformative Theory and Practice

Editors
Francisco J. Villegas
Anthropology and Sociology
Kalamazoo College
Kalamazoo, MI, USA

Janelle Brady
University of Toronto
Toronto, ON, Canada

ISBN 978-3-030-00715-7   ISBN 978-3-030-00716-4 (eBook)
https://doi.org/10.1007/978-3-030-00716-4

Library of Congress Control Number: 2018956817

© The Editor(s) (if applicable) and The Author(s) 2019
This work is subject to copyright. All rights are solely and exclusively licensed by the Publisher, whether the whole or part of the material is concerned, specifically the rights of translation, reprinting, reuse of illustrations, recitation, broadcasting, reproduction on microfilms or in any other physical way, and transmission or information storage and retrieval, electronic adaptation, computer software, or by similar or dissimilar methodology now known or hereafter developed.
The use of general descriptive names, registered names, trademarks, service marks, etc. in this publication does not imply, even in the absence of a specific statement, that such names are exempt from the relevant protective laws and regulations and therefore free for general use.
The publisher, the authors and the editors are safe to assume that the advice and information in this book are believed to be true and accurate at the date of publication. Neither the publisher nor the authors or the editors give a warranty, express or implied, with respect to the material contained herein or for any errors or omissions that may have been made. The publisher remains neutral with regard to jurisdictional claims in published maps and institutional affiliations.

Cover illustration: © Paloma E. Villegas

This Palgrave Macmillan imprint is published by the registered company Springer Nature Switzerland AG
The registered company address is: Gewerbestrasse 11, 6330 Cham, Switzerland

This book is dedicated to our mothers Amelia Jimenez and Sheryl Brady who taught us the value of breaking down barriers and sacrificed everything to further our schooling.

Acknowledgements

This book, like many others before it, originated from a meeting with George Dei's learning community. It came as a desire to connect what we knew were important topics to schooling in Canada and globally.

We are fortunate to have the ability to work and experience life among individuals who make so many things possible. We would first like to thank Dr. George Dei (Nana) for providing the space to imagine this volume and providing a transformative space to so many of us. He has created many avenues for new scholars and activists to learn grow and thrive, not only as individuals, but as a collective. One of those outlets is his monthly Study Group, a learning circle where members of the community can come together to share in knowledge, resources, community news and receive guidance at various stages of our degrees. We are grateful to Nana and all those before me who have created a space where people who often would not feel they belong, can create new opportunities for each other to share, grow, and collaborate. Thank you so much for writing the foreword, it is the perfect beginning for this book.

We would also like to thank our 15 contributors. It has been a joy to work with you. The breadth, depth, and intersections present in the volume are a testament to your understanding that transformation and liberation must be multifaceted. We are lucky to know your academic and community work as well as counting you among our friends.

A special thank you to Harriet Akanmori who played a pivotal role in connecting contributors as well as early conceptions of the book.

We appreciate your tenacious approach in getting this project off the ground by encouraging others that their work is valued, and they ought to contribute.

We are grateful to have the ability to bookend this book with two individuals that have transformed the landscape of schooling equity in Canada and across the globe. Thank you, Carl James for a critical and thoughtful postscript. Your work was instrumental in the conceptualization and organization of this book and we appreciate the ways you connected our project.

A subsection of this book was presented at the 2017 Decolonization Conference in Toronto. Eight total papers were presented in two panels and we received valuable feedback from various attendees. We would like to thank everyone who participated.

Finally, we are very grateful to our editors at Palgrave USA Milana Vernikova and Linda Braus for their tireless efforts to bring this book to completion. Their patience and guidance were invaluable to this project.

Francisco's Acknowledgements

Este libro es dedicado a mi Mamá en reconocimiento que el libro y todo lo que he logrado es gracias a sus sacrificios. Ella ha sido y sigue siendo mi inspiración, mi primera maestra, y me sigue enseñando tanto. Te quiero mucho Mamá.

It is rare to have someone experience difficulties simultaneously. I am blessed to have my sister Paloma Villegas be part of my journey as we go through every stage of academia together. She has read everything I've written and supported every endeavor I've undertaken. I owe everything I am to her unwavering belief and while she is my little sister, I continue to look up to her.

I would like to extend my thanks to my colleagues, Adriana, Espy, Kiran, and Aman at the Department of Anthropology and Sociology at Kalamazoo College. I am very lucky to work alongside you and appreciate the space we've developed. A very heartfelt thank you to Natalia Carvalho-Pinto and Giuliana Bush. I am indebted to the two of you and grateful for the role you play in my life. Thank you for allowing me to share time and space with you. I love you. I would also like to thank Shanna Salinas and Mia Henry for providing multiple forms of support in my transition to Kalamazoo. I appreciate your warmth and valuable input.

A special thank you to my mentors Jeanett Castellanos, Julia Curry Rodriguez, and Patricia Landolt. You showed me the way to get here and supported me every step of the way. I am lucky to call myself your student and endeavor to emulate you. You have taught me to do more than survive in academia and the value of connecting our labor to students, community, and justice.

Academia can often be an isolating environment and I would like to extend my thanks to my students who continuously keep me grounded and co-construct a space where we can learn and grow. Thank you to Marilyn Yogarajah, Fatima Chakroun, Celine Gibbons-Taylor, Steven Shivcharan, Christina Hutchinson, Coral Cervantes, Jose Lopez, Libby Munoz, Ashley Santana, Mireli Hernandez, Madie Butler, Neelam Lal, Michelle Alba, Shadaijah Grandberry-Payton, Eli Quinones, Marco Ponce, and Anthony Soria. There's no way I can write everyone's name and I apologize for the many I've missed.

I would also be remiss if I did not mention the instrumental support received from Yessica Rostan, Kate Partridge, Katherine Johnston, Derik Chica, Catalina Calero, Ricardo Bocanegra Meza, Jesus Maya, Tara Beverly, Sabrine Azraq, Frank Ortega, Ismael Lara, Silvia Argentina Arauz, and Andrea Vasquez Jimenez. Thank you for all the love and caring throughout the years. I appreciate and love you.

Finally, a very big thank you to my co-editor Janelle Brady. It has been a pleasure working and learning with you. You came into this project at a difficult time and took up the challenge. Thank you for believing in the project.

Janelle's Acknowledgements

I am grateful to Francisco Villegas for taking this project on and seeing a need for this type of dialogue when it comes to critical schooling. Beyond that, even though Francisco has completed his doctoral degree, and, is in another country, he still finds meaningful ways to stay engaged and continue to mentor folks like myself throughout the process of navigating graduate school as a person of color.

Thank you to my sisters I have met in graduate school Shukri Hilowle, Shirleen Datt, Zuhra Abawi, Shawnee Hardware, Cindy Sinclair, Ezi Odozor, Andrea Vasquez, and Tammy George. Thank you for your mentorship and encouragement Deborah Davidson, Danielle Kwan-Lafond, Njoki Wane, Alana Butler, and Louise Gormley.

There are some people outside of the institution or the organizing world that without them my academic-activist journey would not be possible. I am forever grateful to my late mother, Sheryl Brady, for fighting for me and so many in our community just to get through kindergarten to grade 12, challenging anti-Black racism and sexism at every turn, while facing it in her own day-to-day life. I am thankful to my late grandmother, Nana Jessie, who continuously volunteered her time for a better world and pushed me to do the same. I am thankful to my Nana Lynn for giving me a sense of hard work and organization to carry through. I am also grateful to my Aunt Nadine for years of treats, laughter, and fun. Thank you to my loving father, aunts, friends, and family members. I am thankful for my beautiful and loving sisters and niece, Kenzie, Leila, Nini, Safy and Naveia and my older sister Diana. The time resources to carry out a book project would not have been possible without my loving partner, Matias. His active commitment to systemic change inspires and helps to recharge me to do the same. Thank you for your love and support.

Foreword

There have been times when I have felt nothing can come out of the incessant calls for educational change. This is largely in part of what I see as the perniciousness of the 'system' defined broadly to include the complex ways politics, economics, culture, education have been webbed into the fabric of the colonial and imperial nation-state. I am definitely not alone in this feeling. But, personally, I have also tried to ignore this unease and uncertainty with a spiritual hope and belief that something different is possible and that we must collectively hang on to the dream of new educational futures and work to actualize it. History is a complex combination of the knowledge of events and ideas and practices. We easily forget history. We do not always work with the lessons of history. And yet, history is always in the present and the future, guiding possibilities and given us the courage, wisdom, agency to work for change. As an educator and community worker operating from an anti-racist and anti-colonial lens, I cannot tell you how often I have expressed exasperation, frustration, and angst when students often question if the work we do will amount to anything given the systems in which we find ourselves. I often respond easily by saying we have no choice as teachers and learners to work with possibilities, and that 'we must pack up our books and go home' if we ever think change is an impossibility. Asking questions is a good starting point. After all, decolonization, no matter how we may contest it or quibble around it, starts by asking new questions. I have come to think of decolonization as the many things we do around Land, space, culture, memory, and spirituality to bring about change. While we should see the power of our speculative imaginaries we should also be courageous to take advantage of opportunities that come our way to create new imaginings. To insist on 'taking up space' with, and sharing, a voice of difference is powerful.

It is a great honor to be asked to write a 'Foreword' to such an important collection on: *Critical Schooling: Transformative Theory and Practice*. I looked at the text and wondered if there is anything new to be said after these conversations. But, many who know me will muse over 'I never saw a microphone I did not like.' And, I never saw a chance to write that I will not gladly welcome. Taking up space in this context is a challenge and opportunity to add voice and share one's experience as a contextual basis of knowledge. We are often told 'this is not about you.' But the personal is intellectual and theorizing begins with self-knowledge. To reiterate, this is speaking personal theory as critical theory that emanates from self, personal, and self-generational knowledge base.

It is without saying that education is too important. Education is more than schooling. It is about coming to learn to know, and to act to bring change to oneself, communities, and nation. Education is a task for all of us not just school teachers, but community and social workers, students, parents, administrators, policy makers, etc. In fact, come to think of it, education is about everything we do. Critical schooling must entail asking tough questions about what teachers do in classrooms and what learners are going to do with the education and knowledge received. Critical schooling has become a focus because there is the tendency for uncritical and colonizing education to serve to maintain the status quo. Too often, learners do not question power and the politics of knowledge. Similarly, educators hardly self-implicate, and the question of responsibility of knowledge received is not made front and center in classroom discussions. Decolonizing such education will require raising some tough questions.

Fortunately, this book allows for just that—to ask some pertinent questions. For example, how do we bring about educational change? What do we see as our respective responsibilities as learners, educators, policy makers, school administrators, parents, youth, cultural and social workers etc.? How do we implicate the structures of educational delivery—structures for teaching, learning, and administration of education in our discussions about educational change? What is the role of curricular and pedagogic change? How effective are our classroom instructional practices and teaching strategies to promote change? And, how do we ensure that what is theoretical does not stand in opposition to what is pragmatic?

A study of current educational practices in school calls for a critical reflection for devising countermeasures that defy neoliberal ideologies and the dictates of global finance capital. Education must be beyond understanding to embrace social action and change. While some educators continually search for ways to improve upon our practice, we must simultaneously turn our gaze onto knowledge more relevant to communities and for social change. Our critical teaching must reflect on broader systemic questions: What must we do as an institutional responsibility and why? What are the specific required changes needed or called for? And, how do we to implement these required changes? These questions offer a challenge for any academic text on schooling and education, especially, one that is intended to promote change. This is more so when a book has 'theory' and 'practice' together in the title.

It is a laudable undertaking to further the existing literature that examines schooling and education offering new possibilities within the Euro-American/Canadian context and far-reaching relevance beyond this context. By engaging a "politics of urgency" and working with the necessity to revisit important conversations (largely informed through the various contributors' social locations and politics), this book makes valuable contributions to the existing literature. The book does not disappoint as it lays bare the falsity of any claim to take a 'neutral/objective' stance when it comes to schooling and education for change. If one believes that the current status quo is not working for everyone then change is an imperative and must be forcefully demanded.

An added value of the book is the attempt to highlight some of the existing issues raised by scholars and activists on the question of educational futurity and then proceeding to also offer viable solutions for communities through resistance and change. We think through new futures collectively. We may not all share the particular strategies we adopt but we can believe in the idea that something different must be envisaged, fought for, and arrived at. How we situate ourselves in this futuristic conversation is something we determine in terms of how the 'politics of urgency' speak to us. The days of merely focusing on 'good intentions' without concrete action or a critical reflection on the outcomes of our current practices have been over long ago. Change must be fought for. It cannot be handed down to us that simply. This, then also counters the prominent ideal that with time comes change. Time does nothing but passes us by and as such, change demands action. Furthermore, equitable change, requires the recognition of collectivity and social location.

The host of educational issues highlighted in this collection demand action. We can only act if we understand the nature and complexity of the problem. I am not one of those who insist we already know the problems that afflict schooling and that what is needed now is action for redress. While this may be true, I also want us to think of new educational futures. To think through new futures, we must work with the lessons of the past and present. Issues are articulated differently given the politics of the knowledge producer. We may contest what we each say on the issues, but the fact is, there are significant voices that are often moved aside to make room for dominant voices. This has been the privileging of certain knowledges. The voices of racialized, Indigenous, and colonized scholars about their own schooling and education are often dismissed and held with deep skepticism. If these voices are validated and legitimized in academia quite often [although with some rare exceptions] it is because they are work with dominant theoretical lenses. Resisting voices are forced to succumb to dominant pressures and become assimilated/liberalized for the liking of those in power.

Euro-American schooling faces shares the ongoing impacts of colonialism, capitalism, and neoliberal ideologies. To argue that schooling and education must be anti-capitalist, anti-colonial, and anti-oppressive one must have the intellectual fortitude to withstand strong critiques of one's scholarship. There are power interests at play in working to sustain the current schooling system, particularly as it promotes the values, ideals, and interests of Western modernity. The political economy of schooling and education also distributes differential rewards and punishment for differently located bodies. This serves as a form of corporate disciplinary or regulation of bodies and knowledge, including the school official curriculum. The neoliberal ideologies of schooling fetishize individualism, individual liberty, rights, freedom, personal responsibility, markets, choice, and Western humanism. While not negating the relevance of these social virtues, there is the reluctance to bring a gaze highlighting corresponding virtues of community, sharing, relationality, social responsibility, institutional accountability, and importance of creating a community of learners, in the pursuit of 'schooling and community.' To espouse these ideas, one is often interpreted to be an advocate for communal education as if it was a bad thing. We fail to hold together simultaneous thinking of individual and community as necessitating each other as one is not existent without the other. The example of a 'co-operative individual' [as opposed to a competitive individual] moved more by the interests of a broader community rather than personal/private self-interests is a best expression of this dialectic.

These ideals are counter-epistemes embedded heavily in non-Western and Indigenous knowledge systems. We need to think of engaging cultural and ancestral funds of knowledge that are counter to dominant knowledges. This will include Indigenous philosophies of education and the teachings about society, culture, and nature nexus that sustain the creation of communities, modes of reciprocity, sharing, mutual interdependence, connections, and relationality. Indigenous spiritual ontologies emphasize the intricate relations of body, mind, soul, and spirit challenge binary modes of thought and the separation of the material from the non-material and the physical from the metaphysical. These teachings create a sense of wholeness of learners in a 'community of schooling' with educators, parents, students, school administrators, and policy all working to ensure collective social success rather than the individual academic achievement of the one 'smart' learner. Unfortunately, Indigenous knowings/epistemes that may hold possibilities of new schooling are often discounted and devalued as not 'knowledge.'

If we are serious about educational change, we must courageously embrace knowledge systems that posit an open challenge and threaten to destabilize dominant or imperial knowledge systems. These ontological and epistemic challenges provide us with myriad possibilities, particularly given their collaborative and interlinked nature. That is, rather than proposing a singularity of thought and truth, they present us with the ability of thinking through problems across diverse perspectives, entry points, goals, and needs, while continuously centering impact.

In an age when anti-Blackness, anti-Black racism, anti-Indigenous, anti-Muslim, xenophobia, and 'anti-difference' have not been mere sentiments and individual expressions but become very overt and violent acts, it is difficult to see the goal of education as anything other than coming to terms with racism, sexism, homophobia, patriarchy, heteronormativity, classism, disableism, and other forms colonial oppression. Furthermore, these issues must be front and center in our processes of reimagining education. New forms of schooling and education must be Blackness, Indigeneity, race, and racialization. These are sites where colonialisms, in their various forms, play out in the education of learners. Schooling and education must no longer be a curious search for knowledge but instead a process of using acquired knowledge to bring about social and political action.

Schools and schooling must not be allowed to target bodies of learners. Schools must deal with the continuing legacies of colonialism and settler colonialism where certain bodies feel comfortable to dominate, regulate, or discipline other bodies. In thinking about new visions of education, we must confront the racist policing of schools, the oppression of placing learners under surveillance, and the meting out differential punishment to racialized bodies for perceived transgressions. If the language of zero tolerance has a place in schools, then zero-tolerance policies should extend beyond questions of individual youth discipline to broader systemic questions of social injustice, structural inequities, and social oppressions. In effect, what we need is zero tolerance of racism, sexism, homophobia, and white privilege and white supremacy. These are never individual acts. They are systemic issues and concerns not just read on particular bodies but enacted throughout the school and educational system for bodies to tap into differently.

Quite often attempts to highlight the saliency of situational and contextual variations of different identities and oppressions are countered with calls for intersectional analysis. This gives the impression that the scholar articulating the saliencies of particular identities at given moments does not understand intersectional analysis. Intersectional theory had its intellectual politics, to make visible and to reaffirm the ignored or marginalized experiences of particularly bodies in dominant literatures. While intersectional analysis is helpful in pointing to the complexity and myriad nature of our identities, we must equally be critical of the selective calls for its engagement. It re-surfaces when one makes claim of saliency of race or Blackness. Sure, there is the multidimensionality of Blackness that can be read through race, gender, class, sexuality, and [dis]ability. Also, the complexity of Blackness reveals itself in the different geographies (African Blackness; Diasporic Blackness, Indigenous Blackness, Black/Afro-Indigenous peoples [see Dei, 2018; Dei, Vasquez, & Odozor, 2019]). Similarly, race is not one thing; it is classed, gendered, [dis]abled, and sexualized. However important these complexities, we must also rethink the ways we deploy intersections and intersectionality theory to dance around the saliency of issues for particular bodies. Thus, in reframing intersections and intersectional theory broadly as a lens for political action, the intent is to interrogate and challenge claims of solidarity work (e.g., the question of allyship) which tend to be framed in the perspective of the seduction of liberal, social oppression work. There is a need to reframe the radical, decolonial, and anti-colonial politics of solidarity in ways that do not further cause spiritual, emotional, and physical wounding of Black/African, Indigenous and racialized bodies. Calls for the recognition of the severity of their lived experiences cannot be dismissed as 'oppression Olympics.' The claim of 'oppression Olympics' is itself very oppressive. In working for transformation, we must see all oppressions as primary rooted in white supremacist capitalist structures and logics and, at the same time, uphold the saliencies of issues for Black and Indigenous bodies irrespective of the intersections of class, gender, sexuality, [dis]ability.

It is not surprising to hear white bodies challenge white supremacy and whiteness with a clarion call that it is a homogenizing claim that fails to distinguish how whiteness, for example, is demarcated by class, gender, sexuality, [dis]ability. This is the real 'race to innocence' (Fellows & Razack, 1998). While whiteness is a structure, it is powerfully signified on white bodies. Racialized bodies who are seduced and claim whiteness are only 'successful' [if ever so] to a point! But for me, the bigger point is that the current rise in 'Alt Right' white supremacy and their conservativism has sought to erase not only the history of colonization, genocide, and enslavement, but also, present-day coloniality, settler colonialism, and the ongoing forms of imperialism and militarism that justify, rationalize, and sustain the ideological and systemic practices of the white supremacist, hetero-patriarchal, capitalist state. The erasure is marked by a difficulty, failure, or refusal to/in acknowledging a white colonial dominant notwithstanding the fact that power is diffused (Foucault, 1978, 2002). The question of new educational futurity demands particular understandings of white supremacist logics and whiteness and the task of thinking about collective lives through, and with, mutual responsibilities and reciprocity in mind.

But seeking educational transformation also demands that we become critical of ourselves. We must be careful of the seduction of knowledge hierarchies in schooling such that we as learners and educators often fall easy prey to creating and sustaining these hierarchies and binaries of 'bright and dumb,' 'intellectual and anti-intellectual,' 'theoretical and atheoretical,' who is being 'scholarly' and who is 'espousing a 'political manifesto.' How can we claim to be progressive intellectuals and yet proceed to critique Afrocentricity and anti-colonial politics using the lens and yardstick of Eurocentric theorizing as we profess our affinity to the discourse of the 'post'? How can we claim to be crusaders against anti-Blackness and fail to see when we exhibit our own Black anti-Blackness in our intellectual praxis (e.g., disconnecting Africanness and Blackness in our analysis)?

How can we insist on our Indigeneity and yet simultaneously bring a suspicion to the claim of Black and African Indigeneities? Furthermore, in the discourse of schooling and education, I have seen racialized scholars and learners succumb to the academic language of 'excellence' that mimics Western tropes of 'success' and meritocracy while downplaying our own Indigenous conceptions with the charge that these racialized scholars' communities and scholars are not bringing an intellectually complex gaze/reading to the issues? A call to acknowledge the severity of issues for certain bodies, and the insistence on Black/African perspectivism is recognition of that fact that we each hold knowledge informed by our identity, politics, histories, and situational contexts.

Critical education must redefine 'citizenship and definitions of belonging' not just because claiming citizenship on Stolen Lands is problematic, but also, because certain bodies (e.g., Black/African bodies) are not deemed worthy of learning or coming into learning spaces in the first place. Troubling citizenship is calling into question history and Land dispossession. It is also about coupling claims of entitlements and belongingness with responsibility, transparency, and accountability. We must also interrogate the extent to which our notions of citizenship and belongingness are framed within neoliberal framework or ideology and thus further marginalizing or disenfranchised some of our communities.

In conclusion, I must reiterate that it is very informing to see how different angles cross with various book chapters, specifically in terms of the varying perspectives of schooling, sites of violence, building identity, community, and reclaiming resistance and agency. The book's call for continuing radical dialogues and conversations about schooling notwithstanding the fact that schools are a reflection of larger systemic oppressions is significant. This intellectual positioning also gestures to change as both happening in small and major places and acts of resistance. Clearly, we need new visions of schooling and education. But, in order for this new futurity to emerge we must be prepared to look critically at what currently exists and offer deep reflections with the hope of not repeating the past and current mistakes.

Toronto, Canada

George J. Sefa Dei
Professor of Social Justice
Education and Director
Centre for Integrative
Anti-Racism Studies OISE
University of Toronto

References

Dei, G. J. S. (2018). Black Like Me: Reframing Blackness and Decolonial Politics. *Educational Studies*, 54(2), 117–142.
Dei, G. J. S., Vasquez, A., & Odozor, E. (2019). *Cartographies of Blackness and Indigeneity*. Gorham, ME: Myers Educational Press.
Fellows, M. L., & Razack, S. (1998). The Race to Innocence: Confronting Hierarchical Relations Among Women. *The Journal of Gender, Race, & Justice, 1*, 335–352.
Foucault, M. (1978). *The History of Sexuality* (Vol. 1). Baltimore, MD and Pointe Claire, QC: Random House.
Foucault, M. (2002). The Subject and Power. In J. D. Faubion (Ed.) and R. Hurley, et al. (Trans.), *Essential Works of Foucault Power* (Vol. 3, pp. 326–348). London: Penguin.

Contents

1   Continuing Important Conversations: An Introduction to This Volume   1
Francisco J. Villegas and Janelle Brady

2   "I'm Just a Friend Now": Community Policing in Toronto Schools   21
Gita Rao Madan

3   Restorative Justice: Moving from Punitive Sanctions to Proactive Interactions   47
Michelle H. A. Bailey

4   Canada's Legacy of Colonialism: Implications in Education   75
Jacqueline Benn-John

5   Resistance Is Our Ancestral Knowledge: Incorporating Roots of Resistance into the Education of Adolescent Afro-Caribbean Girls in the Greater Toronto Area (GTA)   99
Kimberley Moore and Celine D. Gibbons-Taylor

6 Disrupting Princesses: A Pedagogical Moment in Dismantling Colonial Norms and Representations of Beauty Through an Anti-colonial Framework 125
Janelle Brady and Zuhra Abawi

7 The First Three Years of LAEN: From Unity-Seeking to Equity-Seeking 147
Catalina Calero and Derik Chica

8 Active Communities and Practices of Resistance: Brief History of the Use of Schools as Border Zones in Toronto 175
Francisco J. Villegas

9 Be a Good Citizen or Else! Neoliberal Citizenship and the Grade Six 2013 Revised Ontario Social Studies Curriculum 201
Ardavan Eizadirad

10 "What Can I Do?": A Guide for Academics Who (Want to) Support Palestine 225
Sabrine Azraq

11 Bridging Borders: Teaching a Bridging Course with Precarious Status Students Transitioning to the University 245
Paloma E. Villegas

12 Self-Study of an Indigenous Settler in Ontario Schooling: An Exploration of Living Theory 269
Umar Umangay

13 Living Biocultures: A Framework for Building
    Sustainable Community Well-Being, Resilience
    and Innovation   299
    Yessica D. Rostan Aellen

14 Community, Schooling, and the Education of
    Racialized Students: A Postscript   327
    Carl E. James

Index   339

Contributors

Zuhra Abawi University of Toronto, Toronto, ON, Canada

Sabrine Azraq Toronto, ON, Canada

Michelle H. A. Bailey Ontario Institute for Studies in Education, University of Toronto, Toronto, ON, Canada

Jacqueline Benn-John Ontario Institute for Studies in Education, University of Toronto, Toronto, ON, Canada

Janelle Brady University of Toronto, Toronto, ON, Canada

Catalina Calero Toronto, ON, Canada

Derik Chica Toronto, ON, Canada

Ardavan Eizadirad Ontario Institute for Studies in Education, University of Toronto, Toronto, ON, Canada

Celine D. Gibbons-Taylor Queen's University, Kingston, ON, Canada

Carl E. James Jean Augustine Chair in Education, Community & Diaspora, York University, Toronto, ON, Canada

Gita Rao Madan Toronto, ON, Canada

Kimberley Moore Columbia University, New York, NY, USA

Yessica D. Rostan Aellen Ontario Institute for Studies in Education, University of Toronto, Toronto, ON, Canada

Umar Umangay First Nations Technical Institute, Tyendinaga Mohawk Territory, ON, Canada

Francisco J. Villegas Anthropology and Sociology, Kalamazoo College, Kalamazoo, MI, USA

Paloma E. Villegas California State University, San Bernardino, San Bernardino, CA, USA

List of Figures

Fig. 11.1 Joey's body map   262
Fig. 12.1 Visual organization of the chapter as Living Theory   270
Fig. 12.2 ALACT model adapted from Korthagen (2001, p. 130)   278

CHAPTER 1

Continuing Important Conversations: An Introduction to This Volume

Francisco J. Villegas and Janelle Brady

1.1 Schooling as a Site of Violence and Resistance

This book continues important conversations surrounding the recognition of inequities within schools and transformative theory and practice. As a collection of essays, this volume stems from a frustration of limited options for critical examination and a desire to centralize and highlight the agency of marginalized communities in their efforts to address injustice within schooling in Canada. To be clear, we are not unattached academics in this process. Thus, rather than proclaiming objectivity or neutrality, each chapter in this book is presented from the authors' social location. As such, we aim to bring to the fore the systemic violence in

---

Ghosh & Abdi, (2013) *Education and the Politics of Difference* (2nd ed.); Ghosh & Galczynski, (2014) *Redefining Multicultural Education* (3rd ed.); Egbo, Mogadime, etc.

F. J. Villegas (✉)
Anthropology and Sociology, Kalamazoo College, Kalamazoo, MI, USA
e-mail: Francisco.villegas@kzoo.edu

J. Brady
University of Toronto, Toronto, ON, Canada
e-mail: Janelle.baptiste.brady@mail.utoronto.ca

© The Author(s) 2019
F. J. Villegas and J. Brady (eds.), *Critical Schooling*,
https://doi.org/10.1007/978-3-030-00716-4_1

schooling and methods to resolve it, rather than recentering the nation or its myths. In the process of developing this book, we as editors are guided by what Aida Hurtado (2003) calls the "politics of urgency," that is we recognize the ways that lives, futures, and knowledge, have been, and continue to be, pushed out from institutions that were not designed for our communities.[1] In alignment with Hurtado (2003), the purpose of this project is to "subvert rather than perpetuate debates that sabotage the potential for political action" (p. 224). In this way, we sought contributors that are hopeful, transformative, and cognizant of the value of praxis. Grounding the book in this manner facilitates fuller engagement with the problematics of schooling as experienced by peoples who inhabit the intersections of various modes of oppression.

Schooling as an institution is imagined as the space to develop future citizens as well as a meritocratic site that facilitates access to the goods of the nation, including social mobility. However, the process of schooling is mediated by numerous power relations that define what constitutes valuable knowledge, how learning occurs and is evaluated, who is capable of learning, and who exemplifies excellence. Numerous scholars have analyzed the politics of schooling as well as how it betrays the very values it purports to uphold. This includes calls to redefine the individualized and pathologized dropout to the pushout through an anti-racist approach which takes structural barriers into account (Dei, Mazzuca, McIsaac, & Zine, 1997), analyzing the production of "at risk" youth in normalizing discourses of color-blindness and meritocracy through a critical race perspective (James, 2011; James & Taylor, 2010), interrogating the histories of residential schooling and its links to the present (Haig-Brown, 2002; Susan Dion, 2009), proposing alternate pedagogies and curricular designs (Alexander, 2006; Dei, 1996, 2003, 2010) and the need for schooling to have a liberatory intention (Giroux, 2007; Leonardo, 2004). Scholars like Shujaa (1994) articulate the difference between schooling and education by defining schooling as "a societal imperative necessary for the maintenance of existing relations of power and privilege" (p. 11). Shujaa goes on to define education "... as a process that locates the members of a culture within their cultural history, facilitates the transmission of knowledge, and affirms the cultural identity" (p. 11). By engaging this operation of schooling and extending it to the scholarship presented earlier, this book aims to continue these conversations as well as link them to contemporary shifts in the ways schooling is conducted today. In this way, the central questions guiding this volume include: What are current inequities facing youth in schooling and how do community members exercise and enact their agency to organize resistance? What does it mean when we say communities through critical perspectives which seek mutuality, shared responsibility, and solidarity rather than fragmentation and divisions? What are alternate methods of imagining the process of schooling that transform the confines of schooling to education? And how do we maintain accountability to ensure schools' promises to our communities? How can we reenvision the schooling process of preparing citizens that critically departs from anti-difference discourses that often center whiteness and heteropatriarchy to a more complete futurity? While contributors to this book aim to address these questions, the responses presented are not definitive and instead should be considered ongoing through which we reimagine the definition of the learner and teacher, the overseeing of learning, the problematics of school disciplining, the connections between schools and processes of displacement and profiteering, and the histories of resistance emanating from the communities experiencing violence.

Schools are filled with violent processes that produce physical, psychological, and spiritual harm. These processes are couched in colonialism, white supremacy, and patriarchy. In fact, the historical trajectories of criminalization, demands to assimilation, disavowal of diverse knowledge, illegalization, and constructs of deficient bodies and cultures remain prevalent today, sometimes in subtler forms. As George Dei (1996) reminds us, "current discussions and explications about 'culture,' 'nation' and 'heritage' can, and do become new tropes for producing racialized doctrines and reproducing overtly racist discourses" (p. 47). That is, language has shifted to facilitate speaking in codes that allow for racist, sexist, homophobic, and colonialist discourse, while masquerading as egalitarian, multicultural, or as recently seen in the Western landscape, through a practice of "freedom of speech."

Too often, frameworks explicating the differential outcomes experience by people according to race, class, and gender—including racialized poor women—operate under assumptions of deficiency and pathology (Carranza, 2009; Collins, 2000; Dei et al., 1997; hooks, 2015; Hurtado, 1995). Supplementary interventions are often proposed as solutions that will result in the oppressed achieving a similar subjectivity as the dominant. This position assumes a lack, or deficiency rather than acknowledging the historical, and resulting structural, systemic, and institutionalized contexts that result in these differential outcomes. Deficiency theories commonly used range from ideas that individuals must assimilate in myriad ways to find a place within dominant society, to beliefs of inferiority due to biology, familial composition, class, culture, or a combination of all of these factors (Balibar, 1991; Goldberg, 1993; Pon, 2009; Romero, 2008; Thobani, 2007). Assimilatory demands normalize white supremacy and blame those who are deemed non-compliant or refusing to admit their or their culture's presumed inferiority. These frameworks, often imagined solely as speech acts, have material consequences, particularly as they not only shape discourse but also practices, policies, and laws. We can see this in the deployment of respectability politics, claims that marginalized bodies are divisive when they address, protest or challenge inequity, criminalization of dissent and legalized state violence in the form of police brutality, environmental racism, austerity measures, among others.

The employment of the multitude of deficiency theories available (such as and not limited to: culture of poverty, the bell curve, broken windows theories) can become hegemonic and within the context of schooling produce teachers, staff members, and administrators that reproduce violence. For instance, educators mobilize racist discourses regarding racialized communities placing little value on schooling and as such, follow a theory of deficiency that flows from the parent down to the children (Ladson-Billings, 2007). Although these theories have been proven wrong time and time again, they continue to gain currency (James, 2009).

In Canada, the "push out" process of racialized students has been documented (Bernhard, 2009; Carranza, 2009; Dei et al., 1997; Rivas & Duarte, 2009; Schugurensky, 2009). In this process, it is often the racialized student, and by extension their family, who is believed to be deficient, lacking, and neglectful of their schooling. There are myriad ways students, their families, and their communities continue to be constructed as devaluing schooling. The prescribed deficiency of racialized families is extended to schooling in which parents, families, and communities are seen to lack concern about formalized education. As a response, rather than centering schools and their administrators, we hope to reconfigure the line of inquiry regarding the project of schooling. Instead of positioning communities as passive, we highlight the methods communities employ in resisting, which speaks to their concern and commitment to community education through agency, change, and activism which challenges and offers a nuanced perspective into the schooling project.

1.2 Locating Toronto in the Canadian and Global Context

This book is placed within the Canadian context. All of the contributors have undergone significant amounts of schooling within this space and by locating themselves differently to the land, highlight various inequities. Importantly, Canada plays an interesting role in the international landscape; it is imagined locally and abroad as a site of opportunity, as a kinder and gentler neighbor to the USA, as a pacifist nation with a history of peacekeeping rather than warmongering (Razack, 2004). Like all other white settler states, Canada has carefully curated its history to remove the presence of genocide of Indigenous peoples, partaking in the trans-Atlantic slave trade, and banning the migration of peoples of color (Austin, 2010) as well as current heightening of the dislocation of peoples across the globe (Walia, 2013), silence in the disappearance and murder of Indigenous women (Jiwani & Young, 2006; Savarese, 2017), and the more recently selling of military weapons used to target civilians (*The Guardian*, 2016). This work is facilitated through proclamations of equity-driven initiatives such as the Multiculturalism Act, a myth of refugee protection, and constant claims toward addressing the wounds of colonialism. What is striking is that while many peoples across the world can see behind the mirage of countries like the USA and England as locations that produce violence across the globe, Canada has not been recognized to the same degree. That is, if the USA imagines itself as the land of milk and honey, Canada positions itself as a gentle provider of milk and maple syrup.

Toronto serves as an important entry point to these discussions. It is positioned as both an important site within the Canadian landscape as well as an international hub that informs and is informed by transnational processes. For example, Toronto serves as an important case study for the effects of neoliberal restructuring given that the amalgamation of the Toronto District School Board in 1998 (Basu, 2004) made it the largest in Canada[2] and one of the largest in North America.

Toronto is also in constant change, it is one of the primary migrant-receiving locations, with its foreign-born population accounting for 46.1% of its populace (Ontario Ministry of Finance, 2017). The presence of various subjectivities demands that we consider the presence of individuals who speak multiple languages, engage in myriad ways of knowing and belonging, reside in diverse locations in relation to the white settler colonial state. Furthermore, the variance of immigration statuses and the effects on schooling is a topic of discussion across most countries located in the global north. This is not only mirrored in other large metropolitan centers around the globe but also increasingly within the rest of country. Finally, Toronto has also become a minority as the majority city. According to the 2016 census, "51.5% [of respondents] said they're from visible minority communities, a milestone that was narrowly missed when 49 per cent identified that way in 2011" (Ballingall, 2017). While the numerical diversity of the city continues to increase, changes to curriculum, faculty, and pedagogy are seldom reflected in schools. Furthermore, the increase of students of color within schools has been met by a significant backlash that includes their criminalization. The presence of police officers in schools is a not foreign to many students in North America and fears of the racialized body often drive these initiatives, leading to broad fields of study that examine the presence and effects of a school to prison pipeline. This is not to say that there has not been resistance. Toronto is also an important space for resistance related to schooling. Its population has organized to develop Africentric schools to challenge the prominence of a Eurocentric curriculum; pressured the Toronto District School Board and Toronto Catholic District School Board into adopting "Don't Ask, Don't Tell" policies to ensure the availability of schooling for undocumented youth and mobilized to remove the presence of cops in schools. This brings an important point of discussion when we think about the future of schooling both globally and locally (within Toronto specifically, but also Canada in general): What changes will we demand from schools that are informed and located as a site of white supremacy? How might we re-envision schooling in a way that recognizes not only the changing populace, but also the moral and ethical duty to educate? How do we center the work of our communities in our academic writing? And, how do we further the goals of our communities through academic labor? Overall, the contributors describe a need for increased engagement with an ongoing history of colonization and racism.

1.3 Multiple Obstacles and Diverse Methodologies of Resistance: Outlining the Chapters

Schooling is an important institution that maintains and produces the ontological, epistemic, and axiological basis of the nation. That is, the nation and its myths are constantly being produced and reproduced and much of this labor occurs within schools. In this way, schools are a central aspect of nation-building, particularly within the white settler state. In Canada, settlement is mediated by processes of dislocation, dispossession, and claims to innocence. Essays in this volume seek to dismantle these narratives through multiple perspectives, subject locations, and theoretical approaches. This book extends conversations about schooling from critical approaches and engages new and emerging discussions, resistances, and pedagogical practices employed within the Canadian schooling system from critical perspectives. We seek to address the ways Canadian schooling is a site of continuous struggle. While schools and school boards may take on diverse and inclusive measures, if they are not anchored within the critical conversations offered by perspectives such as anti-racism, anti-colonialism, Black feminism, among others, then they are doomed to repeat the histories of oppression which such practices and initiatives purport to escape.

Although there is a central goal present throughout the chapters of this book, there is no singular framework shared by all contributors. Instead, we recognize the need for a multitude of methods, perspectives, and ideas that are based on a project of deconstructing power relations while constructing equitable structures for growth and continued resistance. At the same time, it is important to recognize that we understand the chapters as working in parallel directions and invested in ensuring that modes of oppression are not reproduced while seeking liberation. For instance, in relation to anti-racism, Agnes Calliste and George Dei (2000) remind us anti-racism must be integrative. Therefore, authors employ anti-racism, anti-colonial theory, Black feminist thought, among other frameworks. These frameworks become crucial and important frameworks though which to undertake a critical schooling perspective. Anti-Racism seeks to dismantle racism through an integrative approach that disrupts the racist discourse posing difference as a deficit (Calliste & Dei, 2000). Black feminist thought is operationalized similarly through disrupting anti-difference, white, patriarchal, and classist sentiment through an intersectional framework that centers the raced and gendered locality of Black women through self-articulation and self-definition (Hill Collins, 2000; Wane, Deliovsky, & Lawson, 2002). The anti-colonial theoretical framework is a praxis-orientated framework that engages decolonial acts of resistance in response to over five hundred years of colonialism (Dei, 2006). Often within scholarship, there are tensions between and within various theoretical frameworks in the posing of how to answer significant questions. Thus, this book becomes important for educators, both within and outside of the context of schooling, scholars, and students alike. It provides multiple entry points for dialogue among various subject positions within the milieu of Canadian schooling, through a conversation which extends beyond the Canadian context.

The book is organized into four primary themes that we believe are critical sites of violence and resistance within schooling. The first section, The Politics of Punishment examines the mechanisms created within schooling to police, surveil, and punish students who are deemed criminal, deficient, and "behavioral," based on the readings of their bodies and communities. Discipline is a crucial topic within schooling, particularly as it converges with the pushing out of student, the school to prison pipeline, and the differential rewards and punishments present with a system that masquerades as equitable. The surge of demands to police youth through ever-increasingly criminalizing methods is vibrant in Canada. Whether it be zero-tolerance policies, the construction of students as potential hazards in the jobs of teachers, or the introduction of police officers within schools have maintained the belief of schools out of control and youth in disarray. However, we must ask, in the construction of methodologies for surveillance and policing, which students are deemed "at risk" and in need of additional control? Furthermore, how can we reimagine discipline beyond the punitive and criminalizing norm currently in fashion?

Gita Madan opens the volume by analyzing the presence of armed police officers in select Toronto schools. She delves into the history of introducing uniformed police officers, called School Resource Officers, into schools. This history is located alongside a trajectory of policies that criminalize students of color as well as those with a disability. After providing this context she unfurls her argument, deconstructing the "friendly relationship-building" efforts of the Toronto Police Services Board by pairing it with the school-to-prison pipeline. This process she argues, decontextualizes the present and historical violence experienced by communities of color at the hands of Toronto police. It also normalizes the policing and surveillance of young people of color. Specifically, it aims to humanize individual police officers while removing the possibility of thinking about systemic state-sponsored violence through the act of policing and the effects of discourses of schools as violent and in disarray, which can only be corrected through the presence of uniformed officers. In this way, Madan provides with a temporal and spatial analysis of the ways decontextualized discourse limits the recognition of systemic violence at the hands of cops through the naturalized construction of young people of color as threats to society.

In the second chapter, Michelle Bailey proposes the deployment of restorative justice as an alternate to suspensions for minor breaches of the school's rules and codes of conduct in the Toronto District School Board where Black students have higher suspension rates than their white counterparts (Rankin, Rushowy, & Brown, 2013; James & Turner, 2017). Through a Bourdieuan theoretical framework, she analyzes how the divergence between students' and administrators' habitus facilitates criminalization and beliefs of deviance. Alternatively, she shows that restorative justice offers teaching and learning opportunities. Throughout the chapter, the role of principals is illustrated as pivotal in the practice of restorative justice because their commitment to restitution is what will lead to a decreased rate of suspensions for Black students.

After the discussion on the punishment, the volume moves to analyzing the Politics of Identity. This section centers the ways communities protect their ways of being and belonging, particularly when encountering schools. hooks states that though Black and other women of color may experience sexism in the family at early ages, their encounter of racism occurs later on (2015). This points to the significance of the process of schooling in shaping a raced, gendered, and classed imaginary which is anti-different. As Dei et al. (2002) in *Reconstructing the dropout* and Angela Valenzuela (1999) in *Subtractive schooling* argue, schools are often assimilative institutions that maintain colonial beliefs of singular methods of knowing, naming, and being in the world. These beliefs, couched on the propagation of deficiency theories demand an adherence to a white, male, heterosexual, abled, and Bourgeoisie, subjectivity. Furthermore, those who resist or reject these impositions are often defined as "problems" and "pushed out" or "subtracted" from the schooling process. Rather than continuing the epistemic violence of proving the presence of violence within the schooling space, authors in this section ask, what would schooling defined through our own subjectivities look like? And how do we develop localized initiatives to promote practices of resistance? The chapters in this section are introspective while providing a platform to discuss educational reform, as well as transformative possibilities to counteract the effects of white supremacy in the development of norms regarding the belief of who can be a learner, who has history, how beauty and personal value are defined, and how large community organizations can influence schooling policies.

Jacqueline Benn-John begins this conversation by analyzing the divergence between her parents' belief that Canada's educational system offered limitless opportunities for learning, personal development and knowledge expansion, and the ways the Canadian schooling system betrays these ideals. She approaches this topic from a position of systemic as well as individual subordination and resistance. As a Black woman schooled in Canada, the topic contextualizes her experience of racism, sexism, and invisibility within educational systems. It also frames and elucidates the educational experience of countless Black children and Indigenous students as necessarily connected to colonial ideologies of whiteness, anti-Blackness, and anti-Indigenous racism. The chapter employs anti-colonialism, anti-racism and African feminism discursive frameworks to explore and understand Canada's legacy of colonialism. Particularly, Benn-John focuses on how colonial practices continue to be contemporaneously implicitly and explicitly maintained in educational systems in the twenty-first century. She intentionally makes visible the West's colonial past, as well as its history of domination, exclusion, and the imposition of white superiority within Canada's educational system. Furthermore, she resists "conservative arguments that attribute educational inequality to inherent differences in intelligence and ability" between learners (and communities) of different racialized identities (Wotherspoon, 2009, p. 35) and offers strategies for decolonizing and change.

In their co-authored chapter, Kimberly Moore and Celine Gibbons-Taylor describe a program that draws from the spatial and temporal stories of ancestors to guide initiatives with Afro-Caribbean girls. They demonstrate how and why narratives of resistance by Afro-Caribbean women are a transformative force that needs to be incorporated in the schooling of Afro-Caribbean girls in the Greater Toronto Area (GTA). In their chapter, they discuss how Black women resisted the conditions of enslavement in the Caribbean and follow by situating modern forms of resistance to nuanced engagement with past and present can be used to educate Afro-Caribbean girls. To do so, they propose a strengths-based program for Afro-Caribbean girls that demonstrates how they can mobilize inherited narratives of resistance in strategic, purposeful ways.

Similar to Moore and Gibbons-Taylor, Janelle Brady and Zuhra Abawi's chapter details an intervention to facilitate cross-generational dialogue; however, their chapter is specifically focused on deconstructing standards on beauty and the effects on children of color. They use an anti-colonial theoretical framework to deconstruct whiteness in forms of representation and beauty norms among young learners. They describe working with two sets of young learners and family members in an art project where they created a collage of images of women tracing their own histories and centering their own social locations in the co-creation of knowledge. Then through duoethnography as a method to interrogate their social locations, they discuss the pedagogical moment and how it can be used in educational settings. By discussing topics such as intersectionality and the saliency of race, they highlight the ways young girls are doubly marginalized by dominant discourse based on their gender and race. Finally, their chapter presents future opportunities and analysis from an anti-colonial theoretical framework.

The final chapter in this section is by Catalina Calero and Derik Chica, two cofounders of the Latin American Education Network (LAEN)—now the Latinx, Abya yala, Afro-LAEN—who discuss the formation of this volunteer-led and grassroots community organization in response to the high "drop-out" rate of Latinx students in Toronto. Their chapter outlines the initial efforts by LAEN so seek consensus in advocating to the Toronto District School Board and the Toronto Catholic District School Board, the two largest publicly funded boards in Toronto and the difficulties in including an overt political stance. The authors document the history and growth of this organization from an advocacy-based project to an equity and activist-based one. Some of the pivotal points in this now documented history include the journey for a more inclusive identity label, listening to the voices of community through yearly conferences, and challenging the way history/heritage months are celebrated by the Toronto school boards. This paper concludes with a new hope for the future of the organization through new leadership and equity-led actions.

The third section of the book analyzes the citizenship and definitions of belonging. It highlights and pinpoints varying social locations that dislocate individuals from the spaces of "home" and the ways that being defined as a non-citizen facilitates the propagation of violence. The dangerous and abusive "other" is often constructed along racial, classist, and gendered lines with an increased effect on those who occupy the intersections of such oppressions. This is particularly salient in the ways that citizenship is redefined by policy within the Canadian space, as well as the methods of teaching what constitutes acts of citizenship, the latter of which are often criminalized. While authors in this section do not provide a singular definition of citizenship or what constitutes the citizen, they center the ability to belong and to feel a part of the nation. However, being located within this imagined community (Anderson, 1991) is often precarious and contingent on who makes claims to citizenship (Li, 2001, 2003; Thobani, 2000). That is, citizenship extends beyond the presence of formal documentation and includes demands to have clear allegiance to the nation (Arat-Koc, 2005) and to contribute through economic means. Thus, to speak of citizenship as contingent accounts for the ways different bodies are afforded claims to the nation and the methods that citizenship can be discursively as well as formally removed when engaging in acts that are transgressive of the boundaries of "good" citizenship performance or those that critique the nation. In this way, authors in this section ask, who has historically been imagined the citizen, what are material consequences of falling outside of this conceptualization, and how do non-citizens navigate that space? How are citizenship acts defined in the process of educating future citizens? And how might we reconsider civic engagement as a practice of freedom across multiple spaces? These are large questions that cannot be fully answered within short essays, yet the authors make important contributions toward reconfiguring how we understand the nation and our roles within it and particularly within the context of schooling.

Francisco Villegas begins this section by outlining the history of demands to access to schooling by undocumented migrants in Canada. His chapter details how undocumented migration is often imagined as a new phenomenon in Canada and how this understanding leads to additional bordering of the school site. The Toronto District School Board's "Students Without Legal Status Policy," colloquially known as the Don't Ask, Don't Tell policy, passed in 2007 serves as a platform to forge discussion beyond the politics of providing entry into schools along with the wide invisibilization of an undocumented population within Toronto, and their continued exclusion from schools. By employing a theoretical framework that addresses the social construction of illegality and the processes that illegalize people, Villegas brings to the fore the ways undocumented students are and have been removed from what is often imagined a pivotal social good. In this way, the exclusion from formal citizenship is expanded by internal borders operating within the school site.

Through curriculum document analysis, Ardavan Eizadirad critically analyzes the language, ideologies, and conceptual framework in the 2013 revised Social Studies curriculum in Ontario, Canada, with a focus on the grade six curriculum content. He argues that the new curriculum predominantly promotes citizenship embedded with neoliberal ideologies which equate citizenship with personal responsibility, complicity, and civic participatory engagement associated with acceptable actions permitted by state-sanctioned authority and its institutions. Within this paradigm, being a responsible, active citizen is equated with being complicit and out-spoken only to the extent that it does not challenge state authority and hegemonic status quo policies and practices. There are great additions to the new revised Social Studies curriculum, including the promotion of a student-centered, inquiry-based model of learning and the introduction of the Citizenship Education Framework. Overall, Eizadirad argues that to promote citizenship education for the development of a justice-oriented global citizen, educators can teach citizenship through the lens of Human Rights rather than personal responsibility.

The final chapter in this section is written by Sabrine Azraq who describes tools of resistance for academics supporting Palestine. Through the use of a politics of refusal (Simpson, 2014; Tuck & Yang, 2014) and politics of urgency (Hurtado, 2003), Azraq speaks to the need to "produce work that beneficially changes Palestinian political, material and social current conditions." Throughout the chapter, she describes different projects to support Palestine as well as the discursive tools that have been used to discredit them. She critically engages with these claims and disentangles the contradictions present as well as the differential conferring of power given the Canadian state's positioning. As such, support for Palestine is seldom defined as an act of citizenship, and instead becomes a criminalized and marginalized location both within academia as well as in the political sphere. Specifically, Azraq positions academics as pivotal to the processes of resistance and charges them with deploying a more critical analysis of what constitutes academic freedom and the pursuit of justice.

The last section for this volume focuses on critical pedagogies. It brings together three papers discussing new ways of engaging with the dissemination of knowledge and the need for educators to maintain an introspective analysis. Schooling in Canada has ignored Freire's (1970) warnings and become a site of "banking on education"—a space where students are imagined as empty receptacles with no valuable knowledge awaiting teachers to deposit and impart knowledge into "empty" repositories. Similarly, teachers seldom recognize the context under which learners attend schools. Thus, in the pursuit of schooling as a meritocratic space, students are often invisibilized. This section asks, what are our respective responsibilities to our students and communities as educators? How do we come to better understand their connections to Land, collectivities, and knowledge? And how may we analyze our own roles in the processes of knowledge creation and propagation? These questions demand action and the chapters within this section engage with Freire's (1970) call to praxis.

Umar Umangay's chapter examines the use of unobtrusive research to analyze the complexities of being an Indigenous person from Hawaii teaching in settler schooling environments. He categorizes this method as "an Inidigenous form of autoethnography" with a theoretical framework based on living theory and self-study of professional practice bolstered by data from archival and journal sources and memory provocations. In this essay, Umangay utilizes decolonization as a reflective pathway to make sense of the professional self and to reimagine what it is to be an ethical educator in teacher education and in classrooms. He then describes this process as produced through five phases: the action phase, reflection phase, awareness phase, creating phase, and the trial phase. Specifically, the action phase explored being an anti-racist educator, the reflection phase examined instructional practices, the awareness phase critically confronted decolonization, the creating phase developed alternative models and the trial phase looked at transformation of the self. These introspective journeys deepen and situate the educator as part of teacher education and schooling that reproduces settler constructs. Furthermore, the reflections are discussed as pivotal toward developing living theory, particularly through demands to active transformations, goals of emancipation, acceptance of multiple layers of analysis.

Paloma Villegas continues the discussion on the value of the classroom by reflecting on the process of planning and teaching a bridging course that facilitates the entry of precarious status migrant students to an Ontario university. While students in some US states have had official access to postsecondary schooling since the early 2000s, in Canada, access has been piecemeal if at all existent. The chapter examines how her own history of immigration influenced the development and running of the course, including the assumptions prior to and during the course. Villegas evaluates the role of storytelling and disclosure and conceptualize the role of students as border-crossers or "bridges." In this case, border-crossers or bridges refer to more than their migrant subjectivities but also the recognition that many are first-generation migrants, university students, etc. The chapter provides recommendations about how to facilitate such courses, the specific needs of precarious status students, and the role of instructors in the process.

The last chapter in this book is written by Yessica Rostan. In this essay, Rostan explores anti-colonial biocultura in the context of Canadian schooling in Tkaronto. It describes a kind of learning that prioritizes subjectivity, diversity, community, co-creativity, and change as a path to living together on the Land. It describes schooling in Canada as one of the mechanisms reproducing colonial biocultures, material systems, and ideas about being Alive, including how we interact with the Land, ourselves and each other. Rostan describes anti-colonial biocultura to ground learning to build sustainable relationships that lead to solutions, highlighting the importance of Land and place-based actions. Finally, she envisions what it might look like to build thriving *schools-as-biocultural-Community-learning-centres*, working with the diverse biocultural knowledge of People in our Communities, honoring the Indigenous bioculturas of Turtle Island and building wellness, resilience, and innovation in the Living Communities within these spaces.

In all, the essays within the sections of the book speak to and engage varying specificities of the schooling experience, sites of violence, building of identity, belonging and sites of reclaiming and resistance. Through the scholarship in this book, there are various positionalities and a myriad of theoretical perspectives. This provides an enriched response to the project of schooling which extends the need for anti-difference and the confines of sameness. Through the varying lenses, we reach multiple perspectives and nuanced understandings of schooling. The chapters answer some of the key questions presented at the onset of the introduction. First, current inequities facing youth currently as well as community responses are addressed in all of the sections presented in this volume, from school SROs and restorative justice to Don't Ask Don't Tell policies and the enactment of such. As well, alternate readings and modes of schooling are presented that transgress the confines of schooling through frameworks like biocultura, proposals of asset-based community programs and critical pedagogical interventions. Finally, the question of citizenship and belonging is raised and problematized through multiple epistemic frameworks.

Some might ask, if schooling has and continues to be a violent and harmful space, why bother engaging with it anyway? Why would interrogating a structure that is functioning in the way it ought to—by serving white, middle- and upper-class, heteronormative, abled, and patriarchal interests—be questioned? The schooling project raises larger questions and allows for introspection of how such particularities can be extended to the larger social milieu. This means that what takes place within schools are certainly not confined to schools. Anti-Black, anti-Indigenous, sexist, racist and classist sentiments and such renderings are not limited to the confines of the school walls. As such, it is important not to lose sight through the abandonment of schools as they provide an important entry point into a political project of justice. Instead, communities, scholars, and educators must collectively engage in subversive and political acts that counter these attitudes, built on colonialism, which in turn become school policy and practice. As mentioned earlier, education and schooling are not the same. We as contributors seek ways to ensure that the disjunction between schooling and education be mended by way of reimagining the project of schooling through the trajectory of community resistance. In closing, we thank the many contributors for their tireless work in engaging and critiquing the schooling project and for their contributions to this book, but more importantly for their continuous work and praxis in change-making and awareness-raising. We thank you, the reader, for taking the time and effort to seek out, build upon and add to knowledge for creating new and better futurities for children and youth who have historically and contemporarily are pushed out from the schooling system.

Notes

1. We use "our communities" to describe the multitude of social locations, and by extension, communities that each of the contributors articulate their experiences and work from.
2. Composed of approximately 246,000 students and 38,000 employees (TDSB, 2014).

References

Alexander, M. J. (2006). *Pedagogies of Crossing: Meditations on Feminism, Sexual Politics, Memory, and the Sacred*. Durham, NC: Duke University Press.

Anderson, B. (1991). *Imagined Communities: Reflections on the Origin and Spread of Nationalism*. London and New York: Verso.

Arat-Koc, S. (2005). The Disciplinary Boundaries of Canadian Identity After September 11: Civilizational Identity, Multiculturalism, and the Challenge of Anti-Imperialist Feminism. *Social Justice, 32*(4), 32–49.

Austin, D. (2010). Narrative of Power: Historical Mythologies in Contemporary Quebec and Canada. *Race & Class, 52*(1), 19–32.

Balibar, E. (1991). Is There a Neo-racism. In E. Balibar & I. Wallerstein (Eds.), *Race, Nation, Class: Ambiguous Identities* (pp. 17–28). London: Verso.

Ballingall, A. (2017, October 25). A Majority of Torontonians Now Identify Themselves as Visible Minorities. *The Toronto Star*. Retrieved from https://www.thestar.com/news/gta/2017/10/25/a-majority-of-torontonians-now-identify-themselves-as-visible-minorities-census-shows.html.

Basu, R. (2004). The Rationalization of Neoliberalism in Ontario's Public Education System, 1995–2000. *Geoforum, 35*(5), 621–634.

Bernhard, J. K. (2009). Latin American Students in the TDSB: Research Findings and Recommendations. In D. Mantilla, D. Schugurensky, & J. F. Serrano (Eds.), *Four in Ten: Spanish-Speaking Youth and Early School Leaving in Toronto* (pp. 22–23). Toronto: Latin American Research Education and Development Network and the Transformative Learning Centre, Ontario Institute for the Studies in Education of the University of Toronto.

Calliste, A., & Dei, G. (2000). Introduction. In A. Calliste & G. Dei (Eds.), *Anti-racist Feminism: Critical Race and Gender Studies* (pp. 11–18). Halifax, NS: Fernwood.

Carranza, L. (2009). Humiliation and Schooling. In D. Mantilla, D. Schugurensky, & J. F. Serrano (Eds.), *Four in Ten: Spanish-Speaking Youth and Early School Leaving in Toronto* (pp. 29–31). Toronto: Latin American Research Education and Development Network and the Transformative Learning Centre and Ontario Institute for the Studies in Education of the University of Toronto.

Collins, P. H. (2000). *Black Feminist Thought: Knowledge Consciousness and the Politics of Empowerment*. New York, NY: Routledge.

Dei, G. J. S. (1996). *Anti-racism Education: Theory and Practice*. Halifax, NS: Fernwood.

Dei, G. J. S. (2003). Schooling and the Dilemma of Youth Disengagement. *Mcgill Journal of Education, 38*(2), 241–256.

Dei, G. J. S. (2006). Introduction: Mapping the Terrain—Towards a New Politics of Resistance. In G. J. S. Dei & A. Kempf (Eds.), *Anti-colonialism and Education: The Politics of Resistance* (pp. 1–24). Rotterdam: Sense.

Dei, G. J. S. (2010). The Possibilities of New/Counter Visions of Schooling. *English Quarterly Canada, 41*(3/4), 113–132.

Dei, G. J. S., Mazzuca, J., McIsaac, E., & Zine, J. (1997). *Reconstructing the Dropout: A Critical Ethnography of the Dynamics of Black Students' Disengagement from School.* Toronto: University of Toronto Press.

Dei, G. J. S., Zine, J., & James-Wilson, S. V. (2002). *Inclusive Schooling: A Teacher's Companion to Removing the Margins.* Toronto, ON: Canadian Scholars' Press.

Dion, S. (2009). *Braiding Histories: Learning from Aboriginal Peoples' Experiences and Perspectives.* Vancouver, BC: UBC Press.

Freire, P. (1970). *Pedagogy of the Oppressed.* New York, NY: Herder & Herder.

Giroux, H. (2007). Educated Hope in Dark Times: Critical Pedagogy for Social Justice. *Our Schools, Our Selves, 17*(1), 195–202.

Goldberg, D. T. (1993). *Racist Culture: Philosophy and the Politics of Meaning.* Cambridge, MA: Blackwell Press.

Haig-Brown, C. (2002). *Resistance and Renewal: Surviving the Indian Residential School.* Vancouver, BC: Arsenal Pulp Press.

hooks, b. (2015). *Feminist Theory: From Margin to Center* (3rd ed.). New York, NY: Routledge.

Hurtado, A. (1995). Variations, Combinations, and Evolutions: Latino Families in the United States. In R. E. Zambrana (Ed.), *Understanding Latino Families: Scholarship, Policy, and Practice* (pp. 40–61). Thousand Oaks, CA: Sage.

Hurtado, A. (2003). Theory in the Flesh: Toward an Endarkened Epistemology. *Qualitative Studies in Education, 16*(2), 215–225.

James, C. (2009). African-Caribbean Canadians Working "Harder" to Attain Their Immigrant Dreams: Context, Strategies, and Consequences. *Wadabagei: A Journal of the Caribbean and Its Diaspora, 12*(1), 92–108.

James, C. E. (2011). Multicultural Education in a Color-Blind Society. In A. C. Grant, & P. Agostino, (Eds.), *Intercultural and Multicultural Education: Enhancing Global Interconnectedness* (pp. 191–210). New York, NY: Routledge.

James, C., & Taylor, L. (2010). The Making of at-Risk Students: How Youth See Teachers Thwarting Their Education. *Our Schools, Our Selves, 19*(3), 123–136.

James, C., & Turner, T. (2017). *Towards Race Equity in Education: The Schooling of Black Students in the Greater Toronto Area.* Toronto, ON, Canada: York University.

Jiwani, Y., & Young, M. L. (2006). Missing and Murdered Women: Reproducing Marginality in News Discourse. *Canadian Journal of Communication, 31*(4), 895–917.

Ladson-Billings, G. (2007). Pushing Past the Achievement Gap: An Essay on the Language of Deficit. *The Journal of Negro Education, 76*(3), 316–323.

Leonardo, Z. (2004). Critical Social Theory and Transformative Knowledge: The Functions of Criticism in Quality Education. *Educational Researcher, 33*(6), 11–18.

Li, P. (2001). The Racial Subtext in Canada's Immigration Discourse. *Journal of International Migration and Integration, 2*(1), 77–97.

Li, P. (2003). Deconstructing Canada's Discourse of Immigrant Integration. *Journal of International Migration and Integration, 4*(3), 315–333.

Ontario Ministry of Finance. (2017). *2016 Census Highlights: Factsheet 8*. https://www.fin.gov.on.ca/en/economy/demographics/census/cenhi16-8.html.

Pon, G. (2009). Cutural Competence as New Racism: An Ontology of Forgetting. *Journal of Progressive Human Services, 20*, 59–71.

Rankin, J., Rushowy, K., & Brown, L. (2013, March 22). Toronto School Suspension Rates Highest for Black and Aboriginal Students. *The Toronto Star*. Retrieved from https://www.thestar.com/news/gta/2013/03/22/toronto_school_suspension_rates_highest_for_Black_and_aboriginal_students.html.

Razack, S. (2004). *Dark Threats and White Knights: The Somalia Affair, Peacekeeping, and the New Imperialism*. Toronto, ON: University of Toronto Press.

Rivas, C., & Duarte, J. (2009). Left Behind. In D. Mantilla, D. Schugurensky, & J. F. Serrano (Eds.), *Four in Ten: Spanish-Speaking Youth and Early School Leaving in Toronto* (pp. 89–91). Toronto: Latin American Research Education and Development Network and the Transformative Learning Centre, Ontario Institute for the Studies in Education of the University of Toronto.

Romero, M. (2008). Crossing the Immigration and Race Border: A Critical Race Theory Approach to Immigration Studies. *Contemporary Justice Review, 11*(1), 23–37.

Savarese, J. L. (2017). Challenging Colonial Norms and Attending to Presencing in Stories of Missing and Murdered Inidigenous Women. *Canadian Journal of Women and the Law, 29*(1), 158–181.

Schugurensky, D. (2009). The Educational Experience of Spanish-Speaking Youth: The Brown Report and the Forty Percent Question. In D. Mantilla, D. Schugurensky, & J. F. Serrano (Eds.), *Four in Ten: Spanish-Speaking Youth and Early School Leaving in Toronto* (pp. 3–10). Toronto: Latin American Research Education and Development Network and the Transformative Learning Centre, Ontario Institute for the Studies in Education of the University of Toronto.

Shujaa, M. J. (1994). *Too Much Schooling, Too Little Education: A Paradox of Black Life in White Societies*. Trenton, NJ: Africa World Press.

Simpson, A. (2014). *Mohawk Interruptus: Political Life Across the Borders of Settler States*. Durham, NC: Duke University Press.

The Guardian. (April 13, 2016). Canadian Government 'Lied' over $12bn Arms Sale to Saudi Arabia. *The Guardian.* Retrieved from https://www.theguardian.com/world/2016/apr/13/canadian-government-lied-over-12bn-arms-sale-to-saudi-arabia.

Thobani, S. (2000). Closing Ranks: Racism and Sexism in Canada's Immigration Policy. *Race & Class,* 42(1), 35–55.

Thobani, S. (2007). *Exalted Subjects: Studies in the Making of Race and Nation in Canada.* Toronto, ON: University of Toronto Press.

Toronto District School Board. (2014). About Us. http://www.tdsb.on.ca/About-Us.

Tuck, E., & Yang, K. W. (2014). Unbecoming Claims: Pedagogies of Refusal in Qualitative Research. *Qualitative Inquiry,* 20(6), 811–818.

Valenzuela, A. (1999). *Subtractive Schooling: U.S.-Mexican Youth and the Politics of Caring.* Albany: State University of New York Press.

Walia, H. (2013). *Undoing Border Imperialism.* Oakland: AK Press.

Wane, N. N., Deliovsky, K., & Lawson, E. (2002). *Back to the Drawing Board: African-Canadian Feminisms.* Toronto: Sumach Press.

Wotherspoon, T. (2009). *The Sociology of Education in Canada.* Don Mills, ON: Oxford University Press.

CHAPTER 2

"I'm Just a Friend Now": Community Policing in Toronto Schools

Gita Rao Madan

2.1 Introduction

On June 15, 2017, the Toronto Police Services Board (TPSB) convened to discuss the future of the School Resource Officer program in Toronto, which has placed fully armed and uniformed police officers (SROs) in many of the city's public high schools on a full-time basis (CBC, 2009). This partnership program between the Toronto Police Service (TPS), the Toronto District School Board (TDSB), and the Toronto Catholic District School Board (TCDSB), was first implemented in 2008, primarily targeting schools in the city's designated "priority areas." It was created largely in response to escalated public concerns about school safety following the death of Jordan Manners, who, in 2007, was the first student to be killed on TDSB property (Brown & Rushowy, 2014). Following its inaugural school year, the SRO program expanded from 30 to 50 high schools across the city. Currently, 36 officers are shared between 75 schools (Gillis, 2017).

G. R. Madan (✉)
Toronto, ON, Canada
e-mail: gita.madan@mail.utoronto.ca

© The Author(s) 2019
F. J. Villegas and J. Brady (eds.), *Critical Schooling*,
https://doi.org/10.1007/978-3-030-00716-4_2

The SRO program first appeared on the TPSB agenda as a regular item for annual approval at a sparsely attended public meeting in May 2017. At this time, a small handful of community members from our grassroots organization Education Not Incarceration (ENI) registered as deputants to voice strong opposition to SRO policing (this was ENI's first public action of an organized and strategic campaign for the removal of the SRO program). Taken by surprise, the board nearly voted to suspend the program on the spot, but instead deferred their final decision until June.

At the June meeting, seventy-nine members of the public registered to present deputations. The room was, in fact, so full of people (and police officers) that many community members who registered to express their positions were barred from entering by a row of officers using bicycles to form a barricade. The majority of the first thirty deputants were strongly in favor of the program (TPSB, 2017). One after another, students, teachers, and administrators—largely from the TCDSB—spoke about the personal relationships they had developed with their SROs. They offered praise for the individual officers who had been placed in their schools, recalling events they had organized, sports teams they had coached, school trips they had attended, programs they had initiated, and so on. Several SROs told "feel good" stories in which they described the impacts they feel they have had on young people and the personal and career impacts that they themselves have experienced as officers through their exposure to "disadvantaged" youth in this setting.

The second half of the eight-hour meeting stood in sharp contrast to the first. Parents, youth, educators, lawyers, researchers, and representatives of community organizations recounted stories of abuse, harassment, and violence by SROs, and called for the immediate suspension of the program. They named the anti-Black racism that continues to plague both the policing and the education institutions, questioned the increasing concentration of policing services in particular areas of the city, and criticized the lack of public consultation on the program prior to its implementation. In the deputation I delivered, I spoke to the existing research, as reviewed during the course of my previous academic and community organizing work (Madan, 2016). For example, researchers have shown that there is little evidence to support the premise that policing actually makes schools safer (Campbell, 2009; Justice Policy Institute, 2012); that SRO policing disproportionately targets schools in low-income, racialized, and urban areas (Nolan, 2011); and that it criminalizes Black, Indigenous, racialized, and undocumented students within their schools, fueling the school-to-prison pipeline (Advancement Project, 2013; Hirschfield, 2008; Madan, 2016; Petteruti, 2011). Further, I and others highlighted the ways in which the program violates policy measures meant to protect our most marginalized students, including the established Police-School Board Protocol, school board equity policies, the municipal sanctuary city policy, and the provincial educational policy of progressive discipline.

In the end, the TPSB refused to suspend the program, instead opting to proceed with another review (the third of its kind). In spite of the fact that the systemic injustices and barriers to education produced by the SRO program had been brought fully into view, the narrative emphasizing the "relationship-building" efforts of the police toward marginalized youth—an approach rooted in the model of community policing—was effectively used to uphold the program and silence the concerns of those most adversely affected by it.

This chapter is firmly situated in, and committed to, the ongoing struggle to remove the permanent presence of police from Toronto's schools. Specifically, it asks: In what ways has the discourse of relationship building been used to justify the existence of the SRO program while simultaneously obscuring the material reality of SRO policing on the ground? I argue that we must critically interrogate the idea that the relationship-building approach taken by the Toronto SRO program somehow renders it able to mitigate the harms inherent to it. To do this, I aim to discern the productive function of the discourses used to legitimize the SRO program—that is, to ask what these discourses *do*. A close examination reveals that the shift from an emphasis on "school safety" toward relationship building has effectively and insidiously advanced many of the institutional interests of the police while powerfully decontextualizing the program from the ongoing historical violence that racialized communities experience at their hands. The relationship-building discourse is self-serving for the TPS in various ways: It allows for the extension of their existing community policing model into school spaces; it boosts public relations by framing the program as a mutually beneficial community partnership; it allows for the humanization of individual officers, a process that detracts from systemic analyses of policing as an institution; it provides police with increased access to youth for intelligence-gathering purposes; and it masks the disciplinary and pedagogical functions of SRO policing.

This work of critically interrogating Toronto's SRO program is particularly important for a number of reasons, one of which is that the majority of existing scholarship discussing policing in schools has been produced in the American context. The dearth of scholarship in the Canadian context is significant because there are several key differences. In the USA, formal partnerships between police departments and school boards proliferated in the 1990s as part of a broader "zero-tolerance" approach to misconduct (Petteruti, 2011). This highly punitive approach mandates serious consequences for even minor violations of school rules, including acts with little potential for harm, and permits little room for consideration of mitigating circumstances or alternative disciplinary approaches. This transformed educational regime has predominantly taken the form of sweeping securitization and surveillance in many urban American public schools, including the installation of metal detectors, scanners, and surveillance cameras; random drug sweeps and controlled access to school grounds; and the permanent stationing of security guards and police officers (Nolan, 2011).

In Toronto, while SROs are armed and uniformed, they are not accompanied by the gamut of security strategies characterizing many American SRO programs. In fact, upon consideration of installing further security apparatus in schools, former TDSB Director of Education Donna Quan stated, "Metal detectors are not the answer. We don't want to create fortresses" (Doucette, 2014). In terms of policy, Ontario's Ministry of Education did enact zero-tolerance-based legislation (the *Safe Schools Act*) in 2001 but was forced to shift toward a more progressive disciplinary model in 2007 after the Ontario Human Rights Commission found that the policy was having discriminatory effects on students of color, particularly Black, Indigenous, Tamil, and Latinx students, as well as students with disabilities (OHRC, 2003). The SRO program was implemented in Toronto schools shortly after this time, despite the fact that the existing literature clearly refers to policing in schools as a direct manifestation of a zero-tolerance- and crime-control-based approach to education, not as a constructive alternative.

I argue that the contradiction between the simultaneous rejection of metal detectors in schools, on the one hand, and the enthusiastic acceptance of a permanent police presence, on the other, can only be reconciled if SRO policing is constructed as fundamentally discontinuous with a zero-tolerance approach. This understanding—that SRO policing in Toronto is, at its core, different from the zero-tolerance logic from which contemporary SRO programs have emerged—has been largely achieved through the dominant public and institutional narrative of relationship building. This has effectively led many teachers, administrators, parents, and students to uncritically accept the presence of school-based officers rather than to question the need for them in the first place. However, it is crucial for all educational stakeholders to fully examine what becomes obscured by the relationship-building logic; we must grapple with this question even though, and precisely because, it calls into question the very legitimacy of the program.

2.2 Theoretical Framework

My understanding of racial violence in the context of SRO policing extends beyond sensational acts of police brutality. I draw from the work of Ferreira da Silva (2010), who refers to police violence as the "most perverse and elusive form of race injustice" (p. 441). This is because the effects of racial power that manifest themselves in forms such as police brutality go far beyond easily documented instances of racial discrimination, exclusion, or prejudice. The hegemonic construction of race presumes that race must be invoked (explicitly or implicitly) in order to justify practices that produce exclusion. She argues that this view, still retained by many scholars, limits considerations to whether and how racism plays a role in specific social encounters, processes, and structures.[1] However, there are more slippery forms of racial injustice left uncaptured by this framework. For Ferreira da Silva, police terror is the most elusive instance of race injustice precisely because it operates fully and effectively *without* the invocation of race. Accordingly, in order for the effects of racial power to be fully grasped, the logic that race only becomes significant when it is invoked to justify practices of discrimination must be challenged. In doing so, it is possible to articulate claims of racial injustice that are otherwise rendered unheard or irrelevant on the grounds that they fail to invoke race.

Goldberg (2009) argues that in the modern imagination, race is assumed to be an obsolete notion, a vestige of the premodern past. Contemporary forces of racial order insist on formal equality under the law, producing state-mandated race neutrality that has effectively "saved" racism through the categorical abandonment of race. Goldberg refers to this redirection of the racial as born-again racism: "Racism without race, racism gone private, racism without the categories to name it as such. It is racism shorn of the charge, a racism that cannot be named because nothing abounds with which to name it. It is a racism purged of historical roots, of its groundedness, a racism whose history is lost" (p. 23). Born-again racism is transparent and faceless, always operating in denial. A regime of racelessness, while appearing to extend openness and accessibility, ensures the covert and totalizing extension of the racial—a logic that now rests on discourses of security maintenance, crime control, and the like.

Menter's (1987) discursive analysis of the literature on police-school relationships in England identifies this erasure, revealing that police in schools are often framed by institutions in ways that obscure the central role of the police in the broader machinery of security and surveillance. He identifies in institutional documents a common pattern of carefully crafted and race-neutral language, including words such as "cooperation," "respect," "responsibility," and "cultural diversity." These policies are "carved very precisely, and with a very sharp edge, around the contours of race, ethnicity, and class; ironically in the name of public safety, educational accountability, and personal responsibility" (Fine & Ruglis, 2009, p. 22). Here, the glaring omission of race is not merely an effect of power; it is the very mechanism through which it operates.

In Toronto, the implementation of the SRO program has been accomplished in an institutional context that makes no mention of race or the historical relationship between police and racialized communities. Race is absent from all of the official communications related to the program, an omission that is also echoed in public discourse. In this chapter, I explore the ways in which the Toronto SRO program is fundamentally rooted in racial injustice, operating through racially coded discourses that allow it to persist while eliding the criterion of racial invocation. Further, I examine how the absence of an explicit or implicit invocation of race in dominant explanations for the existence of Toronto's SRO program actually works to obscure its most harmful functions—namely, the production and reproduction of social inequalities within school spaces.

2.3 RELATIONSHIP BUILDING AND SROS

As an SRO, I am also an educator, an informal counselor, a mentor, a role model, and a friend.

In particular, he's well known for Star Wars breakfast, where he engages students while preparing Star Wars toast and waffles for students weekly at the school.

—TPSB deputations, June 2017

Two of the primary goals of the Toronto SRO program are to "improve the perception of the police amongst youth in the community" and to "improve the relationship between students and police" (Public Safety Canada, 2013). What does the relationship-building approach actually look like in Toronto schools? "Officers don't just patrol the halls, they also develop a relationship with students," said police spokesperson Mark Pugash (Aulakh & Dobbs, 2009). SROs have actively integrated themselves into all aspects of school life, taking on roles such as coaching sports teams, running homework clubs, participating in talent shows, attending graduations, delivering anti-bullying presentations, attending field trips, running charity fundraising events, speaking to law and civics classes, DJing at pep rallies, and attending student council meetings (Gee, 2009; Kauri, 2012; Rushowy, 2009). They also actively foster relationships with other members of the school community by attending staff meetings, parent council meetings, and parent information sessions, and by making efforts to integrate themselves into school management teams. SROs report that the most successful strategies they have used to establish and strengthen relationships within schools include showing students respect and considering their needs, being approachable and non-authoritarian, being friendly and positive, fostering informal conversation, offering prize incentives (especially food), identifying popular students to promote and lead events, coaching or participating in sports, and being visible in the halls and at lunch (TPS, 2009, 2011).

Some SROs have developed elaborate programs involving large inputs of time, energy, and funding. One such initiative is the Cooking with Cops program, started at a high school in Toronto's west end several years ago by an SRO who was tired of seeing fast food takeout containers in the hallways of the school (Chu, 2014). "Eager to make a change," she started a program that would allow youth to learn recipes, cook food together for school events, serve meals at a seniors' center in the area, and visit local restaurants for kitchen tours and cooking classes (Rainford, 2014). Of the program, the SRO said, "I like the experience it gives the students, plus it teaches them about teamwork, hard work, dedication and commitment. I truly love it...They don't see me as a police officer half the time, I'm just a friend now" (Chu, 2014).

The SRO program has created an abundance of new opportunities for police to access and interact with young people. Interestingly, some SROs report that they have sometimes found it challenging to perform their duties in the school because other staff-led activities and programs compete for student participation (TPS, 2011). Does the TPS-driven mandate of building relationships align with the best interests of students or with the educational mandates of the school boards in which SROs have been placed? Both curricular and extracurricular programming and pedagogy should arguably be fulfilled by professional educators and support staff who have devoted their careers to building skills, training, knowledge, and experience in the fields of education, schooling, and youth work. What is accomplished by the assumption of these responsibilities by *police officers*? Further, how does the seemingly benign relationship-building approach obscure the more insidious policing functions of the SRO?

2.4 WHAT IS CONCEALED BY THE RELATIONSHIP-BUILDING DISCOURSE?

You remember me? You arrested me in the summertime.
—A Toronto student, upon meeting the SRO who was assigned to his high school. (Rushowy, 2009)

2.4.1 *Race, Place, and Youth "at Risk"*

The narrative of relationship building not only masks the naturalization of police presence but also enables and obscures the violence that accompanies it. Though the SRO program may at first seem innocuous, well intentioned, and mutually beneficial, it emerged from a broader community policing model that was applied in a targeted way to racialized and low-income areas of the city through the TPS' (recently disbanded) Toronto Anti-Violence Intervention Strategy (TAVIS) (Public Safety Canada, 2013; Vivanco, 2009). Under the guise of relationship building and becoming familiar faces in the community, TAVIS officers aggressively assaulted and drew guns on young people on the streets of their neighborhoods, performed strip searches in broad daylight, and arbitrarily stopped hundreds of racialized people without cause in public areas to question them and gather intelligence—a practice known as carding, which has been targeted primarily at Toronto's Black community (Winsa, 2013). One study of Toronto high-school students shows that Black students who are not involved in delinquent behavior are much more likely to be stopped and treated as suspects by the police than white youth who actually *admit involvement* in illegal activity (Fine et al., 2003). The SRO program extends the TPS' community policing practices into the school spaces of these same youth, producing a continuity across institutional boundaries that denies them the possibility of escape. Indeed, one of the explicit goals of TAVIS was "normalized policing" (TPS, 2015).

Under the integrated TAVIS model, policing services converged on the bodies of youth who have been deemed "at risk" because they reside in neighborhoods designated as "priority areas" (since renamed as "neighbourhood improvement areas") (Public Safety Canada, 2013). The discursive association of lawlessness and other "problem" behaviors with residence in stigmatized urban neighborhoods in Toronto is discussed by James (2012), who argues that police intervention into the lives of youth is recurrently justified by pervasive discourses of at-riskness. "Risk," which serves as a euphemism for race/place and other interlocking constructs including class, gender, and immigration status, is not an abstract concept; it is a category used to identify racialized youth, to label them as in need of saving, and to justify mechanisms of social control. The at-risk designation is powerful in its ability to mask institutionally structured relations in ways that pin responsibility for circumstances and life opportunities back onto youth, their families, and their communities. The institutions that then mobilize this designation are absolved from responsibility, understood only as well intentioned in their provision of additional community "supports" such as extra police.

Chapman-Nyaho, James, and Kwan-Lafond (2012) have investigated another TPS program rooted in similar objectives and discourses as the SRO Program: The Youth in Policing Initiative (YIPI). Every summer since 2006, YIPI has offered 150 predominantly racialized (over 93%, with over half identifying as Black) youth from Toronto's designated priority neighborhoods six weeks of full-time employment in various police divisions. The purpose of the program is to provide work experience for youth who are deemed "at risk" and to improve the historically tense relationship between these youth and their communities, on the one hand, and the police, on the other. Both YIPI and the SRO program fall under the TPS' community mobilization strategy and both are listed under the *City of Toronto*'s broader strategy for addressing "youth who are at the greatest risk of marginalization" in Toronto (Brillinger, 2013, p. 1).

The racialized spatial nature of the at-risk designation is evident in the selection criteria for the YIPI program (Chapman-Nyaho et al., 2012). All youth accepted into the program must reside in priority neighborhoods. However, youth cannot have a criminal record to participate in the program, and very few who are selected have a history of encounters with law enforcement or trouble at school. Therefore, regardless of their individual circumstances and histories, all youth from priority areas are labeled as "at risk" and in need of guidance and attention solely based on geographic location. In other words, violence and criminality are always already understood as inherent to these racialized spaces and, by extension, to the bodies that move through them. When faced with the reality of the irrelevance of the at-risk designation that is applied to all the individual young people with whom they work, YIPI officers frame the intervention as preemptive: While the youth may not *seem* "bad," considering their environment and lack of opportunity, you "never know what would happen" without programs like this (p. 89).

James (2012) argues that initiatives such as YIPI and the SRO program—those that involve educational support, guidance, mentorship, and relationship building—are frequently the precise outcome of the mobilization of at-risk discourses. In other words, the very existence of these programs is dependent on this racialized construct. Specifically, when it comes to policing, this rhetoric is routinely used to justify interventions that extend beyond the law enforcement capacity of the police—this is the very premise upon which the model of community policing is based. However, it is critical to understand how these programs continue to produce and sustain racial hierarchies. Chapman-Nyaho et al. (2012) argue that they are actually "premised on a need to guide, govern, and surveil young people from priority areas, and, in the process, protect and advance the material, moral, and psychological interests of the police" (p. 84). The creation of the at-risk designation allows the police to declare racialized and low-income youth as in need of special intervention to fill the void of positive influence in their lives. When the police swoop in to help, they establish their moral authority through efforts to reach out to marginalized youth, a redemptive gesture that reflects positively on their public image. The mentorship of the police is said to provide valuable opportunities and experience that youth from these communities would otherwise be lost without, and only the guidance of the police can transform them into responsible adults and good citizens. The framing of these initiatives through a language of opportunity has facilitated the widespread adoption of a paradigm that pathologizes and criminalizes young racialized people, garnering enthusiastic support from policymakers; authority figures in young people's lives, including teachers and school administrators; and many from the wider community. This framing of policing as benevolent effectively resolves any public anxieties that may have been induced by the idea that students are now being policed in their schools. The portrayal of YIPI and SRO officers as savior-like has been successful in pacifying criticism even from some of those who are critical of the harsh and aggressive tactics employed by Toronto police elsewhere.

2.4.2 Who Benefits?

At the June 15 TPSB meeting, almost every school administrator, educator, and student who celebrated the success of the SRO program spoke predominantly of the extracurricular programming that their individual officer(s) had not only initiated and run in the school, but also funded (TPSB, 2017). It became very apparent that the perceived benefits brought by the program to the school community had far more to do with a lack of funding for full-time caring adults and supportive programming than a need for officers in particular. In the face of neoliberal cuts to public education, the SRO program—funded entirely through the police budget—represents additional adults in the school who may provide access to extracurricular programs that are desirable for students as part of their high-school experience. Further, because of the financial resources available to SROs, participation in some of their initiatives is incentivized with prizes for students such as free bicycles and even trips to Disneyland (Park, 2015). For this reason, it is true that some students in schools with SROs may gain some material and social benefits as a result of the program and come to see it as a valuable experience overall. When it comes to choosing between having an extracurricular activity or team run by a police officer or not having it at all, for many students, the choice is clear. For example, I asked one of my former students how he felt about his junior boys' baseball team being scheduled to play several games against a team of police officers. He said, "I'd rather just play against another school. I don't wanna shake their hands because they're the ones who are constantly looking at me every time I'm walking down the street." For him, being forced to interact with police officers in this way was the personal cost of being able to play sports at school. Although a full examination of the prison industrial complex as it relates to SRO policing is beyond the scope of this chapter, it is critical to ask why the police are so *invested* in providing these opportunities, and why so many educational stakeholders are defending the redirection of public education funds into criminal justice security and surveillance, an investment that ultimately benefits private and carceral interests.

Does SRO policing foster mutual understanding and respect? The discourse of relationship building rests on an assumption that bringing "at-risk" youth and police together in a "get-to-know-you" setting will improve the historically problematic relationship between them. The TPS argues: "Young people get to see police officers in a different light, and police officers get to see young people in a different light—when the program works well, both sides can take away something positive" (TPS, 2011). However, the claim that this is a mutually beneficial exchange where understandings flow freely and equally between youth and the police is utterly false and serves to obscure the gross power differential between the two parties. Instead, the way that the YIPI and SRO programs are structured works primarily to advance the institutional interests of the police—they do so by using relationship building to bring the beliefs and practices of racialized youth in line with those of the policing institution. Importantly, this occurs while the police are able to carry on as usual without sacrificing any of their practices or assumptions, and without having to examine or confront the ongoing historical violence that racialized communities experience at the hands of the police. The relationship-building approach is powerfully effective at decontextualizing the SRO program from its social and historical reality, ignoring the ongoing struggles for justice by racialized communities in the city for whom police violence is a daily reality. It precludes a systemic analysis of policing that would first and foremost ask, why is the relationship between police and racialized youth in need of improvement in the first place? When police speak of the strained relationships that exist between them and marginalized communities, no responsibility is taken for the violence that has led to such mistrust—on the contrary, the violence is actively invisibilized by such discourses. Instead, inadequacy and disadvantage are located on the bodies of racialized youth as both blame and responsibility are deflected from the structural to the individual.

Further, the relationship-building approach encourages liberal understandings of policing in which some police officers are "good" and harmful police practices are ascribed to other individuals who strayed from protocol. Chapman-Nyaho et al. (2012) noted that over the course of the six-week YIPI program, there was a profound change in the way the youth conceptualized policing. Youth reported feeling highly influenced by the interpersonal relationships they developed with officers in the program, describing officers as being very relatable, having a great sense of humor, and going out of their way to make the youth comfortable. Regardless of their previous attitudes toward the police, by the end of the program almost every youth concluded that the police are good people: "Now I see how they are; they're human just like us. They're doing a job just like everybody else" (p. 90). This enthusiastic admiration for individual officers quickly translated, however, into an increased belief that the institution of policing as a whole is friendly, helpful, and just. The effect of this form of governance was thus a drastic shift in the beliefs and attitudes of youth into alignment with the interests and objectives of the police. This paradigmatic shift on the part of young people resulted in switched allegiances, with youth taking on an ambassadorial role for policing in their communities and defending police practices that are often criticized by others: "Now, when I see a cop car, I don't look to see who's in it, I look to see who's driving it" (p. 91).

A similarly profound realignment has been accomplished with respect to student attitudes toward SRO police:

> When he came to NACI [North Albion Collegiate Institute] as a school resource officer—one of 50 now in Toronto schools to maintain security and reach out to troubled kids—many saw him as the enemy. They turned away when he came down the hall, muttering among themselves or sucking their teeth in disdain. "No one would talk to me," recalls Constable Chhinzer, an athletic 27-year-old with a shaved head and an open manner. One day he saw some boys playing football in the gym. He put up a notice calling a football practice and, to his astonishment, 70 kids came out. As he put them through their paces in after-school drills that lasted three hours and more, they gradually learned to trust him and see the man behind the blue uniform and flak jacket. (Gee, 2009)

"If anything, I'd rather have him inside the school than outside," said Lovejeet, a Grade 12 student. "It changed the perception of police officers," she said. "My cousins don't like the cops and now they talk to him and stuff." (Rushowy, 2009)

The teens said they didn't always have this positive attitude towards police. "Honestly, I thought they were assholes," said Farooq. "I'd be chillin' with my friends and they'd harass me for no reason." "The cop in our school is normal, he's the complete opposite of that," he added. (Benitah, 2009)

The students no longer care that Chhinzer wears a uniform and carries a gun. To them, he's part counselor, mentor, ego-booster and founder and coach of a football team with no uniforms or equipment but enough enthusiasm that 60 boys come out on a regular basis—rain, shine, even hail—just to scrimmage. ... He jokes with the students, and they with him; on the rare occasion he brings his patrol car to school, students put their hands on the hood as if under arrest. (Rushowy, 2009)

A student that I work with closely wanted nothing to do with a police officer, didn't want to speak to him. He had questions surrounding an issue that I thought this officer could possibly help with. Didn't want anything to do with it. So I said, "Ok well can you tell me why?" And he said, "I don't want to talk to any cops ever. Never." Eventually he came to understand through some of his peers that the officer in question at our school wasn't a negative influence. Yeah, he's not gonna sit with him right now either, but he's lightened that opinion slightly and my hope is to just eventually build on that and maybe he can see our officer as a person and not just "that cop." (TPSB deputation, June 2017)

These improved perceptions of police among youth are considered one of the greatest successes of the SRO program (TPS, 2009, 2011). Though framed largely as an opportunity for youth—an opportunity to attend a school that is "safe," an opportunity to build closer relationships with the police, an opportunity to access sports and other extracurriculars that may otherwise not be offered at the school—the opportunities provided to the TPS by the SRO program far outweigh any benefits proffered to students. Through the relationship-building initiatives of the program, the exposure of police to youth in a non-conflictual setting has allowed for the humanization of individual officers, allowing them to be seen as regular people who can relate to the struggles of youth.

In other words, it has enabled youth to divorce the personalities of individual SROs from their fundamental role as representatives of the police. In this way, the interests of the institution are not only protected but entrenched through programs such as these.

2.4.3   Student Surveillance

If you are going through something, talk to me.
—Toronto SRO to high school student (Rushowy, 2009)

The SRO program is a critical tool for increased government surveillance of the youth population at large. The TPS' community policing projects are intelligence-led; information collected about individuals from racially targeted street stops is retained in a burgeoning database that can be accessed by any security force in Canada, as well as the FBI and US Homeland Security (Saczkowski, 2015). If intelligence gathering was not already taking place informally, in 2011, the responsibilities of Toronto SROs were officially expanded to explicitly include this practice (TPS, 2012). According to the TPS, every SRO is now a member of a police Tactical Intelligence Strategy team that meets weekly to share information specifically about youth. Other members of this team have included frontline enforcement, intelligence, TAVIS street policing teams, and the Canada Border Services Agency (CBSA). SROs play a critical role on this team because they are uniquely positioned to collect sensitive information about young people, and they actively encourage students to disclose information to them and to see them as confidants and allies (Benitah, 2009). This "get-to-know-you" approach serves to conceal the intelligence-gathering mandate of SROs, allowing them to develop intimate and familiar relationships with students, who may share personal information with officers while remaining wholly unaware of the potentially grave consequences of doing so.

The SRO's intelligence mandate is particularly threatening for the thousands of students (and their families) in Toronto who have precarious immigration status.[2] In May 2007, under pressure from school groups and community organizations, the TDSB adopted a "Students Without Legal Immigration Status" (or "Don't Ask, Don't Tell") policy (P.061 SCH) stating that all children are welcome at school regardless of status and that status-related information would not be shared with immigration officials (No One Is Illegal, 2010; TDSB, 2007; Villegas, Chapter 8). Under this policy, schools are instructed not to require information about immigration status for student enrollment and, if it becomes known, not to provide this information to immigration authorities. Further, the policy is supported by a directive that denies immigration authorities access to TDSB property. However, through the SRO program, the CBSA is effectively able to access personal information about students and their families that could lead to apprehension, detention, and deportation. The collusion between SROs and CBSA is a clear violation of the board's commitment to the "Don't Ask, Don't Tell" policy. Even if the policy was enforced for SROs, it would conflict not only with the SRO mandate but also with current policing practices under subsection 5 of Ontario Regulation 265/98 (Government of Ontario, 2005). Although this regulation states that it is legally within the discretion of police to report any personal information gathered in their investigations to federal agencies for "bona fide" reasons, it has been found that the TPS reports individuals to CBSA on a high-volume basis (Moffette & Gardner, 2015). In other words, the routinized flow of information from the police to CBSA means that the only way to address the dangers posed by the SRO program to students who are undocumented or have precarious status is to remove officers from schools altogether.

2.4.4   SRO Disciplinary Practices

I've seen officers pick up students who were skipping first period.
—A Toronto high school teacher, TPSB deputation, June 2017

This is a case of a Black child, railroaded by the Toronto District School Board and the Toronto Police, whose negligence damaged his life. This case points to why Black students are 3 times more likely to be suspended, 3.5 times more likely to be carded, 4 times more likely to be charged.
—Parent, TPSB deputation, June 2017

Nolan (2011) describes the series of events typical of most school-based arrests she observed in high schools in New York City: These confrontations begin with the violation of a school rule that has little or no impact on school safety, such as the dress code or taking too long to get to class. Students are criminalized for these behaviors, and in responding to the provocation they often end up getting arrested for insubordination or disorderly conduct. The presence of police in the school creates an excessive reliance on law enforcement, meaning that minor incidents previously dealt with by the school administration escalate into criminal justice matters.

The relationship-building discourse of the Toronto SRO program is extremely effective at detracting attention from the disciplinary and enforcement functions of SROs. The polished public image of Toronto SROs seems to stand in contradiction to the harsh and aggressive tactics characterizing SRO programs in many American schools; it has been shown that SROs in Toronto prefer to see themselves as relationship builders rather than enforcers (Rushowy, 2009; TPS, 2009, 2011). However, reports of police intimidation, harassment, arrests, and assault of students by Toronto SROs were confirmed by the organization Educators for Peace and Justice as far back as 2009 (Jennie, 2009). They claimed that SROs create a climate of fear and repression in schools and that while the media prefers to focus on students who may benefit from the presence of police officers, many marginalized students feel further alienated by this program.

One cell phone video of an incident in a Toronto school went viral after it was posted to YouTube: the arrest of a sixteen-year-old Black male in the stairway of his high school in October 2009. The video, called "Student Arrested at Northern Secondary School for No Reason," begins following a confrontation that was reportedly initiated when the SRO asked the student for identification (even though he was wearing an ID lanyard around his neck) and the student responded using the word "bacon" (Friesen & Appleby, 2009; MajorKraze, 2009). As the situation escalates, the officer repeatedly demands that the student put his hands behind his back. The student responds with, "I've done nothing wrong to get arrested," and, "Don't you have to let me know what I've done first?" The student's friends also demand that the officer let the student go. With no justification given, the officer handcuffs the student and proceeds to violently push him through a packed hallway of the school, making a public spectacle of the incident for all the other students to see. The student was subsequently charged for assaulting an officer and resisting arrest, and then suspended (TPAC, 2009).

What message is sent to students who are under tight and constant scrutiny, repeatedly being asked to identify themselves in their own schools, the very places where they are supposed to be? Discipline is powerfully pedagogical. Noguera (1995) asserts that the disciplining event itself functions to reactivate power, both by demonstrating where it lies and also by perpetuating its authority. Quoting Foucault, he writes that the "ceremony of punishment ... is to make everyone aware, through the body of the criminal, of the unrestrained presence of the sovereign" (p. 49). In this sort of altercation between students and SROs, there is a reactivation of power that takes place that is imprinted on the bodies of students. Racial hierarchies in the school are reinscribed through the encounter: The targeted youth is produced as a criminalized subject, as a threat that must be contained and removed from the school, while the groups of white students (and staff) bearing witness to this performance in the hallway are able to affirm that they are *not* him, and are therefore deserving of protection *from* him at any cost. Lipman (2011) writes that repeated police encounters serve as a "powerful signifier that youth of colour are dangerous and need to be locked up or removed from public space" (p. 85). Spectacles of this sort serve to confirm the perception that there is indeed a need for the SRO in the school. The rest of the school community can be assured that although the vast majority of the time the presence of an SRO is unnecessary, rare incidents do arise that only the police can handle.

This racial boundary is enforced even when SROs are not engaged in disciplinary action. Until now, throughout all SRO activities, there has been a strong emphasis on the visibility of officers. Former Police Chief Bill Blair insisted that officers be in uniform at all times and that they maintain an active and visible presence in the school (Blatchford, 2009). When SROs are engaged in other activities or even just standing around, their uniformed presence still ensures a constant visual reminder not only of the power they wield as police officers but also of a constant threat of criminality that lurks in school spaces. The result is a culture of control that constantly codes the bodies of racialized students in particular ways, teaching students about themselves and their place within the hierarchy of the school. It also sends a clear message to the broader school community about the students who attend the school. For example, at one school located on a major street, the SRO often insists on parking his police car directly in front of the school instead of in his assigned spot in the parking lot behind the building. This move has resulted in passersby frequently asking what just happened at the school. In the few instances when SROs perform their duties in civilian clothes, this decision is made very strategically. For instance, an SRO who visited a school to make a special presentation explained, "I do the same job as Candy [the school's SRO]. I purposely didn't dress up like a cop today because I wanted you to see Candy as a cop in a uniform and me as a cop not in a uniform. We're both just people. And we're both here to help" (Mills, 2012).

2.5 Born-Again Racism

The race-based discrimination characterizing Ontario's former zero-tolerance disciplinary policy has in many ways been "born again" through the SRO policing program in Toronto schools. The characteristically neoliberal purging of race from the public sphere in the name of racelessness does not make it disappear; instead, it unhinges race from the domain of state delimitation, allowing it to circulate freely under discourses of individual merit, effort, ability, and choice. Because the relationship-building strategy relies on these discourses, it is a particularly insidious example of how racism continues to operate without race invocation—in this case, under a veneer of opportunity and mutual benefit. In fact, racial power is manifestly secured in the *absence* of this invocation, as the central organizing logic of race becomes hidden by race-absent institutional discourses of safety, risk, opportunity, and relationship building. Goldberg (2009) writes, "As race evaporates from the socio-conceptual landscape, racisms (in their plurality) are pushed further and further out of sight, out of "existence," unmentionable because the terms by which to recognize and reference them recede, fade from view and memory" (p. 360). Racial power assumes new strategies and modes of management in order to ensure its continuity; this is evident in the discursive evolution of the SRO program from safety and security to relationship building, each subsequent strategy more thoroughly raceless and thus farther away from the explanatory grasp of dominant conceptions of racism.

2.6 Conclusion

In this chapter, I have challenged the assumption that the injustice inherent to SRO policing can be addressed by reframing it through the discourse and practice of relationship building. The TPS has invested large sums of time, money, and energy into implementing and defending the program, creating and mobilizing discourses of safety, at-riskness, and opportunity in order to present the project as beneficial for the youth targeted by SRO policing. However, a close examination of this discursive framing reveals that it in fact works to produce and reproduce racial hierarchies in a myriad of ways. In this context, one of the greatest "accomplishments" of this approach has been its relative success at engulfing critique and suppressing resistance. Since its inception, the SRO program has quickly become normalized within the schooling fabric of the city and, until very recently, has managed to fly largely under the radar both in conversations about education and about policing. Here, I have aimed to articulate what is suppressed by official discourses in order to more fully grasp what is at stake in the continued existence and expansion of the program.

On May 4, 2016, the TPS unveiled the newest development in police-school partnerships in Toronto: "May the Police 4th Be with You"—a day of fun, games, and relationship building between TPS officers and elementary school students from 22 schools in Scarborough, a largely racialized suburb of Toronto (CTV Toronto, 2016). News coverage of the event depicts children as young as nine years old participating in a "Mock Police Academy," which included being coached by officers to hit mats with batons while yelling, "Get down!" as well as learning how to place each other into handcuffs. Speaking at the event, Chief of Police Mark Saunders said, "Instead of seeing us in the uniform, they see us as human beings. We're interacting in a social environment and having a good time together."

As the expansion of TPS' school-based policing strategy continues, youth, parents, educators, community members, and community organizations including Education Not Incarceration, Jane and Finch Action Against Poverty, Black Lives Matter—Toronto, Educators for Peace and Justice, and the Latinx Afro-Latin-America Abya Yala Education Network, are organizing in resistance. In the past few months, these organizations have mounted a mainstream media and public education campaign; lobbied officials at the TPS, the school boards, and elected political representatives; and collected over 1000 signatures for a petition to end the SRO program. In the coming months, as the fate of the program is decided, it is the responsibility of educators, administrators, school boards, policy-makers, parents, community members, and all those invested in an equitable and just education system to center the experiences of those most harmed by its historical and ongoing racial violence. I conclude with the eloquent observations of Toronto high-school student Rayon:

> The feelings among most of the students at Weston C.I. is that they do not want a cop in their school and they feel threatened by the presence of an armed police officer in the school for numerous reasons. The students cannot identify with an individual who wears a massive bullet proof vest and carries a loaded gun and taser, which is quite intimidating particularly for people coming from T.O.'s "priority neighbourhoods"—let's be honest,

ghettoes—who witness and experience police activity in a whole different light than youth from more affluent areas. On a day-to-day basis, the police harass, bully, and brutalize people from our communities and get away without being held to account for their actions. How can we accept having police in our schools to "build relations" with us if they are getting away with daily brutality and sometimes murder in our communities? (Rayon, 2009)

2.7 Addendum

This chapter was written at a particular political moment, within the depths of a collective community-based struggle for the removal of the SRO program. Shortly after the time of writing, we redirected our campaign strategy away from the TPSB and toward the two school boards. As a result, on November 22, 2017, students and communities in Toronto won a historic victory: the permanent removal of the SRO program from the TDSB (the largest school board in Canada). The program still operates in TCDSB schools.

Notes

1. Ferreira da Silva's (2010) analytics of raciality theory, which is beyond the scope of this chapter, traces the racial as a strategy of power in the production of modernity itself.
2. There are approximately 200,000 non-status migrants currently living in the Greater Toronto Area (Keung, 2013).

References

Advancement Project. (2013). *Police in Schools Are Not the Answer to the Newtown Shooting*. http://b.3cdn.net/advancement/a24bfe0e82e0a37d66_1zm6bkclv.pdf.
Aulakh, R., & Dobbs, K. (2009, October 24). Officer Attacked at High School Hailed as Hero. *The Toronto Star*. https://www.thestar.com/news/crime/2009/10/24/officer_attacked_at_high_school_hailed_as_hero.html.
Benitah, S. (2009, October 24). Police School Program: Hit-and-Miss with Teens. *CTV Toronto News*. http://toronto.ctvnews.ca/police-school-program-hit-and-miss-with-teens-1.446653.
Blatchford, C. (2009, September 9). Cops in Schools: Sometimes Needed, If Not Always Trusted. *The Globe and Mail*. http://www.theglobeandmail.com/news/national/cops-in-schools/article4285256/.

Brillinger, C. (2013). Review of City Service Levels Supporting Toronto's at Risk Youth. *City of Toronto.* http://www.toronto.ca/legdocs/mmis/2013/cd/bgrd/backgroundfile-61255.pdf.
Brown, L., & Rushowy, K. (2014, September 23). School Stabbing Revives Trauma of Jordan Manners Shooting. *The Toronto Star.* https://www.thestar.com/yourtoronto/education/2014/09/23/toronto_school_stabbing_death_deja_vu_seven_years_later.html.
Campbell, J. (2009, April 16). Numerous Studies Show Cops in Schools Make Matters Worse. *Basics News.* http://basicsnews.ca/numerous-studies-show-cops-in-schools-make-matters-worse/.
CBC. (2009, June 29). 50 Toronto High Schools to Have Police Presence. *CBC News.* http://www.cbc.ca/news/Canada/toronto/50-toronto-high-schools-to-have-police-presence-1.785021.
Chapman-Nyaho, S., James, C. E., & Kwan-Lafond, D. (2012). "We Expect Much of You": Enlisting Youth in the Policing of Marginalized Communities. *Canadian Ethnic Studies, 43–44*(3–1), 81–98.
Chu, N. (2014, June 25). Cooking with Cops Brings Police Officer and Students Together in the Kitchen. *Bloor West Villager.* http://www.insidetoronto.com/news-story/4597428-cooking-with-cops-brings-police-officer-and-students-together-in-the-kitchen/.
CTV Toronto. (2016, May 4). *Mock Police Academy for Students* [video file]. http://toronto.ctvnews.ca/video?clipId=862989&playlistId=1.2888308&binId=1.815892&playlistPageNum=1&binPageNum=1.
Doucette, C. (2014, September 24). Metal Detectors 'Not the Answer' to School Safety Concerns: Donna Quan. *Toronto Sun.* http://www.torontosun.com/2014/09/24/metal-detectors-not-the-answer-to-school-safety-concerns-donna-quan.
Ferreira Da Silva, D. (2010). Towards a Critique of the Socio-Logos of Justice: The Analytics of Raciality and the Production of Universality. *Social Identities, 7*(3), 421–454.
Fine, M., Freudenberg, N., Payne, Y., Perkins, T., Smith, K., & Wanzer, K. (2003). "Anything Can Happen with Police Around": Urban Youth Evaluate Strategies of Surveillance in Public Places. *Journal of Social Issues, 59*(1), 141–158.
Fine, M., & Ruglis, J. (2009). Circuits and Consequences of Dispossession: The Racialized Realignment of the Public Sphere for U.S. Youth. *Transforming Anthropology, 17*(1), 20–33.
Friesen, J., & Appleby, T. (2009). Teen's Arrest in High School Hallway Sparks Debate About Police Program. *The Globe and Mail.* https://www.theglobeandmail.com/news/toronto/teens-arrest-in-high-school-hallway-sparks-debate-about-police-program/article4288376/.

Gee, M. (2009, October 7). A Police Drama with a Happy Ending. *The Globe and Mail*. http://www.theglobeandmail.com/news/toronto/a-police-drama-with-a-happy-ending/article791109/.

Gillis, W. (2017). Toronto Police Board to Consider Suspending School Resource Officer Program. *The Toronto Star*. https://www.thestar.com/news/crime/2017/05/23/toronto-police-board-to-consider-suspending-school-officer-program.html.

Goldberg, D. (2009). *The Threat of Race: Reflections on Racial Neoliberalism*. Malden, MA: Blackwell.

Government of Ontario. (2005). *O. Reg. 265/98: Disclosure of Personal Information*. http://www.ontario.ca/laws/regulation/980265.

Hirschfield, P. (2008). Preparing for Prison? The Criminalization of School Discipline in the USA. *Theoretical Criminology, 12*(1), 79–101.

James, C. (2012). Students at "Risk": Stereotypes and the Schooling of Black Boys. *Urban Education, 47*(2), 464–494.

Jennie. (2009, June 9). Letter to the TDSB Regarding Police in Schools. *Educators for Peace and Justice*. http://epjweb.org/campaigns/sanctuary-schools/letter-to-the-tdsb-regarding-police-in-schools/.

Justice Policy Institute. (2012). Measured Responses: Why Increasing Law Enforcement in Schools Is Not an Effective Public Safety Response to the Newtown Tragedy. *Justice Policy Institute*. http://www.justicepolicy.org/uploads/justicepolicy/documents/schoolsafetyfactsheet.pdf.

Kauri, V. (2012, November 13). Trustees, Principals Fear Loss of Officer Program. *The Globe and Mail*. http://www.theglobeandmail.com/news/toronto/trustees-principals-fear-loss-of-officer-program/article5266272/.

Keung, N. (2013, February 22). Toronto Declared 'Sanctuary City' to Non-Status Migrants. *The Toronto Star*. https://www.thestar.com/news/gta/2013/02/21/cisanctuarycity21.html.

Lipman, P. (2011). Cracking Down: Chicago School Policy and the Regulation of Black and Latino Youth. In K. J. Saltman & D. A. Gabbard (Eds.), *Education as Enforcement: The Militarization and Corporatization of Schools* (pp. 73–91). New York: Routledge.

Madan, G. R. (2016). *Policing in Toronto Schools: Race-ing the Conversation* (Masters thesis). OISE, University of Toronto, Toronto.

MajorKraze. (2009, October 2). *Student Arrested at Northern Secondary School for No Reason* [video file]. http://youtu.be/rhfh8P0FomI.

Menter, I. (1987). The Long Arm of Education: A Review of Recent Documents on Police/School Liaison. *Critical Social Policy, 7*(21), 68–77.

Mills, S. (2012). *"Coolest Cop in Canada" School Cop Candy @PCGraham9655 Bishop Marrocco Social Media Success & Safety* [video file]. https://youtu.be/dLZdKJIML6o.

Moffette, D., & Gardner, K. (2015). *Often Asking, Always Telling: The Toronto Police Service and the Sanctuary City Policy.* Toronto: No One Is Illegal.
Noguera, P. A. (1995). Preventing and Producing Violence: A Critical Analysis of Responses to School Violence. *Harvard Educational Review,* 65(2), 189–212.
Nolan, K. (2011). *Police in the Hallways: Discipline in an Urban High School.* Minneapolis: University of Minnesota Press.
No One Is Illegal. (2010, September 3). Toronto Schools a Little More Welcoming for Undocumented Students. *No One Is Illegal.* http://toronto.nooneisillegal.org/node/497.
Ontario Human Rights Commission [OHRC]. (2003, July 8). *The Ontario Safe Schools Act: School Discipline and Discrimination.* http://www.ohrc.on.ca/en/ontario-safe-schools-act-school-discipline-and-discrimination.
Park, R. [zeebraCop]. (2015). Retrieved from https://twitter.com/zeebraCop.
Petteruti, A. (2011). Education Under Arrest: The Case Against Police in Schools. *Justice Policy Institute.* http://www.justicepolicy.org/uploads/justicepolicy/documents/educationunderarrest_fullreport.pdf.
Public Safety Canada. (2013). *School Resource Officer Program (Details).* https://www.publicsafety.gc.ca/cnt/cntrng-crm/plcng/cnmcs-plcng/ndx/dtls-en.aspx?n=71.
Rainford, L. (2014, October 20). Students and Seniors Bond Through Bishop Marrocco's Intergenerational Program. *Bloor West Villager.* http://www.insidetoronto.com/news-story/4923670-students-and-seniors-bond-through-bishop-marrocco-s-intergenerational-program/.
Rayon. (2009, April 16). 'They Don't Belong': The Solution Is Not the Cops. *Basics News.* http://basicsnews.ca/%E2%80%98they-don%E2%80%99t-belong%E2%80%99-the-solution-is-not-cops/.
Rushowy, K. (2009, January 11). The Kids Are All Right, Says Cop. *The Toronto Star.* http://www.thestar.com/life/parent/2009/01/11/the_kids_are_all_right_says_cop.html.
Saczkowski, T. (2015, August 31). Carding and Toronto Police Practices Called into Question. *Rabble News.* http://rabble.ca/news/2015/08/carding-and-toronto-police-practices-spotlight.
Toronto District School Board [TDSB]. (2007). *Policy P.061 SCH: Students Without Legal Immigration Status.* http://www2.tdsb.on.ca/ppf/uploads/files/live/98/1555.pdf.
Toronto Police Accountability Coalition [TPAC]. (2009). *Toronto Police Accountability Coalition, Bulletin #50.* http://www.tpac.ca/show_bulletin.cfm?id=139.
Toronto Police Service [TPS]. (2009). School Resource Officer Program: 2008/2009 Evaluation. *Toronto Police Service.* https://www.torontopolice.on.ca/publications/files/reports/2008,2009-sro_evaluation_program.pdf.

Toronto Police Service [TPS]. (2011, December). School Resource Officer Program: 2011 Follow-Up Evaluation. *Toronto Police Service.* http://www.torontopolice.on.ca/publications/files/reports/2008,2009-sro_program_follow-up_evaluation.pdf.

Toronto Police Service [TPS]. (2012). 2011 Service Performance Year End Report. *Toronto Police Service.* http://www.torontopolice.on.ca/publications/files/reports/2011performancereport.pdf.

Toronto Police Service [TPS]. (2015). TAVIS. *Toronto Police Service.* http://www.torontopolice.on.ca/tavis/.

Toronto Police Services Board [TPSB]. (2017, June 15). *Toronto Police Services Board Livestream Thursday June 15th 1 pm* [video file]. https://www.youtube.com/watch?v=J6lVDtmlATk.

Vivanco, P. A. (2009). *'Safe' Schools: Safe for Who?: Latinas, Thugs, and Other Deviant Bodies* (Masters thesis). OISE, University of Toronto, Toronto.

Winsa, P. (2013, September 27). TAVIS Police Unit in Eye of the Storm. *The Toronto Star.* http://www.thestar.com/news/gta/knowntopolice2013/2013/09/27/tavis_police_unit_in_eye_of_the_storm.html.

CHAPTER 3

Restorative Justice: Moving from Punitive Sanctions to Proactive Interactions

Michelle H. A. Bailey

3.1 Introduction

Restorative justice emphasizes mediation between the accused, the victim, and those involved (Costello, Wachtel, & Watchel, 2009). The use of restorative justice in schools is a progressive shift in discipline from the traditional reactive practice of suspension, to an intervention and preventative model (Costello et al., 2009; Costello, Wachtel, & Watchel, 2010). Suspension is the disciplinary action commonly taken by schools when students commit an infraction. According to the philosophy of restorative justice, empathy, accountability, responsibility, and fairness are salient tenets used in addressing infractions (Arnott, 2007; Costello et al., 2010; Payne & Welch, 2010). Restorative justice is a proactive approach to discipline. It is about teaching students conflict management and resolution skills, in addition to accepting responsibility for their actions (Costello et al., 2009). Therefore, restorative justice has pedagogical relevance in addressing inappropriate behaviors, conflicts, crises, and teaching

M. H. A. Bailey (✉)
Ontario Institute for Studies in Education,
University of Toronto, Toronto, ON, Canada
e-mail: elle.bailey@mail.utoronto.ca

© The Author(s) 2019
F. J. Villegas and J. Brady (eds.), *Critical Schooling*,
https://doi.org/10.1007/978-3-030-00716-4_3

appropriate social relations (Gonzalez, 2012; Lewis, 2006; Sumner, Silverman, & Frampton, 2010). Restorative justice can be included in the elementary and secondary social science curriculum. Both curriculum expectations state that students should demonstrate an understanding of respect, building healthy relationships, empathy, personal and interpersonal skills, anger management, and conflict resolution skills (Ministry of Education, 2013a, b). Furthermore, the curriculum expectations also emphasize students should know how to analyze situations and develop appropriate responses (Ministry of Education, 2013a, b). When minor issues arise, marginalized, and academically struggling students, who are the most vulnerable are suspended from school (Ontario Human Rights Commission, 2005a; Toronto District School Board, 2013a, b).

This paper has five sections. In the first section, I explain the support for using restorative justice in schools for minor infractions. The suspension of Black students in the TDSB is an entry point for discussing the need for a paradigm shift in discipline. In the second part, I discuss an overview of the suspension process and highlight the offenses most suitable for restorative justice. The third section reviews the assessment of documents in the Ontario Student Records (OSR), to surmise the student's educational habitus and capital. An examination of the formation of the principal's habitus, use of capital, logic of practice in the field (school), and symbolic power are instrumental factors in the process leading up to a suspension. In the fourth section, I examine the interactive function between habitus, cultural capital, field, and practice. I demonstrate how these characteristics interact in the social regulation that occurs in schools. In the fifth section, I argue that the philosophy of restorative justice is a beneficial alternative to suspensions since it utilizes forums where corrective, intervention and preventative learning occurs. I assert that when teachers, students, and principals are committed to restitution, a reduction in suspension and social inequalities will occur.

Being a teacher/guidance counselor has enabled me to understand that some students make decisions without thinking them through. These decisions can result in an infraction, which can be punishable by suspension. Based on the severity of the infraction, there may be the opportunity to approach the incident in a manner that will educate the students; or, exert punitive actions. Therefore, out of school suspensions for minor infractions are counterproductive. For example, the three- to five-day suspension interrupts the students and parental schedules because they will have to attend an intake meeting at the suspension program that is set during school hours. If a parent/guardian cannot attend the intake meeting to sign the required documents, a delay in attendance may occur. Further, teachers are required to send all relevant materials and assignments the student was working on to the suspension program. When these tasks do not occur in a timely manner, it disrupts regular scheduled activities, which is annoying especially if the student has to return to school within a week. Instead of a suspension, the use of restorative justice in such cases can be of instrumental value. However, a respectful and empathetic attitude toward all students is required from the teacher/facilitator of the restorative justice forum. The use of restorative justice provides a space for insightful conversations about how to handle situations without a conflict. During restorative justice forums/circles participants learn about respect for self and others, healthy relationships, empathy, anger management, and how to de-escalate conflicts—social and civil responsibilities are inculcated. Critics argue this is not the role of teachers or the function of schools. However, as previously mentioned, learning about social relations is included in elementary and secondary social science curriculum. In elementary schools, curriculum expectations include learning positive traits and values to cultivate positive character development (Ministry of Education, 2013a, 2018). The secondary curriculum expectations are more extensive as they move beyond developing character traits to analyzing social justice, equity, and policies issues, which relate to conflict resolution (Ministry of Education, 2013a, b).

Restorative justice or practice is transformative pedagogy, which teaches social responsibility and conflict resolution in a communal setting with a shared code of conduct (Ball, 2003). To restore order, restorative justice will engage students in knowing why their behavior was inappropriate, and other students felt as observers of the incident (Macready, 2009). The process of restorative justice for students and educational staff encourages cooperative and co-constructed learning, problem-solving, and conflict management skills (Ball, 2003). Restorative justice highlights the importance of fairness and the student returning to the classroom after addressing the situation (Costello et al., 2009).

3.2 Is Racism the Vehicle Driving Suspensions?

The Ontario Human Rights Commission (OHRC) filed a complaint against the TDSB in 2005. OHRC argued that Black students were disproportionately suspended and expelled from the TDSB schools (Ontario Human

Rights Commission, 2005a, b). In November 2005, the OHRC, the Ministry of Education (MOE), and the TDSB finalized an agreement that included the implementation of equitable services for students, increased representation of persons from minority groups in schools, intervention and alternative school programs for suspended and expelled students (Ontario Human Rights Commission, 2005a, b). As a result, Safe and Caring Schools began to provide educational programs for suspended and expelled students. Concerning discipline, the OHRC recommended the avoidance of suspensions and expulsions especially for racialized students and those with learning exceptionalities (Ontario Human Rights Commission, 2005a, b). In addition, the OHRC recommend that, the TDSB adhere to the principles of progressive discipline and suggest "detention, peer mediation, restorative justice, referrals for consultation and transfers as part of the process" to reduce suspensions and expulsions (Ontario Human Rights Commission, 2005a, b; Toronto District School Board, 2017). It is difficult to know the utilization of these recommendations within schools in the TDSB.

In March of 2013, Rankin, Rushowy, and Brown's article in the Toronto Star stated, "Black students were three times more likely to be suspended than white students" and the pattern of suspending Black students continued. James and Turner (2017) report that of the "students who were expelled over the 5-year period (2011–2012 and 2015–2016), 48% were Black students" (p. 33). They also affirmed that "by the time they finished high school, 42% of all Black students had been suspended at least once, compared with only 18% of White students and 18% of other racialized students" (James & Turner, 2017, p. 34). It is against this background that the extent of racism toward Black students becomes clear.

According to Welch and Payne (2010), Black students were disproportionately subject to hostile discipline and exclusionary policies. Furthermore, students were introduced to the school to prison pipeline, because criminal charges were laid in most circumstances (Fronius, Persson, Guckenburg, Hurley, & Petrosino, 2016). In addition, the presence of school resource officers (SROs) also contributed to the school to prison pipeline. As a result of increased surveillance, harassment, bullying, and arrest were critical concerns raised about the TDSB partnership with Toronto Police Services (Madan, Chapter 2). According to Madan, "the presence of police in the school creates an excessive reliance on law enforcement, meaning that minor incidents previously dealt with by the school administration escalate into criminal justice matters"

(Madan, Chapter 2). While safety concerns were the reason for introducing SROs in schools (SROs have since been removed from all school under TDSB), interestingly, they were not part of the programs for expelled students who allegedly commit the most concerning infractions. To mitigate the impact of the school to prison pipeline on marginalized communities, Payne and Welch (2013) call for "implementing a more restorative approach to addressing student—one that has been shown to reduce recidivism and boost the number of students who complete their education—would be a paramount priority" (p. 5). Studies show that the use of restorative justice in schools reduced inappropriate behaviors and suspension rates in schools in Australia, New Zealand, and the USA (Fronius et al., 2016; Szymanski, 2016; Varnham, 2005).

Anti-Black racism is the primary factor preventing students from utilizing the educational opportunities in schools (Lewis, 1992). Dei, Mazzuca, McIsaac, and Zine (1997) conducted an ethnographic research with Black students in the TDSB and noted that "student narratives revealed that racial issues and a Eurocentric curriculum play a large role in discouraging Black students from pursuing their education" (p. 69). Furthermore, students felt alienated by negating differentiated treatment from the educational staff and believed the disciplinary actions that they received were much harsher (Dei et al., 1997).

James and Turner (2017) state:

> suspension rates are an important indicator of school success, as they reflect lost instructional time, which reduces students' opportunities to learn. Moreover, suspension can undermine the attachment of students to their school, particularly if they feel they have been unfairly treated. (p. 35)

When students are disengaged, they may become disruptive and default on the school's rules and the code of conduct. Thus, suspensions do not address student disengagement; it is an immediate dismissive reaction to the infraction.

Since 2005, stakeholders have pressured the TDSB to reduce the suspension rates of Black students. It is against this background that if implemented restorative justice can be an alternative to suspension while also teaching positive social relations. According to Hopkins (2013), "a restorative approach in a school shifts the emphasis from managing behaviour to focusing on the building, nurturing and repairing of relationships" (p. 3). When school personnel shift their attitude from being punitive to caring, they will become knowledgeable about the challenges, antecedents, and triggers that vulnerable students encounter. Caring adults are the foundation for student success because their expectations can change the outcome of the student's behavior.

3.3 An Overview of the Suspension Process

When a student commits an act that contravenes the school's code of conduct, the principal has the authority to decide if the student should be suspended (Education Act, R. S. O., 1990; Ministry of Education, 2009). The suspension process begins with an assessment of the following factors: the antecedent, the event, and the overall impact of the behavior on other students and on the culture/climate of the school (Education Act, R. S. O., 1990). The number of previous suspensions, the severity of the situation, previous disciplinary actions and progressive discipline account in the decision to suspend a student (Roher, 2008). Winton (2011) states, "progressive discipline also involves responding to misbehaviour in ways that are developmentally appropriate, supportive, and corrective rather than punitive" (p. 248). This means schools utilize progressive discipline, while taking into consideration mitigating factors such as, the student's age, grade, attitude, cognitive abilities, and the socio-emotional issues that are occurring in their life (Winton, 2011). While the mitigating factors can influence the decision to suspend students, in Ontario, the Education Act mandates suspendable behaviors. Every school board has a code of conduct that governs the schools. For example, the Education Act states:

A principal shall consider whether to suspend a pupil if he or she believes that the pupil has engaged in any of the following activities while at school, at a school-related activity or in other circumstances where engaging in the activity will have an impact on the school climate:

1. Uttering a threat to inflict serious bodily harm on another person.
2. Possessing alcohol or illegal drugs.
3. Being under the influence of alcohol.
4. Swearing at a teacher or at another person in a position of authority.
5. Committing an act of vandalism that causes extensive damage to school property at the pupil's school or to property located on the premises of the pupil's school.

6. Bullying.
7. Any other activity that is an activity for which a principal may suspend a pupil under a policy of the board (Education Act, Section 360 (1), 1990).

A suspension can be the penalty for any offense listed above. However, the principal can decide the extent of the punishment after assessing the context and severity of the situation as well as the harm done (Education Act, 1990). If, schools implement restorative justice forums/circles and no harm occurred to another person, behaviours one, two, and three listed above can easily qualify for restorative practices. However, an investigation and documentation of the threat must occur since the situation can quickly change and become a future incident. While seven of the offenses outlined above are provisions in the Education Act, the TDSB expanded on this list and identified 16 behaviors that may lead to suspension. They are:

1. willful destruction of school property; vandalism causing damage to school or District property; or property located on school or District premises;
2. use of profane or improper language;
3. use of tobacco;
4. theft;
5. aid/incite harmful behavior;
6. physical assault;
7. being under the influence of illegal drugs;
8. sexual harassment;
9. racial harassment;
10. fighting;
11. possession or misuse of any harmful substances;
12. hate-motivated violence;
13. extortion;
14. distribution of hate material;
15. inappropriate use of electronic communications/media; and
16. an act considered by the principal to be a breach of the District's Code of Conduct (Zuker & Kirwin, 2015; Toronto District School Board, "Chart of Consequences of Inappropriate Student Behaviour").

For this discussion, offenses two, three, and seven can warrant the use of restorative justice depending on the context. Similarly, depending on the severity of the situation and the student's attitude at the time of the incident, offenses five and ten can also qualify for restorative justice. If any injury happened during the incident (i.e., in a fight), the teacher/principal has a duty to report the incident to the parent/guardian, fill out the incident reporting form, and in some cases call the police. When the police get involved, a charge of assault or assault causing bodily harm for causing an injury usually occurs.

A suspension can range from a day to twenty days. The maximum suspension time of twenty days is for serious infractions, and an expulsion from the school or all schools of the board may occur after the twenty days (Toronto District School Board, 2009). Before each suspension, and to determine the facts of the situation the principal does an investigation (Toronto District School Board, 2009). However, sometimes that investigation occurs during the suspension especially if multiple students were involved. The investigation may involve multiple factors: interviewing staff, parent/guardian(s) and students, reviewing recorded evidence and the academic history of the student kept in the Ontario Student Record (OSR). The OSR "is established for each student who enrolls in a school operated by a school board or the Ministry of Education" (Ontario Ministry of Education, 2000). The OSR is a folder, which has all the educational documents mandated by the Ministry of Education as being important in the student's educational career (Ontario Ministry of Education, 2000). A hearing to determine a school only or all schools of the board expulsion will take place. If the parent/s gets a lawyer, this process can get messy and take a while.

3.4 Conception of the Habitus and Capital from Educational Documents

The documents in the OSR provide biographical information about the student. From reading the following documents: Index Card, Individual Education Plan (IEP), Ontario Student Transcript (OST), Report Cards, Psychological Assessments Reports, Social Worker's Reports, Safety Plans and custody agreements (Ontario Ministry of Education, 2000), educators make inference about the student's habitus and educational abilities. The information in the above documents includes the name and contact information of the parent/guardian, number of schools that the student attended, attendance records, academic history, and achievement. The academic interventions and behavioral strategies used to accommodate the student's learning are also included in the above educational reports. Therefore, a conception of the student's educational habitus results from information contained in the OSR.

According to Bourdieu (1977), habitus is "an acquired system of generative schemes objectively adjusted to the particular conditions in which it is constituted, the habitus engenders all the thoughts, all the perceptions, and all the actions consistent with those conditions" (p. 95). Accordingly, habitus develops during socialization; social interactions and responses to situations become internalized, which contribute to the complexity or flexibility of its trajectory, which is ongoing (Bourdieu, 1977). Bourdieu (1990) affirms "the habitus is also expressed by the way one stands, speaks, walks, feels and thinks, these bodily expressions are also culturally related" (p. 170). In relation to habitus, educators judge students based on the socioeconomic position of their parents, their current circumstances, and cultural expressions. Accordingly, educators must desist from using deficit models when assessing student's abilities and as the under-lining reason for students' behaviors. Educators must become aware of the diverse cultural expressions and differences that exist in the student population as demonstrated through the habitus. According to Reay (2004), "Bourdieu developed the concept of habitus to demonstrate the ways in which not only is the body in the social world, but also the ways in which the social world is in the body" (p. 432). From this perspective, the habitus provides insight into the student's "past and present circumstances, such as, family upbringing and educational experiences" (Grenfell, 2008, p. 51). Subsequently, cultural values and perspectives are also part of the habitus. Reay (2004) asserts, "a person's individual history is constitutive of habitus, but so also is the whole collective history of family and class that the individual is a member of" (p. 434). The documents in the OSR assist in confirming the habitus, the sociocultural positioning of family, and their cultural affiliates.

From the aforementioned documents in the OSR, educators can also gain insight about the capital that the student embodies or can access. According to Wacquant (1998),

> capital is any resource effective in a given social arena that enables one to appropriate the specific profits arising out of participation and contest in it. Capital comes in three principal species: economic (material and

financial assets), cultural (scarce symbolic goods, skills and titles) and social (resources accrued by virtue of membership in a group). A fourth species, symbolic capital designates the effects of any form of capital when people do not perceive them as such. (p. 221)

This confers that an individual's background conveys predictive information, which signals being included, and or, excluded, in the culture of the school (Bourdieu, 1991; Grenfell & Kelly, 1999; Horvat, 2001; Reay et al., 2001). For example, the parent's job title and their residential address are indicators of the family's capital. The job title implies the educational attainment of the parent(s) while their address connotes their geographic location, type of residence, and value of the property. Economic, cultural, social, and symbolic capital can correlate with the outcome of how students experience school. Educational staff responds to infractions according to an assessment of the student's reaction and their family's capital. In discussing how capital functions in society, Lareau and Weininger (2003) contend "the concept of capital has enabled researchers to view culture as a resource - in that it provides access to scarce rewards, is subject to monopolization, and, under certain conditions, may be transmitted from one generation to the next" (p. 556). Within schools, the rewards of capital influence the quality of staff–student relationships, the student's educational achievements, and the number of suspensions a student receives (Lareau & Weininger, 2003).

The rewards of capital connect with race, learning abilities, socioeconomic status, and influence suspension rates. TDSB's (2013) report, "Suspension Rates by Students' Demographic and Family Background Characteristics" confirms this claim by stating in both Census years 2006–2007 and 2011–2012

> for Kindergarten to Grade 6 students, the higher the students' family income, the lower the suspension rates. In Grades 7-8 and Grades 9-12, students whose parents held professional and senior management positions had the lowest suspension rates than other student groups. On the other hand, students whose parents held unskilled clerical, and trades, or non-remunerative positions, held higher suspension rates in both Census years. (p. 4)

Racialized students from "priority neighborhoods" are predominantly suspended. The data showed that their parents have little to no capital to challenge the school board. When parents possess little or no capital to oppose suspensions, the directives and judgments of the school board subjugate them. Parents with capital navigate the school system to discuss the matter with school board representatives such as superintendents and trustees who are above than the principal in the bureaucratic chain. If needed, these parents will retain a lawyer to resolve the situation. The interpretation of documents in the OSR can be consequential, as one can gain insight about a student's habitus and capital. Therefore, it is important for educators to utilize an equity focused and culturally sensitive lens, which recognizes the hegemony embedded in the school system.

3.5 The Interaction Between Habitus, Capital, Field, and Symbolic Power

The above discussion revealed that the biographical information in the OSR conveys information about the student's habitus and capital. However, the dialectic of the process to suspend a student is reflective of hegemonic practices. During the investigative process, the habitus, cultural and symbolic capital are inseparable they comprise the student's and principal's personality. The discussion that follows demonstrates the relevance of the link between habitus and capital compounded in the field (school) to culminate into practice. Bourdieu's equation [(habitus) (capital)]+field=practice] enables an understanding of the aggregating factors that intersect as convergent or divergent factors in the suspension process (Grenfell, 2008; Horvat, 2001).

During the investigative process when the principal interviews the student, the inseparability between habitus, capital, and symbolic power is evident in the interaction. Other signifiers of the student's identity: race, class, gender, physical abilities, and sexual orientation will implicitly influence the perception about the student and the social interactions that will occur. During their dialogue, the habitus and cultural capital will be interactive; as in the fluency of speech: knowing how to answer questions eloquently, or, deflecting them, engaging in positive body language or negating body gestures, and avoiding or maintaining eye contact. These nonverbal skills along with an eyewitness and or evidence can incriminate or alleviate culpability according to dominant social norms. The communicative skills demonstrated during the investigation confirm Lash's (1993), claims that the "habitus is made up of cultural capital" (cited by Reay, 2004, p. 435). Similarly, Reay (2004) concurs that the "relationship between habitus and cultural capital is more enmeshed," and the entanglement between habitus and cultural capital is indicative of a person's social history (Reay, 2004, p. 435). Therefore, the habitus and capital of the student and principal are relationally implicit during their interaction. The implied meaning is the social history of the student; as well as, that of the principal will influence the suspension process especially if there was a verbal altercation.

However, Reay (2004) cautions that whereas the "habitus reflects the social position in which it was constructed; it also carries within it the genesis of new creative responses that are capable of transcending the social conditions in which it was produced" (pp. 434–435). Reay's (2004) declaration suggests that the habitus is capable of shifting according to changes in belief, attitude, and exposure to other cultural capital. Accordingly, racism can be unlearned if there is a willingness to understand the manifestations of power and its effects of marginalization on people (Ontario Human Right Commission, 2005a, b). For Black students, the social injuries that can accompany race remain profoundly oppressive in its consequences. Interactions with socializing agents and their experiences in school shape student's attitude toward education (Dei et al., 1997). Students lose motivation when they realize that educators have low academic and conduct expectations for them (Dei et al., 1997). Projected through dialogue, these ideals become part of the student's educational experience.

A discussion of the principal's habitus suggests multiple factors converge and diverge, to illustrate leadership of the school as an equitable place, or, a space, which reproduce social inequalities. The principal's acquired habitus is a cumulative process, which produced his/her personality. Wacquant (1998) asserts that

> the mediation between past influences and present stimuli, habitus is at once structured, by the patterned social forces that produced it, and structuring: it gives form and coherence to the various activities of an individual across the separate spheres of life. This is why Bourdieu defines it variously as 'the product of structure, producer of practice, and reproducer of structure', the 'unchosen principle of all choices', or the 'practice-unifying and practice-generating principle' that permits 'regulated improvisation' and the 'conductorless orchestration' of conduct. (p. 221)

These ideas of habitus explain the shaping of its trajectory as a continuum from socialization to professional practice. Therefore, embedded in the habitus are cultural values about gender, class, race, abilities, and sexual orientation, which determine how the principal perceives and reacts to students.

Similarly, location of residence, teaching experiences, length and quality of academic achievement, leadership proficiency, beliefs, and attitudes toward people from different racial and ethnic background are all salient characteristics that comprise the principal's habitus, capital, and symbolic power (Reay, 2004). In addition, the principal's habitus includes knowledge and experience gained from their social status, cultural affiliations, and sensitivities to people from diverse ethnic background. The principal's "logic of practice" and how they use symbolic power is demonstrated in the contributions to the mission of the school, the school's improvement plan, as well as their history of disciplinary actions against students.

Within schools, the logic of practice also refers to the quality of interactions between the principal, students, teachers, other staff members, as well as the culture of the school. These interactions are daily rituals and practices that determine how students feel and how they will participate in the culture of the school. Horvat (2001) argues, "practice can be conceived of as individual action situated in a social setting". In this context, "students who are perceived as future criminals by their teachers and school administrators tend to receive more punitive sanctions, regardless of the actual infractions committed" (Payne & Welch, 2010). As repeatedly documented, the logic of practice reveals how punitive sanctions, anti-Black racism and the maintenance of a culture of dominance contributes to the disenfranchisement of racialized students (James & Turner, 2017; Lewis, 1992; Ontario Human Rights Commission, 2005a, b; Giroux, 2003; Dei, 1995, 1996, 2010). This is the reality of daily life, inequitable actions, and practices toward racialized students (James & Turner, 2017; Welch & Payne, 2012).

The principal's logic of practice implicates their position and complicity in the disciplinary process. The principal's use of symbolic power emerges during managerial interactions, and actions, subjective or objective approach, discretion, and engagement in school activities. Therefore, an analysis of the principal's logic of practice must include the history of their academic repertoire, the intervening and preventative strategies implemented, as well as the number of suspensions, expulsions, and other disciplinary actions. In addition, empirical evidence of academic or social improvements associated with the school and an account of the immediate stakeholders' perspective as documented in reports and illustrated in the environment will also provide evidence of the principal's commitment to the School Board's Improvement Plan. The logic of practice has to be a comprehensive analysis of how the principal acted as a leader. While being a principal is a symbolic position of authority, the power that resonates from the position must not be a dominating, but mediating.

Creating an environment where more learning and less discipline occur depends on the morale of the educational staff under the directive of the principal. The principal is responsible for cultivating and fostering a climate of progressive academic success and social responsibility. The school's culture is established and maintained when the principal, teachers, and other educational personnel demonstrate appropriate social relations. The rules and the code of conduct are in students' agendas discussed in classes, at staff meetings and must appear visually around the school.

A progressive principal will implement proactive strategies to accommodate students with academic challenges and those who are most likely to fail. Students who are vulnerable wander the hallway, have poor marks, and oftentimes have learning exceptionalities such as Attention Deficit Disorder, Communication Disorder, and Dyscalculia. Such students have difficulty focusing on tasks and act out their frustrations via infractions. In such circumstances, teachers need extra time to explore innovative ways to engage these students in learning. Differentiated strategies and targeting student's interest signal an intention to nurture their learning abilities. When students are wandering in the hallway during class time, their behaviour shows that they are disengaged. This is a sign that the students needs academic intervention. Suspending these students for swearing will not change their behaviour, which emphasizes the necessity for academic mediation and alternative forms of discipline.

The principal's authority is to secure access to equitable learning for all students. This includes knowing how to navigate instrumental changes to promote progressive teaching and learning initiatives and reduce punitive reactionary suspensions. In summation, the principal's embodied habitus, capital, and symbolic authority produce a narrative of practice which include the students' academic achievement, and the number of suspensions and expulsions. This evidence signifies the reproduction of social inequalities or proactive and appropriate responses to minor infractions.

As it relates to the examination of the school being a field, "Bourdieu calls field in the first instance, a structured space of positions, a force field that imposes its specific determinations upon all those who enter it" (Wacquant, 1998, p. 221). The school is both a structured physical place, and a social space, and this "space is implicated in the production of individual identities and social inequalities" (Shilling, 1991, p. 23). Social regulation consists of screening all persons who attend the school. Students perceived as not possessing the capital to "belong" in affluent schools and are always under surveillance. Further, Shilling (1991) confers the school as a space, "a resource which simultaneously structures and is structured by individuals in the course of their day-to-day lives. As such, it is central to the production and reproduction of social relationships and the life-chances of different groups of people" (p. 23). From this perspective, I argue that education is a field; and that schools are institutions engaged in that field. The school is a structured space where people occupy various social positions, and each social position has an explicit role, with rules, expectations, and a code of conduct to follow. As a social space, the school is comprised of symbolic artifacts and monuments that indicate its tone, customs, and prestige. The curriculum, explicit and hidden, also indicates the culture of the school. Nora Dewar Allingham (1992) defines curriculum as,

> the textbooks and storybooks, and the pictures, and the seating plan, and the group work, and the posters and the music, the announcements, the prayers and readings, the languages spoken in the school, the food in the cafeteria, the visitors to the classroom, the reception of the parents in the office, the race (or races) of the office staff, the custodial staff, the teachers, the administration, the displays of students' work, the school teams and sports played, the clubs, the school logo or emblem, the field trips, the assignments and projects, the facial expression and body language of everybody, the clothes everybody wears...it is the whole environment. (p. 20)

This definition of curriculum is inclusive since it explains a holistic school as a social setting; a micro-society where culture and environment impact on and influence learning and behaviors. The school represents a space subject to re-evaluation; therefore, there is hope for transformation. However, not all schools have an inclusive model of curriculum; consequently, issues of culturally relevant pedagogy, cultural sensitivity, and the need for a diverse staff population are critical concerns that are ongoing. Moreover, in schools, the hidden curriculum has influence on learning and behaviors. Accordingly, Marsh and Willis (2007) state:

the hidden curriculum for students includes more than the personal likes and dislikes of their teachers and the attitudes and values embedded in what their teacher do. It also includes the priorities of educational and political authorities about the power relationships between adults and students in schools, about controls over future employment opportunities, and about how such abstract concepts as justice and equity function concretely in the society at large. (p. 14)

The representations in the hidden curriculum are instrumental in conveying ideas to students about how valued they are in the school. Students also compare how teachers speak to other students, and the attitude of the educational staff toward them, to conclude if they are in a caring or negating school. The hidden curriculum includes the school's code of conduct, attitudes, beliefs, reactions, interactions, and the inclusion and exclusion of students in classroom and outdoor activities (Marsh & Willis, 2007). The hidden curriculum also involves implied language and attitudes about class, gender, race, sexual orientation, and the abilities of each student. The combination of the principal's habitus and capital along with the demonstration of symbolic power indicate the level of ethnocentrism imposed and embedded in the culture of the school.

3.6   Restorative Justice, the Philosophy of Hope

Can we expect a reduction in suspensions to occur when it is the primary method of discipline used to correct students' behavior? A reduction in suspension can only occur when principals change their attitude from punitive and allow discipline to become a restorative learning experience. Restorative justice offers a space where learning can occur. In defining restorative justice, Costello et al. (2009) state it is "the belief that decisions are best made, and conflicts are best resolved by those directly involved in them" (p. 7). From this perspective, restorative justice is a community-based response to a wrongful activity which sees inappropriate behaviors as being separate from the personal history and characteristics of the individual (Costello et al., 2009, 2010). This means the focus of school discipline should be on the present infraction, not on the personal history or previous infractions. By focusing on the immediate infraction, there is less risk for stigmatizing the student and being excessive with discipline.

To suspend a student for a minor infraction will not effectively address the impact the incident had on those involved or the climate of the classroom or school. Nor, does the suspension provide a cohesive learning opportunity for other students who saw what happened. For example, students in the classroom witness a student swearing at a teacher and kicking the chair over. The teacher sends the student to the office; the principal suspended the student for a couple of days. Although the student recognizes that the behavior is inappropriate, he/she may not be aware of the impact the behavior had on the teacher and other students. On their part, restorative justice procedures provide a forum to address inappropriate behaviors so that students are aware of the effects of their action in disrupting the class. The student has the opportunity to explain what caused the inappropriate action and listen to advice and suggestions from their peers about alternative ways to express their frustration and anger (Costello et al., 2009). Restorative justice does not acknowledge the use of the deficit model, which focuses on socioeconomic circumstances and pathologies the individual, instead, it builds respectful relationships, supports positive behavioral changes and cultivates a process of forgiveness while inculcating in students' problem-solving and conflict resolution skills (Costello et al., 2009).

The implementation of the practice of restorative justice is a concerted process directed by the principal, practiced by educational, and support staff in the school. The procedural process of restorative justice begins with building relationships before having to deal with conflicts. Building relationships include inviting students to sit in a circle and participate in team building activities before working toward addressing conflicts in a community forum (Costello et al., 2009). Before restorative justice circle is used, a positive rapport between teachers and students based on safety and competency must be established, as the restorative process requires active participation from the offender in a nonjudgmental process of a student forum (Costello et al., 2009, 2010). In practice, all involved in the process will sit in a circle, and both the victim and the offender are encouraged to express their feelings about what happened so that the offender comes to understand how their actions affected not only the victim, but also, other students who were in the vicinity (Costello et al., 2009, 2010). This is a powerful process in self-realization, growth, and personal development (Costello et al., 2009, 2010). Undoubtedly, it also fosters group cohesion, understanding, mentorship, and promotes a peaceful school climate for all involved in the process. Thus, restorative justice cultivates practical interpersonal skills and maintains school safety; as all involved in the incident come to realize that collective action is better than isolated punishments (Costello et al., 2009).

While the practice of restorative justice promotes conflict management and resolution skills, the avenues leading to a shift in disciplinary sanctions begin with classroom teachers. It takes an exceptional teacher to stop teaching and use the misbehavior of a student as an opportune learning moment for all. When misbehaviors and victimless infractions are discussed in a whole class forum, timely intervention occurs, the students are involved in promoting accountability as they participate in the decision-making process. Similarly, when peer mediation occurs, learning happens, as students are able to dialogue from a commonly shared experience. These moments are valuable.

Conversely, when students are sent to the principal's office, "emotions are aroused, and judgments are made. Comfort and discomfort levels are established well in advance of verbal communication. We unconsciously or consciously register and make judgments about stature and voice" (Darder, 2009). Further, when students go to the office to see the principal, their reaction can be explosive or accepting. The behavioral expression of the student reactively depends on the personality of the principal, their attitude, and the type of comments he or she makes to the student. If the interaction with the student is authoritarian and abrasive, then ego, resentment, prejudice, and an escalation of words can result. However, when the principal demonstrates concern and takes a "need to understand" approach, the situation does not escalate but is likely to highlight areas where the student may be experiencing challenges (Costello et al., 2009, 2010).

The first principle of restorative practice involves identifying the students that are altering the climate of the school and those that are "at risk" to leave school early (Costello et al., 2009, 2010). Costello et al. (2009, 2010) state that these students are disengaged; they disrupt class and wander the hallways. When proactive administrators meet regularly, but separately with each student, these non-confrontational, almost egalitarian meetings enable personal relationship building. During these meetings, the principal supportively explains how the student can use their strengths positively, how their behavior is affecting other students, and the options of staying or leaving the school before another breach in the school's code of conduct occurs (Costello et al., 2009, 2010). This strategy is useful because students get to know the principal outside of the disciplinarian role. The principal is also able to discuss and clarify the expectations of being a student while initiating a supportive caring relationship. According to Costello et al. (2010), there is misconception that disengaged students want to leave school early, in fact, none of the students who met regularly with an administrator wanted to become a dropout. Further, when students are provided with concise educational options they will choose to change their behavior and stay in school.

The second principle of restorative practice uses affective statements to solicit thoughtful reactive responses from students. By explicitly expressing their feelings, the teacher fosters an environment of authenticity, whereby students learn how to use and respond to affective statements in a different context (Costello et al., 2010). Consequently, students can develop diverse methods of effective communication through practice with affective statements. Costello et al. (2010) suggests that educators should use the following questions to address students involved in challenging situations:

What happened?
What were you thinking of at the time?
What have you thought about since?
Who has been affected by what you have done?
In what way have they been affected?
What do you think you need to do to make things right? (Costello et al., 2009)

> These questions initiate critical thinking and prepare the student to take responsibility for their actions. Those affected by the incident should be asked the following questions:
> What did you think when you realized what had happened?
> What impact has this incident had on you and others?
> Who has been affected by what you have done?
> What has been the hardest thing for you?
> What do you think needs to happen to make things right? (Costello et al., 2009, 2010)

The questions above get students to reflect and acknowledge their behavior using the restorative process and may apply to all involved; the offender, victim, and witnesses who are responsible for restoring balance. These questions are also useful in one-on-one counseling sessions.

The third principle of restorative justice utilizes circles and is the most recognized form of restorative justice in schools. Circles are part of the tradition of First Nations Peoples in Canada and North America whose value system includes healing and restoring balance to the community (Ryals, 2004). As part of their tradition, First Nations Peoples use circles to discuss the effects of violence, crime, and other negative situations on their lifestyle (Ryals, 2004). In some Aboriginal communities, the structure of circles are used at meetings, sentencing circles, elders' or community sentencing panels, and in sentence advisory and mediation committees (Green, 1998). Driving Hawk-Sneve (1987), as cited by Moeser (1999) states, "the circle is a sacred symbol of life... individual parts within the circle connect with every other; and what happens to one, or what one part does, affects all within the circle" (p. 130). Being in/part of a circle invokes feelings of equality and connectedness and supports collective interest in resolving the issue (Moeser, 1999).

Using restorative justice circles in schools is an innovative response to infractions because the offender is encouraged to accept responsibility and to ask for forgiveness. Furthermore, the witnesses are involved in the process to address and support a resolution of the situation. Schachter (2010) affirms that restorative justice programs when implemented in schools create a caring, accountable environment as the learning community holds students accountable for their actions. Using restorative justice circles offers a productive process to cultivate social responsibility, and those involved will express their feelings about the issue in a nonjudgmental, but critical manner that focuses on moving beyond the infraction and restoring a harmonious environment. Under restorative justice circles are effective in addressing confrontations with educators and peers.

There are no known negative outcomes associated with restorative justice. Zaslaw (2010) affirms,

> school suspension and expulsion result in a number of negative outcomes for both schools and students. Some students see out of school suspension as a vacation. If they realize that nothing will be done at home, they will continue to try to get suspended. Despite the packets of homework that are sent home, they usually do not get done, because many parents will not enforce the student's responsibility to complete them. (p. 10)

Students can lose credits for the semester if they neglect to complete their academic work while being suspended because they fall behind in their assignments and have incomplete marks. Aforementioned, multiple suspensions, expulsion, and disengagement with schooling diminish opportunities for students to achieve the Ontario Secondary School Diploma or Certificate. Further, students cannot enter a post-secondary institution or trade school unless they attend and pass an upgrading program. To enhance student success, restorative justice as an alternative approach promotes respectful progressive conflict resolution practices.

3.7 The Embodiment of Restorative Philosophy in the Classroom

What follows is a discussion about the demonstration of restorative justice in the classroom. While this discussion may appear basic in nature, the absence of these professional practices leads to the silencing of marginalized students. Restorative justice in the classroom and in the school must therefore be a reciprocal process of respect, which recognize and value the presence of all students (Costello et al., 2010). The social location and experience of each student along with their personality can be delicate or abrasive according to the attitude they exhibit. Conversations with other teachers and school personnel can lead to personal bias and prejudice, which interferes with how educators interact with students. Most importantly, when these conversations are negative toward the student, it destroys the opportunity for authentic interpersonal relations to occur. When teachers can only think of students in a negative way, they close the door to influencing positive change because it is difficult to affect change from a place of resentment. Accordingly, it becomes extremely important that teachers do not prejudice their interactions with students by internalizing and reacting from comments made by previous teachers, or what is in their OSR, because students can change their attitude.

Teachers' attitude, speech, and body language signal powerful messages to students who will connect or disconnect with teachers depending on their feelings of safety, this is a dual process (Allingham, 1992). When students are involved in a mutually respected relationship, they feel secure and safe, and are focus, cooperative, and engaged in learning. When students do not feel safe, they are hesitant to participate in classroom activities, ask for help with their assignments, contribute to classroom discussions, and they often wander in and out of the classroom. One can describe the absence of a safe learning environment as the absence of soul in the classroom. For example, Kessler (1999) states, "when soul is present in education, we listen with great care not only to what is spoken but also to the message between the words-tones, gestures, the flicker of feeling across the face," this process of reading the body is reciprocal as both teacher and student form an idea about each other. This initial observation of a new teacher is what students do, followed by a discussion with their peers, to decide if the teacher has respect, shows empathy, kindness, forgiveness, and honesty. It is also the initiation process, which predicates whether the relationship can be mutually reciprocal. This mutual reciprocal process is instrumental in determining whether transformational learning will occur or any learning at all.

In order to teach students, we have to be prepared to listen and learn. The combination of empathetic listening and communication is salient in getting to know the student by building a genuine relationship. Genuine relationships involve transparency in the classrooms where the teacher will answer yes, to the following questions. Should I share my goals with the students? Should I talk about my struggles in the education system? Should I share the challenges I overcame during the teenage years? Should I share the challenges I face as a parent? Some questions we are told are personal and irrelevant in the classroom, yet it is the answers to these questions that will connect us with our students, who will see us as individuals who also struggle with real-life issues. These questions when discussed provide context, meaning, and purpose to all those involved in the teaching and learning environment. These conversations contribute to personal awareness and development, foster reciprocal attitudes, "and extend the quality of the relationship that is developed between the person and the world" (Kessler, 1999). When we share our experiences with students, they see us as being human, and breaks down the dividing wall as students begin to see that we also contemplate and share common experiences. The classroom becomes united, learning happens and the collective tries to find resolutions to problems and ultimately attends class every day because they are aware that there is a caring adult in the room who is not afraid to get personal. This is "when soul enters the classroom, the masks drop away....students discover compassion and begin to learn about forgiveness" (Kessler, 1999). This is a transparent process, which teachers need to practice more with students to build better relationship and teaching communities (Allingham, 1992). When better relationships and learning communities are present in the classroom, the culture of progressive change begins, and students radiate pride in learning and are always smiling. Students who experience positive interactions are less likely to drop out of school; they will approach the teacher to talk about stressors in their lives because a positive relationship already exists (Dei et al., 1997).

3.8 Restorative Justice
the Bridge Over Troubled Water

This paper employed some of Bourdieu's concepts to illustrate the process and practice of suspending students. Anti-Black racism was the primary reason cited for the disproportionate rates of Black students suspended from the TDSB. An overview of the suspension process discussed the investigative assessments used to decide on the course of disciplinary action. I explained how the documents in the OSR indicate students' abilities, academic history, inherited social and provide conception of student's habitus and capital to the principal. Wacquant (1998), argues that "position in the field inclines agents toward particular patterns of conduct: those who occupy the dominant position in a field tend to use strategies of conservation (of the existing distribution of capital) while those relegated to subordinate locations are more liable to deploy strategies of subversion" (Wacquant, 1998, p. 221). The combination of the principal's habitus, capital, and symbolic power illustrate the school as an inclusive or dismissive space through the logic of practice (Horvat, 2001, p. 214). Accordingly, the suspension data from schools can be an indicator of how the principal chooses to manage discipline. Bourdieu's equation [(habitus) (capital) + field = practice] explains the relational dynamics in the suspension process. It illustrates the trajectory of social patterns, of inequities or equity according to the use of capital and regulation in schools. Therefore, the principal being the highest authority in the school embodies symbolic power, which demonstrates their actions as equitable or inequitable.

I also suggest that the actions taken by parents involve the use of capital to secure a favorable or different outcome to the initial suspension. Affluent parents will use their capital and status to contact, mobilize, and retain persons who can assist them to reduce the length of the suspension or expunge the suspension from the student's record. These parents know how to navigate the system because they are familiar with the hierarchy and procedures. However, not all parents will challenge the suspension; some parents may actually see it as a suitable form of discipline.

Low-income parents are constrained by the lack of resources needed to navigate this field. Often times, they will follow the directive of the principal (Lareau & Horvat, 1999, p. 43). Finally, exclusion and inequalities are challenges low-income parents and their children face in schools, especially if they do not possess the capital needed to interact with educators (Horvat, 2001; Lareau & Horvat, 1999).

I have suggested that restorative justice is an equitable alternative to address minor infractions; it has the potential to promote social justice within schools. Restorative justice is a student-centered approach, which focuses on building relationships, personal accountability and maintaining a harmonious balance (Ball, 2003; Costello et al., 2010). I have argued that if implemented in all schools in the TDSB, the practice of restorative justice will teach students to take responsibility for their actions, resolve and mediate conflicts. Restorative justice is proactive pedagogy, students learn prosocial skills which leads to healthy relationships in accordance with the expectations in Ontario's Elementary and Secondary curriculum.

REFERENCES

Allingham, N. (1992). *Anti-racist Education and the Curriculum—A Privilege Perspective in Racism and Education: Different Perspectives and Experiences.* Ottawa, ON: Canadian Teachers Federation.

Arnott, K. (2007). Restorative Justice Making Brand New Endings. *Education Today, 18*(2), 22.

Ball, R. (2003). Restorative Justice as Strength-Based Accountability. *Reclaiming Children and Youth, 12*(1), 49–52.

Bourdieu, P. (1977). *Outline of a Theory of Practice.* Cambridge: Cambridge University Press.

Bourdieu, P. (1990). *The Logic of Practice.* Cambridge: Polity Press.

Bourdieu, P. (1991). *Language and Symbolic Power.* Harvard University Press.

Costello, B., Wachtel, J., & Wachtel, T. (2009). *The Restorative Practices Handbook for Teachers, Disciplinarians and Administrators Building a Culture of Community in Schools.* Bethlehem, PA, USA: International Institute for Restorative Practices.

Costello, B., Wachtel, J., & Wachtel, T. (2010). *Restorative Circles in Schools Building Community and Enhancing Learning, A Practical Guide for Educators.* Bethlehem, PA, USA: International Institute for Restorative Practices.

Darder, A. (2009). Decolonizing the Flesh: The Body, Pedagogy and Inequality. In R. S. Coloma (Ed.), *Postcolonial Challenges in Education* (pp. 217–234). New York: Peter Lang.

Dei, G. J. S. (1995). *Disengaging from School* (ERIC Document Reproduction Service No. 389808). San Francisco, CA: Annual Meeting of the American Educational Research Association.

Dei, G. J. S. (1996). *Anti-racism Education: Theory and Practice*. Halifax, NS: Fernwood Publishing.

Dei, G. J. S. (2010). Schooling and the Dilemma of Youth Disengagement. *Mcgill Journal of Education, 38*(2), 241–256.

Dei, G. J. S., Mazzuca, J., McIsaac, E., & Zine, J. (1997). *Reconstructing 'Dropout': A Critical Ethnography of the Dynamics of Black Students' Disengagement from School*. Toronto: University of Toronto Press.

Fronius, T., Persson, H., Guckenburg, S., Hurley, N., & Petrosino, A. (2016). *Restorative Justice in U.S. Schools: A Research Review*. Retrieved from West End Justice & Prevention Research Center. http://jprc.wested.org.

Giroux, H. A. (2003). Racial Injustice and Disposable Youth in the Age of Zero Tolerance. *International Journal of Qualitative Studies in Education, 16*, 553–565.

Gonzalez, T. (2012). Keeping Kids in Schools: Restorative Justice, Punitive Justice and the School to Prison Pipeline. *Journal of Law & Education, 4*(2).

Green, R. G. (1998). *Justice in Aboriginal Communities: Sentencing Alternatives*. Saskatoon: Purich.

Grenfell, M. (2008). *Pierre Bourdieu: Key Concepts*. Durham: Acumen Publishing Limited.

Grenfell, M., & Kelly, M. (1999). *Pierre Bourdieu: Language Culture and Education: Theory into Practice*. New York: Peter Lang.

Hopkins, B. (2013). Restorative Justice in Schools'. *Mediation in Practice*, pp. 4–9.

Horvat, E. (2001). Understanding Equity and Access in Higher Education: The Potential Contribution of Pierre Bourdieu. In J. C. Smart & W. Tierney (Eds.), *Higher Education: Handbook of Theory and Research* (p. 17). New York: Agathon Press.

James, C. E., & Turner, T. (2017). *Towards Race Equity in Education: The Schooling of Black Students in the Greater Toronto Area*. Toronto, ON, Canada: York University.

Kessler, R. (1999). Nourishing Students in Secular Schools. *Educational Leadership, 56*(4), 49–52.

Lareau, A., & Horvat, E. M. (1999). Moments of Social Inclusion and Exclusion Race, Class and Cultural Capital in Family-School Relationships. *Sociology of Education, 72*, 37–53.

Lareau, A., & Weininger, E. B. (2003). Cultural Capital in Educational Research: A Critical Assessment. *Theory and Society, 32*(5–6), 567–606.

Lewis, L. (2006). *The Glasgow RJS: Restorative Practices in Schools* (p. 24). Resolution: News from the Restorative Justice Consortium.

Lewis, S. (1992). *Report on Race Relations and Policing Task Force in Ontario.* Toronto: Government of Ontario.

Macready, T. (2009). Learning Social Responsibility in Schools: A Restorative Practice. *Educational Psychology in Practice, 25*(3), 211–220.

Marsh, J., & Willis, G. (2007). *Curriculum Alternative Approaches, Ongoing Issues.* Pearson Columbus, OH: Merrill Prentice Hall. www.legalrightscenter.org/uploads/2/5/7/3/25735760/lrc_umn_report-final.pdf.

Ministry of Education. (2000). *Ontario Student Record (OSR) Guideline.* Queens Printer for Ontario.

Ministry of Education. (2009). Suspension and Expulsion: What Parents Need to Know. Queen's Printer for Ontario. Retrieved from http://www.edu.gov.on.ca/eng/safeschools/NeedtoKnowSExp.pdf.

Ministry of Education. (2013a, revised). The Ontario Curriculum, Social Studies, Grades 1–6; History and Geography, Grades 7–8. Queen's Printer for Ontario.

Ministry of Education. (2013b, revised). The Ontario Curriculum Grades 9–12 Secondary, Social Sciences and Humanities. Queen's Printer for Ontario.

Ministry of Education. (2018, revised). The Ontario Curriculum, Social Studies, Grade 1–6; History and Geography, Grades 7–8. Queens Printer Ontario.

Moeser, J. P. (1999). Reclaiming Juvenile Justice for the 21st Century: Balanced and Restorative Justice. *Reclaiming Children and Youth, 8*(3), 162–164.

Ontario Human Rights Commission. (2005a). *The Ontario Safe Schools Act: School Discipline and Discrimination. VII Disproportionate impact in Ontario.* Retrieved from http://www.ohrc.on.ca/en/ontario-safe-schools-act-school-discipline-and-discrimination.

Ontario Human Rights Commission. (2005b). *Human Rights Settlement Reached with Ministry of Education on Safe Schools-Terms of Settlement.* Retrieved from http://www.ohrc.on.ca/en/human-rights-settlement-reached-ministry-education-safe-schools.

Ontario Ministry of Education. (2009). *Who's Responsible for Your Child's Education?* Retrieved from http://www.edu.gov.on.ca/eng/document/brochure/whosresp.html.

Payne, A. A., & Welch, K. (2010). Modeling the Effects of Racial Threat on Punitive and Restorative School Discipline Practices. *Criminology, 48,* 1019–1062.

Payne, A. A., & Welch, K. (2013). Restorative Justice in Schools: The Influence of Race on Restorative Discipline. *Youth & Society, XX*(X), 1–26.

Rankin, J., Rushowy, K., & Brown, L. (2013, March 22). Toronto School Suspension Rates Highest for Black and Aboriginal Students. *The Toronto Star.* Retrieved from https://www.thestar.com/news/gta/2013/03/22/toronto_school_suspension_rates_highest_for_Black_and_aboriginal_students.html.

Reay, D. (2004). 'It's All Becoming a Habitus': Beyond the Habitual Use of Habitus in Educational Research. *British Journal of Sociology of Education*, 25(4), 431–444.
Reay, D., David, M., Ball, S. (2001). Making a Difference? Institutional Habituses and Higher Education Choice. *Sociological Research Online*, 5(4).
Roher, E. M. (2008). Progressive Discipline: Totally Rethinking Safe Schools. *Principal Connections*, 11(2), 203–221.
Ryals, H. S. (2004). Restorative Justice: New Horizons in Juvenile Offender Counselling. *Journal of Addictions & Offender Counselling*, 25(1), 18–25.
Schachter, R. (2010). Discipline Gets the Boot. *District Administration*, 46(1), 26–28.
Shilling, C. (1991). Social Space, Gender Inequalities and Educational Differentiation. *British Journal of Sociology of Education*, 12, 23–44.
Sumner, M. D., Silverman, C. J., & Frampton, M. L. (2010). *School Based Restorative Justice as an Alternative to Zero Tolerance Policies: Lessons from West Oakland*. Thelton E. Henderson Center for Social Justice. Berkeley: University of California, Berkeley, School of Law.
Szymanski, M. (2016). *Restorative Justice Program Drastically Lowers Days Lost to Suspensions in LAUSD* (LA School Report). Retrieved from http://laschoolreport.com/restorative-justice-program-drastically-lowers-days-lost-to-suspensions-in-lausd/.
Toronto District School Board. *Chart of Consequences of Inappropriate Student Behaviour*. Retrieved from: http://northern-secondary.com/Joomla/attachments/article/60/Chart%20of%20Consequences.pdf.
Toronto District School Board. (2013a). *TDSB Facts. Programs of Study: An Overview*. Retrieved from http://www.tdsb.on.ca/Portals/research/docs/reports/ProgramsOfStudyAnOverview%20FS-%20FINAL.pdf.
Toronto District School Board. (2013b). *Caring and Safe Schools Suspension Rates by Students Demographic and Family Background Characteristics*. Retrieved from http://www.tdsb.on.ca/Portals/research/docs/reports/CaringSafeSchoolsCensus201112.pdf.
Toronto District School Board. (2017, April). *Expulsion Decision-Making Process and Expelled Students' Transition Experience in the Toronto District School Board's Caring and Safe Schools Programs and Their Graduation Outcomes*. Toronto: Toronto District School Board, Research and Information Services.
Varnham, S. (2005). Seeing Things Differently: Restorative Justice and School Discipline. *Education and the Law*, 17(3), 87–104.
Wacquant, L. (1998). Pierre Bourdieu. In Rob Stones (Ed.), *Key Sociological Thinkers*. London: Macmillan.
Welch, K., & Payne, A. A. (2012). Exclusionary School Punishment. *Youth Violence and Juvenile Justice*, 10(2), 155–171.

Winton, S. (2011). Managing Conduct: A Comparative Policy Analysis of Safe Schools Policies in Toronto, Canada and Buffalo, USA. *Comparative Education, 47*(2), 247–263.

Zaslaw, J. (2010). Restorative Resolution. Principal Leadership, the National Association of Elementary School Principals.

Zuker, M., & Kirwin, L. M. (2015). *Children's Law Handbook Third Edition.* Carswell Thomson Reuter Canada Limited.

CHAPTER 4

Canada's Legacy of Colonialism: Implications in Education

Jacqueline Benn-John

4.1 Introduction

My understanding of the purpose of formal education was influenced by my parent's belief that the Canadian educational system offered limitless opportunities for learning and knowledge expansion. Undoubtedly, they said, this learning would lead to career success later in life. Terry Wotherspoon (2009) draws on Emile Durkheim's (1956) early work on formal education, which according to Wotherspoon is still relevant today and states that the purpose of education is "to provide each individual with the knowledge and capabilities that are essential for meaningful participation in particular societal contexts" (21). I concur with this structural-functionalist view and appreciate Talcott Parsons' (1959) extension, where he recognizes that education does more than transmit values and knowledge to students: rather, "such knowledge and values are to be internalized by individuals as part of their personalities" (21).

J. Benn-John (✉)
Ontario Institute for Studies in Education,
University of Toronto, Toronto, ON, Canada
e-mail: Jacqueline.benn.john@mail.utoronto.ca

© The Author(s) 2019
F. J. Villegas and J. Brady (eds.), *Critical Schooling*,
https://doi.org/10.1007/978-3-030-00716-4_4

Yet, the question is, whose knowledges and values are reflected in the Canadian curriculum? Despite the common Canadian claim to embracing social diversity and multicultural values, Eurocentric knowledges and values continue to implicitly dominate the curriculum, structure and schooling philosophy. Despite the availability of different axiologies and epistemologies, Eurocentrism has nonetheless been superimposed in many—if not most—educational systems, resulting in the colonization of education. Evidence of this colonialist influence is present in my parents' mistaken conviction in privileging the educational system in the global North. This leads me to consider that it "follows then that educational systems, curriculum, and teaching are shaped in context-specific ways by legacies of colonialism" (Asher, 2009, p. 67). My parents' beliefs—and those that I learned from them growing up—are a concrete example of this. Overall, these colonial influences have had an implicit impact on both the curriculum contained in educational systems and how racialized and white students experience them.

To this end, I approach this topic from a position of systemic as well as individual subordination and resistance. As a Black woman schooled in Canada, this topic contextualizes my experience of racism, sexism and invisibility within educational systems. It also frames and elucidates the educational experience of countless Black children and Aboriginal students as necessarily connected to colonial ideologies of whiteness, anti-Blackness and anti-Indigenous racism. This paper intentionally makes visible the West's colonial past, as well as its history of domination, exclusion and the imposition of white superiority within Canada's educational system. Finally, this paper resists simple and "conservative arguments that attribute educational inequality to inherent differences in intelligence and ability" between learners (and communities) of different racialized identities (Wotherspoon, 2009, p. 35).

4.2 DISCURSIVE FRAMEWORKS: VISIBILITY, INCLUSIVENESS & RESISTANCE

Within this paper, I use *anti-colonialism, anti-racism* and *African feminism* discursive frameworks to explore and understand Canada's legacy of imperialism. Particularly, I focus on how colonial practices continue to be contemporaneously implicitly and explicitly maintained in educational systems in the twenty-first century. Together, these frameworks challenge the institutional powers and structures established by and maintained through ongoing colonialism.

Anti-colonialism is defined as "the political struggle and active resistance of colonized peoples against the ideology and practice of colonialism. It emphasizes decolonization and affirming Indigenous knowledge and culture, while establishing Indigenous control over Indigenous national territories" (Pon, Gosine, & Phillips, 2011, p. 400). Dei (2006) posits that, unlike dominant Eurocentric discourses, anti-colonial thought outlines:

> an approach to theorizing colonial and re-colonial relations and the implications of imperial structures on the process of knowledge production and validation, the understanding of Indigeneity, and the pursuit of agency, resistance and subjective politics. (p. 2)[1]

In this way, this framework articulates the *validity* and *strengths* of Indigenous educational systems, while simultaneously identifying rhetoric of colonizer supremacy embedded in other (more hegemonic) systems. Anti-colonialism further aims to establish and foster educational opportunities that are rooted in traditions of Indigenous nations (Hart, 2009).

Anti-racism is defined as "an action-oriented, educational and political strategy for institutional and systemic change that addresses the issues of racism and the interlocking systems of social oppression (sexism, classism, heterosexism and ableism)" (Dei & Calliste, 2000, p. 11). Integrating an integrative anti-racism discursive framework to my analysis of Canada's educational system illuminates the way in which Indigenous and racialized bodies continue to experience racism and other systems of oppression within Canadian institutions, workplaces and community spaces. An integrative anti-racism framework centres and articulates the experience of marginalized groups from their own standpoint. In the case of Black students, integrative anti-racism framework examines the lived experience of the students through their "personal experiential knowledge" (Dei, 1996, p. 63) and thereby works to expose historical and current sociopolitical factors that re-produce the construction of Black students as subordinate.

Building upon these frameworks, *African feminism* creates an inclusive brand of feminism that "is about people, their children, their work, their day to day experiences, their stories of the past" (Wane, 2011, p. 9). Particularly, African feminism encourages African women to tell and record their histories and to produce and reproduce Indigenous knowledge—much as I briefly did in this essay's introduction. In doing so, African feminism shares commonly marginalized narratives and "challenges the institutional powers and imperial structures that have kept African women and their Indigenous knowledges buried under the weight of modernity"—as well as under interlocking manifestations of sexism and racism (Wane, 2011, p. 14).[2]

Together, these frameworks support a critical analysis of colonial history and practice, while fostering the consciousness to engage in alternative decolonizing works of resistance in education. The concurrent application of anti-colonial, anti-racism and African feminist theory combines to raise different yet interlocking issues implicit in hegemonic (i.e. South and Western) educational structures and content. Anti-racist theory surfaces and identifies often invisibilized iterations of colonizer privilege embedded in hegemonic systems, while anti-colonial theory operates to point to the cogency and strengths of othered (Indigenous) systems. African feminism brings capacity to understand these issues through a lens of intersectional identities—in my case, the lens of race and gender; however, the co-occurrence of additional social locations may contribute to one's lived experience—found in personal narratives.

In this work, I employ a textual analysis of selected works from feminist, racialized and Western scholars that address the lived experiences of Black and Indigenous students. I compare how these lived experiences of racialized persons—including experiences of racism, sexism and Indigenous truths—are or *are not* commonly present in educational curriculum or structures. The review of various texts, as above, helps to surface themes of *hegemonic* (i.e. colonizer) *narratives, missing narratives* (i.e. the histories and perspectives of marginalized communities) and implicit *bias* in educational curriculum and structures. Certainly, these themes are not simply structural; more, they have direct impacts upon the day-to-day learning experiences (and learned content) that students acquire. To unpack this further, I will critically reflect on my own experiences of marginalization, identifying similarities within the educational experience of the marginalized groups studied in the text analysis. I also offer decolonizing strategies for the future. A textual analysis allows me to employ the theoretical frameworks identified above—*African feminism, anti-racism theory, anti-colonial theory*—to raise threefold issues: (1) to employ the lived experiences of marginalized persons in order to raise narratives that are commonly invisibilized in the hegemony; (2) to identify racist or white superiority implicit in hegemonic educational systems; and (3) to posit additional systems and system components, based on the strengths and values of racialized communities.

4.3 Strategic Omission: Canada's Legacy of Colonialism

Colonization refers to "the occupation and control of one nation by another" (Asher, 2009, p. 71). As conceptualized by Fanon, colonialism occurs when foreign people or government imposes its will on the original inhabitants (Mucina, 2011). In the Canadian context, Europeans established white settler societies on non-European soil. These settlers saw themselves as superior to the non-European Indigenous inhabitants, who originally occupied the land. Historically, white settler societies were structured by a racial hierarchy, wherein murderous violence, rape and slavery were justified and normalized (Razack, 2002). European settlers felt entitled to newly discovered lands and to the resources of its inhabitants. Thus, Razack (2002) argues that, consequently, "a white settler mythology is, both an ongoing enactment of exploitation of persons of colour, as well as a disavowal of conquest, genocide, slavery and exploitation of the labour of peoples of color" (p. 2). Colonial history maintains the supremacist myth that "white people came first [to Canada] and that it is they who principally developed the land." Moreover, Razack identifies, "Indigenous people are presumed to be mostly dead or assimilated" (2002, p. 2).

Black people in Canada were enslaved in order to provide cheap or free labour to fuel the colonizers' capitalist pursuits, and they provided a means to confirm and consolidate white privilege and an assumed superior identity. To justify the enslavement of Blacks, colonizers created a racial hierarchy that subordinated the status of Blacks and elevated whites; within this social construct, Blackness connoted invisibility, inferiority and being marked as dirty (Razack, 2002). Black people were the colonizers' property and objects for exploitation. On the other hand, and in contrast, whiteness connoted visibility, power and privilege. White colonizers not only had control over their lives and bodies, but also control over the colonized, and marked them as the inferior, worthless, evil, and backward "Other" (Goldberg, 1996). Goldberg (1996) describes "Whiteness as being characterized in terms of light and learning, Blackness in terms of darkness and degeneration" (p. 179). Furthermore, whites were *un*marked and free, and had the authority to make, change and manipulate rules; these rules invariably favoured them and gave them privilege, especially economic gain.

The ongoing oppression and economic exploitation of Blacks during slavery were institutionalized and supported by law. Cheryl Harris (1995) argues that "slavery as a legal institution treated slaves as property that could be transferred, assigned, inherited, or posted as collateral" (p. 279). This raises an interesting contradiction about the supposed worthlessness of Blacks as a racial category: their bodies held value as property to slave owners and slave owner families, yet, institutionally, no value was accorded to Black persons themselves. The Black body was an asset to the colonizer, yet a liability to both the Black person and the society that was designed to produce, and perpetuate, white racial domination. The Black slave had no rights as "Black" racial identity marked them as subject to enslavement; whereas "white" racial identity marked whites as free, or at the minimum, as not enslaved to another (Harris, 1995, p. 278). Furthering Harris's argument, the gender of Black female slaves marked them as available for rape and other forms of abuse and exploitation, all sanctioned under law, through racial oppression and patriarchy (Pietsch, 2004). Indeed, the white racial subject was free to do what it wanted with their "property", including rape, murder and trafficking of Black women and girls.

Protected under law and through a system of patriarchy, slave owners also exploited and violated Black women's bodies by using them to breed more slaves. This form of emotional, psychological and physical torture produced more assets and wealth for the slave owners, guaranteeing them a steady flow of labour. This again presents a stark contradiction about the value of the Black body—here, the female body in particular: within this racialized system, slave owners and their families depended on the Black woman's reproductive abilities to guarantee their wealth and intergenerational financial security; bell hooks (1998) argues that "to justify breeding, the institutionalized sanctioning of ongoing rape of enslaved Black females to produce future laborers, white supremacist patriarchs had to position the Black female in the cultural imagination as always 'sexually suspect'" (p. 69). These stereotypes negatively portrayed Black women as whores, sapphires, jezebels, sluts and mammies, serving to further degrade them (Ladson-Billings, 2009). These socially constructed images of the Black race were internalized not just within white communities, but also within Black communities, where by extension, Black men exercised patriarchal privilege, justifying the control, rape and violation of the bodies of Black women and girls (Benn-John, 2016). In this way, the intersection of Blackness and womanhood is pronounced and increases the vulnerability of Black women and girls, "leaving them more susceptible to exploitation in all forms by the enslavers and Black men" argues Moore and Gibbons-Taylor (2018, Chapter 5). This vulnerability to exploitation continues today, despite its roots in dated negative stereotypes from decades before.

In view of these historical facts, how is Canada's national history of genocide and colonialism being accurately told or not told? What version of Canada's history is being told, and who is the storyteller? Finally, who is listening to these stories—and via which Canadian systems? It is important to recognize the potential role of the Canadian educational system in telling our history consistently, in telling the story of *multiple histories* and in understanding histories' impact on Canada's many educators, parents and students. In the next section, I focus on how colonialism manifests in the educational system.

4.4 Colonial Practices in Education

Canada's history of imperialism, white racial superiority and discrimination, and accompanying colonial practices, is strategically left out of national narratives. In the school curriculum, we are taught and reminded only of the great white north and the hardworking white settlers who built this nation: this is the mythology that has become our national narrative. These stories perpetuate the myth of Indigenous and Black people's invisibility and assume their lack of contribution to the development of the state of Canada. The suppressed histories and knowledges of Black and Indigenous people further serve to constitute and validate the identity of the colonizing white settler as founding fathers who were, and continue to be, racially superior, and therefore worthy of entitlements over the "Other." While these colonial narratives dominate in all places and spaces in Canada, in particular, the erasure of race from the dominant national narrative is a colonial practice that continues to be perpetuated in governmental institutions and, as a matter of interest to this paper, in the educational system. Kempf (2011) argues that "formal education is among the key mechanisms through which colonial epistemic programs proceed" (p. 94)—and is therefore manifested in various educational processes, hegemonic narratives and practices.

Despite dedicated efforts by white colonizers to portray Indigenous societies as lacking in formal systems, Wotherspoon (2009) offers an account of Indigenous education in Canada prior to colonialism:

It [Indigenous education] was an education in which the community and the natural environment were the classroom, and the land was seen as mother of people. Members of the community were the teachers, and each adult was responsible for ensuring that each child learned how to live a good life. (p. 5)

Many African Indigenous systems are similar: "oral traditional teachings facilitate the inculcation of socially desirable values such as hard work, honesty, thrift, and wisdom" (Aliyu, 1997, p. 149). "African women are the guardians of traditional knowledge" (Wane, 2011, p. 15) and through narration, African women pass on knowledges of African cultures and ways of knowing. These examples of pre-colonial Indigenous education, knowledge and value systems underscore that Indigenous societies had sophisticated and formalized ways of educating children for generations. Thus, Canada's national narrative, which purports that the earliest "formal" schooling was established by missionaries and religious orders (Wotherspoon, 2009), is false and was devised with the goal of "replacing Indigenous lifestyles and knowledge with European concepts and consciousness" (p. 58). Inherent in this structure and supposed act of benevolence is the belief that Indigenous people are backward and need civilizing from themselves.

I share Kempf's (2011) contention that the dismantling of Indigenous education systems commenced with the onset of educational imperialism. This was a crucial element of colonialism, with profound effects on the colonized and the colonizer. One such effect is observed through the introduction of residential schooling which is defined as follows:

a colonial system of schooling enforced on Indigenous nations aimed at effecting cultural genocide and assimilation on children, many of whom were forcibly removed and abducted from their families and communities. This experience is characterized by forced removal from families; systemic and ritualized physical and sexual assault; spiritual, psychological, and emotional abuse; and malnutrition, inhumane living conditions, death and murder. (Cannon & Sunseri, 2011, p. 278)

Another effect of education has been that "mainstream schooling socializes and indeed formalizes inequitable relations along lines of race, gender, ability, language, anti-religion, class gender, sexual orientation and geographic status" (Kempf, 2011, p. 94). Likewise, Eurocentric education promotes individualism and privileges individual accomplishment and achievement through testing, grading and ongoing assessment of overall scholastic achievement (Wotherspoon, 2009). In contrast, knowledge systems that are communitarian or shared in nature, as in most Indigenous models, are devalued in favour of institutionalized knowledges in the academy (see Wotherspoon, 2009). Eurocentric knowledge and values are further promoted through a Eurocentric curriculum in the classroom and the hiring of predominantly white teachers as bastions and promoters of Eurocentric knowledge and values: this occurs in classrooms, lecture halls and even through online distance learning media, ensuring the consolidation of Eurocentric ways of knowing and epistemic hegemony. We can see the influence of the economic pursuit by the colonizers manifest in how children are made to understand achievement and are groomed to compete in the marketplace: the individual student's performance is characterized by individualism and separateness from others, fostering competitiveness (Wotherspoon, 2009). This educational imperialism began with the dismantling of Indigenous educational systems and the imposition of colonial practices in education. Altogether, continuing to today, this has had a marked effect on both the colonized and the colonizer (Kempf, 2011). The examples cited above offer a representation of colonial practices in education.

In order to evaluate the full impact of Canada's legacy of colonialism contemporaneously, it is important to take stock today and ask, "how far have we come?" An examination of the unequal educational outcomes for Indigenous and African/Black students that have been recorded in Canada's educational system garners a resounding and unapologetic response: Not far enough! As Francisco Villegas and Janelle Brady, in the introduction to this volume, remind us, "schools are filled with violent processes that produce physical, psychological, and spiritual harm. These processes are couched in colonialism, white supremacy, and patriarchy." As these processes are both pervasive and implicit, they have implications for communities of colour.

In the next section, I review the notion of educational outcomes and identify unequal outcomes for racialized students *and* educators in Euro-American spaces of learning. Certainly, structures informed by colonialism will have impacts on students and educators. In this system, it is learners and educators from communities of colour that experience this implicit inequity most negatively.

4.5 Unequal Educational Outcomes for Whom?

In his chapter *Colonial Stains on Our Existence*, Alfred Taiaiake (2011) asserts that colonial legacy is maintained today by both those with racial privilege (who accept a privileged role) and those who internalize colonial myths such as racist histories, notions of white superiority, notions that hegemonic knowledge is more "important" than subjugated knowledges, and the lie of Eurocentric ideas of what constitutes progress. This last point refers to the constructed and populist North American immigrant narrative, in which the new immigrants hope that material accumulation and expansion of wealth are the formula for happiness, and that being both accepted by the white man, and attaining legitimacy through citizenship constitutes immigrants' progress.

In the context of the educational system, Wotherspoon (2009) offers an account of how an ongoing dynamic of regulation and resistance produces distinct social and educational experiences (p. 117), such as streaming, official knowledge, hegemony and silencing. As Wotherspoon (2009) explains, *streaming* is a process in which students are channelled into specific programmes and learning groups, for channelling them into more focused, skill-specific educational and employment goals in future. I can recall sitting in the guidance office in high school, discussing my career possibilities. I informed the guidance counsellor that I wanted to attend university. Although I did not really have a clear focus of what I wanted to study, I had envisioned the possibility of university studies for myself. The guidance counsellor took a long look at me from under her thick-rimmed glasses and said "ohhhh noooo...you did not take advanced math. You must have advanced math to go to university. Your typing speed is not too bad, why don't you give secretarial work some thought? You can take a course to help you increase your typing speed." I responded that I didn't really like typing, and my parents said I had to go to university. The guidance counsellor pointed out that I did not continue with French and I did not do well in science either. "It is very hard to get into universities and your marks were not high enough", she asserted.

Clearly, this guidance counsellor had a preconceived idea as to what Black female students could and could not achieve academically, and where, as a woman of colour, I belonged in the labour force. She attempted to stream me into those directions. This example of streaming also illustrates the intersecting nature of oppression based on race and gender. I received clear cues from the guidance counsellor about her expectations of me, my abilities and what she perceived should be my goals. This experience is not unique to me. Many Black friends and family members of mine who were similarly marginalized were aware of their perceived status in relation to others, as well as the academic and labour stereotypes attributed to them based on their particular intersectional social locations. It is therefore unsurprising that Wotherspoon (2009) points out that streaming produces results that "tend to correspond to existing patterns of social inequality" (pp. 118–119), such as race, class and gender achievements.

The halls of higher learning—colleges and universities—are not exempt from colonial practices in education. Felly Nkweto Simmonds (1997) points out that she "cannot ignore the fact of her Blackness, even if she wanted to, and neither can her colleagues or students, even if they wanted to" (p. 52). This awareness leaves us especially vulnerable to being targeted by—and repeating—colonial scripts: Nkweto Simmonds might be an academic, but she "carries an embodied self that is at odds with expectations of who she is" (p. 52). Expectations are connected to a colonial script, while the racialized bodies (and minds) carry future goals and skills, educational and otherwise, that diverge from socially constructed definitions. In the context of racism and white supremacy, Nkweto Simmonds is out of place and time within the academy, as she is fixed through her race as being inferior to all whites, regardless of class. In this way, Black female academics face multiple layers of oppression, as their overall scholarship, contribution to knowledge production and teaching abilities present as divergent from, if not alien to, the normative colonial script for Black women. As a result, they are under constant surveillance by white students and faculty, as well as subject to internal oppression by African/Black students and faculty. Illustrating this very dynamic, Bannerji (1995) reflects on the first time she applied for a teaching job in 1988: she determined that got the job because "they had a tremendous necessity for hiring people in certain areas, and I got hired to teach about Third World women and feminist theories about gender, race and class" (p. 192). Consequentially, academically achieving persons of colour do not fit the image of non-white persons constructed by colonialism: "Aboriginal people and racialized minorities are perceived as 'outsiders within' the 'hallowed halls' of the academy. They are expected to know their limitations and stay in their ascribed 'place'" (Dei, 2000, p. 146).

Not only do racialized persons appear not to fit in higher education spaces, they also do not appear as readily as their white counterparts as knowledge brokers, subject-matter experts or active agents in developing educational content. Wotherspoon (2009) contends that official knowledge determines which topics, information and content are regarded as worth knowing and legitimate. In colonial education systems, official knowledge is intertwined with education while educational institutes are sites where knowledge is transmitted or disseminated (Wotherspoon, 2009), thus perpetuating the official discourses. It is not surprising then that the colonizer disseminates official knowledge and the colonized are the recipients of this "official knowledge." When my five-year-old daughter came home with her weekly show and tell homework assignment, I was struck by the omission of Indigenous and female inventors from the list of inventors she was expected to research. On another occasion, the show and tell assignment was on the topic of famous artists. A list of at least ten artists did not include even one Indigenous or female artist. Why would a private school education mirror the same omissions I experienced as a student in Canadian public and Catholic schools? It was almost four decades interval, and yet, the hegemonic narratives in the educational curriculum had not changed. My eight-year-old son who attends the same private school as his sister also came home with an assignment to prepare a project report on Pioneer Life in Canada. In this assignment, he was required to address why the settlers came to Canada, where they came from, who were the early inhabitants of Canada, and how did they help the settlers. This assignment also served to perpetuate the myth of Canada's official colonial narrative. Although it did acknowledge the existence of Indigenous people, albeit minimally, the usefulness of Indigenous people was only recognized in relation to how far they "helped" the settlers. Thus, a critical view of the notion of "usefulness," as denoted by the colonial settlers, reveals the extent of exploitation of Indigenous knowledge that was required to help implement the colonial project: in effect, if there had been no settlers to offer help to, would the contributions of these Indigenous persons to Canada have been noted? In the assignment's overall query, the work, social and economic contribution of Indigenous persons appears significant only for what it benefitted to the white settlers. A trip to our local library further corroborated this dominant script: the books we signed out promoted stereotypical images of Indigenous people as primitive, passive, loyal and fixed within a historical context. Conversely, the national narrative portrayed

European settlers as hardworking, family oriented, peaceful and friendly. Kempf (2011) poignantly asks: "Why do students and classrooms need these knowledges?" (p. 94). According to Brady and Abawi (Chapter 6), decolonizing narratives and knowledges are needed to "challenge the divide-and-conquer politics of reading our bodies as 'settler-colonials' as we operate from an understanding of colonialism beyond the North American boundaries." Certainly, this deliberate misinformation serves to exclude non-European knowledges from the classroom which simultaneously legitimizes (Kempf, 2011). According to Dei (1996), this misinformation impedes the social growth of marginalized students. Kawano (2011) argues that "Eurocentric ways of knowing have come to be reproduced, and, at the same time, Indigenous ways of knowing have come to be devalued and marginalized" (p. 83). The example of my son's experience at the public library characterizes the prevalence of narratives of exclusion in the Canadian curriculum, and how easily such omissive information is accessed in our communities without critique. Consequently, of great concern to me is what my children are *not* learning—that is, what has been systematically or strategically omitted from the curriculum that is essential for them to know in order to affirm their identity and give them knowledge that is true and whole.

Colonial hegemonic scripts inform, reproduce and foster a status quo of social inequity. Wotherspoon (2009) asserts that hegemony is domination that people experience in day-to-day life experiences. Similarly, hegemony also refers to a process of domination by consent, in which the general population adopts a worldview that reflects the interests of the dominant classes (Gramsci, 1971, in Wotherspoon, 2009, p. 130). Identifying hegemony helps us to see how what we do and do not question or accept on a commonsense basis is grounded in our day-to-day experiences; indeed, tradition is "constructed so that ruling practices are maintained without usually being evident to us." Wotherspoon (2009) provides two clear examples to demonstrate how educational practices are hegemonic. The first is related to how schools are organized and how knowledge is presented in the classroom, primarily through curriculum. Curriculum is "understood, arranged and transmitted to pupils, and often to teachers in pre-arranged units" (Wotherspoon, p. 130). This is reminiscent of a child sitting down to the dinner table in front of a plate of food; the reality is the child has no choice in whether or not they want to take in what is on the plate. It is, in effect, the only plate offered to them.

Wotherspoon's (2009) second example of hegemony in the schooling process is the socially constructed ethic of individualism so evident in Western educational systems. In the Western world, we are consciously and unconsciously taught the importance of individualism. Messages related to being self-reliant, independent, and taking initiative is reinforced through schooling. This worldview does not recognize other ways of being and producing knowledge in the world, in particular, Indigenous and African societies with a "social origin of practices and ideas"—for example, traditions of collectivism and knowledge co-creation (Wotherspoon, 2009, p. 131). In the case of African societies, Indigenous knowledge is created through lived experience of intersectional identities that are context specific (Dei, 2008) and shared through common experiences then passed on from generation to generation. On the other hand, in Western educational systems, we continue to see a devaluing of knowledge systems that are communitarian or shared in nature, characteristic of most Indigenous ways of knowing, in favour of the individualism promoted by institutionalized values in the academy (Catungal, 2011). For example, the notion of student achievement and success is posited as an individual's accomplishment (or failure) based on their ambition, steadfast work and ability to transcend barriers. This common narrative (also present in the previously mentioned "immigrant dream" or "immigrant story") does little to identify the role of systemic barriers, social marginalization or discrimination operating in the lives of racialized persons—nor the practical impacts of these social contexts upon their successes, achievements or limitations. I concur with Wotherspoon (2009) in his assertion that:

> when social inequality is not discussed as a central part of curricula and when the world is seen as a collection of individuals rather than a system based on distinct social positions, one consequence is that prevailing patterns of domination and subordination come to be understood and experienced as natural and inevitable rather than as something to be questioned. (p. 131)

Certainly, dynamics of subordination and domination will likely also be invisibilized: visible only to individuals, communities and society at large as *individuals'* failings or limitations. Another consequence of education is that, under this hegemonic system, repressed histories and subjugated knowledges will never see the opportunity to enlighten the colonized nor the colonizer. Colonial practices in education remain unchallenged and enjoy the opportunity to be continually reproduced. Correspondingly, Kawano (2011) understands ongoing colonialism in the educational system as "reproducing the colonialism imprint and perpetuating whiteness" (p. 84).

Silencing is put forward by Wotherspoon (2009) as another example of how relations of regulation and resistance produce distinct social and educational experiences. Silencing operates in two interrelated ways: first, when discussion on particular issues relevant to marginalized students are excluded from or discouraged in the classroom, and second, when the lives, experiences and interests of particular groups are made irrelevant to the educational process (Wotherspoon, 2009).

Experiences of silencing can occur at different points in one's educational journey. As a young racialized woman, not only was I invisible in the curriculum, but I found that the storybooks and history books alike depicted gross stereotypes of African people as inferior and incapable. The questions that I faced included: Where are the African/Black scientists and inventors? Why do the storybooks present the white nuclear family as the *only* type of family? There were no answers from the education I was receiving, and before long, I stopped questioning my invisibility in the history books and other learning materials. Instead, I accepted those that portrayed healthy and happy white children with two-parent families, straight noses, blue eyes and blonde hair as the norm. This acceptance, however, resulted in continually identifying as having a family, body or physical traits that could not align with the norm. As of consequence, for example, I asked myself: "why did I end up with 'bad' hair?" I begged my mother to have my African hair hot combed and later chemically straightened so I could have "good" hair and look as white as possible.

Unable to recognize the impact of colonialism on Black children's self-perception and, later, academic success, my parents, like many other West Indian parents, encouraged me to compensate for my Blackness by working and studying "twice as hard." I studied French and Canadian history until I no longer noticed that Indigenous peoples and other people that looked like me were invisible. I came to believe that African/Black people had no history and no role models, as we were portrayed as though this was true and we did not contribute anything to the development of Canadian society. Furthermore, our teachers did not "groom" my siblings and I for post-secondary education, nor were we encouraged to actively participate in class discussions, as were white students. When I recently contacted a past professor to request a reference to support my application for graduate studies in the PhD programme, I was advised that my A-grade average in her course meant I was not at the top of the class and therefore the professor did not know me; consequently, she could not provide a reference. I was subsequently encouraged to contact another professor and told that only if I was not successful there would she assist me with a reference. The term "silenced" is not strong enough to describe how this interaction left me feeling. I agree with Wotherspoon's (2009) account of how a dynamic of regulation and resistance produces distinct social and educational experiences for racialized students. Of course, I also believe that intentional querying of and resistance to this dynamic can create anti-colonial opportunities for both colonized and colonizer communities alike. In the next section of this chapter, I will discuss practical strategies towards these opportunities.

4.6 Decolonization Starts with Me

Every day, women, men, elders, students, community activists, academic warriors, scholars and allies rebel, challenge and resist Canada's legacy of imperialism, including colonial practices in education. From colonial through to post-colonial periods, resistance has included paying homage to our racialized ancestors; passing Indigenous and African traditions onto generations of Indigenous and African people through oral traditions; researching and creating knowledge that promotes non-Western values, knowledges and standpoints (Mucina, 2011). Such people have worked to provide an alternative to the existing narrative and have documented the collective experience of marginalized groups through embodied experiences, art or music (Outerbridge, 2011). Despite the dominant colonial narrative, many marginalized people continue to pursue ambitious careers in education and create holistic, healthy and happy intimate partner and family relations. At the root of these acts of resistance is *decolonization*. Decolonization does not have a single definition: overall, it is generally understood that it is the process of undoing the atrocities of colonialism, as well as resistance of the colonizer's ideas that promoted the inferiority of colonized peoples.

Decolonization is also the most powerful and effective form of resistance in response to Canada's legacy of imperialism and colonial practices in education.

Decolonization empowers Indigenous people by providing an alternate narrative that does not align with colonial expectations and limitations. It offers Indigenous persons entitlement to speak for themselves, tell their own stories and challenge what colonizers have asserted and legitimized as theory. Smith (1999) further emphasizes this point with her assertion that "decolonization is about centering our [Indigenous and other racialized persons'] concerns and world views, and then coming to know and understand theory and research, from our own perspectives and for our own purposes" (p. 39). The process of decolonizing is a powerful form of resistance that is also political and as Fanon argues, "sets out to change the order of the world and is, obviously, a programme of complete disorder" (Smith, 27). The process is also about finding oneself *in between stories*. We have a "his story"—a story constructed by the colonizer—that we can dismantle. From here, we can "re-right" and reconstruct our Ancestors' story, which is our own story. Elements of these stories shape our current and future stories. Since decolonizing is a lifelong journey, there will always be a story to "right."

In this paper, I contend that decolonization *as an act of resistance* must be a project for colonized and colonizer alike. Following my presentation on the topic of this paper in the classroom, a student asked me where she would start with the project of decolonization. My response was very simple: start with you. Read the works of non-Western scholars, meditate, ask yourself how you have come to know what you know, ask your community library and children's schools critical questions about the tools made available for learning, continue to take courses with scholars who include subjugated knowledge in his curriculum, and provide safe spaces for students to dialogue and ask critical questions. Further, one can resist colonizing forces in our communities, workplaces and schools, and participate in uplifting and empowering others instead. Envision the decolonizing project as a body of water and place yourself in the centre. When you start with yourself, there will be a ripple from within that will spread outward to your immediate family, friends, community, schools and then beyond.

I propose a decolonization framework with the following four strategies:

i. *Honour and Practice the Traditions of Our Ancient Ancestors*

This strategy is quite broad and calls for a commitment to mourn, rediscover, reclaim, remember and celebrate our ancestral practices and traditions. My interpretation of traditions encompasses African culture, spirituality, language, social and political structures. Certainly, "we must learn again to acknowledge our Ancestors, for they walk with us and can light the path" (Arewa, 1998, p. 48). I continue to feel great pride and draw inner strength from my African history and African proverbs. Indigenous and African/Black students can also begin to acknowledge their Ancestors by taking the time to learn our history, and to meditate on their achievements. In addition, we can incorporate subjugated knowledges in our work as educators, leaders, mentors and activists. Our Ancestors' "light" has been a comfort, and it continues to inform the unanswered and challenging questions that will emerge through the decolonizing journey.

ii. *Acquire and Practice Critical Analytical Skills*

Critical analysis skills are crucial to supporting Indigenous and African/Black students decolonize. These skills enable us to interrogate existing dominant theory, information, misrepresentation, misappropriation, images and practices, and make visible the invisible. The development of an "oppositional gaze" that will stare our oppressor in the eye, thereby changing our own reality is a necessary condition for Black women's liberation (hooks, 1992, p. 116). Similarly, Dei, Karumanchery, and Karumanchery-Luik (2004) argue that "the critical gaze is a necessity of liberatory praxis"; without it, the oppressed "remain blind to the reality of their oppression" (pp. 6–7). As soon as we recognize we are in the midst of repressive power relations, then the possibility of resistance is created.

iii. *Formation of Theoretical Frameworks*

A theoretical framework grounds us. At the same time, it calls us to take action. In Scheurich and Young's (2002) *Coloring Epistemology*, the authors argue that "we need to create epistemologies that speak to our reality" (p. 50). This allows us to resist fitting into epistemologies that are inherently racist. Also, important in Scheurich and Young's (2002) argument is the act of Indigenous people participating in knowledge production. This action empowers us to speak for ourselves, control how we are represented and who represents us, offer alternative narratives to the colonizer's rhetoric, and gives voice to our ideas and stories within the academy. Creating our own epistemologies also enables Indigenous students to access and benefit from our ancestors' wisdom. If this important wisdom was included, our learning institutions and curriculums would reflect other ways of knowing and being in the world. A theoretical framework is also a necessary strategy for decolonizing Indigenous people, as it calls on marginalized populations to take action and draw attention to the oppression they experience. Dei et al. (2004) identify that raising the consciousness of the oppressed—and not assuming that we are all starting from the same place—is a necessary step to resist the oppression of others and ourselves. We are called not just to seek *our* interests, but to shape our world so it is a better place for our sisters and brothers to come.

iv. *Development of an Indigenous Network*

I propose an Indigenous network—that is, social, academic, professional or other networks, in which racialized persons intentionally connect for sharing resistance strategies, mentoring and positive support. A network of like persons can buffer the isolation experienced during the decolonization process. Andrew Okolie (2002) argues that "alliances with other anti-oppression groups and organizations should be forged with those groups that share the vision" (p. 14). Such partnerships can increase morale, promote interpersonal support and create safe space for decolonizing discussion. Moreover, partnerships, like alliances, "pool together and lend support where necessary but not displacing your issues or not taking over others' issues in a manner that denies them control" (Okolie, p. 14). Similarly, Carby (1997) argues that networks such as this help to develop survival strategies and cultures of resistance that "embody important alternative ways of organizing production and reproduction and value systems critical of the oppressor" (p. 52). An Indigenous network can also provide easier access to resources, including funds and skills, which are needed to recreate, implement, teach and sustain some of our Ancestors' traditions. In addition, a network such as this can be co-created by all its members, so to ensure it is collaborative and meets the needs of its member.

In an effort to restore wholeness in our lives and environments, decolonizing strategies ought to be approached by individuals at their own pace. However, skills, will and support are strengthened while doing so in collectivity with others who are engaged in similar processes.

4.7 Conclusion

This paper has interrogated colonialism as an expression of imperialism in education. I argue that reverberations from the atrocities of colonization are still experienced in the twenty-first century, with particular systemic implications for colonial practices in education. Educational systems continue to see colonial and post-colonial practices in their structures, educational content, subject-matter experts and in the culture of educational institutions. My research explores the continued experiences of marginalization and exclusion of Indigenous and Black students at different sites in the educational system: for example, we are not recorded in national stories as historical or present-day contributors, our stories of resistance remain untold, we are denied opportunities for career advancement in the workplace, our knowledges are subjugated in the academy, and we are underrepresented as faculty. These marginalizing experiences reveal that the personal (experience) is political. When considering ways in which Blacks in Canada can resist and heal from the negative effects of colonization, allies and academic warriors must ensure their theories and concepts represent the experiences of Black peoples. It must also aim to reflect the intersectional nature of Black peoples' in/visibility, so to shed light on the experiences of Black women, Black youth and other Black persons.

Increased understandings about Canada's legacy of colonialism and its impact can lead to real possibilities for the recognition of Black peoples, their knowledges and expertise, and constitute a valid basis for their resistance and healing (see Benn-John, 2017). This understanding can also lead to collaboration across and within other anti-oppression movements (e.g. feminist, anti-colonial and anti-racist) and for the conceptualization of ideologies that represent the experiences of Black peoples. To this end, allies and academic warriors must also consider ways to employ their power to transform education to create spaces so as to ensure no one is left behind. Certainly, this manner of scholarship and activism will provide insights that shape and create possibilities for educational policies and practices that benefit all learners.

NOTES

1. This comprehensive definition appears in J. Benn-John (2017).
2. Also see J. Benn-John (2017).

REFERENCES

Aliyu, S. (1997). Hansa Women as Oral Storytellers in Northern Nigeria. In S. Newell (Ed.), *Writing African Women* (pp. 149–158). London: Zed Books.

Arewa, C. (1998). Honoring the Ancestors: Re-membering the First Ancestors. *Opening to Spirit* (pp. 47–59). London: Thorsons Publishers.

Asher, N. (2009). Decolonization and Education: Locating Pedagogy and Self at the Interstices in Global Times. In R. S. Coloma (Ed.), *Post Colonial Challenges in Education* (pp. 67–78). New York: Peter Lang Publishing.

Bannerji, H. (1995). *Thinking Through: Essays on Feminism, Marxism and Anti-racism.* Toronto: Women's Press.

Benn-John, J. (2016). (Re)Colonizing Black Canadian Women & Routes to Resistance. *Race, Gender and Class Journal, 23*(1/2), 150–165.

Benn-John, J. (2017). Critical Intervention: Black Women (Re)Defining Feminist Resistance, Activism, and Empowerment in Feminist Organizing Within Ontario. In P. Albanese, L. Tepperman, E. Alexander, & Canadian Sociological Association (Eds.), *Reading Sociology Canadian Perspectives* (pp. 288–291). Don Mills, ON: Oxford University Press.

Cannon, M. J., & Sunseri, L. (2011). *Racism, Colonialism, and Indigeneity in Canada: A Reader.* Don Mills, ON: Oxford University Press.

Carby, H. (1997). White Woman Listen! Black Feminism and the Boundaries of Sisterhood. In H. S. Mirza (Ed.), *Blacks British Feminism* (pp. 45–53). London: Routledge.

Catungal, J. (2011). Circulating Western Notions: Implicating Myself in the Transnational Traffic of 'Progress' and Commodities. In N. Wane, A. Kempf, & M. Simmons (Eds.), *The Politics of Cultural Knowledge* (pp. 23–36). Rotterdam: Sense Publishers.

Dei, G. J. S. (1996). The Role of Afrocentricity in the Inclusive Curriculum in Canadian Schools. *Canadian Journal of Education, 21*(2), 170–186.

Dei, G. J. S. (2000). Rethinking the Role of Indigenous Knowledges in the Academy. *International Journal of Inclusive Education, 4*(2), 111–132.

Dei, G. J. S. (2006). Introduction: Mapping the Terrain—Towards a New Politics of Resistance. In G. J. S. Dei & A. Kempf (Eds.), *Anti-colonialism and Education: The Politics of Resistance* (pp. 1–24). Rotterdam: Sense Publishers.

Dei, G. J. S. (2008). Inidigenous Knowledge Studies and the Next Generation: Pedagogical Possibilities for Anti-colonial Education. *Australian Journal of Inidigenous Education, 37*(Suppl.), 5–3.

Dei, G. J. S., & Calliste, A. (2000). Mapping the Terrain: Power Knowledge and Anti-racism Education. In G. J. S. Dei & A. Calliste (Eds.), *Power, Knowledge and Anti-racism Education* (pp. 11–22). Halifax, NS: Fernwood.

Dei, G. J. S., Karumanchery, L., & Karumanchery-Luik, N. (2004). Introduction: Anti-racist Tapestries: Threads of Theory and Practice. In G. J. S. Dei, L. Karumanchery, & N. Karumanchery-Luik (Eds.), *Playing the Race Card: Exposing White Power and Privilege* (pp. 1–20). New York: Peter Lang Publishing.

Goldberg, D. T. (1996). In/Visibility and Super/Vision: Fanon on Race, Veils and Discourses of Resistance. In L. R. Gordon, T. D. Sharpley-Whiting, & R. T. White (Eds.), *Fanon: A Critical Reader* (pp. 179–200). Oxford: Blackwell.

Harris, C. (1995). Whiteness as Property. In K. Crenshaw, G. Peller, & K. Thomas (Eds.), *Critical Race Theory: The Key Writings that Formed the Movement* (pp. 276–291). New York: The New Press.

Hart, M. A. (2009). Anti-colonial Indigenous Social Work: Reflections on an Aboriginal Approach. In R. Sinclair, M. A. Hart, & G. Bruyere (Eds.), *Wicihitowin: Aboriginal Social Work in Canada* (pp. 25–41). Halifax, NS: Fernwood.

hooks, b. (1992). Black Looks: Race and Representation. In *The Oppositional Gaze, and Representations of Whiteness* (pp. 115–132). New York: Routledge.

hooks, b. (1998). Naked Without Shame: A Counter-Hegemonic Body Politic. In E. Shohat (Ed.), *Talking Visions* (pp. 65–74). Cambridge, MA: MIT Press.

Kawano, Y. (2011). Being Part of the Cultural Chain. In N. Wane, A. Kempf, & M. Simmons (Eds.), *The Politics of Cultural Knowledge* (pp. 83–92). Rotterdam: Sense Publishers.

Kempf, A. (2011). North African Knowledges and the Western Classroom: Situating Selected Literature. In N. Wane, A. Kempf, & M. Simmons (Eds.), *The Politics of Cultural Knowledge* (pp. 93–110). Rotterdam: Sense Publishers.

Ladson-Billings, G. (2009). 'Who You Callin' Nappy-Headed?' A Critical Race Theory Look at the Construction of Black Women. *Race Ethnicity and Education, 12*(1), 87–99. https://doi.org/10.1080/13613320802651012.

Mucina, D. (2011). Moving Beyond Neo-Colonialism to Ubuntu Governance. In N. Wane, A. Kempf, & M. Simmons (Eds.), *The Politics of Cultural Knowledge* (pp. 71–82). Rotterdam: Sense Publishers.

Okolie, A. C. (2002). Beyond Courtesy Curriculum: A Contribution to the Debate on Inclusive Education in Canadian Universities. Draft Paper Delivered at the *Annual Conference of the Canadian Sociology and Anthropology Association*, Held at the University of Toronto.

Outerbridge, D. (2011). What Might We Learn If We Silence the Colonial Voice? Finding Our Own Keys. In N. Wane, A. Kempf, & M. Simmons (Eds.), *The Politics of Cultural Knowledge* (pp. 111–120). Rotterdam: Sense Publishers.

Parsons, T. (1959). The Social Class as a Social System: Some of Its Functions in American Society. *Harvard Educational Review, 29,* 297–318.

Pietsch, N. (2004). Un/Titled: Constructions of Illegitimate Motherhood as Gender Insurrection. In A. O'Reilly (Ed.), *Mothers Matter: Motherhood as Discourse and Practice* (pp. 65–78). Toronto: Association for Research on Mothering, pp. 65–78.

Pon, G., Gosine, K., & Phillips, D. (2011). Immediate Response: Addressing Anti-Native and Anti-Black Racism in Child Welfare. *International Journal of Child, Youth and Family Studies, 2*(3/4), 385–409.

Razack, S. (2002). When Place Becomes Race. In *Race, Space and the Law: Unmapping a White Settler Society* (pp. 1–20). Toronto: Between the Lines.

Scheurich, J., & Young, M. (2002). Coloring Epistemology: Are Our Research Epistemologies Racially Biased? *Anti-racist Scholarship: An Advocacy* (pp. 51–73). New York: State University of New York Press.

Simmonds, F. N. (1997). My Body, Myself: How Does a Black Woman Do Sociology? In H. S. Mirza (Ed.), *Black British Feminism: A Reader* (pp. 50–63). London: Routledge.

Smith, L. T. (1999). *Decolonizing Methodologies: Research and Inidigenous Peoples.* London: Zed Books.

Taiaiake, A. (2011). Colonial Stains on Our Existence. In M. J. Cannon et al. (Eds.), *Racism, Colonialism and Indigeneity in Canada* (pp. 3–11). Oxford University Press.

Wane, N. (2011). African Inidigenous Feminist Thought: An Anti-colonial Project. In N. Wane, A. Kempf, & M. Simmons (Eds.), *The Politics of Cultural Knowledge* (pp. 7–22). Rotterdam: Sense Publishers.

Wikipedia. *Decolonisation.* http://www.jstor.org.myaccess.library.utoronto.ca/topic/decolonization/ and https://en.wikipedia.org/wiki/Decolonization. Retrieved on August 18, 2017.

Wotherspoon, T. (2009). *The Sociology of Education in Canada.* Don Mills, ON: Oxford University Press.

CHAPTER 5

Resistance Is Our Ancestral Knowledge: Incorporating Roots of Resistance into the Education of Adolescent Afro-Caribbean Girls in the Greater Toronto Area (GTA)

Kimberley Moore and Celine D. Gibbons-Taylor

5.1 Introduction

> Black women are expected to use our anger only in the service of other people's salvation or learning. But that time is over. My anger has meant pain to me but it has also meant survival, and before I give it up I'm going to be sure that there is something at least as powerful to replace it on the road to clarity. (Lorde, 1984, p. 132)

K. Moore (✉)
Columbia University, New York, NY, USA

C. D. Gibbons-Taylor
Queen's University, Kingston, ON, Canada
e-mail: 16cdgt@queensu.ca

© The Author(s) 2019
F. J. Villegas and J. Brady (eds.), *Critical Schooling*,
https://doi.org/10.1007/978-3-030-00716-4_5

If schooling is to be inextricably linked to the formation of identities, we owe it to individuals being schooled to use every possible resource to support this process, particularly as it takes place for girls in secondary schools. Afro-Caribbean culture contains a wealth of narratives of resistance that demonstrate how Afro-Caribbean women resist the social conditions that exacerbate experiences of gendered-racism, oppression based on the intersection of race and gender, within institutions (Andersen & Collins, 2004). As Audre Lorde expresses in the excerpt above, many of these experiences are streaked with pain and anger. These experiences are particularly prevalent in schools and the institutionalized education that Afro-Caribbean girls receive. Like Lorde, we believe there are immeasurable power, resilience, and brilliance within these experiences; power that should only be wielded in the service of individuals whose experiences generated it. In this paper, we explore how to address the gendered-racism Afro-Caribbean girls experience in high schools in the Greater Toronto Area (GTA). We review historical and contemporary literature on methods Afro-Caribbean women have used to resist similar conditions in order to explore the problem. In addition, we draw on our lived experiences and literature on the experiences of Black youth in Canadian schools. We propose that developing and implementing a culturally informed, strengths-based program using our narratives of resistance is the best possible response to the challenges facing Afro-Caribbean girls in schools. We conclude by outlining this program, which provides participants with a foundation of ancestral knowledge and the opportunity to develop skills that will support them in resisting and navigating institutions like schooling in the future.

By acknowledging the ongoing resistance practices of Afro-Caribbean girls within the current educational system that perpetuates anti-Black racism, and by working with them to create spaces of/for resistance, albeit individually or collectively, we will be able to actively contest this violence Afro-Caribbean girls face navigating the school system. Curriculum/programming that centers both historical and contemporary acts of resistance provides a space for young Afro-Caribbean girls to openly and, more importantly, unapologetically contest the structures that confine and control their means to define themselves. As outlined by Katherine McKittrick (2000): "repeated patriarchal defilement and violences against Black women's bodies/minds have summoned Black feminists, authors, academics and poets to comment on and redraw the place of femininity, Black womanhood, race and nation(s) in modernity" (pp. 223–224). Therefore—whether through practicing ancestral methods of healing and spirituality, creating or participating in oral histories, or engaging in the literature of scholars such as M. Nourbese Philip, Dionne Brand, and Audre Lorde—the creative work of Black women is indicative of the transformative, self-affirming power of resistance wherever Black women express themselves in community with eachother. The ways in which these women have conceptualized their identity, contesting the creation of Black womanhood that has a strong foothold in racist, colonial configurations of deficiency and otherness, are valid knowledge that must be integrated to better serve Afro-Caribbean girls within the GTA.

5.2 THE ROOTS FROM WHICH OUR LEGACIES STEM: HISTORICAL MODES OF RESISTANCE

Resistance, whether maroon, material, personal, private, legal, or cultural, illustrates that Black women understood deeply their predicaments and used these particular forms of resistance either in isolation or in some combination to define, as much as possible, the terms of their existence in the Americas. (Elgersman, 1999, p. 101)

Girls whose foremothers are Caribbean women of African ancestry descend from women and girls who survived the largest forced migration in history, the transatlantic slave trade. Institutions, governments, and other social bodies mobilized against Black individuals indiscriminate of age or gender. Our use of the term "Black" to identify this group of individuals is evidence of the omnipresent brutality of this process. Europeans invented "race" for the purpose of eternally subjugating masses of Black people globally, utilizing preexisting systems of slavery within Africa (Lovejoy, 2012). The intersection of geopolitics and economy during this era is of extreme importance in communicating the dismal conditions individuals enslaved in the Caribbean lived through. The ceaseless demand for sugar in Europe, and later the USA, increased the fervor with which enslavers exploited the conditions of the individuals who labored under them. The production of sugarcane and other cash crops like tobacco, coffee, and later cotton on plantations in the Caribbean fueled the brutality inflicted on labor, particularly women (Walters, 1999).

The exploitive structural foundations in the colonies did not expunge the milieu of cultures, ethnicities, languages, tribes, and other groups Africans brought to the Caribbean. There is one reality that becomes particularly clear when examining this cultural milieu; each culture was instrumental in shaping the experiences of Black women who resisted the conditions of their enslavement in Maroon communities. Maroon communities existed in multiple islands during the slave trade; one of the most documented of these communities was in Jamaica (Gottlieb, 2000). Many children in Jamaica often hear tales of marronage; these tales are coupled with powerful, public symbols like the image of Queen Nanny of the Maroons on the 500 Jamaican dollar bill.

One of the most thorough accounts of Queen Nanny's life and similar narratives of Maroon women in Jamaica can be found in Karla Gottlieb's (2000) *The Mother of Us All: A History of Queen Nanny*. Women's roles in Maroon communities were largely influenced by the cultures, villages, ethnic, and language groups from which they or their foremothers came. Though accounts vary in terms of detail, most note that Queen Nanny was born in present-day Ghana and descended from an Akan group, most likely Asante. Through an extensive review of Jamaican literature, Gottlieb (2000) writes that: "around 1728, Queen Nanny emerged as the primary general, leader, and obeah woman of the Windward Maroons, her reign extending until around 1740, shortly after the Maroons signed a peace treaty with the British" (p. 1). According to many accounts, including oral accounts passed down to me from family members[1,2] in Jamaica, her reign coincides with the most effective periods of marronage in Jamaica.

Generally, the role of women is uncontested among scholars. Much of Gottlieb's work focuses on consolidating data collected by historians from different backgrounds. On the overall role of women as agents of resistance in Jamaica, she finds that like Queen Nanny, much of their role was rooted in how they maintained ancestral knowledge, in spite of the Spanish and British efforts to quell it. This was particularly true of women, whose status as freedom fighters was inextricably tied to the African cultures from which they descended, Gottlieb (2000) posits:

> The Maroons of Jamaica preserved many aspects of the language and culture of the Akan and Ashanti peoples of the Gold Coast [current day Ghana]. They also retained many of the matrilineal and matrilocal aspects of these cultures. Kinship was passed down through the mother's side of

the family...Another important role that women played in Maroon communities was through their enormous contribution to agriculture...women were responsible for producing nearly the entire agricultural output of the Maroon communities. (pp. 27–28)

In addition to reigning as queens and revered spiritual leaders, women picked up arms in combat during wars with the British and plantation raids to free other enslaved individuals (Gottlieb, 2000). The stories of Queen Nanny and other women in marronage are one example of many narratives of resistance that characterized Black women's existence in the Caribbean during slavery. Tales of Queen Nanny were coupled with tales of Toussaint Louverture and what my elders referred to as the world's first Black republic, Haiti. Though the role of women in the Haitian Revolution is not thoroughly documented, historical paintings and visual depictions of women in arms alongside men from that time warrant further investigation. Furthermore, plantation records in nearby islands, like Jamaica, consistently show that the number of women enslaved outnumbered the number of men by 1807 (Elgersman, 1999). We can infer that records in Haiti show a similar trend; as such, it is impossible to imagine a successful revolution without women.

In her book titled *Unyielding Spirits Black Women and Slavery in Early Canada and Jamaica*, Maureen G. Elgersman (1999) provides an impeccably thorough account of the myriad ways Black women resisted the conditions of enslavement. As she poignantly points out, the power in these narratives does not exist on a spectrum of success or failure. On the contrary, the power rests in the persistence of the acts themselves. The fact that Black women took actions of resistance says far more about their self-concept of existence than whether or not actions were "successful". The tendency to conceptualize resistance and revolution on this spectrum of "success" leaves Black women at a disadvantage[3] (Elgersman, 1999). Patriarchal literature on slavery is widely accepted and employed as the main means of teaching high school students about slavery, if taught at all. With the exception of figures from the USA like Harriet Tubman and Sojourner Truth, widely accepted depictions of resistance are often characterized as being inherently masculine. These Black patriarchal depictions of revolutions are also prevalent in literature on Decolonization in Africa and the Caribbean, the Civil Rights Era, and the Anti-Apartheid Movement. This literature mobilizes misogynoir—the term created by Black Queer Feminist Dr. Moya Bailey to describe a particular form of anti-Black racist misogyny (Anyangwe, 2015) which disempowers Black women who were enslaved. It implies that the intersection of Blackness and womanhood reduced their existence solely to tragic, passive sexual exploits—existence that could only be salvaged through the efforts of respectable Black male saviors. Considering the emotional, sexual, reproductive, and domestic labor that Black women were forced to fulfill during and after slavery throughout the diaspora, the movements and revolutions, we imagine are ones in which Black women were just as, if not more, invested in resisting by any means as Black men. Additionally, this Black patriarchal savior defined by "success" reflects measures of value rooted in capitalism and imperialism. The notion that an act of Black resistance should be masculine centered, documented, respectable, and quantifiably successful in order to be given space and merit within educational literature robs validity from acts of resistance that do not uphold that capitalist formula.

The problem here does not lay in any one element of the narrative; Black women were sexually exploited and the intersectionality in their social location left them more susceptible to enslavers' exploitation, in all forms, than Black men. The relationships and bonds between Black women and men were indescribably complex. However, more comprehensive literature like Elgersman's demonstrates the commonality, variety, and emotional depths of Black women's resistance, independent of Black male saviors. To romanticize the savior trope, then teach it in schools as "slavery literature" is a heinous crime against Afro-Caribbean girls today whose foremothers resisted so that they might exist. Thinking about resistance as it existed outside of this trope becomes even more important when examining the more negative elements of mass resistance, like marronage. Many scholars, Afro-Caribbean included, argue that some women were kidnapped and forced into marronage during plantation raids (Elgersman, 1999); effectively, exchanging an oppressive system based on race for one based on gender. Marronage refers to escaping enslavement to contribute to the formation of independent communities as a form of resistance (Kars, 2016). Women who were forced into marronage were simultaneously forced to enact resistance in ways that fit this specific narrative. This distinction is particularly vital considering the current realities of many Afro-Caribbean girls, whose Blackness does not shelter them from acts of violence within their own homes and communities.

Elgersman (1999) writes that Afro-Caribbean women resisted in a number of ways of varying emotional, material, and physical consequences. Some used "arson, insolence, and confrontation" which involved murder, assaulting exploiters verbally and physically, insolence or inflicting material property damage. In Jamaica, for example, the use of poison by Black women was quite common (Elgersman, 1999). Indeed, Black women enslaved in Jamaica often had a reputation for being "troublesome and confrontational"; some enslavers communicated enduring "constant insubordination of the plantations' slave women" (Elgersman, 1999). Elgersman (1999) also describes "private and cultural resistance…constructed as resistance of the sexual invasion of women's bodies" stating that:

> Acts of contraception, abortion, and even infanticide have been noted as the essential forms of the private resistance of Black women in Jamaica. In both a temporal and a spatial sense, private resistance illustrated the inability of planters and overseers to control all of the slaves' time and all aspects of slave women's lives…practices of abortion helped Black slave women create and maintain a private sphere of control. (p. 119)

One may choose to conceptualize these acts of resistance as early displays of reproductive rights and clear acts of sexual agency. Imagine if current events or politics programs and classes taught to Afro-Caribbean girls in high schools pulled from these acts,[4] as examples of reproductive rights instead of popular depictions that pull from narratives of the birth control movement among married, upper middle-class white women in the USA during the 1940s. These and other intimate acts of resistance are intergenerational threads within our communities; woven powerfully, beautifully, and abundantly, unyielding in the histories of the Black women we descend from.

The quotation from Elgersman's work featured at the start of this section communicates the fervor with which Black women enslaved in the Caribbean took measures to define the terms of their existence. If they were to exist enslaved, their existence would be one of resistance. There is no greater proof of the magnitude of this resistance than the existence of millions of Afro-Caribbean people today, in the Caribbean and Canada, including Celine and myself. Although we carry the names of the white men who owned our foremothers, we would not exist had they not taken every measure possible to survive for over half a century in societies built to destroy them.

Although the transatlantic slave trade and slavery as it existed during that era no longer exist, Afro-Caribbean women resist the gendered-racist remnants of that era today. As Audre Lorde (1984), the daughter of immigrants from Barbados and Curaçao, once wrote, "…unless one lives and loves in the trenches it is difficult to remember that the war against dehumanization is ceaseless. But Black women and our children know the fabric of our lives is stitched with violence and with hatred, that there is no rest" (p. 119). The ceaseless resistance against dehumanization persists; particularly today, as Afro-Caribbean girls and women resist what bell hooks, with edits from Laverne Cox, refers to as the hetero-imperialist white supremacist capitalist patriarchy (hooks & Cox, 2014).

This particular patriarchy takes form in agendas, institutions, systems, and socialization; this patriarchy has not "broken" systems, nor has it "infiltrated" institutions. On the contrary, these systems and institutions are functioning exactly how they were designed to function. We are not resisting broken systems or corrupt institutions; we are resisting systems and institutions that were built to subjugate us to uphold white supremacy by any means. Hence, we charge forward with our mission to support Afro-Caribbean girls in developing tangible tools[5] to utilize the legacies they come from and are a part of today. In the section that follows, we further our discussion of narratives of resistance by exploring how Afro-Caribbean women today resist modern hetero-imperialist white supremacist capitalist patriarchal systems.

5.3 The Limbs of Our Existence: Contemporary Modes of Resistance

Resistance was often more subtle than revolts, escapes and sabotage. It involved, for example, the clandestine acquisition of reading/writing skills and the imparting of this knowledge to others. (Davis, 1983, p. 22)

Considering these historic resistances that have been quintessential to the survival of Afro-Caribbean women's psychological and material well-being, Davis' sentiments are still very much applicable to understanding contemporary forms of resistance, existing as both communal or singular acts of self-making. As Davis notes, the illicit act of learning during enslavement was a means for the Black enslaved class to articulate their humanity amidst the inherent violence of the plantocracy

(1983). What is most transformative about this act is the sharing of this acquired knowledge with others, who may not have access to it otherwise, as a means to rehumanize themselves. Taking these acts alongside those outlined above reveals how necessary it is to acknowledge both the explicit and more subtle ways of resisting "white supremacist capitalist [hetero]patriarchy" (hooks, 1994, p. 134). These acts, though they may not always challenge hegemony, articulate counterhegemonic possibilities that act as a means to grapple with the historical violences Afro-Caribbean women and girls were forced to endure.[6] Thus, decontextualizing these acts through ignoring the aforementioned histories that mark a trajectory of Afro-Caribbean resilience, much like the mainstream educational system within the GTA that is devoid of Afro-Caribbean history, delegitimizes Afro-Caribbean women and girls' self-making work as it is articulated through the means most available to them.[7] Instead, these instances of self-authorship must be situated within a longer history of resistance that is situated within anti-colonial, anti-racist, feminist teachings and should be understood as a means of survival, regardless if they are subversive or reinforce one's own subjugation. Self-/community-making is riddled with complexity and, therefore, should not be trivialized. Patricia Hill Collins (1986) reminds us that:

> If Black women find themselves in settings where total conformity is expected [or necessary], and where traditional forms of activism such as voting, participating in collective movements, and office holding are impossible, then the individual women who in their consciousness choose to be self-defined and self-evaluating are, in fact, activists. (p. S24)

As such, the impact of contemporary forms of resistance, and more generally Blackness and Black cultural production, is "a site of strategic contestation" (Hall, 1996, p. 473) and often does not necessarily subscribe to the common understanding of resistance whereby individuals collectively organize to challenge hegemony. Instead, we hold these individual actions of Afro-Caribbean women and girls who may not be in a position to collectively organize yet still negotiate these daily contestations to a high esteem as their methods of self-making reveal the malleability of their subjugation. These negotiations are arguably most visible within communities of healing and creative expression whereby Afro-Caribbean women and girls purposefully contend with and challenge the daily anti-Black sexism that permeates society.

Healing methods are among many of the practices that survived the Middle Passage and are a direct result of the resilience of our ancestors. Through this, our foremothers were able to spiritually sustain themselves within spaces built to violate them. This form of resistance, taken alongside other self-making practices (present-day vernacular, food, music, or Caribbean cultural production overall), should be viewed as the fervor with which our ancestors fought—a tenacity with which they endured violent, dehumanizing conditions to ensure their survival and our existence. As such, traditional forms of healing and spiritual methods utilized by Grenadian women are an example of this survival and the translation of historical forms of resistance into contemporary practice. As Sutherland (2011) notes:

> These religions provided the cultural resources that were critical for reconstructing the social bonds ruptured by colonialism and slavery, and for fashioning new identities and belief systems to cope with the devastating conditions of new and cruel social contexts. African styles of worship, rituals, and belief systems survived because they were transformed to creatively adapt to new environments and is indicative of the will of the human spirit to endure and resist. (p. 46)

These communities of healing allow Afro-Grenadian women to reconstruct their humanity amidst the ongoing victimization they experience. The existence of these communities of women is especially important as limited resources for healing exist for these women otherwise (Sutherland, 2011).

Similarly, the current education system within the GTA violates young Black girls who must constantly grapple with the anti-Black racism and sexism that is ingrained within an institution that forcibly delegitimizes their existence. An example of this is the case where a young Black girl in the TDSB was continuously chastised for her natural hair by the school's principal (*CityNews*, 2015, November 10). Natural Black hair was, and continues to be, a site of regulation and control (Browne, 2015). To combat this, what would it mean for us to channel communal healing methods as a means to contend with these historically rooted violences so as to prioritize the self-care for these young Black girls? Embedding spaces of healing that center Black humanity as the care and support networks discussed through the example of Afro-Grenadian women, which extend beyond kinship and friendship ties, can be pivotal to the education of young Afro-Caribbean girls as they foster the resources needed to navigate the inadequacies current education system.

The reverberations of historical resistance are also evident within expressions of sexuality and sexual agency. Premised on its juxtaposition to white womanhood as a means to legitimize white supremacist colonial and capitalist logics, Black womanhood has historically been rendered a site of inherent deviance deficiency[8] (Hill Collins, 2002). Thus, geography, colonialism, capitalism, white supremacy, and heteropatriarchy interlock to produce a homogenized, and violent, construction of Black womanhood. These narratives continue to manifest throughout history and are, arguably, most visible within the media and discourses surrounding Black women's sexuality. Furthermore, these systems have distorted current understandings of the Black woman's body and erased the social and cosmic significance of Black womanhood within a pre-colonial society (Welsh Asante, 1994). With this, the Afro-Caribbean women's body, by virtue of the oversimplification of Black womanhood, is rendered hypersexual, excessive, and accessible, with the violent tropes of the Mammy, Jezebel, and/or Sapphire delineating our exploitation for capitalist gain and sanctioning the structural violence we experience (Ladson-Billings, 2009). This reveals the simultaneity of hypervisibility and invisibility that characterizes Black women's existence and how this dynamic complicates our complex lived realities. Acknowledgment must be given to the ways this dynamic impacts how "the complexity and ambiguity of history, race, racism and place are inscribed" on the bodies of Black women and girls and the spaces we enter (McKittrick, 2000, p. 225). This dynamic also "reflects the reality that the body is imbued with social meanings that are simultaneously written and read onto it" (Lawson, 2011, p. 108). Due to the lack of education on these histories in the classroom, Afro-Caribbean girls are especially vulnerable to the violence enacted on and through their bodies, just as it was on the bodies of their foremothers' through the intersection of race, gender, sexuality, and class.

For these reasons, instances where the body is revalued in spaces such as carnival, dancehall, and fete settings, contest the colonial understandings of the Black body. Whether Afro-Caribbean women serve as cultural producers, participants, or consumers, these spaces can provide avenues for expressing, defining, contesting, and negotiating facets of one's identity and history. These creative processes combat the heteropatriarchal violence that renders Black women objects of desire or consumption. In that sense, these spaces prove to be crucial not only for self-valuation but belonging; they are extremely valuable. As such, we must remain critical of regulatory practices that undercut the spaces Caribbean people create to express themselves. In Canada, these regulating practices include increased public scrutiny through securitization and discourses of violence and terror (Burman, 2010; Jackson, 1992). This type of scrutiny demonstrates the ways in which Canada's multicultural agenda constrains self-authorship and expression through capitalist endeavors. Therefore, considering Caribbean cultural production like Toronto's Caribbean Carnival parade—previously, but still, referred to as Caribana—which is a diasporic Carnival reminiscent of its parent festival in Trinidad, capitalizing this space significantly impacts how the histories that this cultural product emerges from are understood. By marketing, this festival as an experience within a cosmopolitan, multicultural (white-settler nation), removes from the collective conscious the possibilities of this space post-independence in terms of Afro-Caribbean self-making and resistance (Barnes, 2006). This history, if taken in tandem with that of this land to unpack Canada's nation-building project that constructs whiteness as natural and having claims to this land (McKittrick, 2014), demonstrates why the inclusion of resistance-based knowledge within programming for Afro-Caribbean girls is extremely crucial.

Lastly, recognition must be given to the many ways in which Canada was built on anti-Blackness and how the Black community is constructed as outside of, but necessary to this nation (McKittrick, 2014; Walcott, 2001). As McKittrick (2014) states:

> ...the bureaucratic working of Multiculturalism demand a predetermined Eurocentric terrain that the Black diaspora enters or is mapped upon;... Blackness is, instead an addendum. With this comes the reminder that the originary logic of multiculturalism–an extension of western democracy and freedom–was engendered by slavery, colonialism, and indentureship and is therefore a policy that, in fact, contains asymmetrical emancipatory tools. (pp. 243–244)

Thinking about Canada in this way complicates the national mythology that this country is an accepting, hyper-benevolent space where diversity is its strength. Instead, it is evident that the legacies and violence of colonialism manifest to contradict this notion of Canada. For instance, as Canada premises itself on multiculturalism and hyper-benevolence, this nation consistently fails to acknowledge its history of anti-Black racism and exclusion through migration policies that constructed Afro-Caribbean live-in caregivers as undesirable or "bad" migrants when they negotiated their own sense of citizenship (Stasiulis and Bakan, 1997). We remember stories from our mothers and other Afro-Caribbean women, of the hardships and struggles they endured during migration. Resilience and the importance of networks of resistance when their spouse or partner was all they had in this country characterize the ways that these women, our mothers included, fought to live here. Again, these networks of resistance are quintessential to our survival. It is worth mentioning that these stories of resistance are not kept from us—it may very well be that my mother, our mothers, did not conceptualize their experiences as resistance. They may have gravitated more toward articulating these experiences in terms of duty and responsibility to their families. Even the smallest forms of resistance, especially those close to home, should be acknowledged as ancestral, experiential, and historical knowledge that can produce transformative results if included in educational programming for Afro-Caribbean girls.

5.4 A Programmatic Response to the Issue

This is what I think is beautiful. You can spend a lifetime discovering African-style hairdresses, there are so many of them, and so many creative, natural styles yet to be invented. For me, it was important not just because of how good it made me feel but because of the world in which I lived. In a country that is trying to completely negate the image of Black people, that constantly tells us we are nothing, our culture is nothing, I felt and still feel that we have got to constantly make positive statements about ourselves. Our desire to be free has got to manifest itself in everything we are and do. (Shakur, 1987, pp. 174–175)

5.4.1 Shortcomings to Other Responses to the Issue

Individuals and groups have proposed literary and programmatic responses to some of the issues Afro-Caribbean girls face in education. Our review of Canadian literature on the experiences of Black youth in schools revealed that these responses are in silos; none employ the intersectionality needed for students who exist in bodies located at the intersection of multiple oppressions. One of the more common literary responses to the oppressive conditions students of color face in schools is curricular reform. Two issues in this literature are: the influence of teacher's discretion in dispensing the material and the space itself as an environment unconducive to learning. We acknowledge the vital role reform can play and the value of proposed curriculum that acknowledges the racism and other oppressions students face. Simultaneously, we recognize that for many students, schools are sites of violence. In their three-year study on Black Canadian youth and the politics of negotiating identity in schools, George J. Sefa Dei and Irma Marcia James' findings demonstrate how alienating school environments can be for Black students in Canada. They conclude that, "this alienation negatively affects students' learning, possibly entailing significant emotional and social costs, and may also precipitate premature school leaving" (Dei & James, 1998).

Though these findings are over ten years old, they provide valuable context to the current negative experiences of Black youth in Canadian schools. Even with the establishment of educational alternatives, such as Africentric schools, programs like the one we propose later in this chapter provide a valuable supplement.[9] In a more recent article titled "Race and the Production of Identity in the Schooling Experiences of African-Canadian Youth", Dei (1997) writes that "African-Canadian youths are offered very limited (if any) choices in terms of identity production from the schools they attend". Our personal and professional lived experiences align with Dei's claim here. However, we believe that youth, girls in particular, must be provided with options for identity production outside of school. A space outside of the confines and administrative barriers of school buildings; a safer space, where students can further explore their identities and develop transformational relationships. Furthermore, programs like ours prioritize the intersections that larger institutions do not have the capacity to target effectively. Theoretically, removing white supremacy from schools does not simultaneously remove patriarchy, heterocentrism, colonialism, imperialism, or capitalism. Even in circumstances where Black youth are not othered in school because they have access to Africentric schooling that is intersectional, providing programming like ours creates an additional, solid community of resources youth can pull from for comprehensive support and identity formation.[10]

During my [Kimberley] time working with the New York City Department of Education (DOE), one of my key responsibilities was developing curriculum and lesson plans for teachers. The topics of the curriculum I developed were either directly, or closely related to the themes listed as areas in need of elaboration in Aoki et al.'s "Blurred Vision: Rethinking the Ontario Curriculum"; specifically, I covered the areas Aoki, Baker, Hallman-Chong, Morgan, and Walker (2001) term "Media Literacy", "Diversity in Education", and "Critical Thinking". Aoki et al. aim to address the general holes in Ontario's curriculum by advising the incorporation of broad social justice issues into curriculum. My curriculum, which included interactive activities and in-class exercises, was classified as "Advisory" and was dispensed by teachers weekly. Invariably, I observed that Advisories varied dramatically based on the teachers tasked with dispensing the material.

Though my experience in curriculum development was not with a Canadian school,[11] it parallels the gendered-racist biases in schools discussed in literature on Black students and pedagogy. The following excerpt from Paulo Freire's (1970) *Pedagogy of the Oppressed* communicates much of my experience with the DOE: "Education thus becomes an act of depositing, in which the students are depositories and the teacher is the depositor. Instead of communicating, the teacher issues communiques and makes the deposits in which the students patiently receive, memorize and repeat" (p. 72). I developed the content teachers deposited into the information banks of students. As Freire posits, instead of creating a transformative dialogue with students about the material, teachers dispensed information coated in hetero-imperialist white supremacist capitalist patriarchal ideals. An initiative designed to facilitate an enhanced learning environment through which students could develop knowledge became a swift transaction. A transaction whereby teachers deposited information to students, and students confirmed the transaction by "patiently receiving, memorizing, and repeating" (Freire, 1970) said information. In the process of this transaction, students were traumatized and re-traumatized; school, the site where they are obligated to invest the majority of their time during adolescence, became another site of violence and oppression. Our review of literature on pedagogy and education for Black Canadian students demonstrates the importance of exploring the possibility of implementing programs like the one we describe in the sections that follow.

5.4.2 Program Theory

The theoretical journey that led us toward a programmatic response to existing shortcomings was complex. Upon further reflection for the purpose of creating this chapter, we understand one overarching element as being integral to this theoretical journey: our lived experiences over the past seven years. These experiences have been shaped largely by how we have navigated academia and the nonprofit industrial complex. We navigated these regimes in community with other Black cis and trans women and nonbinary mentors, peers, and chosen family who we love and revere. In varying ways, we were all excruciatingly vulnerable to cis-hetero-capitalist patriarchal anti-Blackness as we navigated these regimes. As a result, one of the experiences we currently share within our community is the intragenerational pursuit to imagine and organize spaces for us, by us that aim to liberate and heal our people from the complex anti-Black violence that is inflicted on us. Currently, we experience and witness this violence as folks who have survived academia and the nonprofit industrial complex only to become working professionals within these regimes. Furthermore, as Black women who hold privileges including but certainly not limited to access to formal education, our duty involves an additional two-part process. First, we must remain critical of the ways we may be complicit in the violence and suppression that is inflicted on the communities that reared us. Second, we must be unyieldingly creative in our individual and collective approaches to organizing with our communities to imagine liberated healing, educational spaces outside of the confines of the regimes that oppress us.

We highlight this second point to uphold the work of one of the Black women who we are in spiritual community with, Audre Lorde (1984). These are the regimes we are socialized to believe are the only viable options for our communities to heal and grow, the same regimes that socialize us to internalize hatred and inferiority so that the regime may remain intact, so that the regime may continue to exploit us, our Black trauma and Black brilliance while simultaneously training us to be complicit in exploiting the Black brilliance and Black trauma of folks in our own communities. Numerous Black women whom we share spiritual, virtual, and physical community with have imagined and organized healing spaces outside of the rigidity of academia and nonprofit institutions. Our arrival at a program as an end point is an extension of the imagining and re-imagining of liberated futures that *is* our existence as Black women in community with our people.

The program we imagine will be built on the findings of collaborative, holistic, equitable research completed in community with adolescent girls of Afro-Caribbean descent living in the GTA who are currently enrolled in schools in the GTA. We imagine combining these findings with three main concepts derived from our review of literature on current responses to the issue to formulate the program theory: transformational relationships, strengths-based practice, and Black history and current events education.

Strengths-based practice with youth involves two processes: recognition and respect. Recognizing and respecting that participants come to youth programming with creativity, intellect, resilience, natural propensities for critical thinking, and many other capacities that make them optimal agents of change and advocates for their own personal and community development (Freire, 1970; GEMS, 2009). Strengths-based approaches to programming parallel pedagogical literature that emphasizes the utility of experiential and ancestral knowledge. Facilitators of our program will respect and recognize the experiences that program participants bring in with them, supporting participants in their own social, cognitive, and emotional development as collaborators instead of directors.

Black history and current events education is the final concept behind the program we propose. Recent research on mental health and coping among Black youth in the USA reveals the utility of Black history education. Chapman-Hilliard and Adams-Bass (2015) developed a "Black history knowledge (BHK) model of coping and mental health" (p. 16) that demonstrates how awareness of BHK builds on Black youth's resilience and provides a pathway to navigating challenges they face. Access to historical and current knowledge provides context; it helps youth develop a more comprehensive lens through which they may view the vulnerabilities they face. Chapman-Hillard and Adams-Bass find that using BHK:

> ...the lens through which one assesses and consequently responds to vulnerabilities associated with African enslavement and subjugation is contingent on the psychosocial resources one possesses, including an understanding of particular strengths and resistance evident prior to, during, and after African enslavement. (Chapman-Hillard & Adams-Bass, 2015, p. 16)

These findings hold special implications for Afro-Caribbean girls in the GTA today who are directly and indirectly exposed to anti-Black state-sanctioned violence worldwide, Canada included. More often than not, Canadian government responses to the Black Canadian community's Afro-Caribbean girls belong to are characterized by denial or passivity. In the foreword of *The Hanging of Angelique: The Untold Story of Canadian Slavery and the Burning of Old Montreal*, George Elliott Clarke refers to this silence:

> ...we make liars out of our "coloured" – that is, "visible minority"- citizens, as our federal government did in 2003. In that year. When the United Nations released a report stating that Africans and Aboriginals suffer racism in Canada, the response of the Liberal government of Canada was that the UN was wrong. (Elliott Clarke, 2005, p. XXIII)

Our program addresses the social challenges that Elliott Clarke makes reference to. Furthermore, it provides participants with resources for their personal journeys of identity formation and growth; the same personal journey Assata Shakur speaks to in the excerpt from her autobiography that starts this section. Her words demonstrate the importance of incorporating current events and contemporary contexts into any education on history. By extending Chapman-Hillard and Adams-Bass' model to include current events, we provide program participants with education on the history their government and the schools it funds, denies, and context around the current realities they live.

5.4.3 Preliminary Program Description

Here, we think it wise to restate our purpose with this section of the paper: The purpose is to provide a conceivable, clear, tangible solution to the findings and challenges raised in previous sections and in the literature we review. As such, what follows is not a formal program proposal; it is a possible course of action. We propose a strengths-based program whereby Facilitators develop transformative relationships with girls who identify as female, Black, and as having Afro-Caribbean heritage currently enrolled in high school in the GTA. The program will not exclude Black girls who do not have Afro-Caribbean heritage, however, girls who do will be the focus of outreach efforts and program development due to the culturally informed nature of the program. The program will include lessons, workshops, activities, excursions, storytelling, sister circles, and expression circles—consisting of whichever means of expression participants feel best represents them. Each section and element of the program will build on previous sections and subjects; as such, the foundation of the program is Black history and current events as it pertains to Afro-Caribbean girlhood. In beginning with these topics, we provide participants with context, ancestral knowledge, and the experiential knowledge of facilitators. They may choose to use these tools in their identity formation, and the development of the lenses they use in the lives they live and work they will do.

The program will be held three days a week, for two hours each day, after-school during the school year and continue into the summer months, using the same schedule. Although space will vary based on a number of factors, the program is designed to be implemented in a variety of accessible public spaces including but not limited to libraries, community centers, community hubs, parks, and recreational spaces. The program can also be held in schools, particularly during the school year, with the cooperation of school boards. This point is one we imagine debating seriously as we recognize that many participants within the demographic experience school buildings as sites of violence. The program will operate using a collaborative model where the purpose of positions and levels is for organization and stakeholder accountability, not to recreate authoritative hierarchies commonly used in the nonprofit industrial complex.

5.4.4 Program Participation Incentives

Though previous sections of this paper allude to positive outcomes and benefits for program participants, we recognize that providing participation incentives holds value on more than one level. The use and form of incentives will vary largely based on the collaborative research findings, funding and program capacities. Ideally, we hope to implement a stipend system whereby coordinators set up scholarship savings accounts for each participant; upon full participation in daily programming, coordinators will deposit a stipend into each account. After program completion and high school graduation, students will be permitted to access these accounts to further their education. We believe that scholarship and study is an extremely individual journey; pathways may include trade school, internships, fellowships, certification courses, college, bridging programs, or university. As such, students will be permitted to use their savings to pursue any pathway to postsecondary academic or professional development. In addition to building on personal saving and financial management skills, this system demonstrates a respect for participant agency, choice, and self-determination.

With the cooperation of schools, we will provide participants with volunteer hours for participating in the fourth quarter of the program. Here, participants will be provided with the opportunity to earn the 40 volunteer hours they require to graduate by doing purposeful work. Earning hours in this way clearly demonstrates each participant's personal and community development in a way that does not silo the two. Participants will earn well over the 40-hour requirement, which will contribute to their graduation and eligibility for merit-based government scholarships for university based on volunteerism.

5.4.5 Program Evaluation

We envision using an empowerment evaluation whereby all stakeholders in the program work collaboratively as full participants in the process. In accordance with Rossi et al.'s definition of empowerment evaluations, program participants' role in the program evaluation will involve the following process:

> Consultation and facilitation directed toward developing the capabilities of the participating stakeholders to conduct evaluations on their own, to use the results effectively for advocacy and change, and to experience some sense of control over a program that affects their lives. The evaluation process, therefore, is directed not only at producing informative and useful findings but also at enhancing the self-development and political influence of the participants. (Rossie, Lipsey, & Freeman, 2004, p. 51)

In opting for an empowerment evaluation directed by the Executive Director, we hope to accomplish two things. We do not want the evaluator to be totally removed from the program or the theories behind it; the Executive Director's proximity is a healthy medium. Secondly, we want to optimize sustainability and agency; ensuring the evaluation provides program participants with evaluation and capacity building skills is one more means of ensuring the time they invest in participating is productive and self-serving.

5.4.6 Additional Considerations

Thorough, equitable research should be designed and conducted prior to finalizing the program design and implementation strategy. This assessment would likely utilize mixed methods including individualized interviews, focus groups, and surveys to gauge the demand, need, utility, and special considerations. A study of this kind will help measure the counterfactual—what would happen if we did not implement the program and how the development of participants would differ without it (Stiglitz, 1998). We can hypothesize and extrapolate theories from literature and experiential knowledge, but an empirical counterfactual will assist us in communicating why our program is a good investment for stakeholders. Although it is difficult to gauge at this time, funding sources will ideally include a variety ranging from government grants to community fundraising, in order to optimize sustainability.

5.5 Conclusion

However contentious these dialogic initiatives may be, they are framed by a feminist politics that insists on the inclusive, critical, and liberatory value of education and classroom pedagogical practices. (Lawson, 2011, p. 109)

Our review of literature on historical and contemporary literature on resilience among Afro-Caribbean women demonstrates the wealth of knowledge that Afro-Caribbean girls should be given access to as they engage in processes of identity formation. We conclude that schooling and education have an incomparable influence on this process. Moreover, we find that the equity work used to "better serve" Afro-Caribbean girls often removes their agency by employing the very politics that continue to disempower and subordinate them. As such, we propose culturally informed, strengths-based programming be implemented in order to secure Afro-Caribbean girls' access to ancestral knowledge; the program we propose provides an opportunity to develop transformative relationships and skills that will serve as resources for girls in the long term. Literature on the schooling experiences of Black youth in Canada was used throughout the paper to contextualize our lived experiences as Afro-Caribbean women who have attended and worked in primary and secondary schools in the GTA and abroad. By pulling from these experiences, we do not seek to empower or inspire. Nor do we seek to contribute to current fervor to provide a pseudo-respectable example of what is possible for Afro-Caribbean girls currently faced with the task of learning in spite of the institutions that school them. In urging for the implementation of this program, we aim to add another weapon to the arsenal these girls use to combat the gendered-racism they experience in primary and secondary schooling. Investing in equity seeking spaces that do not fulfill this mandate adds another layer to the cultural imperialism these girls already navigate in school. By utilizing narratives of resistance through pedagogy in the way we propose, these girls will be agentic architects in the systems that so acutely impact their trajectories.

Notes

1. Oral histories and storytelling within families are integral elements of dismantling and rebuilding within Afro-Caribbean communities; these histories also served as a means of resistance during enslavement and colonization.
2. The introduction of Chapter 6 highlights the critical role female-identifying family members and matriarchs play in facilitating these discussions with younger girls in families and communities.
3. Furthermore, using these tropes of success and productivity to categorize more subtle, intimate forms of resistance is an act of capitalism and imperialism.
4. Janelle Brady and Zuhra Abawi analyze similar themes around the gendered norms girls in school are subjected to in, Chapter 6.
5. Janelle Brady discusses the utility of representation in learning processes with an Afro-Caribbean lens; situating her own identity as a descendant of the transatlantic slave trade in Chapter 6, she demonstrates how representation can be used as a tool for transgressing the oppressive, colonial ideals young learners are subjected to in school.
6. Additionally, the act of acknowledging the power within these subtleties is an additional form of resisting the capitalist imperialist tendency to delegitimize acts that do not categorically contribute to profit or nation-building.
7. Acknowledgment also honors current day forms of self-making, community-making, unpaid emotional labor, and unseen precarious labor Afro-Caribbean women continue perform within their own communities and for other communities; within this section, this acknowledgment is an intentional act of intergenerational solidarity.
8. This assumed inherent deviance intersects with culture within Afro-Caribbean communities in the Caribbean and the diaspora; deviance associated with womanhood and Blackness intersects with the

hypersexualization of Afro-Caribbean women's' self-expression and self-actualization during Carnival, Crop Over, Caribana, and Passa Passa.
9. Proposing a programmatic supplement to Africentric schools in the GTA provides a space for students to expand on the conversations they have with instructors, conversations that operate with necessary degrees of partiality that allow for "productive tension". A programmatic response provides young people with a space to build on reflections they have in class, as a result of the unique relationship between educators and students. Paloma Villegas explores this in Chapter 11, where she reflects on her own experiences as an educator and the importance of providing space for students to participate in "re-negotiation" in courses where instructors and students experience parallels in positionality and identity with the actual course content.
10. The reflections in Chapter 11 emphasize the complexity of positionality and identity where course content mirrors the identity-related experiences of the instructor. The discussion highlights the role of intentional partiality for course instructors teaching under these circumstances and the importance of being mindful of making assumptions around shared experience, and "claiming full commonality" with students in these courses.
11. Chapter 7 provides more in depth exploration of these and other themes involving discrimination and equity in curriculum in a Canadian context, within Toronto schools; Calero and Chica's parallel the conversation in this section, on the inequities students are subjected to through various points of interaction with schooling in Toronto.

REFERENCES

Anderson, M. L., & Collins, P. H. (2004). *Race, Class, and Gender: An Anthology* (5th ed.). Belmont, CA: Wadsworth/Thompson.

Anyangwe, E. (2015, October 5). Misogynoir: Where Racism and Sexism Meet. https://www.theguardian.com/lifeandstyle/2015/oct/05/what-is-misogynoir. Accessed 22 October 2015.

Aoki-Barrlett, J., Baker, B., Hallman-Chong, S., Morgan, V., & Walker, P. (2001). *Blurred Vision Rethinking the Ontario Curriculum*. Toronto, ON: Elementary Teacher's Federation of Ontario.

Barnes, N. (2006). *Cultural Conundrums: Gender, Race, Nation, & the Making of Caribbean Cultural Politics*. Ann Arbor: The University of Michigan Press.

Browne, S. (2015). *Dark Matters: On the Surveillance of Blackness*. Durham, NC: Duke University Press.

Burman, J. (2010). *Transnational Yearnings*. Vancouver: UBC Press.

Chapman-Hillard, C., & Adams-Bass, V. (2015). A Conceptual Framework for Utilizing Black History Knowledge as a Path to Psychological Liberation for Black Youth. *Journal of Black Psychology, 42*, 1–29.

CityNews. (2015, November 10). Video: TDSB Principal Under Fire After Chastising Black Need About Her Natural Hair. *CityNews.* Retrieved from http://www.citynews.ca/video/2015/11/10/video-tdsb-principal-under-fire-after-chastising-Black-teen-about-her-natural-hair/.

Davis, A. (1983). *Women, Race & Class.* New York: Vintage Books.

Dei, G. J. S. (1997). Race and the Politics of Identity in the Schooling Experiences of African-Canadian Youth. *Discourse: Studies in the Cultural Politics of Education, 18*(2), 241–257.

Dei, G. J. S., & James, I. M. (1998). 'Becoming Black': African-Canadian Youth and the Politics of Negotiating Racial and Racialized Identities. *Race, Ethnicity and Education, 1*(1), 91–107.

Elgersman, M. G. (1999). *Unyielding Spirits Black Women and Slavery in Early Canada and Jamaica.* New York, NY: Garland Publishing.

Elliott Clarke, G. (2005). Forward. In A. Cooper (Ed.), *The Hanging of Angelique the Untold Story of Canadian Slavery and the Burning of Old Montreal (I–IVIII).* Toronto, ON: HarperCollins.

Freire, P. (1970). *Pedagogy of the Oppressed.* New York, NY: Continuum International Publishing Group.

GEMS. (2009). Victim, Survivor, Leader (VSL) Curriculum. Girls Educational and Mentoring Services (GEMS).

Gottlieb, K. (2000). *The Mother of Us All: The History of Queen Nanny Leader of the Windward Jamaican Maroons.* Trenton: Africa World Press.

Hall, S. (1996). New Ethnicities. In D. Morley & K. Chen (Eds.), *Stuart Hall: Critical Dialogues and Cultural Studies* (pp. 442–451). London: Routledge.

Hill Collins, P. (1986). Learning from the Outside Within: The Sociological Significance of Black Feminist Thought. *Social Problems, 33*(6), S14–S32.

Hill Collins, P. (2002). The Sexual Politics of Black Womanhood. In C. L. Williams & A. Stein (Eds.), *Sexuality and Gender* (pp. 193–206). Oxford: Blackwell.

hooks, b. (1994). Gangsta Culture–Sexism and Misogyny: Who Will Take the Rap? In *Outlaw Culture: Resisting Representations* (pp. 134–144). New York: Routledge.

hooks, b., & Cox, L. (2014, October 13). *bell hooks and Laverne Cox at a Public Dialogue at the New School.* Retrieved from https://www.youtube.com/watch?v=9oMmZIJijgY.

Jackson, P. (1992). The Politics of the Streets: A Geography of Caribana. *Political Geography, 11*(2), 130–151.

Kars, M. (2016). *Maroons and Marronage. Oxford Bibliographies in Atlantic History.* New York: Oxford University Press.

Ladson-Billings, G. (2009). "Who You Callin' Nappy Headed?" A Critical Race Theory Look at the Construction of Black Women. *Race, Ethnicity and Education, 12*(1), 87–99.

Lawson, E. (2011). Feminist Pedagogies: The Textuality of the Racialized Body in the Feminist Classroom. *Atlantis, 35*(2), 107–117.

Lorde, A. (1984). *Sister Outsider Essays & Speeches by Audre Lorde*. New York, NY: Random House.

Lovejoy, P. E. (2012). *Transformations of Slavery: A History of Slavery in Africa*. London: Cambridge University Press.

McKittrick, K. (2000). 'Who Do You Talk to, When a Body's in Trouble?': M. Nourbese Philip's (Un)Silencing of Black Bodies in the Diaspora. *Social and Cultural Geography, 1*(2), 223–236. https://doi.org/10.1080/14649360020010220.

McKittrick, K. (2014). Wait Canada Anticipate Black. *The CLR James Journal, 20*(1), 243–249.

Rossie, P. H., Lipsey, M. W., & Freeman, H. E. (2004). *Evaluation a Systematic Approach* (7th ed.). Thousand Oaks, CA: Sage.

Shakur, A. (1987). *Assata an Autobiography*. Chicaco, IL: Zed Books Ltd.

Stasiulis, D., & Bakan, A. (1997). Negotiating Citizenship: The Case of Foreign Domestic Workers in Canada. *Feminist Review, 57*, 112–139.

Stiglitz, J. (1998). 14 Evaluation as an Incentive Investment. In R. Picciotto & E. Wiesner (Eds.), *Evaluation & Development the Institutional Dimension* (pp. 287–290). New Brunswick, NJ: The World Bank.

Sutherland, P. (2011). Traditional Healing and Spirituality Among Grenadian Women: A Source of Resistance and Empowerment. *Canadian Woman Studies, 29*(1/2), 43–49.

Walcott, R. (2001). Caribbean Pop Culture in Canada; Or, the Impossibility of Belonging to the Nation. *Small Axe, 9*, 123–139.

Waters, M. C. (1999). *Black Identities West Indian Immigrant Dreams and American Realities*. New York, NY: The Russell Sage Foundation.

Welsh Asante, K. (1994). Images of Women in African Dance: Sexuality and Sensuality as Dual Unity. *Sage, 8*(2), 16–19.

CHAPTER 6

Disrupting Princesses: A Pedagogical Moment in Dismantling Colonial Norms and Representations of Beauty Through an Anti-colonial Framework

Janelle Brady and Zuhra Abawi

6.1 Introduction

Through representation, Black and Brown women and girls are reminded that they are not part of a larger, dominant narrative. Such reminders of difference that women and girls encounter, subtle as they may seem, permeate into everyday representations of women vis-à-vis the parameters of whiteness, within a hetero-patriarchal structure. As a result, women of colour walk along the margins of the larger dominant narrative. We ask: how does this impact even younger learners and recipients of such colonial messages? To explore this, we carry out a critical, pedagogical project that dismantles the idea of taken-for-granted whiteness within patriarchal contexts.

J. Brady (✉) · Z. Abawi
University of Toronto, Toronto, ON, Canada
e-mail: Janelle.baptiste.brady@mail.utoronto.ca

Z. Abawi
e-mail: zuhra.abawi@mail.utoronto.ca

© The Author(s) 2019
F. J. Villegas and J. Brady (eds.), *Critical Schooling*,
https://doi.org/10.1007/978-3-030-00716-4_6

Our roles as mothers/older sisters and aunts prompted us to complete an artistic project with our nieces, sisters and daughters. At the onset, the idea of the project was to use decolonial pedagogical to disrupt taken-for-granted representations of princesses embedded in the media. By this, we mean that our younger family members are often exposed to images idealizing whiteness and a very particular femininity under a male gaze, so we deployed the project to unpack these representations and provide our nieces, sisters and daughters with exposure to new images not easily accessed through the mainstream media outlets.

Our project challenges Eurocentric representations and norms of beauty as we deploy an anti-colonial theoretical framework. First, the project was carried out by artistic means. Beyond the artistic undertaking, we deploy a duo-ethnographic study between ourselves. Through this method, we engage in a dialogue about our learning and unlearning from the art projects. The final art projects were produced with our daughters, nieces and sisters (who will be referred to as *young learners*) who were all between the ages of 4 and 6 during the time of the project, in late 2015. The project represents a pedagogical moment of disruption for the young learners as well as for ourselves. The final products are collages of "princesses of the world" with many histories and identities previously unavailable. The final collages (referred to as *art project/s*) centres histories of Blackness, Indigeneity and conceptions of Brownness. Centring multiple histories moves away from whiteness[1] as an ideal and can be used in curriculum by educators to move beyond multicultural othering discourses through the centring learners' social locations in their own knowledge and education. We chose to centre young learners' history and identity, when often in schooling, such histories can instead be forgotten, ignored or compartmentalized and marginalized by dominant narratives, through the application of "difference" (Ladson-Billings, 1996) in a larger colonial message. As highlighted by scholars such as Ladson-Billings (1996), young learners come to know that they are "different" when they enter the schooling system. To subvert this, we worked within and through a liberatory research praxis approach (King, 2015). This approach centres the histories and identities of Black and Indigenous people and is passed down from generation to generation, especially through art. This undertaking is fundamentally anti-colonial and questions the fragmenting nature of colonialism. Fitting within our anti-colonial framework, the art project provides an entry point for the young learners to use their social locations and identities in knowledge production.

We contemplate: how have colonial representations of anti-Blackness and anti-Indigeneity affected younger girls through colonization of the mind in their own identity formation? How can we as an aunt, mother and older sister facilitate a pedagogical moment to disrupt and decolonize such young people without causing them to rebel from these decolonizing efforts? In order to answer these questions, this chapter begins with our social locations as in duo-ethnography it is important to which engage and interrogate our social locations in relation to one another. In this case, we explore the pedagogical impact of the art project on the young learners and ourselves. This is important, as in decolonial work, we are not concerned with appearing objective and all-knowing, but instead are aware of the ways that our social locations, experiences and lived realities impact our knowledge production, sharing and learning.

By deploying a duo-ethnographic approach, together we explore our "situated knowledges" (Collins, 1990; Dei & Kempf, 2006; hooks, 1991), which brings about an understanding of our respective social locations, subjectivities, positionalities and histories. As such, we have been able to interrogate our privileges in being placed in higher education settings. We also understand our diasporic histories, which led to both of us from different corners of the globe to be emplaced on the Indigenous Land of Turtle Island appropriated by the mythology of the Canadian nation state (Coulthard, 2014). Coming together, we both challenged the divide-and-conquer-politics of reading our bodies as "settler-colonials" as we operate from an understanding of colonialism beyond the North American boundaries. Thus, we see that we have come from different colonial diasporic collisions collectively come to be on Turtle Island from the brutalities of European enslavement, dominance, imperialism and violence. While at the same time understanding that we are not complicit, but instead implicated by ongoing forms of colonialism (Dei, 2017). There is an understanding of our role in being part of a colonial state, and with that our responsibility to Indigenous communities of Turtle Island so sovereignty and self-determination. What does this look like? When it comes to pedagogical projects with our young learners that means we have important conversations about the history of Turtle Island and ongoing forms of colonialism and provide examples that can resonate with them, given their age. Moreover, we aligned theory to praxis in not only talking about awareness, but also having them come to their own understanding of how they too can take action and stand up with Indigenous communities on Turtle Island.

6.2 LOCATING OURSELVES

Location of the self will appear throughout the chapter, and not only in this section because we take an approach, like many Black feminist and anti-colonial theorists (Collins, 1990; Crenshaw, 1991; hooks, 2015; King, 2015; Ladson-Billings, 1996) which actively engages our subject-locations by shedding light on the intersections of race, class and gender in our analysis of our engagement in the art projects with the young learners and how this relates to a larger decolonial milieu.

6.2.1 Janelle

As a first-generation child born on Turtle Island to parents and ancestors who were brought to the Caribbean through the trans-Atlantic slave trade, I cannot forget the impact of loss. Loss in this context refers to the loss of histories, locality and "roots" in my African ancestry. This is quite unsettling as I am confronted with images, symbols and messages, which devalue my African history and cultural knowledge, prioritizing whiteness and Othering Blackness. Dei (2009) states that we must theorize Africa beyond its boundaries. What this means, is for people like myself who have experienced loss and displacement, an African approach takes a holistic reading and understanding of Africa beyond the continent and thus includes diasporic identities. Representation is important, as according to Hall (1997) it is an integral part of the process by which meaning is produced and exchanged between members. These constant cues and reminders not only impact me as an adult, but also, of course impact young learners (Moore & Gibbons-Taylor, Chapter 5). As I embark on my own decolonizing journey, I deal with the wounds of colonization of the mind internally and see its affects most aptly when I am around my nieces and younger siblings. They are all born in Turtle Island and "mixed" race (Kanienkehaka, Trinidadian, Canadian [British/Scottish/Irish], Jamaican, Uruguayan). I felt it very important to do an art project with the young learners to transgress some of the colonial ideals of beauty, knowledge and history from an early age.

Upon interrogation, my own journey to "go natural" with my hair a few years ago was originally rooted in a desire to "start over" and have the perfect Black girl, but "not too Black girl curl" or what is referred to as the "mixed girl curl". I am now decolonizing my own internal/personal ideals of what "good" natural hair is. Looking back, I recall my sister and nieces' reactions to my cutting my hair. They were upset with me, unsettled, and demonstrated this through their reactions of repugnance and even hurt. Not only were these reactions of my younger family members, but also of elders around me, young Black girls in after-school programs I had worked out of and countless others. Their reactions showed the multitude of ways that gender expectations are enacted upon. The idea of me having short, natural hair was unsettling to many people as it challenged the tropes of gender expectations as well as race expectations. Their unsettling thoughts led me to see the reality of colonization and one of its deepest effects, colonization of the mind. As Wane noted:

> The encounter between the colonizer and the colonized disrupted ways of knowing, learning and teaching for most Indigenous peoples of the world. It also requires a loss of lands, erosion of cultures and ideas, and most importantly, the colonization of minds. (Wane, 2008)

Such colonization of the mind was something I thought I should begin to disrupt through small pedagogical acts within the family and beyond.

6.2.2 Zuhra

I address my positionality in a white, settler state as a product of a colonizer/colonized fusion, the daughter of a white British (English/Scottish) mother and an Indigenous Pashtun father from the Yousafzai tribe. My family comes from Bajaur, which was a part of British India until 1947, and now, part of modern-day Pakistan. The British were intent on dividing the Pashtun tribes straddling the Afghan-British Indian border, effectively separating brothers and sisters. In the early 1900s, my great-grandfather left Bajaur after the British destroyed much of it and migrated north to Afghanistan to be free of British rule. Although my father was born in Kabul, Afghanistan in 1946 one year before the partition of India, I have always grown up hearing stories of the mountains and valleys of Bajaur nestled in the fabled Himalayan chain. Throughout my childhood, it was a peaceful place I would daydream about in class. In the news, however, it has been portrayed as a place of violence, radicalism and the infamous shooting of my fellow tribeswoman and cousin Malala Yousafzai.

I look at my daughters who are also mixed with Persian heritage from their father, their dark, almost Black hair and eyes and olive skin does not match the dolls or mainstream female cartoon characters, and Disney Princesses on television. At such an early age, they already remark on blonde hair, blue-eyed features as "beautiful" while I search for more "culturally" appropriate dolls, movies and media. Colonization, self-hatred and internalized oppression are deeply problematic processes, which arise from an early age. Being mixed, my sister and I have different axes of power and oppression, my skin is whiter than hers, my hair is fairer, however, she was provided with an English name. The same phenomenon is true regarding my young daughters. My daughters are a mix of Pashtun, Iranian and Irish/British. My oldest daughter has darker skin and my youngest is fairer, my older daughter has often remarked that she dislikes her skin colour. She tells me: "I don't like my skin colour…I want white skin like Sophia" (in reference to the Disney show "Sophia the First"). These remarks and obsession she has with describing other people's skin colour in relation to whiteness both trouble and disturb me. She has described her skin colour as being "dirty" and refers to beauty in terms of those who have blonde hair and blue eyes. I try everyday to decolonize this internalized oppression that has already enveloped her, it is an ongoing and pervasive struggle, one that we must engage in continuously.

6.3 Theoretical Framework

We entered this project by looking at disruptive, critical pedagogical practices with young learners through art to decolonize the mind. Furthermore, our focus was not only turned towards the young as we also interrogate ourselves and do so by way of self-location and dialogue. Our approach this topic came from an anti-colonial framework as it helps us understand the deep-rooted impacts of colonialism and provides forms of resistance leading to decolonization, in this case the resistance is through art projects. Importantly, the anti-colonial framework provides new imaginaries and horizons grounded in hope. Moving away from colonial forms of education, we work to deploy an anti-colonial form of education, which addresses power/privilege dichotomies, and the operatives of such pertaining to representation of women and beauty. Dei and Kempf (2006) suggests that the academic project of anti-colonial thinking and practice:

> …is to challenge and resist Eurocentric theorizing of the colonial encounter. Such Eurocentric theorizing is best captured in representations of minoritized/colonized bodies and their knowledges, and through the power of colonial imageries. The anti-colonial critique also deals with

interrogations of colonial representations and imaginaries examining processes and representations of legitimacy and degeneracy through the mutually constitutive relations of power. (p. 4)

Anti-colonial thinking deconstructs hetero-normative, grand narratives about the histories of the colonial encounter and interrogates the forms of representations of minoritized/colonized and racialized bodies. Indigenous people and people of colour are often portrayed as deficient and are measured against a beauty standard which centres whiteness that is inherently anti-Black and anti-Indigenous. Such ideals of beauty are represented, and people of all ages are exposed to them. For example, the well-known *Clark & Clark Doll Study*, an experiment highlighting representations and perceptions of race, young Black children viewed the white doll as good and beautiful and the Black doll as bad and ugly (Clark & Clark, 1947). The study demonstrates that perceptions of beauty, goodness and pureness are being associated with whiteness and how this takes shape across all age groups and affects young learners just as much as it does adults and elders. This also shows how early on internalized oppression and colonization of the mind can manifest in children of colour. And so, it is important that we as educators and family members disrupt messages that extend beyond superficial beauty and reinforce systems and practices of historical erasure, othering and subjugation. Similar acts to disrupt the colonial messages presented to girls of colour have been carried out through the Songhoy Princess Club, established by Dr. Joyce E. King and started from the Songhoy Club, which provides Black girls with a sense of their African history and ancestry (Swartz & King, 2014). Pedagogical projects which uncover the histories and identities, which are often limited and misrepresented in colonial representations, create space for young learners to engage critically and see themselves from a more empowering perspective. As Fanon (1961) highlights, "the settler makes history and is conscious of making it" (pp. 39–40). Thus, it is critical to undertake projects that reclaim Indigenous and African history as the colonial system only operates as it was intended to.

It is fundamental to move beyond the axiology of beauty and quantification of representation of whiteness. Beyond the axiology, a knowledge system is produced and reproduced. Such a knowledge system centres some knowledge, some histories and some identities, while devaluing, de-historizing, romanticizing and delegitimizing others. Moving beyond the axiology, to the epistemology of colonial systems of oppression reminds us that knowledge and histories have been centred upon white-Eurocentric, patriarchal narratives and have not considered the fluidity and multiplicity of knowing and in the process, have devalued Indigenous and African knowledge, especially from and by women. To challenge these systems of oppression, scholars like Dillard (2006) call for an *Endarkened Feminist Epistemology*. By this, Dillard moves beyond feminist theorizing beyond national boundaries and reclaims Indigenous ways of knowing in a reclaiming of spirituality, community, research and praxis, which continues to face fragmentation from Euro-colonial projects of oppression. Another example is presented by Wane and Chandler (2002) who describe the cultural knowledge held by Embu women between the 70–100 years old on the environment, biodiversity and land degradation. This outlines how Indigenous women's cultural knowledge is contextual, interdependent, vital and scientifically rooted in lived experiences (Wane & Chandler, 2002). Women's knowledge is degraded in a larger web of colonial hetero-patriarchy. Applying an intersectional approach reminds us that women of colour are further marginalized in such a system as they are doubly oppressed both based on their race and their gender (Collins & Bilge, 2016; Davis, 1983; hooks, 2015). Thus, it is important to engage in pedagogical projects to disrupt the "normative" white and hetero-patriarchal order, which doubly displaces oppressed girls of colour. Black feminists who have applied an intersectional approach (Collins & Bilge, 2016; Crenshaw, 1991) look particularly at the intersections of the raced and gendered realities of Black women both historically and contemporarily. Kolawole (1997) speaks of like-minded African womanist/feminist scholars like Ogundipe-Leslia in asserting that:

> African women have always spoken out and decries simplistic false images of African women, especially the so-called muted rural women portrayed as having no mind of their own. She maintains that the problem is the refusal of scholars to search for African women's voices. (p. 9)

However, pedagogical conversations and projects about Indigeneity and decolonizing intentionally centre the knowledge and portrayals of Indigenous and racialized bodies. Thus, this art project draws on an anti-colonial theoretical approach in identifying forms of colonialism and its impacts. As we have stated, our young learners, at such an early age are immune to colonialism and it in turn affects, whom they see as valid, beautiful and smart and importantly how they see themselves. In this project, we reclaim knowledge production, reproduction and the politics of representation through anti-colonial and decolonial disruptive acts with our young daughters, sisters and nieces by intentionally centring and reclaiming their histories and social locations through art. We say disruptive because decolonization is about unlearning, and is not an arrival, but a journey (Wane, 2008). We recall countless times family members would say, "well, you can't change what kids are exposed to anyway, so you may as well just let them watch Disney movies and just enjoy it" or "they will learn this in school anyways". We contest these statements which are rooted in the status quo and do not enact the children's agency and our responsibility to challenge and resist the tropes of colonialism. Instead, by reimagining new futurities, we say no to passively "just letting things be" and instead, disrupt the usual order by having young learners exercise their own agency and learn more about their history, identity and Indigenous and African knowledge.

6.4 Method

In this section, we discuss the art project so to provide further contextual background and then we will address duo-ethnography and the dialogue between us (Janelle and Zuhra) in carrying out this project.

6.4.1 *The Art Project*

Originally, we decided to locate several photos on the Internet via Google search of princesses beyond the mainstream, white-Eurocentric characters that are prominent in dominant media. We planned to print these preselected images and engage in an art project that included critical conversations about the various histories and identities of each princess. However, in the week leading up to the project, prior to printing, we were confronted by offensive images when trying to locate women from various cultural backgrounds (on Google images). Through our Google search, we witnessed grand narratives reinforcing whose histories are told and easily accessible—the colonizer's histories—and whose histories were essentialized, devalued, left untold, missing and erased—the histories of the colonized. We originally framed this project around princesses, since this could be an entry point to engage younger family members with a topic of interest to them. They are bombarded by images of Disney princesses, Barbie and other characters that do not represent them and leave feelings of angst to look and become these characters. We used princesses only as an entry point given their ages and interests at the time of the art project. Our idea about this project emerged because of our unlearning of the dominant and hegemonic Eurocentric norms of beauty. As we confronted our own ideas and experiences of beauty, we thought this would be an effective way to disrupt and decolonize our daughters', younger sisters and niece's understanding of themselves and their own histories, while learning and unlearning with them in the process. Despite the difficulties we encountered, we continued to search via Google for women and girls that were more reflective of their histories.

Upon reflection, we understood that it was a challenge for of us to easily locate images of Indigenous, Black and Brown women who were not overly sexualized, exoticized and dehumanized through the white colonial gaze. Eventually, we extended the images used for the project to not only include princesses and instead reframed the meaning of princess and located various photos of women and girls across the globe. We started primarily by searching within the localities of our children's ancestral backgrounds, and then we branched off into searching for Indigenous women from Turtle Island and other women from communities who face genocide and displacement. We centred the voices and stories of women and girls that are often left untold, unrepresented and misrepresented in the types of exposure the girls currently get through television, film and in the classroom. We independently created two complete collages of images with the young learners; then, we discussed the project with them, while pasting the images onto poster boards. Though oral storytelling, we explained—to the best of our own knowledge—what each image meant and whom they represented.

We completed each final art collage separately with the young learners separately to allow for maximum comfort in a usual setting that they are used to. The meaning of posting the photos to the board was the idea of coming together and collaboratively engaging in a form of expression where they are using their hands and their minds to explore their creativity. Also, while pasting photos onto the poster, it provided an opportunity to have conversation. Often, their reactions would be "that's my background". Just hearing that as a reaction was refreshing because that is usually not the reaction they have when watching television and movies. They had an opportunity to see themselves and were very vocal about who they were. As well, they would say: "I'm that girl". This was an important reaction because it showed that a simple art project could disrupt and challenge the mainstream and status quo. Instead of them longing to have straighter hair and more white features, they were engaged and interested in the histories and identities of Black, Brown and Indigenous women and that resonated with them. This is important because it demonstrates the process of decolonization in that, it is a process and not an arrival, and it can happen at any age or stage in life. Importantly, decolonial methodologies are also not an arrival, but a process, and thus, we did not have guided instructions or questions, but instead employed the feedback we gained from the young learners so to apply it to the duo-ethnographic study. As Smith (1999) highlights:

> Decolonization is a process, which engages with imperialism and colonialism at multiple levels. For researchers, one of those levels is concerned with having a more critical understanding of the underlying assumptions, motivations and values which inform research practices. (p. 20)

By taking a decolonial research approach, we question "typical" Western research practices and identify ways of decolonizing our approach to remain grounded in an anti-colonial framework. As well, we were very critical about our role as facilitators in the art project and followed a Freirean model, where learners can see themselves through their histories and identities and come to knowledge through guidance and facilitation (Freire, 1970). Thus, we acted as facilitators and not all-knowing, unquestionable subjects and this allowed for the young learners to share their reactions openly and freely and come to their own knowledge and understanding through our aid.

6.4.2   *Duo-Ethnography*

Utilizing a duo-ethnographic methodology was helpful in this project as we met before creating the collages to discuss and analyze our social locations and the role they would play in the project. Upon completion of the collages, we met again and interrogated how our life histories led us to locating images through the means of representation. We looked at both collages and could understand the convergences and divergences in our own understandings of our histories.

The dialogic method used in this project is a duo-ethnography (MacDonald & Markides, 2016; Sawyer & Norris, 2013). The purpose of the duo-ethnography is to examine and disrupt the Eurocentric dominance embedded in narratives of beauty and acceptance among young learners and to delve deeper into the epistemological and ontological implications of such ideals. The duo-ethnography research method allows two scholars to engage in dialogue with one another about a certain topic. In this case our topic is the anti-colonial art project which disrupts the mainstream portrayal of princesses with our daughters, siblings and nieces. Latz and Murray (2012) described duo-ethnographic method as the following "Each researcher/dialoguer uses his or her life's curriculum, which is inevitably steeped in some 'culture(s)', as a starting point for dialogical contributions" (p. 2). The duo-ethnographic method is thus a transformational exchange between researchers, in which the purpose of open-ended exchange is to provide varying and alternate perspectives concerning a topic that would not otherwise be reflected through the voice of one identity (Lund et al., 2017). Sawyer and Norris (2013) drew on the transformational purpose of the duo-ethnography in relation to the interaction between the researchers in conversation. The authors described the relationship as one in which each scholar comes to "regard each other as both their teacher and student, assisting the Other in reconceptualising their own meanings" (p. 22) thus, providing a narrative that is informed by a myriad of exchanges that transform the dialogue.

The purpose of our collaboration is to understand how gendered, colonial histories, subjectivities and locations are deeply implicated by dominant Eurocentric hegemonic conceptions and representations of beauty of acceptance. These hegemonic conceptions of beauty encompass one of the plethora of ways in which ongoing forms of colonialism continues to be enacted, internalized and passed down vis-à-vis generational trauma. By this, we mean that colonial thinking around Euro-colonial expectations of beauty can be passed down across generations. For instance, as a child unquestioningly straightening our hair and being rewarded by compliments by family and community members for having straight hair or being expected to present ourselves in this way is an example of how the colonial logic is passed down. Our social locations, experiences and positionalities framed our study, while simultaneously resisting quintessentially Eurocentric and white supremacist epistemological methodological practices. Here we mean that we resist the idea of being all-knowing and "objective" without understanding how our social locations, histories and identity impact our understanding. We move beyond a white-Eurocentric view of whiteness as the norm, or whiteness as universal under the veil of neutrality (King, 2015). Rather, through the duo-ethnographic study, we engage in a dialogue, which unquestionably engages our own localities. Our utilization of the duo-ethnography provides an informal and oral storytelling approach to the challenges, interactions and colonial dichotomies of both standards of beauty as well as gendered binaries, power and privilege. Our oral storytelling approach was done with the young learners, as we pasted various pictures onto the collage, they would ask questions or provide information about the woman or girl in the picture. We found creative ways to link the identities of those in the project to their own and a larger web, by engaging the South African philosophy of *ubuntu*, demonstrating that our humanity is intrinsically linked. Beyond dissemination through this paper, we also displayed the final art projects on our wall, to have the young learners be proud of their work, as well, we shared it with our family members. As Dei (2012) states, "knowledge is about sharing" (p. 14). Here Dei looks at new imaginaries in Indigenous knowledge. For us as new scholars, it is important that we do not gain access to knowledge and garner it for individual pursuit of enlightenment, but that we instead look at ways we can share knowledge with our friends, family members and community members towards a larger political pursuit of decolonization. A duo-ethnographic project seemed one way to transform theory to practice and ground our conversations with action, starting with ourselves and with young learners in our families.

6.5 Duo-Ethnographic Dialogic Exchange

Zuhra: As the mother of two daughters, white privilege and supremacy hegemonically inform perceptions of beauty and acceptance, settler-colonial conceptions of femininity. I have often discussed with the young girls we raise in our personal lives how Black and Brown women are sexualized and exoticized. During the past two years, since my oldest daughter started kindergarten in a predominantly white, high-income neighbourhood, she has started saying that she hates her Brown skin. My younger daughter has fairer skin like myself and my oldest said she wished she had white skin because Brown skin is ugly. At first, I was heartbroken that she felt this way, but rather than feeling upset about it,

I decided to problematize the glorification of white skin with her. She named off all the people in her class that had white skin and the frozen characters: Elsa and Anna. I realized that there were not a lot of people that looked like her not only at her school, but also among the teaching staff and administration.

Janelle: As an aunt and older sister to several sisters, three of whom who spend more time with me; I've also experienced firsthand the resulting trauma associated with over 500 years of colonization. Like you Zuhra, I can identify with the reactions that your daughters have when seeing similar reactions from my sisters and nieces. They often voice the disdain they have with their hair and long for the hair type they see on television, when they are bombarded with depictions of cisgendered thin white women with straight hair. I too, try to help facilitate their interrogation of white supremacist ideals of beauty. I have paused the television and asked the oldest to explain "what is off?" with a movie or television scene when a person with darker hair and skin is displayed in a negative light and a person with lighter skin and hair is portrayed more positively. I am often amazed and learn from her reaction and ability to do such heavy unpacking at such an early age. It breaks my heart that your daughters, and many other young people go through this to this day, but I am confident that decolonization and change is a process and is ongoing. So, these conversations must also be ongoing, challenging and continuous.

Zuhra: I have made a conscious effort to have critical discussions with my daughters about how characters in Disney movies and other mainstream shows often have a very white, female character that is meant to represent the epitome of settler colonial beauty, while the "bad" characters are often darker and villainized. When films depict a racialized woman or girl as the main character, she is often scantily clothed and sexualized. Disney's Princess Jasmine is stereotyped and eroticized, she is confined her palace walls at the mercy of her father's arranged marriage to an array of misogynistic prospective suitors. The popular Disney movie now is Moana, who, just as Jasmine is wearing far less clothing than their white princess counterparts. The colonial depiction of Black and Brown women as being inseparable from "nature" is evident in Moana as the women are portrayed in an animalistic manner and through the Eurocentric colonial gaze that renders them as "uncivilized".

Janelle: The portrayal of Moana reminds me of Pocahontas and it was not until I was much older that I realized the anti-Indigenous message the movie portrayed which reproduces the ongoing narrative of colonialism and the white-male saviour helping to "civilize" backwards Indigenous and racialized women. I was glad to show the girls one of the Miss Navajo in the art project. They reacted proudly to see a portrayal of an Indigenous woman; I explained that the competition was also grounded in her role in community and ancestral knowledge and not solely beauty like in Western contexts. My nieces and sisters instantly claimed Miss Navajo's identity as part of their own. Such anti-colonial moments remind you to continue to have hope. Zuhra, I certainly find it refreshing that you not only talk about the "good" vs. "bad" dichotomy as portrayed in Disney movies and other television shows, but that you have also highlighted who is worthy of being a princess or not. When my sisters and nieces choose characters for role-play, rarely do they choose Disney character, Princess Tiana. This is likely because they do not find her story beautiful, inspiring or of interest because of her transformation into a Frog, and her "rags to riches" story. Through the advancement of white feminism on the backs of women of colour, films and TV shows have made great strides in addressing greater gender equality like in the newest Disney's Rapunzel, but an anti-racist lens is still very much lacking. From an intersectional approach, Black and Brown girls are reminded all too often that their beauty doesn't count and that their role models are only sexualized, not entirely and always for empowerment, but instead for a white supremacist, hetero-patriarch male gaze. In what way was an art project important to do with the kids?

Zuhra: Janelle, the art project was important to do with the kids because it was so essential to show my girls that women who look like them are not limited to over-sexualized, exoticized women that are barely clothed, most recently: Moana. My older daughter mentions that she wants to dress like Moana or Pocahontas because she feels that they look like her. I found it very important to show her what princesses and women from various parts of the world look like beyond the tokenistic and colonial depictions perpetuated by Disney. I took on another project that was quite like this with my Grade 8 girls health class this past year, we were talking about the way Black and Brown female bodies are portrayed by the media through derogatory imagery such as in music videos and films. Most of my students were Black and Brown girls and they had a lot to say about the subject and the way that certain body parts are constantly scrutinized within popular culture. I found this a good opportunity to discuss Sarah Baartman and show the film in class. I was as expected, faced with criticism from my administrators, but as this was a health class I strongly made the point that these are significant issues facing racialized women and have faced Black and Brown women from the time of overt European colonialism to modern-day colonialism in Canada.

Janelle: It was difficult, yet at the same time, much simpler to go about this project with our own family members, than having institutional pressures. Though we both agree that this is a good project for the classroom, having critical discussions like these can pose very straining in a formal schooling setting—though important. It was important that we completed this art project with our younger family members. The project was significant because it was not only used as a pedagogical tool for them, but also for us as adults. I went into the project expecting my sisters and nieces to only be negative about it; however, I was shocked to see their interest and excitement about learning and linking their own histories to the histories of others through non-traditional princesses. I found the project very empowering for them, through their exclamations, "I'm that girl!" This time, they were identifying more so with women they would grow up to more closely to resemble, rather than their constant need for identification with the white, thin, blue-eyed princess. Instead now, they learned about different regions and diverse women, including the hardships that many women face and their resilience. As they get older, I hope to do a follow-up project, which interrogates the intersections of race, class and the role of gender, and turns the entire idea of princesses and all the elitism it comes with on its head! However, for now, it was important to begin with something they have an interest in currently and can identify with. Zuhra, could you have used this type of a project when you were a child?

Zuhra: Yes, I certainly could have although I must acknowledge my white privilege. Because of my white skin, I had the privilege of identifying with a lot of the Disney princesses such as Belle in Beauty and the Beast. I felt so happy when Aladdin came out because my father had told me the tale many times and I so badly wanted to identify with Jasmine, but my older cousin who is a Brown woman told me that I was too white to be Jasmine. I imagine that my younger daughter who has fairer skin will feel similar being mixed but also embodying white privilege, I can already see that the Disney princesses affect my daughters in diverse ways. Our acts to disrupt these images are small, but I think important, because children and their families are bombarded with these images through one of the pillars of colonialism, capitalism. Did you do such a project as a child?

Janelle: No, but this sort of a moment as a child would have helped to disrupt the unrealistic beauty ideals I was confronted with then. Lucky enough, my mom when raising me tried to disrupt taken-for-granted ideas and have me think more critically. She especially gave me a strong sense of empowerment and balance, so I would not need to "look for love" as she'd say, which in retrospect supports the idea of empowerment vis-à-vis female chastity, which I do not agree with now as an adult. However, it is worth noting that her pedagogical practices for me was amazing and brilliant I might add. When I started university, I would often come home in shock and say, "my professor says the same thing as you about *x* or *y* about injustices in the world". She certainly was a critical thinker and pillar of strength, but like myself, and us all, she had her own colonial traumas which she faced head-on, or which were just part of her life unknowingly. With that, I could have certainly benefited from such a discussion explicitly early on. It wasn't until I was in completing graduate school and reading, falling in love with thinkers who are like me, Black, African feminist and womanist scholars that I started to question why wearing weave or straightening my hair was so routine. This outward expression became so entrenched and part of my life and that of my mother's, without question. Early and intentional interrogation could have helped me value every single kink and curl in my hair from a very early age, which I am coming to now. As an adult, I continue to learn and unlearn and have learned to be okay with that.

Zuhra: Janelle, your mother is a remarkable woman and although we are all colonized what your mother did is brilliant as you say because she raised an awareness in you about beauty, love and acceptance in a Euro-colonial society where we are constantly socially conditioned to believe that slim, petite white women are the only women deserving of love and happiness. Growing up in a very white neighbourhood with a white British mother, I often tried to escape my roots and ascribe to whiteness. Going to high school in a post 9/11 world, I would capitalize on my white skin and claim that my father was from one of the former Soviet republics. I was not taught to embrace my heritage, or to learn our language, or what my father called a "useless" language. I see now how colonized my father is. My ancestors lived in British India and the British tried to occupy Afghanistan three times officially granting the country independence on 19 August 1919, and yet he is so fascinated with the colonizer and married the colonizer. I have spent a lot of time unlearning and decolonizing the emphasis on the WASP work ethic and success and embracing my Pashtun heritage.

Janelle: Zuhra, when I talk to you, I am always reminded that there is so much to be done. The reactions of my nieces and sisters reminds me that the art project is one moment in time, one-weekend visit, but what happens when they turn the TV on again? I am constantly left reminded, that in the work of anti-colonial education, though we must look ahead to new horizons, futurities and possibilities, we cannot be discouraged, but must also continuously have the flexibility to learn and unlearn and critically self-interrogate. Though the project was more than I would imagine, I am trying to be reflexive in thinking through new decolonial pedagogical moments as an educator in the classroom, in community and with family.

Zuhra: Yes, I agree. And we are learners too…

Janelle: Very true. Decolonization starts from within, so the learning and unlearning is difficult, but starts with me.

6.6 Results and Conclusion

As indicated, we were apprehensive to have our younger family members partake in this art project because we worried about their reactions. However, instead, we were inspired by their reactions and both saw their very vocal claim of their own identities through the identities of all the "cultures" they saw displayed in the final collage. This also created an opportunity for us to unlearn our own expectations and engage in pedagogical processes as facilitators with openness to relearn. They demonstrated a sense of pride to have representation, which reflected them. In both cases, they would say, "That's my background" to the many images they pasted onto their collage. In both cases, they reacted with excitement towards the project and as it was later displayed on the walls, pointed to it with pride to other family members. It was truly a moving project and helped us to understand our own histories, its complexity, shifting locality because of colonialism (Benn-John, Chapter 4) and deep roots in the strength of Indigenous women throughout time. Through an anti-colonial framework, we used oral storytelling and shared through images, to demonstrate their diverse histories, bringing their layered representation and knowledge production to the forefront.

Following an anti-colonial theoretical framework, this project unraveled the impacts of colonialism, and rather than passively accepting them, we could engage in decolonial forms of resistance. Our resistance was grounded in critical and transformative pedagogy. Here, linked reactions of young learners to a larger web of colonialism, and challenge these taken-for-granted representations and their epistemological and ontological placement historically and contemporarily through way of art, storytelling and collaboration. The young learners' reactions such as "I'm her" or "That's me" demonstrate how they claim their identity and histories which have been and continue to be stolen from them by way of current beauty standards and representation. Also, oral storytelling and collaborating with our young highlight Indigenous knowledge which is not solely about "telling" them about their histories, but instead, we learn from them, their reactions and share in a co-creation of our knowledge coming together.

In the process, we also interrogated our subjectivities in the searches we conducted for images. We learned that we both used our own histories and social location as entry points. Though our entry points seem divergent because of national borders, we were reminded through our sharing of stories the ways in which our past histories converged and met again. Our point of return being Turtle Island, and histories of ongoing colonization and imperialism. As our daughters, sisters and nieces are all mixed race, the project allowed for us to go beyond the exoticization of mixedness of our young family members and uncritical notions of their bodies being read as the end of racism by centring their own histories, discussing them through anti-colonizing discourses rather than through the guise of multiculturalism (Mahtani, Kwan-Lafond, & Taylor, 2014).

The discourse and narratives surrounding the term "princesses" are problematic as highlighted earlier but were used to engage them in working collectively on the art project. This project certainly reminds us very starkly, that decolonization is a process of learning and unlearning, both personally and collectively. We as educators beyond the classroom need to locate ways of employing *multicentric* ways of knowing (Dei, 2008, p. 12). Using a multicentric approach centres the voices of Indigenous and African people whose axiology, epistemology and ontology are left on sidelines and misrepresented. This motivated us to take up an art project collectively with younger family members to help with diverse types of representation in their understanding of themselves, or at least just a small portion of it. The implications of this project are quite complex, we have highlighted some of the transformative results of it, but it does not involve an explicit discussion of ableism and works within the confines of heteronormativity or at least to an extent does so. Also, we would caution that the goal was not to demonstrate colour blindness, pluralism and multiculturalism, but instead to show complexity, layers and centre/value theirs and other Indigenous cultural representations and language. We will certainly follow-up with another project surrounding this art project in about three years with our family members when we can hopefully take an even more critical look at the project. A more critical project, will be one which interrogates the idea of princesses in the first place, using an anti-colonial framework, we can come to an understanding of how princesses are part of hierarchy, and of a classed, abled, raced and gendered history of oppression. However, as previously stated, for the purposes of this project, we decided to engage the young learners from their own level of interest and entry point so to engage in a small decolonial act.

This decolonizing art project poses as a simple, yet critical exercise, which educators can use in the classroom or with two classrooms and two educators, or two families and two homes, as Zuhra and I have done. Having two educators allows for duo-ethnography where both can understand their social location throughout the course of the project and critically understand the convergences and divergences with their colleague based on their histories. Both educators can compare the end products. The project allows for transformative learning where students are co-creators of their own knowledge by centring their own social locations and histories. The project also is rooted in theoretical framing and praxis, so students can be intentional about their own identities and thus disrupt and dismantle colonial forms of representation. However, it is important that the educators who partake in this important anti-colonial work have themselves interrogated their own identities and positions of power/oppression to allow for a constructive and critical learning experience.

NOTE

1. Note, we capitalize the terms Black, Brown and Indigenous and not white for the sake of subverting the dominant colonial axes of power by way of language.

REFERENCES

Clark, K. B., & Clark, M. K. (1947). Racial Identification and Preference Among Negro Children. In E. L. Hartley (Ed.), *Readings in Social Psychology*. New York, NY: Holt, Rinehart, and Winston.
Collins, P. H. (1990). *Black Feminist Thought: Knowledge Consciousness and the Politics of Empowerment*. New York: Routledge.
Collins, P. H., & Bilge, S. (2016). *Intersectionality*. Cambridge, UK: Polity.
Coulthard, G. (2014). *Red Skin, White Masks: Rejecting Colonial Politics of Recognition*. Minneapolis: University of Minnesota Press.
Crenshaw, K. (1991). Mapping the Margins: Intersectionality, Identity Politics, and Violence Against Women of Color. *Stanford Law Review, 43*, 1241–1299.
Davis, A. Y. (1983). *Women, Race and Class*. New York, NY: Vintage Books.
Dei, G. J. S. (2008). Indigenous Knowledge Studies and the Next Generation: Pedagogical Possibilities for Anti-colonial Education. *The Australian Journal of Indigenous Education, 37*(S), 5–13.
Dei, G. J. S. (2009). Theorizing Africa Beyond Its Boundaries. In G. J. S. Dei (Ed.), *Teaching Africa: Towards a Transgressive Pedagogy* (pp. 47–60). London, UK: Springer.
Dei, G. J. S. (2012). "Suahunu," the Trialectic Space. *Journal of Black Studies, 43*(8), 823–846.
Dei, G. J. S. (2017). *Reframing Blackness and Black Solidarities Through Anti-colonial and Decolonial Prisms*. New York, NY: Springer.
Dei, G. J. S., & Kempf, A. (2006). *Anti-colonialism and Education: The Politics of Resistance*. Rotterdam, NL: Sense Publishers.
Dillard, C. B. (2006). *On Spiritual Strivings: Transforming and African American Woman's Academic Life*. Albany, NY: Suny Press.
Fanon, F. (1961). *The Wretched of the Earth*. New York, NY: Grove Press.
Freire, P. (1970). *Pedagogy of the Oppressed*. New York, NY: Herder & Herder.
Hall, S. (1997). *Representation: Cultural Representations and Signifying Practices*. London: Sage.
hooks, b. (1991). *Feminist Theory: From Margin to Center*. Boston, MA: South End Press.
hooks, b. (2015). *Feminist Theory: From Margin to Center* (2nd ed.). New York, NY: Routledge.
King, J. E. (2015). *Dysconscious Racism, Afrocentric Praxis, and Education for Human Freedom: Through the Years I Keep on Toiling*. New York, NY: Routledge.
Kolawole, M. E. M. (1997). *Womanism and African Consciousness*. Trenton, NJ: Africa World Press.

Ladson-Billings, G. (1996). Your Blues Ain't Like Mine: Keeping Issues of Race and Racism on the Multicultural Agenda. *Theory into Practice, 35*(4), 248–255.

Latz, A. O., & Murray, J. L. (2012). A Duoethnography on Duoethnography: More Than a Book Review. *The Qualitative Report, 17*(36), 1–8. Retrieved from http://nsuworks.nova.edu/tqr/vol17/iss36/3.

Lund, D. E., Holmes, K., Hanson, A., Sitter, K., Scott, D., & Grain, K. (2017). Exploring Duoethnography in Graduate Research Courses. In J. Norris & R. Sawyer (Eds.), *Theorizing Curriculum Studies, Teacher Education, and Research Through Duoethnographic Pedagogy*. New York: Palgrave Macmillan.

MacDonald, J., & Markides, J. (2016). *Negotiating the Truths Between Us: A Duoethnographic Reading of the Truth and Reconciliation Commission's Calls to Action*. Unpublished manuscript, Werklund School of Education, University of Calgary, Calgary, AB.

Mahtani, M., Kwan-Lafond, D., & Taylor, L. (2014). Exporting the Mixed-Race Nation: Mixed Race Identities in the Canadian Context. In R. C. King O'Riain, S. Small, M. Mahtani, M. Song, & P. Spickard (Eds.), *Global Mixed Race* (pp. 238–262). New York, NY: New York University Press.

Sawyer, R. D., & Norris, J. (2013). *Duoethnography: Understanding Qualitative Research*. New York, NY: Oxford University Press.

Smith, L. T. (1999). *Decolonizing Methodologies: Research and Indigenous Peoples*. London, UK: Zed Books Ltd.

Swartz, E., & King, J. E. (2014). *Re-Membering History in Student and Teacher Learning*. New York, NY: Routledge.

Wane, N. N. (2008). Mapping the Field of Indigenous Knowledges in Anti-colonial Discourse: A Transformative Journey in Education. *Race Ethnicity and Education, 11*(2), 183–197.

Wane, N. N., & Chandler, D. J. (2002). African Women, Cultural Knowledge, and Environmental Education with a Focus on Kenya's Indigenous Women. *Canadian Journal of Environmental Education, 7*(1), 86–98.

CHAPTER 7

The First Three Years of LAEN: From Unity-Seeking to Equity-Seeking

Catalina Calero and Derik Chica

7.1   Introduction

This paper examines the evolution of a grass-roots community organization called the Latin American Education Network (LAEN)—renamed to the Latinx, Afro-Latin-America, Abya Yala Education Network (LAEN)—created in Toronto, Ontario, in June 2012. We discuss our barriers and limitations working with the Toronto District School Board (TDSB) and the Toronto Catholic District School Board (TCDSB) and the need for greater community organizing in addition to advocacy towards these established institutions. As volunteers and two of the many co-founders within the group, we discuss the limitations of our initial vision, "a united and strengthened Latin American community in Toronto supported by a network of diverse educational initiatives" (Appendix A), and its impact on our organization. It also serves as part of the institutional memory (Linde, 2009) of our network: to document important historical achievements and failures, so that future leaders may continue to build from us.

C. Calero (✉) · D. Chica
Toronto, ON, Canada

© The Author(s) 2019
F. J. Villegas and J. Brady (eds.), *Critical Schooling*,
https://doi.org/10.1007/978-3-030-00716-4_7

We primarily focus on the first few years of LAEN as it is the time period when we were most active (2012–2015). Since then, LAEN has continued to evolve with great new leadership and expanding anti-oppressive and anti-racist initiatives and memberships. Hence, the focus of this paper is the evolution of our organization from unity-seeking to equity-seeking. Using a social movement theory framework, we discuss our engagements with bureaucratic schooling institutions, our members and our community. Kertzer (1998), as cited by Tarrow (2011), defines social movements as "…repositories of knowledge of particular routines in a society's history, which helps them to overcome the deficits in resources and communication typically found among disorganized people" (p. 29). While we refuse to use a deficiency lens and aim to avoid objectifying our community as "disorganized", we choose to use this framework because of the collective knowledge we have gained throughout the years which have allowed us to effectively bring different people and sectors of our community together, sharing resources and communicating towards a shared goal. We recognize the importance of sharing the knowledge we have gained in order to document that our community has not been passive in our demands for better access to schooling and we hope that future activism and advocacy will not be viewed as a "new phenomenon", something Villegas (Chapter 8) argues may invisibilize our community's history of resistance.

We begin by contextualizing our perspective and positioning ourselves within this paper, followed by some background information on the complexities of Latinx identity in Toronto. We then provide a brief summary of the conditions of education for Latinx students in Toronto, presented through research on the high push-out rate (Dei, Holmes, Mazzuca, McIsaac, & Campbell, 1995; Schugurensky, Mantilla, & Serrano, 2009) of our students in Toronto schools, which prompted the inception of LAEN. We then outline LAEN's structure, initiatives and work with the TDSB/TCDSB, followed by a discussion of the changes that this community organization has undergone. We conclude with reflections of our experience within the first few years of LAEN.

We also note that given the organization of the paper, we do not follow a chronological timeline. We do this to facilitate a focus on the changing structure and evolving lens with which we approach issues, rather than a recounting of history. Finally, we employ the term "Latinx" instead of Latina/Latino or Latin@ throughout this paper, and this change is a significant part of the evolution of our organization.

The main function of the "x" is to be more inclusive of gender nonconforming and gender-fluid people (Scharron-Del Rio & Aja, 2015). Hence, we adopted the term Latinx because of its conceptual ability to encompass greater inclusivity.

7.2 The Authors

Catalina Calero was born in Toronto to immigrant parents from Colombia and Ecuador. She completed her high school and post-secondary education in Toronto and throughout university was very involved with the Latinx community, particularly surrounding issues of student success in the Toronto secondary school system. She has worked with students directly in the school system through various organizations. As a settlement worker assistant working with "at risk" students and through different community initiatives, she has witnessed the many barriers and forms of oppression these students experience regularly in the school system. She has been a volunteer/member and supporter of LAEN since its inception.

Derik Chica identifies as a Latino cis-gender male with many privileges, including light skin. He was born in Toronto, and his parents immigrated to Canada from Ecuador. He spent most of his schooling in the TDSB before moving to the York Region District School Board for secondary studies. Beginning his career in education in Toronto, he underwent political transformation through social justice work with the Latinx community. He volunteered with Student Aid and Learning Opportunities (SALO) and Organization of Latin American Students (OLAS) and was one of the founders and the first Co-Chair of LAEN for three years. He now teaches for the TDSB and uses lessons he has learned from his mentors to seek sustainable and equitable action-oriented solutions to improve systemic education for his community. We must note that due to Derik Chica's position within the TDSB and local organizations, he has also been privy to information from meetings or personal communication which will be used in this paper.

7.3 Complexity of Latinx Identity

Latinx individuals use a variety of labels to identify themselves. Considering that Latinxs originate from a variety of places in the "Americas", including Mexico and the Caribbean, many use their nation of origin or ancestral origin. However, given the low density of Latinxs in Toronto, many employ a more collective term in replacement or in addition to their nation or ancestral identity marker, for example Latina/o, Latin American or Hispanic. Hispanic is "...derived from the Latin word for Spain, Hispania and means Spanish..." (Yankauer, 1987, p. 15). It is problematic because it serves to centre our conversations on our colonial roots and trivializes the genocide of Indigenous peoples since 1492. "Hispanic" places emphasis on an identity with Spain and the anti-indigenous and anti-blackness it entails. As such, it erases our Indigenous and Afrocentric roots, through the assumption that our peoples and cultures originate from Spain or by centring this location. This colonial practice of focusing on Eurocentric identity and representation is also seen within the education system. As Behn-John (Chapter 4) argues, "educational systems continue to see colonial and post-colonial practices in their structures, educational content, subject matter experts, and in the culture of educational institutions". By framing a discussion in colonial terms, we are only further subjugating ourselves to the shackles of colonialism.

Identity has been central to the organizing of LAEN and eventually defined our position on equity and inclusivity in our community. This has fueled a series of complicated and dynamic discussions around the term "Latin American" as opposed to "Hispanic". As a collective, we recognize that the language we use to identify ourselves and our community limits or enhances access to spaces in which we can organize. For our community, the choice of language can also highlight our history of oppression, and the use of "Hispanic", as previously mentioned, centralizes our colonizer (Alcoff, 2005). Thus, in schooling, using "Hispanic" and the Eurocentric discourse that is tied to it enables the potential for oppressive representations that centre white supremacy.

7.4 THE INCEPTION OF LAEN: COMMUNITY RESPONSE TO THE NEEDS OF LATINX STUDENTS AND FAMILIES

In the literature, the difference in levels of academic achievement between different racial and socio-economic groups is referred to as the "achievement gap" (Schugurensky et al., 2009), educational debt (Ladson-Billings, 2007) and more recently the "opportunity gap" by the TDSB (as Derik has learned from the TDSB Equity Policy Advisory Committee (EPAC)). Similarly, we use the term "push out" rather than "drop out" to interrogate the various institutional mechanisms that force our students out of schools (Dei et al., 1995). There has been ample evidence in the literature surrounding the issue of the "drop out" or push-out rate for Latinx students, both within and outside the Toronto context; for example, Valenzuela (1999) and Valenzuela, Garcia, Romo, & Perez (2012) discuss this issue within the context of the USA while Schugurensky et al. (2009) provide context for the TDSB.

According to the TDSB's 2006 Publication: *The Grade 9 Cohort Study: A Five Year Analysis, 2000–2005*, the "dropout rate" among Spanish-speaking[1] students was near 40%, compared to the average dropout rate of 23% (Schugurensky et al., 2009). This issue is of great importance to our community, because of not only the high likelihood that any given student may not complete their secondary education, but also the underrepresentation of our community in post-secondary education and the probable negative consequences on the future prospects of these students.

Reports have revealed many erroneous perceptions of Spanish-speaking youth as deficient, misconceived as being "low-achieving" and "drop out", or as lazy or dumb (Gaztambide-Fernández & Guerrero, 2011; Schugurensky et al., 2009). The reality is that many of these students have become disengaged from a system that has placed them in the margins, as seen in the USA (Valenzuela et al., 2012). Racism, discrimination and a Eurocentric curriculum are some of the main causes for this disengagement and marginalization (Dei, Mazzuca, McIsaac, & Zine, 1997; Schugurensky et al., 2009; Valenzuela et al., 2012), and these negative perceptions have contributed to the micro- and macro-aggressions they frequently experience. Furthermore, the inaccessibility of resources, both from within the school system and outside, is another contributing factor (Moreno & Gaytan, 2013; Valenzuela et al., 2012).

Our students are subjected to racism and discrimination from peers, teachers and other school staff alike. According to Valenzuela et al. (2012), even teachers with good intentions may have an "...uncritical embrace of covert racist ideologies and deficit thinking" (p. 26) as well as the lack of "...experience and understanding of the obstacles facing urban and migrant students" (Valenzuela et al., 2012, p. 26). For example, many of these students receive advice from guidance counsellors to pursue an "applied" (college-bound) or "workplace" (no post-secondary potential) pathways instead of "academic" (university-bound) programmes, with the assumption that these students are not capable of success. Streaming is common and places students in limiting pathways early in their lives (Parekh, Killoran & Crawford, 2011). While streaming was to be discontinued in the 1990s (Curtis, Smaller, & Livingstone, 1992) evidence shows it continues today (TDSB, 2015).

In addition to lowered expectations of students from teachers and other staff, the curriculum creates a barrier to engagement. The Eurocentric curriculum reflects what Valenzuela (1999) calls "subtractive" schooling, describing educational practice in which "policies, practices, school staff, and teachers ignore or devalue the home culture and linguistic knowledge...of minority students, thus effectively stripping them of much of the social and cultural capital, potential and perspective that they could potentially bring to the classroom" (p. 26). According to Dei (2010), the Eurocentricity of the Ontario school system is problematic because of its inability to give students a well-rounded view of the world. Further, Shankar et al. (2013) looked at the educational experiences of low income, Indigenous and visible minority Canadian youth and found that the Eurocentric format of education delivery did not meet the needs of these students. This demonstrates a need for students' experiences to be placed at the centre of their education, as well as the role that diversity plays in knowledge production to challenge dominant ways of knowing (Dei, 2010).

In Toronto, sixty secondary students from high schools across the city provided their experiences and perspectives on schooling through a collaborative participatory action research initiative between the Ontario Institute for Studies in Education and the TDSB. This initiative was called Proyecto Latin@ and was a major step forward in education research for our community (Gaztambide-Fernández & Guerrero, 2011). Students spoke about issues they faced such as curriculum they do not relate to, streaming, unfair disciplinary processes, lack of extracurricular activities specifically for Latina/o students, financial barriers, racism and a lack of understanding from teachers with regard to language acquisition in ESL classes. The students then provided advice on how to improve schools. For example, they listed positive teacher qualities that supported them, requested that part-time jobs for students be available in schools, requested for community-based programming in schools and asked for the use of alternative pedagogies in classrooms such as student-centred approaches and critical pedagogies.

LAEN was formed in 2012 when members of the Latinx community in the TDSB and the TCDSB, Toronto's two largest school boards, recognized the lack of a collective approach to advocating for Latinx students at the various schools. As Tarrow (2011) mentions, "the coordination of collective action depends on the trust and cooperation that are generated among participants by shared understanding and identities" (p. 29). Our community had both a shared understanding and shared identity at this time and so we were able to generate trust among us and coordinate that trust into action; thus, LAEN was born. It is important to note that this shared sense of identity became precarious as LAEN evolved an equity lens and questioned who was included and excluded with the identity markers we were using. We will discuss this in a future section of this paper, titled "Evolution of LAEN".

In summary, there have been various institutional mechanisms that push students out of schools and have resulted in the high push-out rate of Latinx students (near 40% in 2006). This provides context for the inception of LAEN, when Latinx community members in both school boards realized the lack of collective approach to advocating for Latinx students. We have also highlighted the Proyecto Latin@ initiative and the suggestions the students made for improving schools. A couple of these suggestions were community-based programming and alternative, student-centred and critical pedagogies in classrooms.

7.5 Structure and Initiatives of LAEN

LAEN was created as a volunteer-run, grass-roots community-based, non-hierarchical organization with elected Co-Chairs meant to facilitate conversations and support LAEN's administrative tasks. For the first two years (2012–2014), the Co-Chairs of LAEN were Derik Chica and Alexandra Arraiz. For the third year, the Co-Chairs were Derik Chica and Tatiana Penuela. Our Terms of Reference (Appendix A) were created with a broader understanding of the term "education": to support community and popular education initiatives. In our first three years, we created a social media platform and a monthly electronic newsletter to support community by promoting various community events and initiatives. We also held monthly general meetings, in addition to work group/committee meetings, to discuss educational issues, LAEN initiatives, and plan future events/initiatives. These meetings were public, although were generally populated by members of LAEN, including Latinx community organizations, parents and youth. LAEN also advocated for our community to the board through the TDSB's EPAC, and the TCDSB Advisory Committee for Spanish Speaking Communities (ACSSC), in addition to Latin@/Hispanic Heritage Month committees in both boards.

LAEN's initial Terms of Reference (Appendix A) allowed us to create a space to network and share the plethora of initiatives in our community, and to collect and organize ideas and issues we faced and use them to advocate for change in the educational systems. With a focus on unity, we generally worked through consensus. The Terms of Reference were created through the participation of several organizations with different levels of political engagement with our community. Initially there was disagreement in how to refer to our community, however at the time we desired to "not get bogged down with language". We did not foresee the inequitable space we would be creating by putting words such as "Spanish-Speaking" (not all of our community speaks Spanish) and "Latin@" (a gender binary term limiting gender fluidity). Thus, our community is referred to as "Latin@/Spanish-speaking" in our initial documents.

Our first annual education conference, named "Education and Our Community" in October 2012, was focused on displaying the numerous services and initiatives for families in our community. It engaged youth, parents, and community through workshops about identity, equity, human rights, gender-based violence, and navigating the education system. Our second annual education conference, named "Strengthening Our Community" in November 2013, moved towards a more action-oriented and community organizing approach, concluding with a peer-reviewed report published by Latin American Encounters (Matute & Chica, 2014). This report showcases past issues our community has encountered in the school boards, and outlines their continued influence on our community, as discussed at the forum. Over 100 community members, including students, educators and parents, participated in workshops dialoguing around questions such as: "What challenges does our community face in the public education system?", "What can the School Boards do to help us overcome these challenges?" and "What can we do as a community to address these challenges?" In the documented responses, our community identified three overarching themes as barriers: stereotypes and prejudice, lack of support in schools, and language and identity (Matute & Chica, 2014).

Community educators, the youth, and parents spoke out stating that teachers held racist stereotypes about Latinx students and thus, lowered their academic expectations of them, solidifying the findings by Proyecto Latin@ and paralleling research done in the United States (both previously discussed). They felt these low expectations led to a scenario of "self-fulfilling prophecies" for many youth, which resulted in poor outcomes and disengagement from schooling. They also felt there was a lack of adequate communication between the school and Latinx families, and in addition to this, a lack of academic support and required resources. The students and their parents expressed facing difficulty in navigating the educational system and their experiences with the negative effects of streaming. Lastly, they spoke about the challenge of newcomers not being able to speak English and the resulting deficiency framework with which the staff operated towards the students (Matute & Chica, 2014). Through this research, it was clear that both students and parents/caregivers were not apathetic towards education as some in society believe. They were able to clearly outline their barriers, their needs, and their strengths with the correct facilitation.

It is important to note that the 2013 LAEN Education Forum was not solely about barriers, but also about brainstorming solutions. As a result, school boards were asked to provide meaningful equity and anti-oppression training for educational staff and consider hiring teachers that "better reflect the diverse population of students in Toronto" (Matute & Chica, 2014, p. 34), specifically, hiring teachers with "relevant backgrounds, culture, language and histories" (p. 34). In addition, school boards were asked to provide resources and additional supports to Latinx youth, and support the building of positive, nurturing relationships between Latinx youth and teachers. Curriculum was brought up as an area needing much improvement, and the boards were asked to include more content from Latin American studies and other Latin American based themes. Lastly, parents requested concrete, tangible changes that could facilitate parent involvement in school/board-run events or meetings. For example, they indicated that transportation assistance and child minding would go a long way to enable them to attend events (Matute & Chica, 2014).

At this event, our community also spoke at length of the need to act as a collective. Attendees felt it critical to "accept and understand that community advocacy, within individual and collective power, is important, indispensable, and inevitable to improve our life conditions" (Matute & Chica, 2014, p. 36). There was a dire need to push for more Latinx representation in positions of authority in the city, and in addition, there was a need to "work with other communities to support each other and demand higher education levels for our youths" (p. 36). Parents spoke of how important it was to "promote participation between families and friends as well as members of the community" (p. 36) and the youth spoke of the "need to unite and mobilize their agency and resources" (p. 36). As previously mentioned, there is a dominant belief that our community is deficient and unengaged (Gaztambide-Fernández & Guerrero, 2011; Schugurensky et al., 2009). These quotes contradict this idea and demonstrate the awareness and knowledge that parents and youth have on the issues faced by our community and their willingness to participate in collective activities.

In February 2015, LAEN hosted its third annual forum named "From Dialogue to Action". This conference was also focused on a community organizing approach, but instead of producing a report, the decision was made to provide a more accessible means of communicating the results: a single page document with a table summarizing the discussions and outcomes of the forum (Appendix B). With a larger community turnout than previous years, the conference proved a resounding success, with approximately 150 people in attendance. The resulting one-page document reflected both similar barriers and needs as previous forums had identified, as well as newly identified issues. This document is also only a brief summary of the many discussions had at the conference. For example, barriers/needs/issues raised in these discussions range from the need for more spaces where Latinxs feel included inside schools, to the issue of anti-Blackness towards and within the Latinx community (demonstrated by the lack of representation of Black Latinxs in community initiatives and posters, and the lack of awareness about the racist origins and uses of the term "Hispanic"). We presented this document to the TDSB and the TCDSB and continue to work towards improvements across the educational system.

An action plan was also presented to the TDSB and TCDSB, outlining seven key areas of focus, based on our previous community forum: anti-streaming; employment equity; removing School Resource Officers (police officers) from schools (Madan, Chapter 2); better implementation of the "don't ask, don't tell" policy in regards to immigration status (Villegas, Chapter 8); increased community partnerships and greater access to board resources; moving away from a Eurocentric curriculum; and a review of punitive practices that disproportionately targets racialized youth (Bailey, Chapter 3), particularly Black and Indigenous youth and the potential in adopting progressive discipline remedies. These are all important steps for the improvement of the Latinx student experience, as they each address one of the various factors that negatively impacts the schooling experiences for these students and are tied to the previously discussed disengagement from school. Presenting this action plan to the TDSB and the TCDSB was an important step because it demonstrated our organization as a movement and as devoted to community organizing, and applied political pressure using our established relationships to dialogue.

One of the important successes our forums have achieved, with the support of key partnering community organizations, is the high turnout of Latinx youth, debunking the stereotype that youth simply "do not care". The youth took the time to come out on a Saturday morning to drive these conversations, and thus, LAEN succeeded in stimulating meaningful participation through the creation of youth civic spaces. Richards-Schuster and Dobbie (2011) define youth civic spaces as "…pathways, structures and vehicles that provide opportunities for young people to engage in critical discussion, dialogue and action". (p. 234). These spaces have allowed youth to share their experiences in the education system with their peers and community members in a safe environment, as well as given them an opportunity to tell us what they need to achieve better educational outcomes in school and what changes they would like to see. This important outcome could not have been achieved without the support and integration of many individuals, organizations, the youth and their parents. Interestingly, this type of "civic engagement" parallels Eizadirad's (Chapter 9) idea of citizenship being more active engagement and a right to "oppose, resist, and challenge injustice". Contributions made by our community have provided us with clearer pathways for setting our future goals and action plans.

Despite the successes of this approach, we acknowledge there are still some limitations. Although dialoguing with students is a necessary step in seeking change, it is important that their involvement does not end there. In these first few conferences, students were given the opportunity to be involved in critical discussion and dialogue, but there was not sufficient emphasis on students being involved in the action that came after the conferences. On the other hand, more recent initiatives with the new Co-Chairs have focused more on long-term student leadership and action.

To summarize, we have described LAEN as a volunteer-run, grassroots community-based, non-hierarchical organization with elected Co-Chairs. In the first three years, aside from promoting community events and initiatives we have also advocated to the school boards through various school board committees and organized yearly education forums/conferences. We have highlighted the progression of the conferences and their positive outcomes for our students and community, such as providing spaces for community, family and students to voice their needs and experiences, and give them an opportunity to suggest solutions. Further, the creation of summarizing documents and an action plan from these conferences have assisted us in advocating to the boards for the improvement of our schools.

7.5.1 Working with the TDSB and TCDSB

In the following paragraphs, we outline the successes and challenges resulting from our collaborative approach to working with senior-level staff from the two largest school boards in Toronto for the past few years. One of the most important aspects of running an organization is funding, and funding has always been a positive factor/outcome in this collaborative work. Since LAEN is volunteer-run and does not have its own financial resources, we depend on funding to be able to make our events accessible and keep our work sustainable. For example, the education conferences we have organized have required funding for food, honorariums for facilitators, MC's, and artists/entertainment, public transportation tokens and child minding to support parental involvement.

Fortunately, both the TDSB and TCDSB—alongside organizations such as the Ontario Secondary School Teachers Federation, Elementary Teachers of Toronto, and Ontario English Catholic Teachers—have financially supported our work through the first 3 years. This willingness to fund our activities has been highly recognized, especially in the light of austerity, chronic underfunding of school boards from the province, and the declining enrolment in schools in Toronto (affecting both union and school board funding).

Another issue of importance has been access to relevant information that has allowed us to operate on evidence-based data. The TDSB has been collecting student race-based data for many years and has been publishing and sharing these vital statistics that have been useful to our community (Yau, Rosolen, & Archer, 2015). During an EPAC meeting, we learned that students are given the choice to self-identify as "Latin American", separate from the categories of "Black", "Aboriginal" or "Mixed". We must note that there are limits to this type of data collection and categorization. There is a lack of intersectionality, as all "Latin American" students are lumped into one category, resulting in difficulty if a Black/Afro-Latinx student, for example, would need to choose between "Black" or "Latin American". Therefore, it does not take into consideration that an ethnicity can include multiple races, as well as the resulting differences in the students' experiences. However, current LAEN Co-Chairs have been in discussion with senior staff regarding the global intersectionalities of Blackness, including but not limited to Black/Afro-Latinx identities. Despite these needed improvements, this data has still been useful for community organizing, and has allowed us to see where, geographically, we should focus our efforts. LAEN has consistently advocated to the school boards for the sharing of updated demographic statistics for Toronto schools in order for us to share such data with other organizations who are looking to build similar partnerships with local schools based on the population and concentration of Latin American students.

Through meetings with the TCDSB, Derik learned that the TCDSB, on the other hand, does not collect race-based data, and their data is limited to school-based information, not student-based information. For this reason, we have been unable to effectively ascertain how Latinx students are doing in their schools, though we can still see where Spanish-speaking students, as they identify them, are concentrated in their schools. We shared this information with community groups knowing that both the concentration and population of Spanish-speaking students is useful to select schools for their initiatives. However, our contention is that labelling our youth solely as Spanish-speaking students ignores not only the distinction of second generation Latinxs who may only speak English, but also disregards the existence of any other languages spoken in Latin-America aside from Spanish, the colonizer's language.

As such, naming the TCDSB "Advisory Committee for Spanish Speaking Communities", while accepted at the time of its birth, fails to acknowledge the reality of the barriers we face as a racialized people, and seeks to emphasize our identity as a community as being simply language-based. This limits the scope of such an Advisory Committee to one that discusses issues that Spanish-speaking youth face, meanwhile, excluding other Latinx youth who do not speak Spanish and therefore, the racism and other intersectional systemic barriers that are placed in front of these excluded students. Nonetheless, there is a positive aspect to the work of this Advisory committee. Their commitment to our community has been demonstrated by their most senior staff and some trustees meeting us four times a year, allowing us to bring any issues of concern to the table for discussion.

Despite the successes we have enjoyed in working with the school boards, there have also been clear limitations to the support we have received. School Board actions on issues discussed have not been as forthcoming as expected, and it has required several efforts and friendly follow-ups, including various emails to ensure tasks were completed and support was provided as agreed on in meetings. These limitations became more prominent, especially with the TCDSB, as we began to take positions further from dominant ideologies.

LAEN also had a consistent presence in the TDSB and TCDSB Heritage/History months. While heritage/history months provide a platform to create awareness of and launch important initiatives, they can also be turned into tokenistic "multicultural" celebratory events, ignoring both power and privilege within society. As a member of heritage month planning committees, LAEN has worked hard to avoid contributing to the tokenistic side of this celebratory month. However, the planning committees for these events do not control local school planning and thus, local schools continue to organize tokenistic multicultural events involving our community. In school board planning committees, we have persistently proposed having meaningful conferences where important information can be collected, valuable networks can be created, relevant community services promoted, and action-based workshops can be facilitated. These are ways in which we can enrich the celebration of our heritage/history months to positively impact the community. Through these heritage/history months, we hoped to place pressure on educational institutions to integrate our community and our needs into their annual strategic planning. We hope that future planning in these history/heritage month committees allow for, as Brady and Abawi (Chapter 6) reveal, an opportunity for young learners to "claim their identity and histories which have been and continue to be stolen from them" (p. 143).

We also faced challenges in working with the TDSB and TCDSB as separate entities. When we first began LAEN, a joint "Hispanic Heritage Month" committee existed, but after a controversial incident regarding a racist presentation by a TCDSB teacher during "Hispanic Heritage

Month", the committee was disbanded, and the school boards reverted to working independently. For LAEN, working separately with the TDSB and TCDSB creates certain limitations in our work with Latinx youth for our community, in that it becomes more difficult to create community initiatives as we must target and navigate approvals for various initiatives with each board separately and through their bureaucracies, instead of vetting them through a single committee. This has placed the onus of time needed to advocate to the boards on voluntary community members instead of paid board staff members. Each of the planning committees in the TDSB and TCDSB also plan separate education conferences, which often lack a clear equitable direction.

Near the end of the first three years of LAEN, we also faced barriers in working with the TCDSB. While we continued to have a positive presence in the ACSSC, our new equity-seeking focus seemed to create more resistance from central staff within the board. While our social movement actively tried to frame our identity in an equitable fashion, we needed to compete with, as Gamson (2004), cited by Tarrow (2011) writes, the framing that goes on through other means, "which transmit messages that movements must attempt to shape and influence" (p. 32). The TCDSB also continued to request for more information regarding the issues around identifying our community as Hispanic or Spanish-Speaking, regardless of the repetitive dialogue at advisory committee meetings surrounding community voice and research on the limitations of those identity labels. It is unfortunate that while the LAEN has progressed to seek equity, the TCDSB has not done the same with our community.

Working with the school boards has brought both successes and difficulties. On the one hand, funding has been a positive factor, as well as access to relevant information and data from the TDSB and TCDSB which we have been able to use as a community. On the other hand, advocating to the TCDSB became more difficult as our positions grew further from dominant ideologies. Further, working with the two boards as separate entities has also slowed down the process of approving school initiatives due to the need to navigate two separate bureaucracies.

7.6 Evolution of LAEN

The progression of the forums/conferences as well as our initiatives and group discussions demonstrate our realization of the importance to move from unity to equity. As we grew, the importance of equity-driven actions became more of a focus than the romanticized idea of unity in our community. Through our forums and dialogue, we realized the complex solutions needed to improve our collective experience in schools and the need for a greater equity lens for our community.

Our conferences, "Education and Our Community", "Strengthening Our Community", and "From Dialogue to Action", demonstrates the slow evolution of LAEN and the growing needs of complex solutions to the systemic barriers our community faces in education. We began as a grass-roots group, focused entirely on our community at our first conference, to recognizing the importance of advocacy for our community to the school boards, to recognizing the need for more equitable community action, through diverse means, towards the school boards.

On February 19, 2014, with little community consultation, the City of Toronto proclaimed October as Hispanic Heritage Month (Member Motion 48.14). Then on May 5, 2015, again without any appreciable community consultation, the Province of Ontario proclaimed October as Hispanic Heritage Month (Bill 28). Both motions/bills were passed because a few individuals claiming to represent the community's voice approached these government institutions and made unilateral proposals to this effect.

In the 2014 TDSB/TCDSB Hispanic/Latin@ Heritage Month Celebration, including "Hispanic" in the name of the month enabled a TCDSB teacher to present a Eurocentric and anti-Indigenous PowerPoint (as previously mentioned in the section "Working with TDSB and TCDSB), titled "Enigmas and Paradoxes", which explicitly praised European people and culture while calling various Indigenous cultures "enigmas". This resulted in some students and teachers feeling offended and upset and leaving the assembly early in protest. This is a concrete example of the danger of framing a celebratory month with Eurocentric identity markers like "Hispanic".

It was at this point where we began to realize that our vision of unity was limiting our engagement in equity-seeking initiatives. We began to realize that our evolved commitment to equity and social justice meant we needed to engage in dialogue and education within our own community to ensure we did not engage in the marginalization of our peoples in our resistance to the marginalization we experienced from dominant society. We needed to explore the future of our resistance to marginalization and ways in which we can express our agency as a community without oppressing those intersectional identities in our own community.

The dialogue within LAEN of labelling our diverse community with a single term was an ongoing discussion throughout the three years, with a substantial turning point near the end of the three years in choosing to change our use of the identity marker "Hispanic" to the more inclusive marker, "Latinx". It was at this time that an interesting discussion and debate occurred within LAEN. Initially, we discussed using the term "Hispanic/Latin American" because in our experiences, much of our community used the term Hispanic and Latin American interchangeably, and, in our search for unity, we wanted to respect the voices of our community. However, as the debates thickened, we realized that we would be oppressing people within our own community by using the term Hispanic with its colonial roots. We also reached a point where we had to vote whether to acknowledge the term Hispanic, because some of our community identified that way, or whether to get rid of it completely. It was after this vote where we recognized the need to take a more substantial role in changing internalized racism and oppression, and after a few months of debate, the term "Hispanic" was rejected from LAEN. We decided we could not be a part of the perpetuation of the oppression of our own community by engaging with a term that is colonial and not equitable nor inclusive.

In 2015, Derik Chica had been the Co-Chair of LAEN for three years and it was time to transition to new Co-Chairs. Andrea Vásquez Jiménez and Silvia-Argentina Arauz have been active with LAEN since the beginning, and as self-identifying Afro-Latinas were advocating for the creation of spaces that would enable more representation and the discussion of systemic issues that affect Black/Afro-Latinxs. As the new Co-Chairs, they were both able to expedite LAEN's transition from a unity-focused to an equity-focused organization with an emphasis on action-oriented initiatives.

That same year, a petition and formal request to elected government bodies to change the name of the month was created by Andrea Vásquez Jiménez. In Andrea's petition, *Change Hispanic Heritage Month to Latin-America History Month: Toronto, Ontario, Canada*, she explicitly highlighted the *geographical region* of Latin-America, stressing the importance of self-identification (rather than being forced to accept a colonial labelling as a group of people) as well as the importance of "… celebrating a land and histories that connect us all" (Vásquez Jiménez, 2015). Both LAEN and the creator of this petition acknowledge that the term "Latin-America" also has its colonial roots (Mignolo, 2005), but it was chosen to counter "Hispanic" and as a way to ignite critical conversations and actions.

After substantial dialogue with community, including LAEN members, and a vote, "Latin-America History Month" was agreed upon as the term to be proposed to the school boards in opposition to "Hispanic Heritage Month", and to vocalize support for the petition. With the direction of the new leadership from Co-Chairs Andrea Vásquez Jiménez and Silvia-Argentina Arauz, LAEN worked with the TDSB to create a Latin-America History Month and to discontinue using the term "Hispanic". As a result, the TDSB celebrates Latin-America History Month in April. The TCDSB unfortunately has continuously refused to do so and continues to celebrate "Hispanic Canadian Heritage Month".

Further, LAEN also moved forward in the decision to hold a vote for an organizational name change in March 2016. The name was changed to the "Latinx, Afro-Latin-America, Abya Yala Education Network" in an effort to be more critical and reflective of our community. As previously mentioned, Latinx is gender neutral and is an alternative to the masculine-centric term "Latino" or gender binary "Latin@". The use of Afro-Latin-America is an effort to centre Black/African identities in the Latin-America diaspora, and Abya Yala is a decolonial term for "the Americas", used as a form of resistance (LAEN Latinx, Afro-Latin-America, Abya Yala Education Network, 2017). Further, in an effort to centre the experiences of those identities marginalized by the education system, the new co-chairs have developed culturally informed, strengths-based initiatives.

Due to the novelty of the term Abya Yala for some readers, we wish to provide some context in the following section. According to del Valle Escalante (2015), the Indigenous term/concept of Abya Yala means "land in its full maturity" in the Kuna language, referring to the whole American continent, and it emerged in the 1970s in Dulenag (a Kuna Tule territory, current day San Blas, Panama). It was suggested by Indigenous leaders in Bolivia (Takir Mamani—Aymara leader—and Tupaj Katari—one of the founders of the Indigenous rights movement in Bolivia) that Indigenous peoples and organizations use the term in their official declarations (del Valle Escalante, 2015), arguing that "placing foreign names on our villages, our cities, and our continents is equivalent to subjecting our identities to the will of our invaders and their heirs" (Arias et al., 2012, as cited in del Valle Escalante, 2015, p. 101).

They also argued that the renaming of the continent is the first step towards epistemic decolonization, autonomy and self-determination of Indigenous peoples. This term is now used by many Indigenous activists, writers and organizations (del Valle Escalante, 2015). Finally, it is also important to note that Abya Yala is not the only term used by Indigenous communities to refer to the whole American continent.

In conclusion, LAEN's evolution over the years has occurred through all of its components. From the progression of its forums/conferences to the initiatives and discussions, realizing that our vision of unity limited our engagement with equity-seeking initiatives. We realized the necessity of dialogue and education within our own community to avoid re-perpetuation of oppression to those within our community who are usually excluded or ignored, hence our change in discourse from Hispanic to Latinx. Under our new current leadership, LAEN worked with the TDSB to create a Latin-America History Month (while the TCDSB continues to celebrate Hispanic Canadian Heritage month in October), and we changed our name from LAEN to Latinx, Afro-Latin-America, Abya Yala Education Network.

7.7 Reflection and Conclusions

In the first three years of LAEN, we made significant growth in our attempts to organize our diverse Latinx community from numerous countries and cultures. We have progressively moved towards a more justice-oriented organization through an equity-seeking lens and away from the romanticized conception of a united community. While we began with an attempt to bring all ideologies and political perspectives together, we soon realized that it was of more importance to adopt an anti-oppressive approach to our organizing. We listened to concerns of marginalized students, families and community members in our community and used this feedback to build a more equitable movement. In addition, we attempted to integrate them into various advocacy and activist spaces, such as during our monthly meetings where we discussed identity markers and strategizing around our annual priorities.

In our first attempts to seek unity, we were able to bring together and get to know many people around our community like activists, community members, agency representatives, youth and parent groups. We were successful in bringing these people to the same space for dialogue, despite historical conflicts between people and organizations. However, in attempting to move forward united, we faced difficulty with some individuals who did not see a problem with ignoring the experiences of "a small portion of our population". While we attempted to explain our new equity-based positionality on issues to these individuals, we did lose some membership based on this new equity lens. However, we did draw some more active membership from Latinx people impassioned and inspired with our new work who also felt more included as a result of our new direction.

We have seen the way trust and cooperation (or lack of) between our organization, school boards and other organizations have facilitated the coordination of collective action (Tarrow, 2011) or have created obstacles to collective action, in particular when we have not shared understanding or identities. Further, we have also seen the way a movement such as LAEN's has to constantly compete with framings of our community that are inequitable (such as Hispanic Heritage months and other oppressive representations of our community) and therefore must attempt to shape them (Gamson, 2004). Hence, this paper has demonstrated the way the evolution of our social movement has grappled the dominant framings of our community as well as working with stakeholders who do and do not share our equitable lens of supporting our students and community.

We have written this paper to support the work of future leaders in our community and to preserve institutional memory, that is, the previous initiatives we have put forward, and the challenges we encountered regarding institutional barriers or bureaucratic systems that inhibited us from moving forward with respect to school board initiatives. We hope this paper will be a reference in future efforts to develop similar projects and initiatives, and that this work will contribute to decolonizing education as a whole. Ultimately, we aim at improving our community's collective experience within the educational system in Toronto, and hope that we have successfully shed light on and created a better understanding of who we are as an organization, the fluidity of our community and the continuous evolution of our initiatives and vision. This paper is not to say that unity is not important; however, we envision a future where true unity and solidarity is achieved with all members of our diverse community, and not by perpetuating the same oppressions we are battling in larger society.

Note

1. "Spanish-speaking" is the category that the TDSB used to collect their data and is not the same as "Latinx", which may include individuals who do not speak Spanish.

Appendix A

Terms of Reference

Vision

A strengthened and united Latin American community in Toronto supported by a network of diverse educational initiatives.

Mission

To support and advance educational initiatives through a diversity of community support groups, organizations and individuals.

Objectives

Promotion—To promote awareness of educational rights and of the services available to the Latin@ community.

Parents—To support parents' involvement in their children's education through a parents' council and enhance parents' participation through workshops, information sessions, etc.

Advocacy—To advocate on behalf of the Latin@ community to various educational institutions.

Children/youth—To provide a platform for children/youth to become proactively involved, share their experiences and influence change in the education system.

Cultural and personal development—To promote and support spaces where culture, as it relates to the Latin American community, is critically explored and celebrated in order to build enriched and renewed understandings within our community.

Supporting families—To promote and strengthen communication and relationship ties between parents and children/youth by connecting them with tools and resources available in the community.

Membership

Participation in meetings is open to the public at large, but membership is restricted to an individual that represents any initiative, form of outreach or non-profit organization that has the advancement of the Latin@/Spanish-speaking community as a goal or objective. This representation must be submitted in writing and is valid for one (1) year starting on each year after the LAEN Annual General Meeting.

- New membership vetted through the six chairs by consensus. It is the responsibility of the Co-Chairs to review the applications of the organizations with due diligence.
- When submitted, it is accepted after 2 weeks unless objections are made.
- If objections are made, a majority vote will determine outcome.
- In exceptional circumstances, any of the Co-Chairs can bring the item to the membership of LAEN.
- In the case a member is found to be in breach of the objectives and mandate of LAEN, their membership can be brought to the members of LAEN for review.
- In order to sustain the membership, the individual or organization must not miss more than three (3) consecutive meetings without giving due notice.

Becoming a Member

In order to become a member of LAEN an organization or individual must:

1. Submit the following statement:
   "I am joining the Latin American Education Network in order to promote the vision of a strengthened and united Latin American community in Toronto supported by a network of diverse educational initiatives. I endorse the mission and objectives of the Latin American Education Network and will work with other members to promote these".
2. Submit their mandate/biography.

Voting

Each member has one vote as per each written submission. Voting members can participate in the election of the Committee Co-Chairs and can participate in decisions that require a vote during committee meetings. Decision will be determined by a simple majority vote.

Co-Chairs

Each year there will be two (2) Co-Chairs elected, one male and one female. Co-Chairs must attend and chair all committee meetings. They are responsible for facilitating debate during committee meetings and ensuring that diversity of opinion and inclusivity is respected. They must meet with the Co-Chairs of all other LAEN Committees as needed and set the agenda and priorities for LAEN.

Co-Chair duties include but are not limited to:

- Agenda preparation
- Outreach and recruitment
- Minute taking and distribution
- Newsletter preparation
- Uphold the mandate of the committee and organization
- Chair meetings
- Meet with Co-Chairs as needed
- Meeting with stakeholders

Appendix B

From Dialogue to Action: Summary Table

Latin American Education Network—"From dialogue to action"—Summary of conference discussions

	Parents	Youth	Community and educators
Barriers			
Barriers in Education and civic society that limit access and participation	• Lack of effective communication (flyers, videos, brochures, etc.) between school and parents • Promoting students without them having an understanding of reading, math, etc. • Parents are tired, many work multiple jobs and many newcomers don't understand the language • Teachers that are too strict and don't differentiate instruction	• Being pushed into ESL classes that aren't necessary • Low-expectations of students • The necessity to work part-time • Stereotypes, racism, and discrimination in schools where staff think Latin@s can't read English, Latin American is full of crime, newcomers have a lower education level • Many youth losing bilingualism because of the emphasis to speak English	• Most ethnic representation comes from the US • Feel perceived as a problem stirrer if bring up issues • Parental presence results in treatment towards kids being different but no presence results in less favorable attitude towards kids • Intimidation from social workers if kids don't attend class adds to stress • Suburbs have lack of public transportation increasing the economic class gaps • Accessibility for non-status students and settlement workers cannot service them

Latin American Education Network—"From dialogue to action"—Summary of conference discussions

	Parents	Youth	Community and educators
Support and resources			
Existing, Lack of/Needs	• Lack of psychological support within schools to combat depression, anger issues, etc. • Lack of social support to combat bullying • Lack of awareness of existing support services • Lack of understanding of the Sex- Ed curriculum	• Lack of understanding of Latin American culture (thinking there are no Latin@s who are Black) • Lack of support for Latin@ students • Lack of support to learn English and lack of patient teachers for ESL learners • Lack of support for newcomers • Subsidies for families (low income, with more children)	• Lack of awareness of barriers newcomers face resulting in lack of patience • Services for newcomers have been cut • Lack of dissemination of existing resources to newcomers especially older parents • Lack of consistency in ESL courses, too dependable on teachers • Lack of awareness about non-status families and the barriers they face
Model education			
A model educational system and alternatives to the current system	• Spaces where bullying can be discussed and bullies can understand a culture of violence is not acceptable • Sex-Ed where same sex relationships are recognized • Parents receive effective communication regarding parent-teacher interviews, information sessions, translation services, etc. • Resources that enhance cultural pride and alliances across races and cultures	• Education about Aboriginal Canadians and mental health • Spanish and English in schools • No stereotyping • Seeing more Latin@s in media by school • Patient teachers who understand their students • More dialogue in classes and a critical look at history • Flexible school hours for students who need to work • Free Post-Secondary Schooling or more scholarships for Latin@ students • Differentiated instruction and evaluations • Tutors paid for by the school system • Parents who are integrated into the school	• Greater representation of the Latin@ community in teaching • Website that is easy to navigate • Recognizing our students as assets (a shift from the deficit approach) • The use of social media, online forums, tutorials, Spanish radio and community organizations as a means to connect with parents and disseminate important information. • Use of clear and concise language in school or Board communications (avoid technical and legal jargon) • Bilingual communication (i.e. newsletter)

Latin American Education Network—"From dialogue to action"—Summary of conference discussions

Action	Parents	Youth	Community and educators
Action to be taken by participants	• Establish groups within Latin@ communities for an exchange of ideas, support, and information • Speak up to local school about concerns and needs	• Support the creation of Latin-American Schools (to parallel the Afro-Centric schools)	• LAEN as a conduit to provide feedback from the community to school boards • Develop spaces that have 'real' power for parents • Better and consistent anti-racist and anti-oppressive training for teachers and staff

References

Alcoff, L. (2005). Latino vs. Hispanic. *Philosophy & Social Criticism, 31*(4), 395–407.
Curtis, B., Smaller, H., & Livingstone, D. W. (1992). *Stacking the Deck: The Streaming of Working Class Kids in Ontario Schools*. Toronto: Our School–Our Selves Education Foundation.
Dei, G. (2010). The Possibilities of New/Counter and Alternative Visions of Schooling. *English Quarterly, 41*(3–4), 113–132.
Dei, G., Mazzuca, J., McIsaac, E., & Zine, J. (1997). *Reconstructing the 'Dropout': A Critical Ethnography of the Dynamics of Black Students' Disengagement from School*. Toronto: University of Toronto Press.
Dei, G. J., Holmes, L., Mazzuca, J., McIsaac, E., & Campbell, R. (1995). *Drop Out or Push Out? The Dynamics of Black Students' Disengagement from School*. Toronto, ON: Ontario Institute for Studies in Education.
del Valle Escalante, E. (2015). Self-Determination: A Perspective from Abya Yala. In M. Woons (Ed.), *Restoring Indigenous Self-Determination: Theoretical and Practical Approaches* (pp. 101–109). Bristol: E-International Relations.
Gaztambide-Fernández, R. A., & Guerrero, C. (2011). *Proyecto Latino Year 1- Exploratory Research: Report to the Toronto District School Board*. Toronto: Ontario Institute for Studies in Education.
Ladson-Billings, G. (2007). Pushing Past the Achievement Gap: An Essay on the Language of Deficit. *The Journal of Negro Education, 76*(3), 316–323.
LAEN Latinx, Afro-Latin-America, Abya Yala Education Network. (2017, March 27). In *Facebook* [Group page]. Retrieved July 20 2017, from https://www.facebook.com/LAENToronto/photos/a.280599908717635.59087.279682355476057/1151077301669887/?type=1&theater.
Linde, C. (2009). Introduction: How Institutions Remember. In C. Linde (Ed.), *Working the Past: Narrative and Institutional Memory* (pp. 3–14). Oxford: Oxford University Press.
Matute, A. A., & Chica, D. (2014). Community Voices, Community Action: Latin American Education Network 2013 Community Education Forum Report. *Latin American Encounters, 2*, 25–39.
Mignolo, W. D. (2005). *The Idea of Latin America*. Malden: Blackwell.
Moreno, G., & Gaytán, F. X. (2013). Focus on Latino Learners: Developing a Foundational Understanding of Latino Cultures to Cultivate Student Success. *Preventing School Failure: Alternative Education for Children and Youth, 57*(1), 7–16.
Parekh, G., Killoran, I., & Crawford, C. (2011). The Toronto Connection: Poverty, Perceived Ability, and Access to Education Equity. *Canadian Journal of Education, 34*(3), 249–279.

Richards-Schuster, K., & Dobbie, D. (2011). Tagging Walls and Planting Seeds: Creating Spaces for Youth Civic Action. *Journal of Community Practice*, *19*, 234–251.

Scharron-Del Rio, M. R., & Aja, A. A. (2015, December 5). The Case FOR 'Latinx': Why Intersectionality Is Not a Choice. *Latino Rebels*. Retrieved from http://www.latinorebels.com/2015/12/05/the-case-for-latinx-why-intersectionality-is-not-a-choice/.

Schugurensky, D., Mantilla, D., & Serrano, J. F. (2009). *Four in Ten: Spanish-Speaking Youth and Early School Leaving in Toronto*. Toronto: Ontario Institute for Studies in Education.

Shankar, J., Ip, E., Khalema, E., Couture, J., Tan, S., Zulla, R., & Lam, G. (2013). Education as a Social Determinant of Health: Issues Facing Indigenous and Visible Minority Students in Postsecondary Education in Western Canada. *International Journal of Environmental Research and Public Health*, *10*(9), 3908–3929.

Tarrow, S. (2011). *Power in Movement: Social Movement and Contentious Politics*. Cambridge: Cambridge University Press.

TDSB, Equity and Inclusive Schools. (2015). *Sifting, Sorting and Selecting: A Collaborative Inquiry on Alternatives to Streaming in the TDSB*. Resource Document. Toronto District School Board. http://www.tdsb.on.ca/Portals/ward3/docs/Sifting,%20Sorting%20and%20Selecting.pdf Accessed 13 Feb 2017.

Valenzuela, A. (1999). *Subtractive Schooling: U.S.–Mexican Youth and the Politics of Caring*. Albany: State University of New York Press.

Valenzuela, A., Garcia, E., Romo, H., & Perez, B. (2012). Institutional and Structural Barriers to Latino/a Achievement. *Journal of the Association of Mexican American Educators*, *6*(3), 22–29.

Vásquez Jiménez, A. (2015). *Change Hispanic Heritage Month to Latin-America History Month: Toronto, Ontario and Canada*. Retrieved from Change.org: https://www.change.org/p/john-tory-cesar-palacio-norm-kelly-cristina-martins-kathleen-wyne-change-hispanic-heritage-month-to-latin-america-history-month-toronto-ontario-canada.

Yankauer, A. (1987). Hispanic/Latino–What's in a Name? *American Journal of Public Health*, *77*(1), 15–17.

Yau, M., Rosolen, L., & Archer, B. (2015). *Census portraits, understanding our students' backgrounds: Latin American students report*. (Report No. 14/15-17). Toronto, Ontario, Canada: Toronto District School Board. Retrieved from http://www.tdsb.on.ca/Portals/research/docs/reports/Portrait_Census2011-12_LatinAmer_FINAL_report.pdf.

CHAPTER 8

Active Communities and Practices of Resistance: Brief History of the Use of Schools as Border Zones in Toronto

Francisco J. Villegas

8.1 Toronto and Its Borders

In 2006, Gerald and Kimberly Lizano Sossa, two Costa Rican high-school students, were detained within their school in Toronto by Canadian Border Service Agency officials. This action, particularly because it occurred within a school, caused significant community response directed at both the Canadian government as well as the public-school boards. In relation to the latter, a coalition made up of different community organizations mobilized toward the creation of a policy facilitating the enrollment of undocumented youth, preventing the sharing of information about their immigration status, and stipulating that all school staff must redirect immigration officials out of a school and to the Board's head office. This policy, passed in the Toronto District School Board (TDSB)

F. J. Villegas (✉)
Anthropology and Sociology,
Kalamazoo College, Kalamazoo, MI, USA
e-mail: Francisco.villegas@kzoo.edu

© The Author(s) 2019
F. J. Villegas and J. Brady (eds.), *Critical Schooling*,
https://doi.org/10.1007/978-3-030-00716-4_8

in 2007 is officially known as the "Students Without Legal Status Policy" but colloquially as the "Don't Ask, Don't Tell" (DADT) policy.

Amidst the work to facilitate the passing of the DADT policy, public figures express dismay at the presence of undocumented migrants in Canada, a phenomenon only believed to happen in the USA. Specifically, trustees and administrators of the TDSB displayed lack of knowledge regarding the need to enroll undocumented students. However, undocumented migration to Canada, is not a new phenomenon (Wright, 2013), nor is the presence of undocumented youth in Canadian schools. At the same time, the presence of both as well as their histories are invisibilized by the discourse of Canada as a "nation of immigrants," a "refugee-accepting country," and a kinder and gentler space than the USA (Fortier, 2013; Wright, 2013).

Canada portrays itself internally and internationally as a multicultural and diverse nation, while simultaneously being worried about the makeup of its citizens and implemented exclusionary immigration policies, particularly toward migrants of color.[1] While Canadians may recognize overt acts like the Chinese Exclusion Act or the presence of race-based immigration categories, they may be less aware of contemporary governmental measures to immigration control. These subtle methods include the erosion of refugee acceptance and protections (Macklin, 2005), the discursive insertion of "bogus refugees" as a means of increasing suspicion and bureaucratic roadblocks (Pratt & Valverde, 2002), and the presence of an immigration system that privileges white males with social mobility (McDonald, 2009; Thobani, 2007; Walia, 2013). The preoccupation with the presence of racialized bodies in the populace has facilitated the mobilization of criminalizing and illegalizing discourse that promotes ideas of undocumented migrants as abusers of Canadian "generosity." The confluence of racist tropes with the undocumented population has led to the creation of roadblocks toward the availability of social goods.

Toronto presents an interesting case as Canada's largest city, a primary destination for migrants, and a self-identified "diverse" city.[2] In fact, Toronto has been known as "the city that works" (Croucher, 1997), that is, a city that values and integrates diversity in its overall structure. Furthermore, Toronto has the largest school board in the country constituting more than 246,000 students across 588 schools and an operating budget of over 3 billion dollars (TDSB, 2014). Thus, while the apprehension of the Lizano-Sossa occurred at a Toronto

Catholic District School Board,[3] local organizers prioritized mobilizations at the TDSB for greatest impact (Villegas, 2014).

There is constant surprise in mainstream media as well as within schools regarding the presence of undocumented migrants and the demand for inclusion in the schooling process. However, through participant interviews, it is evident that community groups have utilized myriad strategies to secure entry into schools since the 1960s. They have, ensured the inclusion of undocumented status as an equity issue in schooling policy, secure entry to the employment of administrators' personal discretion to enroll a student, mobilizing legal challenges to school board practices, and developed grassroots campaigns to pass the DADT campaign. Furthermore, these strategies spanned across jurisdictions ranging from the local school site, to the board level, all the way to the use of international law to change provincial policy. Regardless of this history, when the DADT policy was introduced at the TDSB many individuals within the Board, across the media, and within the DADT Coalition treat the topic as something new. This lack of institutional history would lead to prolonged difficulties in addressing exclusion from schooling for undocumented students, particularly as it took a year for the TDSB to pass the DADT policy and ten years later, it has yet to be fully implemented (Villegas, 2014, 2017).

This paper proposes that questions regarding immigration status and access to schooling had been discussed for a significant period, decades before the DADT policy. As such, it tracks many narratives that debunk the myth that access to schooling for undocumented migrants as a phenomenon exclusive to today's society, rather than an ongoing struggle between "illegalization" and community activism. The chapter begins with a description of the theoretical framework used across the paper. Bordering and the construction of border zones are important analytical tools to understand how institutions exclude individuals through illegalization. Therefore, the process of producing illegalized migrants goes beyond the crossing of the national boundary and includes everyday experiences with social institutions, in this case schooling. Following the theoretical framework, I provide insight on the method deployed to collect and analyze data. Then as means of highlighting activism in this arena by and on behalf of undocumented migrants, I discuss some of the efforts to enroll undocumented students before the passing of DADT. The periods of time covered include the late 1960s (Harriet Tubman Centre), the 1980s (Boards of Education in Toronto pre-amalgamation), 2002–2003 (Development of Section 49.1 of the Ontario Education Act), and post-2006 (DADT policy at the TDSB). Following this discussion, I conclude with a brief description of the genesis of the DADT campaign as described by organizers. In doing so, I outline a student apprehension and deportation case consistently believed to be pivotal to the development of this campaign, that of Kimberly and Gerald Lizano-Sossa.

Prior to unfurling the following sections, it is important to note that the narrative regarding the history of school boards described in this chapter remains fragmented and incomplete. The purpose of this paper is to describe a history of discussions, strategies, resistance, and advocacy regarding access to schooling for undocumented migrants in Toronto. As such, the chapter serves to dispel the myth that the TDSB was the first school board to discuss this issue and "welcome" undocumented students, a theme that remains prevalent today when trustees and politicians talk about the policy. Secondly, the chapter highlights the presence of an active undocumented population who, along with their allies, have continuously resisted exclusion from schools.

8.2 BORDERS AND RESISTANCE

This paper is conceptualized through the lens of bordering and the construction of border zones. This framework facilitates an understanding of the logic and labor of bordering as well as its process of construction and reconstruction. In our current society, borders are seen as a commonsense feature of the world, many of us experience the in/ability to move across borders as dictated by the types of passports we possess and the capital that can be "verified"[4] to border officials. However, borders exist beyond the sites of demarcation between the national space. They are present within the nation and similar to ports of entry serve to filter individuals according to conceptions of membership. Therefore, people can become illegalized beyond the moment they cross the national boundary and illegalization can be experienced on a daily basis across different institutions (De Genova, 2005).

Scholars have shown how borders are found beyond the physical demarcation between nation-states or points of entry and discourse about the border often parallels the social construction of undocumented migrants (Dechaine, 2012; Johnson, 2012; Ono, 2012; Ono & Sloop, 2002). These discussions include how borders are constructed inside a country to determine membership and sites of inclusion/exclusion as well as how such borders are read and carried within bodies. As Fortier (2013) states, "the modern exercise of state border and immigration policy increasingly extends beyond the regulation, disciplining, and exclusion of foreign nationals at points of entry. People also *experience* and *resist* borders in a multitude of ways *inside* the nation-state" (p. 274, emphasis in original). Sites become bordering spaces where applicants must provide documentation to prove eligibility to a social good and where administrators are, through policy or personal discretion, charged with guarding such services from migrants "illegalized" and constructed as "illegitimate", and potential abusers. The presence of border zones also hinders the possibility of creating community. Johnson (2012), states, "borders move with the people who cross them and function as lines of demarcation between and within communities" (p. 35). Consequently, border zones function to develop spaces of belonging and non-belonging and as extension, given the prominence of their impact, produce precarity.

Borders can be eroded, perforated, and circumnavigated. While remarkably sparse, literature has tracked bordering within Canada in women's shelters (Bhuyan, 2012, 2013), health institutions (Magalhaes, Carrasco, & Gastaldo, 2009; Villegas, 2013), schools (Bejan & Sidhu, 2010; Sidhu, 2008; Villegas, 2013), and the workplace (Goldring & Landolt, 2013). In the city of Toronto, we have also seen an attempt to erode bordering practices through the passing of a policy that makes the city into a "sanctuary" or solidarity city (Keung, 2013). These efforts have visibilized the presence, needs, and contributions of undocumented migrants in the city and successfully changed legislation in order to benefit the undocumented population. However, while borders and bordering practices can be challenged and resisted, institutions can also reify or reformulate boundaries. For this reason, it is important to recognize that even when successfully challenged, borders are in a constant state of flux and can be reconstituted. As such, progressive gains can be lost when policy is not implemented, when it is recalled or reinterpreted, or when new procedures are developed as bordering practices. Thus, it may be necessary to think of any gain as a fragile erosion of the border, while still necessitating a broader reconceptualization of the concept of membership that inherently questions the legitimacy of borders and bordering practices.

8.3 Methods

Data for this paper consists of individual and group semi-structured interviews and my experiential knowledge in working with the DADT Coalition and the TDSB to implement the DADT policy. All data stems from a CERIS[5] and Social Science and Humanities Research Council[6] funded project.

Fourteen public figures were interviewed between 2009 and 2012. All interviews were conducted in the spaces of participants' choosing and included conference rooms in the University of Toronto, a library, a pub, and participants' offices. Seven participants were interviewed individually and five were part of group interviews. For the latter, one group consisted of members of the DADT Taskforce and the other were individuals with closer knowledge of the procedures employed by community groups to work with the Board.

All participants served pivotal functions in the work leading to the mobilizations for access to schooling for undocumented students or worked in key locations across the Board and had direct relevance to the implementation of the policy. Participants from the Board were located in prominent spaces across its bureaucratic map and consisted of trustees, heads of departments, and a principal. Participants not affiliated with the Board included grassroots activists and their allies. All were considered public figures in the movement to pass and implement the DADT policy. They consisted of members of the DADT Coalition, No One Is Illegal-Toronto, leadership from the Ontario Secondary School Teachers' Federation, a member of a TDSB Advisory Committee, and a teacher. Interviews were between one and a half to three hours and were subsequently transcribed and coded in NVivo. Codes were developed at multiple stages: while designing the research project, during data collection, and while re-analyzing data. All participants are identified through gender ambiguous or commonly associated female pseudonym to increase participants' confidentiality and as a move against male protagonism that is often employed in research and activism.

8.4 Efforts to Include Undocumented Students Prior to Amalgamation

As part of a neoliberal restructuring process, the six school boards operating in Toronto prior to 1998 were amalgamated into a single entity, the TDSB (Basu, 2004). As a result of this change, school boards had to redefine policies and procedures including enrollment practices. In this section, I discuss the ways enrollment for undocumented students were constructed prior to the creation of the TDSB and in the process of building a single school board.

Participants referenced conversations about access to schooling for undocumented students spanning a significant period of time. The earliest moment described by a participant was the 1960s. When asked when she first heard about undocumented youth facing barriers entering schools, Quinn a manager of a TDSB department said,

> probably about 1967, 68…I started my work in community and there was a large influx of kids coming from the Caribbean…so I'm very aware of kids coming up here… there would be times that when mothers who themselves weren't landed but had been working for a long time would be bringing their children up or a grandmother would finally say "I'm sending them" and you know, these children would come up and depending on the school [and] the situation, all of a sudden the mother realizes that they can't register their child because they don't have landed status themselves. So again, it would be working with schools or the Black Education Project or the Tubman Center.

Quinn's detailed description above demonstrates the long history of undocumented migrants attempting to enroll children in Toronto schools as well as the efforts by community members to facilitate the process. Quinn's quote also depicts a history of negotiation between community actors and schools or school boards. This move was necessitated because of the history of ongoing labor migration to Canada from the Caribbean and what she described as limited options for transnational childcare available.

Similar to today, in the 1960s, enrollment was not automatically assured for undocumented children. Quinn also highlighted some of the strategies employed at the time to enroll students in school. She said, "you did whatever you needed to do if there was an issue with that child getting into school because you [might] happen to have a…principal wanting the letter before they would register a child so certainly I was aware of the issue." According to Quinn, the letter was not about the student, but instead the parent,

> it was mostly for the mother or for the parent, that she was working so sometimes a letter from an employer would do it… I think it was related to the fear that if this person was working for this length of time at a

company then obviously her or his immigration status had been checked so it would be the letter going to the school. Once in a while that's what they would ask for, "can you get a letter from the parent to say that they're working?"

The demand for a letter detailing gainful employment follows a discursive construction of the "good" migrant who benefits the state and the construction of the "bad" migrant as potentially abusing the communal goodwill through illegitimate demands to social goods (Li, 2001, 2003). The latter is also often depicted as a "burden" (Thobani, 2000) and ineligible to receive a social good. This construction was also constituted through discourses of gender and race as some types of labor were not readily recognized. As an example, Quinn described problems arising when many of the women needing letters worked in domestic labor. Domestic work is gendered and part of a history of feminized labor interpreted as not constituting "real work" (Romero, 1999). Additionally, at the time, large numbers of domestic workers coming to Canada originated from the Caribbean. In this way, it is not surprising that domestic workers would experience additional difficulty in proving their standing as "good" migrants, particularly as their labor did not follow expectations of social contribution. Furthermore, it may have been more difficult to obtain a letter of employment given their immigration status, the possibility of being paid "under the table," and the precarity of their labor.

Nearly forty years prior to the introduction of the DADT policy, school boards in Toronto were engaged in dialogue regarding access to schooling for undocumented migrants and grassroots organizers were developing strategies to ensure their enrollment. According to Tanya, a Toronto East TDSB trustee,

> there were two or three downtown trustees...who took that on in the very early '70s. They were right out of the university and...were movers and shakers and they were in their early 20s and so they started working on that very early and Toronto had policies on how immigrants [accessed school] and it wasn't called "Don't Ask Don't Tell" then...We pretty much said we'd rather have them in schools and so we had not only a policy but an understanding that it would be better for them to be there than hiding out.

Similarly, when asked about the first time she heard about undocumented students needing access to schooling, Dena, a Toronto West

TDSB trustee with an institutional memory predating the creation of the TDSB, stated,

> oh, I think we've always known about them....Most of the ones that we were originally involved with were, would be called Romani and they would sort of come and go so they'd just arrive and then they'd disappear, but they knew they could come back.

Tanya and Dena described recognition of the presence of undocumented migrants in the city by school administrators. They also discussed concerted efforts to develop policies and procedures to enroll such students. It is important to note that both trustees represented areas of the city with a longstanding presence of new arrivals to the country.

The Toronto Board of Education and the North York Board of Education employed various tactics to enroll undocumented students. Quinn described the North York Board of Education as a space that employed discretion in the enrollment of undocumented students. According to her, "it was in 1998 when I started with North York... [I] remember getting calls and knowing that there were certain principals that were pretty good about not asking a lot of questions and letting students register for school." At the same time as these strategies were employed at North York, Dena discussed discretionary power at the Toronto Board of Education,[7]

> we always knew that there were you know [undocumented students], but I would say because the Board was much smaller then and because it was more informal situation and particularly because when I was at the west end...they had their own way of dealing with the situation which was basically, we're not going to have anybody not be part of school and actually it was probably much easier for people to feel that they were welcome because it was a smaller organization and I think it's a little better and a little easier to get a personal aspect than I think maybe then it is now.

These discretionary practices demonstrate that despite a lack of a policy for enrolling undocumented students there was a willingness to enroll students at a single school. In the case of the latter school, Dena alluded to the fact that this informal practice was not the norm across all Toronto Board of Education schools when she stated that students would come from different places in the city to enroll at the school where she worked.

8.5 A New Amalgamated Board

While there appeared to be some mechanisms in place to enroll students in some of the schools before amalgamation, this discretionary power was removed post-amalgamation. As Dena stated,

> certainly, once the TDSB came in to place, probably within the first year that the TDSB [was created], so that was 1999, there was actually quite an active discussion amongst administrators, [the] visa student department, and some of us, about the place of people without status and it was quite clear that some people did not believe that they should be in school. That they were visitors.

Addressing the enrollment of undocumented migrants in the newly formed TDSB at such an early stage of the Board's development shows that it was present in people's minds. In analyzing this shift, it is also important to examine the relevant actors discussing the issue. The fact that the visa student department was present and that undocumented students would ultimately be registered as "visitors" speaks to the belief that such students were considered revenue-generating subjects. Therefore, their exclusion from the schooling process as a result of their immigration status and possible inability to pay tuition fees were considered acceptable.

Decision makers regarding access to schooling for undocumented migrants appear to have been divided along geographical and ideological lines. Those representing areas outside the downtown and North York, as well as individuals in charge of business generation within the Board appeared to reject the idea of enrolling undocumented students free of charge. As Dena stated,

> They have very detrimental opinions about who should go to school and who shouldn't… just the fact that if you didn't have your papers and you couldn't fill out the forms completely then you were a visitor…I think the opinions were much clearer [from] people from North York and Scarborough in particular. I think, although not from everywhere in Scarborough because certainly once you get closer to the lake you have no choice and the same thing in Etobicoke. In the south of Etobicoke, you really don't have a choice, you're confronted with it, so you have to decide what to do.

The quote above delineates an ideological and geographic understanding of access for undocumented students. According to Dena, individuals living in Toronto's suburbs, outside of specific migrant hubs in those areas displayed more exclusionary ideas regarding schooling. Tanya further corroborated this claim and identified areas of Scarborough as zones that were unfriendly to undocumented students and remained heavily entrenched in xenophobic ideals. As such, there was a clear geographic rift among trustees from old Boards aware of the presence and needs of undocumented migrants (North York and Toronto School Board) and those from Boards outside the city who were not considered migrant hubs. In the context of a new amalgamated board, it appears that this divide affected the procedures to enrolling undocumented students as well as the development and deployment of an equity agenda.

The ability to practice discretion in the enrollment of students was also present post-amalgamation. In describing when she first learned about the needs of undocumented students as well as her response, Maggie, a TDSB Senior Board Administrator stated,

> I began to learn about this issue before it became a public issue, a media public issue. It was still an issue with community groups because we dealt with the Education Rights Taskforce… I went to several meetings way back then and began to dialogue and began to service that issue and our response at that time was not at the policy level but more as a resolving individual situations that came up that were brought to my attention that in the absence of a policy I would resolve as a staff person on an individual basis and sign admission papers for the students and so on because while it was clear it was a systemic issue it was really raised as an individual. But I began to see where in fact it was a systemic issue to resolve in terms of a policy.

Maggie offers a historical narrative post-amalgamation that speaks to the lack of policy and procedures. In this context, she explains that as a senior member of the Board she had the discretionary power to sign a student's enrollment application, but this practice was limited to an individual basis. As such, we can see that even post-amalgamation, key individuals within the Board were aware of the presence of undocumented migrants and their needs to enroll in school. While Maggie's employment of discretionary power ultimately resulted in the enrollment of some or all students referred to her, it is important to think about those who did not have access or knowledge of this avenue.

While most of the early tactics speak to a legacy of resistance practices, the strategy of finding friendly individuals willing to employ their discretionary power to enroll a student also displays the limited possibilities available when a prevalent discourse that criminalizes and dehumanizes undocumented migrants is present.

8.6 Failure of Policies: The Education Rights Taskforce and the Education Act

While the deployment of informal practices and procedures to enroll undocumented students has left much to be desired, the development of policy, across many jurisdictions, has also proven to be largely ineffective. Prior to DADT, there have been at least two instances in which policy has been engaged to ensure access to schooling for undocumented students. These examples include the TDSB's equity policy and the lack of implementation of Section 49.1 of the Ontario Education Act. For the former, there is an equity policy that considers immigration status, but it has not transferred into practice for the inclusion of undocumented students. In relation to the latter policy, the Ontario Ministry of Education has done little to ensure that school boards adhere to the demands of the Education Act beyond the sending of memos from time to time.

An equity policy within a school board is designed to prompt a consideration of equity when developing and implementing policies and procedures. Equity policies, however, are not as binding as other policies (like budgets) and can fall by the wayside when confronted with personal and institutional discretion. While the TDSB has an equity agenda in place, Quinn, Michael, and Dena and Tanya considered it weak, compared to that of some of the smaller boards pre-amalgamation. The amalgamation of six school boards did not result in the strengthening of these equity agendas or even their maintenance. Instead, people found that the equity-based curriculum and documents developed were not transferred to the new board. Quinn said,

> I think what happened is that, you know when you have six boards and you have two where human rights, equity, were sort of a priority and again with all due respect to all other boards who certainly acknowledged it, but

I think given the diversity of our two boards there was a need to acknowledge and work so that the kids that were sitting in the classroom were acknowledged and programs and curriculum were put in place in order for them to succeed whereas the other boards probably didn't put as much [emphasis on such work]. So, when you have as much of a mixture, it's not at the same level when you're mixing boards that did a lot with those who didn't and then tried to get everybody on board with the same focus on equity human rights. It's taken a lot of work and I'm still not sure whether we're there or not.

The meshing of six distinct boards with different politics, demographics, and priorities, resulted in a bureaucratic policy-making procedure that Quinn, Dena, and Tanya felt marginalized equity and human rights. For example, in relation to undocumented students, Michael, a member of an advisory committee to the TDSB described the ways that members of an old board discussed an equity policy that recognized immigration status as a mode of oppression,

> the whole conversation around access for non-status had been an ongoing issue around the equity policy advisory table and its predecessors... [Before] amalgamation back in 1999...some of us helped craft the equity foundation statement which is the benchmark theoretically of the defined equity in education policy at the Board and within that issues of immigration status were identified as a shared concern of a basis of exclusion.

The goal in developing an equity statement was to go beyond that covered by the Ontario Human Rights code as a mechanism that informed Board policy and practice. In terms of access to schooling for undocumented migrants, it is telling that previous iterations of the TDSB had considered immigration status as an equity concern. However, it is unclear why this was not maintained in the TDSB's equity statement. Beyond the equity statement, the TDSB instituted an Equity Policy Advisory Committee that has no power beyond access to a few trustees and staff members. It was within this space that DADT was introduced to the Board and supported by two trustees. Overall, while it may be naïve to believe an equity statement and advisory board will be included every time a policy is presented to the Board, it is important to recognize that they are often employed to garner positive media coverage while, at least in the context of undocumented migrants, falling short of ensuring equitable access to schools.

Although there was a policy directive and a Board office that recognized immigration status as a barrier to accessing school, these directives did not stop the Board from shutting undocumented students out of school and demanding fees.[8] For example, Dena, a TDSB trustee stated,

> There's some feelings I think, that some people don't really have the right to it [schooling]...I wonder what would happen if you talked to some trustees even today about whether they think that the policy was, not necessary, but whether it was appropriate... You know, "They're not contributing to the system, they're a drain to the system, they're not at this point heading towards being citizens." ...Somebody with immigration status... people see that as being moving towards being responsible citizens. I think the question for some people are whether or not people without status, are they just here because it was easy, did they just do that because it was easy.

In this way, we can see that regardless of the presence of an equity statement that recognized immigration status as an equity concern, dominant discourse constructed undocumented communities as ineligible for a social good. Dena also signals to the criminalization of undocumented migrants, particularly the prominent trope regarding queue-jumping that does not recognize the ways migrants are legally removed from the possibility of formal governmental acceptance to migrate to Canada (Walia, 2013). The construction of "good" and "bad" migrants has social consequences that includes the removal from eligibility to a social good as well as deportability. This is enhanced when undocumented migration is linked to narratives of abuse, particularly as it relates to being a social "drain." In these ways, trustees resorting to this discourse facilitate the exclusion of students from schools, particularly within the context of a policy that lacks full implementation.

In addition to the internal policies of the TDSB, there are also provincial policies that have historically been ignored. Prior to the development of DADT, a group known as the Education Rights Taskforce (ERT) endeavored to change legal policy to ensure the availability of schooling for undocumented children. Specifically, their focus was Ontario's Education Act. The Education Rights Taskforce was established in 1999, primarily by members of the legal community. Drew, a member of the ERT described it as "as an umbrella group for other groups: legal aid clinics, parents, children and educators to advocate for kids whose parents have ambiguous immigration status." According to Drew, the group had a "very defined agenda." Relying on conceptualizations of membership based on legal rights, including international law, the group focused their efforts exclusively on children, and more specifically on undocumented children. However, at the ERT was most active, there was little policy recourse at the provincial level regarding the enrollment of undocumented students. As a result of this absence, the U.N. Convention on the Rights of the Child became a guiding document. Using the Convention, the ERT understood children as having full membership rights to attend school. These efforts led to the creation of Section 49.1 of the Education Act, which stipulated that undocumented students could not be barred from enrolling in schooling because of their immigration status.

Prior to the development of Section 49.1 of the Education Act, schools in Toronto were demanding study permits, according to Drew, a longtime member of the ERT,

> provincial boards were saying to kids "you have to get a federal permit, study permit in order to get into our schools." And of course, the federal study permits wouldn't be available. I mean the act has been changed since that, but that was always …what education boards insisted on, the study permit. And given that that would not be available for kids whose parents had no immigration status…[that] really was an effective bar to that. And, I recall specifically then the immigration minister, Eleanor Kaplan, came out and said, "you know study permits were never intended to be a bar to students from attending school."

Undocumented migrants were unable to receive a federal study permit because such an application would presumably go to Citizenship and Immigration Canada and place a family in a dangerous situation. Other impossible demands have also played a role in barring access for undocumented students to schools. For instance, Drew stated,

> at the time, sort of early on, a lot of work and maybe it's still the case but I think much less so is that schools would insist on certain documents like they would insist on proof that you were paying to the Catholic[9] or public boards or they would insist on proof of application to the immigration department. Or proof that you had a social insurance number.

Similar to the demand for a study permit, the demands to provide proof of an application to the immigration department or providing the school board with a social insurance number are both difficult and dangerous for undocumented migrants. Furthermore, given the high costs of paying international tuition within the school boards, it may also have been difficult for undocumented parents to afford that.

In addition to the structural level barriers imposed on undocumented migrants, individuals within the Board also deployed prominent rhetoric to keep undocumented migrants out of schools, as Drew stated,

> when kids went in to sort of meet the secretaries, or administrators or so on, once there was a letter from a lawyer or some other community member group, that always changed things. And I remember specifically going in with one particular child…and you know the answer they gave at the front is often the easy one, "you know you just have to go to the education department" or in that particular case they gave the parents a number to phone, "and so all you have to do is phone this number" and it was the number of the immigration department. So that sort of, you know the types of things kids were up against, either because people were, you know administrators can be lazy or because they don't want to deal with the issue or they don't understand.

It is clear that in many instances, beyond the limits placed by the school boards to keep undocumented students out of school, school actors were also party to their exclusion. Whether their actions are the result of apathy, ignorance, or xenophobia, the material consequences were the reification of the school site as an unachievable goal for an undocumented student. The role of the office administrator as a gatekeeper can then display the ways that single individuals can reinforce and deploy "illegalizing" procedures. Thus, we can see how beyond the structural ideologies of protecting the school site from students constructed as "illegitimate" recipients or non-members, individuals are also a part of this complex phenomenon of bordering sites away from the border and determining the basis of membership and as such the basis of access to a social good.

Given the continuous deployment of strategies to maintain the school site as a border zone, in the eyes of the ERT, what was needed was a change in the overarching legislation. Such a change would presumably require all boards within the province to include undocumented migrants in the schooling process. However, the process to change provincial policy was not simple. According to Drew, we lobbied the provincial ministry first for, you know for quite a long time, we lobbied them to number one deal with this issue, the fact that schools were still denying access to kids who had no status when the Act was clear that they could not do that...Then when Gerard Kennedy...became the minister, we continued to push because I recall specifically him standing with us outside of the legislature and saying, "this would take ten seconds to change." And of course when he got the job, it took a bit longer...but he ultimately came through...we got changes that we were happy with... [including] the memorandum sent to school boards making it clear to them that they had to allow kids...And what was specifically useful in... [was that] it said specifically you cannot be insisting on social insurance numbers or proof of payment of property tax or applications for immigration status [to enroll children].

The change in the Ontario Education Act was considered a victory on the part of migrant rights workers. ERT members had effectively challenged the legality of keeping undocumented students out of schools and won. However, while the development of Section 49.1 was imagined as demolishing a barrier, in practice it did little to erode it. Regardless of the change to the Act, school board practices did not change, and undocumented students were still systematically kept out of the schooling process. Furthermore, the Ministry of Education, while charged with ensuring the deployment of the Education Act, has to this date done little more than issue memorandums to school boards about the existence of Section 49.1 and the rights of undocumented migrants. In this way, given the lack of political will and the possibility of boards to maintain xenophobic practices, borders can be reconstituted through a lack of action. This remains the case even when bordering practices are challenged effectively through the law. In this instance, responsibility lies on the shoulders of the Ministry for not implementing the Act as well as on the school boards for willfully ignoring it. Therefore, while the challenging of hegemonic structures is a possibility, it is important to recognize the ways that border zones and bordering practices can be reconfigured and reconstituted to maintain a hegemonic understanding of membership and eligibility to receive a social good.

While the efforts outlined above worked to ensure access to schooling for individual undocumented students who had access to these social actors, overall, the efforts did little to change the structural deployment of the school as a border zone. The next phase of activists pushed to ensure access to schooling in Toronto would not come until 2006.

8.7 DEVELOPMENT OF THE DON'T ASK DON'T TELL COALITION AND THE DADT POLICY

The DADT Coalition was not initially involved in a campaign to ensure access to schooling. Prior to its work in schooling, the campaign had worked to develop a DADT policy at the Toronto Police Services Board[10] and another for services delivered by the city of Toronto[11] (neither schooling nor policing fall solely within municipal jurisdiction). At the time, the counternarrative (DADT) had received moderate support within community agencies but a high degree of reluctance by the targeted institutions.

One incident was believed by most participants to be the primary catalyst to the DADT Coalition. The case of Kimberly and Gerald Lizano-Sossa was not the first time that students faced deportation in the city of Toronto, but according to participants, it was the first time people heard of immigration enforcement entering the school site to apprehend students. This case served as a platform for members of the coalition to mobilize a counternarrative that visibilized undocumented migrants' presence, contributions, and needs in a way that did not criminalize or dehumanize (Villegas, 2017).

The detainment of the Lizano-Sossa was an unexpected occurrence. As Gloria, a member of No One is Illegal and the DADT Coalition recounted,

> I was working with no one is illegal in 2006 when Kimberly and Gerald Lizano-Sossa, two students, originally from Costa Rica were arrested in their high school...and we were contacted by a student who...asked that we come to their school to meet with teachers and students to talk about it...during the meeting at the school, students and teachers, the chaplain, wanted to mobilize and have a rally outside of the detention center...we supported the students, their role in organizing the rally was very much to mobilize their school so they got on the phone they called their friends they made sure teachers came out to it, they made signs and banners. We mobilized trade unions teacher unions, other community groups, got the word out within left organizations and community organizations in the city and at the demonstration every news outlet in

the city was covering it from radio to print to tv and a lot of attention was brought to the case.

The detention of Kimberly and Gerald brought a large amount of media exposure as it betrayed a number of liberal ideals including beliefs about the innocence of children and the safety of the school site. Given the public outcry No One Is Illegal—Toronto saw an opportunity to develop a campaign that would facilitate delivering their messaging. Mobilization in this instance included attempting to stay the deportation order for the Lizano-Sossa family through large rallies outside the detention center and during May Day. It also included the development of the DADT policy that would increase access to schooling for undocumented migrants bar immigration officials from entering schools. The need for the latter was highlighted when yet another student was arrested by immigration officials in school, according to Gloria,

> We were contacted by I believe it was OCASI[12] and they informed us that they got a phone call reporting that two more students had been picked up, two sisters, in another school and both the schools were...part of the Catholic School Board. So, we publicized that that happened though we didn't have contact with that family.

Given the working relationship between the DADT Coalition and the Lizano-Sossa family as well as the lack of contact with the second family detained in a school, Kimberly, and Gerald became the poster children for the campaign.

It must be said that there was a high degree of strategy employed in the decisions made by the organization. Because of capacity, No One Is Illegal, and during this time the DADT Coalition, only became involved in casework that was believed to have significant possibilities to change larger structures. Thus, their involvement with the Lizano-Sossa was believed to contain the possibility of achieving numerous effects including stopping a new way of apprehending undocumented migrants[13] and making schools safe from immigration enforcement. The latter would apply to not just for children but also for adults who may be attempting to enroll their children, waiting to pick them up, or enrolled in school themselves. Also, having media outlets available for this case and the subsequent battle within the TDSB provided a large platform.

In the case of the Lizano-Sossa, the organizing efforts of the coalition yielded some results. According to Gloria,

> At the second rally, Kimberly and Gerald were released from detention but the mother and the rest of the family were still inside, the father was at large. Kimberly, who was 15...said to the media...that she was kind of horrified to see that there was a detention center [and] that it was full of other people, families, kids, that what happened to her and her brother wasn't fair and it shouldn't happen to other people, and Kimberly, Gerald, the mom, the whole family they really wanted to take this issue to the school board. And at that point we made a strategic decision even though the arrests happened at a Catholic school we decided that it would make more sense to go to the Toronto District School Board because it is the largest in the country.

While the Lizano-Sossa children were released from the detention center, the adults in the family as well as their baby sibling remained in custody. In addition to the release of the Lizano-Sossa children, the campaign also resulted in structural change. As recounted by Gloria,

> shortly after those rallies, the Canada border services agency issued a statement saying that they would not enter schools to do immigration enforcement and we believe that is because they were shamed in a very public way and so many organizations spoke out against it.

While this may have appeased some individuals, who saw children as innocent and adults as responsible for their undocumented status and legitimate recipients to the violence of detention and deportation, the DADT Coalition employed this small victory to further mobilize the community. The fact that Kimberly's first words out of detention were to express the deplorable and inhuman conditions of immigration detention served to galvanize the coalition and mobilize a humanizing counter-narrative. Sadly, the plea to stay the family's deportation was denied and on Canada Day in 2006 they were deported to Costa Rica.

The case of the Lizano-Sossa serves to display the development of an activist campaign, and highlights how schooling institutions have served as bordering spaces that attempt to exclude the undocumented through policies that exclude them and can facilitate their removal. Thus, while the school site (in this instance in Toronto) was positioned far from the physical border, making students available to immigration enforcement highlights the constant precarity of undocumented students and the ways borders, as sites of exclusion and expulsion, can be reconstituted throughout the country. The case also displays the limits of liberal discourse. While community members worked tirelessly to stop the deportation of these students by proclaiming their "innocence" as children and exalting their qualities as model students, these attempts proved insufficient to sway politicians and the family was forcibly removed.

The DADT policy was passed with an implementation plan in 2007. While the policy was considered a great victory by organizers, it is important to recognize that the people who spurred this campaign were forcefully removed from their communities. Furthermore, the passing of a policy was only the beginning of an arduous process to ensure entry to the TDSB and bordering practices, while at first believed demolished by the passing of the policy were reconstructed by a lack of implementation and the development of new mechanisms that illegalize undocumented migrants (Villegas, 2017).

8.8 Conclusion

In this chapter, I have argued that a lack of institutional history of resistance serves to invisibilize undocumented migrants. A legacy of activism that dates back to the 1960s displays that undocumented migrants and their allies have not been passive in their demands for access to schooling. The invisibilization of this history then serves to make the current iteration of active resistance (through the passing of the DADT policy) as a new phenomenon. It also invisibilizes the degree to which racialized undocumented migrants have perceived schooling to be vital to their children. In this way, the fight for recognition has been present in Toronto for over fifty years. As Rudy Acuña (1998, 2000) reminds us, erasure from history serves not only to portray the dominant as active it also serves to erase collective memories of the presence and struggles of the oppressed.

It is evident that at least since the late 1960s school boards developed mechanisms to keep undocumented migrants out schools. The construction of border zones effectively determined that undocumented students are outside the parameters of membership as designated by the hegemonic perspective that all legitimate recipients of schooling must have one of the documents outlined above. Overall, one can see consistent exclusions of undocumented migrants from the school site, often by employing demands for documentation that is often taken for granted as readily available to all individuals who deserve to receive a social good.

In addition to the Board failing to recognize that the struggle for undocumented migrants to access schooling has been ongoing, there is also a failure in the ways policies are drafted and implemented. Through interventions at different school boards as well as the Ministry, the limited modes of implementation have done little to alleviate the problems on the ground. That 50 years of activism have been devoted to this work displays that the structures in charge have found a myriad of ways to sidestep the efforts of the community. It also highlights the devaluing of undocumented migrants as members of the communities that these structures are meant to serve.

Finally, in this chapter I have detailed the ways that the most current period of activism regarding access to schooling to schooling for undocumented migrants has been deployed. The development of a campaign that is not based on criminalizing or dehumanizing discourse and centers the material consequences on the most affected has shown promise in developing a productive counternarrative.

Notes

1. See Wright (2013), for a more detailed account of Canada's anti-immigrant history.
2. The city's motto is "diversity, our strength."
3. The Toronto Catholic District School Board is separate board that is also publicly funded school board.
4. I place this in quotes to recognize that people have agency in this process and can at times circumnavigate the processes of verification.
5. "Negotiating Access to Public Goods: Education and Health Care for Toronto Immigrants with Precarious Status," funded by CERIS—The Ontario Metropolis Center 2009–2010, Patricia Landolt Principal Investigator.
6. Patricia Landolt and Luin Goldring, Principal Investigators.
7. A pre-amalgamation Board, mainly located in the downtown area of the city.
8. The TDSB equity statement included immigration status as a mode of oppression and was meant to act as a benchmark under which all policies and procedures were addressed and the department of Student and Community Equity is charged with leading the Board in equity issues.
9. The Catholic boards in Ontario are also publicly funded.

10. This work continued for several years and ended in disappointing fashion with the development of a weak "Don't Ask" except for "bonafide" reasons policy and a the maintenance of ties with immigration enforcement (Hanes, 2008).
11. This policy approved in February 21, 2013, made Toronto the first "sanctuary" city in Canada (Keung, 2013).
12. Ontario Council of Agencies Serving Immigrants.
13. The Lizano-Sossa was also used as bait to detain their father.

References

Acuña, R. F. (1998). *Sometimes There Is No Other Side: Chicanos and the Myth of Equality*. Notre Dame, IN: Notre Dame Press.

Acuña, R. F. (2000). *Occupied America: A History of Chicanos* (4th ed.). New York, NY: Longman.

Basu, R. (2004). The Rationalization of Neoliberalism in Ontario's Public Education System, 1995–2000. *Geoforum, 35*(5), 621–634.

Bejan, R., & Sidhu, N. (2010). *Policy Without Practice: Barriers to Enrollment for Non-status Immigrant Students in Toronto's Catholic Schools*. Toronto: Social Planning Toronto.

Bhuyan, R. (2012). Negotiating Citizenship on the Frontlines: How the Devolution of Canadian Immigration Policy Shapes Service Delivery to Women Fleeing Abuse. *Law & Policy, 34*(2), 211–236.

Bhuyan, R. (2013). Negotiating Social Rights and Membership on the Frontlines: the Case of Violence Against Women Services. In L. Goldring & P. Landolt (Eds.), *Producing and Negotiating Non-citizenship: Precarious Legal Status in Canada* (pp. 238–257). Toronto, ON: University of Toronto Press.

Croucher, S. (1997). Constructing the Image of Ethnic Harmony in Toronto, Canada: the Politics of Problem Definition and Nondefinition. *Urban Affairs Review, 32*(3), 319–347.

Dechaine, R. D. (2012). Introduction: For Rhetorical Border Studies. In R. Dechaine (Ed.), *Border Rhetorics: Citizenship and Identity on the US-Mexico Frontier* (pp. 1–18). Tuscaloosa, AL: University of Alabama.

De Genova, N. (2005). *Working the Boundaries: Race, Space, and "Illegality" in Mexican Chicago*. Durham, NC: Duke University Press.

Fortier, C. (2013). No One Is Illegal Movements in Canada and the Negotiation of Counter-National and Anti-colonial Struggles from Within the Nation-State. In L. Goldring & P. Landolt (Eds.), *Producing and Negotiating Non-citizenship: Precarious Legal Status in Canada* (pp. 274–290). Toronto, ON: University of Toronto Press.

Goldring, L., & Landolt, P. (2013). The Conditionality of Legal Status and Rights: Conceptualizing Precarious Non-citizenship in Canada.

In L. Goldring & P. Landolt (Eds.), *Producing and Negotiating Non-citizenship: Precarious Legal Status in Canada* (pp. 3–27). Toronto, ON: University of Toronto Press.

Hanes, A. (2008, November 21). Immigration Policy Gets Cut by Police Chief: 'Don't Tell'; Officers Can't Turn Blind Eye to Suspected Violations. *National Post*.

Johnson, J. R. (2012). Bordering as Social Practice: Intersectional Identifications and Coalitional Possibilities. In R. Dechaine (Ed.), *Border Rhetorics: Citizenship and Identity on the US-Mexico Frontier* (pp. 33–47). Tuscaloosa, AL: University of Alabama.

Keung, N. (2013, February 22). City Declared a 'Sanctuary'. *Toronto Star*.

Li, P. (2001). The Racial Subtext in Canada's Immigration Discourse. *Journal of International Migration and Integration, 2*(1), 77–97.

Li, P. (2003). Deconstructing Canada's Discourse of Immigrant Integration. *Journal of International Migration and Integration, 4*(3), 315–333.

Macklin, A. (2005). Disappearing Refugees: Reflections on the Canada-US Safe Third Country Agreement. *Columbia Human Rights Law Review, 36,* 365–426.

Magalhaes, L., Carrasco, C., & Gastaldo, D. (2009). Undocumented Migrants in Canada: A Scope Literature Review on Health, Access to Services, and Working Conditions. *Journal of Immigrant Minority Health, 12,* 132–151.

McDonald, J. (2009). Migrant Illegality, Nation-Building, and the Politics of Regularization in Canada. *Refuge, 26*(2), 65–77.

Ono, K. A. (2012). Borders That Travel: Matters of the Figural Border. In R. Dechaine (Ed.), *Border Rhetorics: Citizenship and Identity on the US-Mexico Border* (pp. 19–32). Tuscaloosa, AL: University of Alabama.

Ono, K. A., & Sloop, J. M. (2002). *Shifting Borders: Rhetoric, Immigration, and California's Proposition 187*. Philadelphia, PA: Temple University Press.

Pratt, A., & Valverde, M. (2002). From Deserving Victims to 'Masters of Confusion': Redefining Refugees in the 1990s. *The Canadian Journal of Sociology, 27*(2), 135–161.

Romero, M. (1999). Immigration, the Servant Problem, and the Legacy of the Domestic Labor Debate: "Where Can You Find Good Help These Days!". *University of Miami Law Review, 53*(4), 1045–1064.

Sidhu, N. (2008). *The Right to Learn: Access to Public Education for Non-status Immigrants*. Toronto: The Community Social Planning Council of Toronto.

Thobani, S. (2000). Closing Ranks: Racism and Sexism in Canada's Immigration Policy. *Race & Class, 42*(1), 35–55.

Thobani, S. (2007). *Exalted Subjects: Studies in the Making of Race and Nation in Canada*. Toronto, ON: University of Toronto Press.

Toronto District School Board. (2014). *Toronto District School Board Capital Facts: Building Strong and Vibrant School Communities* (p. 13). Toronto: Toronto District School Board.

Villegas, F. J. (2013). Getting to "Don't Ask Don't Tell" at the Toronto District School Board: Mapping the Competing Discourses of Rights and Membership. In L. Goldring & P. Landolt (Eds.), *Producing and Negotiating Non-citizenship: Precarious Legal Status in Canada* (pp. 258–273). Toronto, ON: University of Toronto Press.

Villegas, F. J. (2014). *The Politics of 'Access': Undocumented Students and Enrollment in Toronto Schools.* Unpublished Doctoral Thesis, Ontario Institute for Studies in Education of the University of Toronto.

Villegas, F. J. (2017). Access Without Fear!: Reconceptualizing "Access" to Schooling for Undocumented Students in Toronto. *Critical Sociology, 43*(7–8), 1179–1195.

Villegas, P. E. (2013). Negotiating the Boundaries of Membership: Health Care Providers, Access to Social Goods and Immigration Status. In L. Goldring & P. Landolt (Eds.), *Producing and Negotiating Non-citizenship: Precarious Legal Status in Canada* (pp. 221–237). Toronto, ON: University of Toronto Press.

Walia, H. (2013). *Undoing Border Imperialism*. Oakland, CA: AK Press.

Wright, C. (2013). The Museum of Illegal Immigration: Historical Perspective on the Production of Non-citizens and Challenges to Immigration Controls. In L. Goldring & P. Landolt (Eds.), *Producing and Negotiating Non-Citizenship: Precarious and Legal Status in Canada* (pp. 31–54). Toronto, ON: University of Toronto Press.

CHAPTER 9

Be a Good Citizen or Else! Neoliberal Citizenship and the Grade Six 2013 Revised Ontario Social Studies Curriculum

Ardavan Eizadirad

9.1　Locating the Self

Being born in Iran, my schooling experiences differed drastically compared to Toronto, Canada transitioning from an authoritarian teacher-centred learning environment to a more democratic student-centred atmosphere. As a male, Middle Eastern immigrant from a working-class background, I struggled mastering the English language upon arrival to Canada. I became involved with many extra-curricular activities at school and within my community. My interest in the area of citizenship and social justice was sparked based on attending three different secondary schools within four years each located in different socio-geographical areas in Toronto. It became evident to me that there were profound elements of racism and stratification that were embedded and intrinsic in various aspects of the school board and that each school had its own unique power relations that impacted its everyday functioning.

A. Eizadirad (✉)
Ontario Institute for Studies in Education,
University of Toronto, Toronto, ON, Canada
e-mail: ardavan.eizadirad@mail.utoronto.ca

Two major incidents in my life gravitated me towards questioning major ideas around citizenship and what it means to be a "good" citizen. Both of these interactions involved encounters with violence impacting me directly and indirectly. When I was in high school, I lost one of my friends to gun violence where he was killed by a stray bullet at a party. The news of his death sparked a lot of anger within me. The incident made me begin questioning ideas around citizenship; rights and responsibilities of individuals to themselves, their families and communities, and the larger nation. Another major incident which impacted me severely was the imprisonment of my best friend for committing a series of crimes. These events inspired and guided me to become a teacher and pursue graduate studies. These experiences remain with me and impact my pedagogy. I often engage students and young adults, many who are racialized and living in high-priority neighbourhoods, in conversations about what it means to be a good person in their immediate lives and in larger context of their neighbourhoods.

9.2　Neoliberalism and Citizenship

Under the current North American economic system and its neoliberal market-driven ideologies of citizenship and individualistic notions of personal responsibility, many of today's young children from an early age are socialized to equate citizenship exclusively with voting and being complicit and passive. Within this paradigm, citizenship is framed as accepting established systems of authority and hierarchical power relations without questioning institutional practices or laws, even if the outcome of such practices and laws results in injustice and inequity. Thus, it is critical to question how have we arrived at a narrowing of the problematic so that it is solely individualistic and often economic determinist where profit has more currency than justice and equity?

From kindergarten, the explicit and hidden curriculum and routine nature of schooling diminishes the capacity of students to be curious and ask critical questions; instead moulding them through a rewards and punishment system that equates being "good" to following instructions and not deviating from the "norm" imposed by dominant culture. Dominant hegemonic culture positions systemic and institutional structures such as schools to function in "neutrality" while proclaiming equal service is provided to all members of society (Apple, 2004; Au, 2013; Giroux, 2003). Schools serve as an Ideological State Apparatus that promotes dominant ideology (Althusser, 2006) while masquerading as equitable. Yet, how can equality of outcomes be achieved when everyone does not have the same starting point or access to opportunities?

Under a market-driven capitalist economy, neoliberal ideologies place blame on individuals (Giroux, 2003; Pinto, 2015; Portelli & Sharma, 2014) and their decisions as the direct cause of their lived circumstances, contributing to a disregard for the salience of race in defining social order in society. As Giroux (2003) argues,

> Within this market-driven perspective, the exchange of capital takes precedence over social justice, the making of socially responsible citizens, and the building of democratic communities. There is no language here for recognizing antidemocratic forms of power, developing nonmarket values, or fighting against substantive injustices in a society founded on deep inequalities, particularly those based on race and class. (196)

When institutions prioritize market needs, internal decisions are often guided by monetary values, leading to perpetuation of various forms of oppression predominantly impacting racialized identities. This leads to dehumanizing practices where human and collective needs of local communities are overlooked for savings and profits. Driven by hierarchical power relations, "colourblind" politics of neoliberalism promote neutrality, which perpetuates the hegemonic status quo and its inequities in pursuit of the market logic while hiding and masking institutional racism (Bailey, Chapter 3; Madan, Chapter 4). Race is "marked as a private manner" signifying a denial that "race is responsible for alleged injustices that reproduce group inequalities, privilege Whites, and negatively impacts on economic mobility, the possession of social resources, and the acquisition of political power" (Giroux, 2003, p. 198). Such neoliberal ideologies permeate social, political, and cultural spheres perpetuating a socially stratified and hierarchical society privileging Whiteness at the expense of suffering and marginalization to others (Apple, 2004; Au, 2013). Pinto (2015) defines neoliberalism by stating,

> Neoliberalism is the dominant political and ideological paradigm of our time, embodied by policies and processes that place political control in a handful of private interests. Its defining characteristics include a shift of shared concern for the common good between the state and citizens to a relationship based on economics whereby citizen roles are limited to "taxpayers" in the social order, and a predominant consensual discourse

whereby contestation and dissent are compromised. Resulting social policies reflect managerialism, privatisation and a preponderance of punitive accountability mechanisms. (p. 142)

Within a neoliberal system, certain social groups, such as the poor and immigrants, become expendable and dispensable for profits, yet ironically, the same groups are blamed for causing many social problems such as crime and violence plaguing communities today. Why are the root causes of social problems plaguing society not attributed to ineffective functioning of systems and institutions which reproduce inequity of access to power, resources, and opportunities? As Giroux (2003) explains,

> Color-blindness is a convenient ideology for enabling Whites to ignore the degree to which race is tangled up with asymmetrical relations of power, functioning as a potent force for patterns of exclusion and discrimination, including, but not limited to, housing, mortgage loans, health care, schools, and the criminal justice system. (p. 199)

The presence of "color-blindness" also robs the ability to proclaim citizenship by those who are scapegoated as responsible for societal social ills.

Being a "good" citizen is a complex notion that requires a framework that prioritizes justice and equity relative to the sociocultural context of the situation and space. Reflexive thinking and development of a social consciousness for elementary students can be facilitated through teaching Social Studies as they transition from elementary to high school, and consequently lead to blossoming of new understandings of what it means to be a global citizen (Bourdieu, 1999; Freire, 1970). As humans, we have the capacity and potential to become informed, inspired, and motivated to break free from socioculturally constructed boundaries and psychological shackles that try to indoctrinate our minds through social institutions such as the education system. This emancipatory process begins by engaging in critical thinking and asking questions from multiple vantage points (Brady & Abawi, Chapter 6). As Mosley (2000) states, "If you can't question the world around you, seeking real answers, then you are trapped by the false answers provided by prejudice" (p. 69).

9.3 Citizenship in the 2013 Revised Ontario Social Studies Curriculum

Prior to 2013, the latest Social Studies curriculum revisions by Ontario Ministry of Education occurred in 2004. This chapter critically analyses the Grade 6 2013 revised Ontario Social Studies curriculum and explores how citizenship is defined and taught; seeking to understand citizenship at the micro-level relative to students' identities and their local communities, as well as at the macro-level relative to their responsibilities to the nation as global citizens. The analysis is guided by two central questions: (1) how citizenship is defined theoretically, ideologically, and conceptually and (2) how citizenship is suggested to be taught pedagogically. Grade 6 is the focus of the analysis because in Ontario, Social Studies is taught as a subject from Grades 1 to 6. Additionally, all students in Grade 6 attending publicly funded schools write the provincial standardized test administered by the Education Quality and Accountability Office (EQAO) which assesses student achievement levels in literacy and numeracy at the end of their primary education relative to established provincial standards (Basu, 2004; EQAO, 2013).

9.4 What Is Citizenship?

In Ontario, Social Studies as a subject is taught from Grades 1 to 6, History and Geography in Grade 7 and 8, and Canadian and World Studies from Grades 9 to 12. The 2013 revised Ontario *Social Studies, History, and Geography* curricula are produced by Ministry of Education as a 212-page document which outlines Grades 1–6 Social Studies and Grade 7 and 8 History and Geography curriculum content and expectations. In comparison, the 2004 edition of the document was only 84 pages. One of the new aspects of the revised document is the realignment of elementary and secondary curriculum through a common vision and unified goals. The unified vision states:

> The social studies, history, geography, and Canadian and world studies programs will enable students to become responsible, active citizens within the diverse communities to which they belong. As well as becoming critically thoughtful and informed citizens who value an inclusive society, students will have the skills they need to solve problems and communicate ideas and decisions about significant developments, events, and issues. (Ontario Ministry of Education, 2013, p. 6)

Within the vision statement, the word citizen is directly associated with words such as "responsible", "active", "critically thoughtful", and "informed". These words situate citizenship as an individualistic concept, thereby promoting the neoliberal ideology of the subject as being responsible for their lived realities and progressing linearly through education to become a "critically thoughtful" and "informed" citizen in order to be a valuable and "active" member of the "communities to which they belong". The language describes and situates citizenship within a limited linear scope that excludes concepts such as collective and shared responsibility and activism as a means of opposing and resisting injustice and inequity. Although it mentions that the goal of the curriculum is to equip students to "solve problems" it is unclear for what purposes or for whose benefits. Does the curriculum promote a stance where problems are solved as a means of maintaining the hegemonic racial and social order and the status quo or as a means of critically altering the racial and social order through social activism guided by justice and equity as its priorities? Giroux (2003) in problematizing the nature of such neoliberal language expresses,

> Lost here is any critical engagement with state power and how it imposes immigration policies, decides who gets resources and access to a quality education, defines what constitutes a crime, how people are punished, how and whether social problems are criminalized, who is worthy of citizenship, and who is responsible for addressing racial injustices. (p. 207)

Westheimer and Kahne's (2004) conceptual framework of different types of citizenship provides an effective lens to examine the type of citizenship promoted in the 2013 revised Ontario Social Studies curriculum. Their research was guided by the question, "What kind of citizen do we need to support an effective democratic society?" (p. 239). Examination of ten programs "aimed to advance the democratic purposes of education" (p. 239) included looking at their visions, values, goals, and practices and led the authors to operationalize three kinds of citizenship, each with its unique ideologies of what it means to be a "good" citizen. The three conceptions of citizenship are defined as the *personally responsible citizen*, the *participatory citizen*, and the *justice-oriented citizen*. According to Westheimer and Kahne (2004), programs that reinforce *personally responsible citizenship* emphasize the importance of character education and personal characteristics such as "honesty, integrity, self-discipline, and hard work" (p. 241). Personally responsible citizenship equates being a "good" citizen as someone who works, pays taxes, obeys laws, recycles, gives blood, and/or volunteers to assist others in times of crisis as a means of demonstrating their responsibility to others and to the environment. *Participatory citizenship* frames the "good" citizen as someone who is constantly active and involved with "civic affair and the social life of the community at the local, state, or national level" (p. 241). Within this paradigm, leadership in the form of organizing events within established systems and structures plays a pivotal role in demonstrating civic engagement. *Justice-oriented citizenship* is characterized as someone who speaks up and acts against what he/she perceives as unjust. The justice-oriented citizen seeks the root causes of problems; synthesizing multiple perspectives and constructively questioning established systems of racial and social order and the role social structures play in creating or perpetuating oppressive policies and practices. Within the justice-oriented conception of citizenship, systemic change might be needed in order to solve a social issue from a grass-roots level. These constructed conceptions of citizenship are not mutually exclusive and can at times overlap in their approaches and practices.

The language of the unified vision statement of the 2013 revised Ontario Social Studies curriculum reinforces predominantly Westheimer and Kahne's (2004) *personally responsible* and *participatory* conceptions of citizenship. By emphasizing the importance of becoming "responsible, active citizens within the diverse communities in which they belong" and becoming "critically thoughtful and informed citizens who value an inclusive society" (Ontario Ministry of Education, 2013, p. 6), the vision statement makes the presumption that Canadian society is equitably diverse and inclusive and that all social groups have an equal voice in the public sphere. The language further reinforces the ideology that it is through the "responsible, active citizen" that an inclusive and diverse society is produced and maintained. Yet, what is not said is just as important. By not mentioning the role of institutions and their systemic policies and practices in creating (in)accessibility to opportunities to succeed, the assumption is made that institutions and systemic structures operate consistently in sync to promote a "diverse" and "inclusive" society, when this is not the lived reality for many social groups within Canadian society particularly for racialized citizens (Apple, 2004; Benn-John, Chapter 4; Block & Galabuzi, 2011). The language of the vision statement does not promote development of a *justice-oriented* citizen, who might question, in solidarity and allyship with others, the established systems of power and their practices.

Along with a unified vision statement, the 2013 revised Ontario Social Studies curriculum outlines five specific goals for the Social Studies curriculum that students will work towards thematically from Grades 1 to 6. The five goals are:

Developing an understanding of responsible citizenship;
Developing an understanding of the diversity within local, national, and global communities, both past and present;
Developing an understanding of interrelationships within and between the natural environment and human communities;
Developing the knowledge, understanding, and skills that lay the foundation for future studies in geography, history, economics, law, and politics; and
Developing the personal attributes that foster curiosity and the skills that enable them to investigate developments, events, and issues. (Ontario Ministry of Education, 2013, p. 7)

Within the goals section, the word "citizenship" is explicitly mentioned and coupled with "responsibility" whereas such statement did not exist in the 2004 curriculum document. In relation to Westheimer and Kahne's (2004) conceptual citizenship frameworks, the language describing the curriculum goals promotes the *personally responsible* and *participatory citizen* with references to "developing an understanding", "knowledge", "skills", and "personal attributes" (p. 7). Although majority of the goals focus on "developing an understanding", what is missing from the discussion in relation to citizenship is exploring what students should do and in what ways with their heightened level of "understanding", such as how to collectively oppose and resist injustices they recognize at the local, provincial, national, and/or global level.

9.5 Citizenship Expectations and Conceptualization in the 2013 Social Studies Curriculum

In order to evaluate the extent which conceptualization of citizenship is further implemented, the focus will shift to specifically examine the Grade 6 Social Studies curriculum content as mandated by Ministry of Education through naming of overall and specific expectations within the document. The expectations for Social Studies in the 2013 revised

Social Studies curriculum from Grades 1 to 6 are organized thematically under two strands; *Heritage and Identity* and *People and Environments* (Ontario Ministry of Education, 2013, p. 21).

In Grade 6, for *Heritage and Identity*, students learn about "Communities in Canada, Past and Present" and for *People and Environments*, students learn about "Canada's Interactions with the Global Community" (Ontario Ministry of Education, 2013, p. 21). In assisting teachers to understand the holistic notion of the overall and specific expectations outlined, an overview for the Grade 6 curriculum is provided which states,

> Students will explore the experiences and perspectives of diverse communities in historical and contemporary Canada and examine how they have contributed to the development of Canadian identity. In addition to developing their understanding of different communities in Canada, students will explore the global economy and Canada's role in it. They will investigate current social, political, economic, and environmental issues, and develop the understanding of the importance of international action and cooperation. (Ontario Ministry of Education, 2013, p. 117)

Although students through exploration of multiple perspectives learn about "experiences and perspective of diverse communities" and their influence in the "development of Canadian identity" what is omitted are discussions about how Europeans had systemic status and state-sponsored power to influence institutional policies and practices to promote their own self-interests. By dominating the public and social sphere of politics, Europeans had the power to inscribe their own identity, values, and way of life onto others through institutions such as the Church and the education system (Grosfoguel, 2011). The power of white settlers to implement change in society led to perpetuation of injustices such as; the development of the reserve system and residential schools for the First Nations; creation of the Chinese head tax as a discriminatory immigration policy; and forced displacement and seizing of property of Japanese Canadians during the Second World War. These injustices perpetuated through the white settler hegemony are also present today and can be seen in the missing and murdered Indigenous women across the country; devaluation of Black lives in encounters with the state and police; and the rise of white supremacist and xenophobic groups.

Nancy Fraser (2004) argues for "reconceptualizing recognition in terms of status" (p. 376). She emphasizes learning about power through the lens of status in society relative to the extent a social group can participate equally in social interactions. Fraser (2004) explains "what is really important is not the demand for recognition of a group's specific identity, but the demand for recognition of people's standing as full partners in social interaction" (p. 377). This is important because validating a group's identity, and their contribution to Canadian identity does not indicate a change in their status and their representation within political, economic, and sociocultural public spheres. Fraser's (2004) status model aligns with Westheimer and Kahne's conception of the *justice-oriented citizenship*, where injustice is located in "institutionalized hierarchies of cultural value that prevent some members of society from participating as peers in social interaction" (p. 377). Therefore, although students in Grade 6 learn about struggles of various social groups that contributed to the development of a Canadian identity, they are not guided to critically analyse the interconnectedness between the current unequal status of various social groups in Canadian society and their lack of representation and power in public spheres relative to access to opportunities and outcomes.

By avoiding discussions and dialogue about how Canada creates and maintains systemic oppression, it creates a utopian mirage which leads to invisibilization of inequity. Inequities in society continue today and have real-life implications for specific social groups and identities such as racialized workers. Block and Galabuzi (2011) emphasize that "racialized Canadians earn only 81.4 cents for every dollar paid to non-racialized Canadians" (p. 3). Contextualizing the data, the authors point out that "racialized Canadians have slightly higher levels of labour market participation, yet they continue to experience higher levels of unemployment and earn less income than non-racialized Canadians" (p. 3). Furthermore, they argue that

> if the labour market continues to relegate workers from racialized groups to the back of the pack, the number of Canadians left behind will only accelerate- calling into question the promise that Canada is a fair and caring society committed to equal opportunities, no matter who you are and where you come from. (p. 4)

The aforementioned statistics demonstrate that racism continues to plague the Canadian labour market and its institutional practices where racialized workers are treated as sub-citizens by being paid less compared to non-racialized workers often with fewer or no benefits. This leads to racialization of poverty where inequality of access to opportunities leads to racialized workers continuing to struggle as a means to survive and provide for their families. A curriculum focused on the merits of the nation does not provide students the necessary tools to comprehend and address the systemic inequities present in Canadian society and the ways power is differentially allocated across social groups.

9.6 Citizenship and National and Global Narratives

As stated earlier, the expectations for Social Studies in the 2013 revised Social Studies curriculum from Grades 1 to 6 are organized under two strands thematically; *Heritage and Identity* and *People and Environments*. As part of *People and Environments: Canada's Interactions with the Global Community* strand, students learn about the "global economy and Canada's role in it" with an emphasis on the "importance of international action and cooperation" (p. 117). Canada is portrayed as a country which often plays a peace-keeping role in various regions around the world. Consequently, by only teaching about selective, positive influences of Canada in the global world, it dismisses and silences inquiries and discussions about national interests and how at times Canada's decision-making has led to perpetuation and reinforcement of violence internationally such as in Somalia, Rwanda, Iraq, and Afghanistan. Framing Canada exclusively in a positive light facilitates the sociocultural construction of Canada as "the helper". This is evident in schools where "fundraising for international charities is often equated with global education, while other aspects of global learning are neglected" (Mundy & Manion, 2008, p. 941).

There are other implications that arise from teaching national Canadian identity in the global context as synonymous with actions of peace-keeping, cooperation, and various forms of help and assistance to less developed nations. For one, this form of representation and metanarrative contributes to creating a "them/us" dichotomous mentality where "violence directed against bodies of colour becomes normalized as a necessary part of the civilizing process" (Razack, 2004, p. 8). These binaries occur linguistically across many levels such as the North and South or developed and developing nations. As a result of reinforcing the ideological image of Canada as "the helper", social issues are simplified and depoliticized taking away from teaching through a critical lens that illustrates complexities in decision-making at the international level where power, status, voice, and representation are unequally distributed leading to tensions and friendships among nations and their leaders. The North often secures a lavish comfortable lifestyle at the expense of exploitation of natural and human resources in the South. Exploitation masks itself behind labels such as "international assistance" and "peace-keeping" yet only one side of the story is often told through dominant media outlets and their mainstream discourses. As Razack (2004) points out in *Dark Threats & White Knights: The Somali Affair, Peace Keeping, and the New Imperialism*,

> As it was in Somalia in 1991, colour-line thinking was certainly in evidence in the American invasions *[with the Canadian army support]* of both Afghanistan in 2002 and Iraq in 2003; invasions justified on the ground that it was necessary to drop thousands of bombs on Afghanis and Iraqis in order to save them from the excesses of their own society. (pp. 7–8)

Razack (2004) deconstructs ideologies about "help" and "assistance" and connects it with notions of power and nation-building pointing out, "Oil, the free market, and the historical support the United States has given to the Taliban and Saddam Hussein, among other despotic regimes, all disappear under 'smart bombs' once the smoke clears and peacekeepers walk in" (p. 8). Similarly, Grosfoguel (2011) emphasizes, "The idea of race organizes the world's population into a hierarchical order of superior and inferior people that becomes an organizing principle of the international division of labour" (p. 10). Hence, through hegemonic metanarratives in education and the media, violence is justified to "assist" the uncivilized in importing capitalism and democracy as a means of transitioning from a "developing" nation to a "developed" nation. National self-interests are at the heart of international assistance to other countries, yet the narrative of the dominant hegemonic discourse, including the Canadian Social Studies curriculum, often depicts a simplistic depoliticized story emphasizing heroism and selflessness of the Canadian nation to assist others without strings attached.

The reinforcement of the *responsible* and *participatory citizen* through dominant ideologies presented in the 2013 revised Social Studies curriculum teaches students monolithically to view Canada as doing a heroic service by helping others experiencing crisis in other parts of the world. On the other hand, the *justice-oriented citizen* would critically question and examine Canada's political, social, economic, and capitalistic agenda particularly whether the assistance they provide in its various forms leads to further exploitation of that country. The *justice-oriented citizen* would raise questions about whether or not the "help" comes with strings attached and who benefits more from this process in long term. As Andreotti (2006) points out, "in order to understand global issues, a complex web of cultural and material local/global processes and contexts need to be examined and unpacked" (p. 41).

How citizenship is defined in the curriculum, in the local and global context, has implications for how learners view the world including the nature and understanding of problems and the extent to which they can make a difference at the macro- and micro-level. Kennelly and Llewellyn (2011) examined keywords associated with terms such as citizenship and democracy within Civics curriculum documents in provinces of Ontario, Alberta, and British Columbia. They concluded that "the formation of the 'active' citizen as a fundamentally neoliberal project" (p. 903). They found that "the constant reiteration of active citizenship as a responsibility and not a right (in and of itself) affirms passive messages about the 'good (young) citizen'" (907). The emphasis on individualistic responsibility, which aligns with Westheimer and Kahne's (2004) conceptions of *responsible* and *participatory citizenship*, frames active citizenship as "consistently coupled with cautions about the importance of compliant behaviour (i.e. ethics, duty, and responsibility) and silenced from seemingly 'inappropriate' participation in civic dissent" (p. 903). From this vantage point, responsible and active citizenship is equated with being complicit and associated with behaviours deemed acceptable within the parameters set by the state, the nation, and its institutions reinforced through laws, policies, and practices.

Neoliberalism places the onus of responsibility on the individual, reinforcing the ideology that it is exclusively their choices and decisions that leads to their circumstances (Giroux, 2003; Pinto, 2015; Portelli & Konecny, 2013). The collective and shared struggle for rights, justice and equity, and various tactics to have one's voice heard is lost in translation in hegemonic discourses about responsible, self-regulating citizens.

The curriculum emphasizes it is the responsibility of the individual to self-regulate themselves and behave in a manner that does not challenge sanctioned rules, laws, and "normative" behaviours established through state authorities and its institutions. As Kennelly and Llewellyn (2011) point out,

> Those who are able to easily take part in traditionally public spheres of activity – which, in Canada, have generally been white, heterosexual, able-bodied, middle class men – continue to benefit from the new 'active citizenship'. Those who have not traditionally had such access – in Canada, typically women, ethnic minorities, sexual and gender minorities, people with disabilities, and Aboriginal peoples – receive no additional assistance in transcending these structural barriers than before the new civics curricula were introduced. (p. 910)

Neoliberal ideologies embedded within the curriculum also extend to global contexts in examination of international affairs, where dominant discourses portray that circumstances of any nation are a reflection of choices made by the country and its government in the past and presently by its leader. This leads to what Andreotti (2006) calls "sanctioned ignorance" referring to,

> [T]he role of colonialism in the creation of the wealth of what is called the 'First World' today, as well as the role of the international division of labour and exploitation of the 'Third World' in the maintenance of this wealth. (p. 44)

Andreotti explains that "this sanctioned ignorance, which disguises the worlding of the world, places the responsibility of poverty upon the poor themselves and justified the project of development of the Other as a 'civilizing mission'" (p. 45). From this viewpoint, values and interests of the North and Western countries are presented "as global and universal which naturalises the myth of Western supremacy in the rest of the world" (p. 44). Colonization is positioned as a thing of the past and situated as non-influential in today's world matters; reinforcing a de-politicization of public spheres.

The language of the new 2013 revised Social Studies curriculum and its embedded neoliberal ideologies about citizenship, through constant references to development of the "responsible, active citizen", contributes to perpetuation of "sanctioned ignorance" (Andreotti, 2006). What is problematic about conceptualizing citizenship through such a narrow and limited lens is that it assumes that all individuals and social groups enter the public sphere as equals; that all have the same access to opportunities and resources and can voice their concerns and be heard. Yet, as Giroux (2003) points out,

> In this view, freedom is no longer linked to a collective effort on the part of individuals to create a democratic society. Instead, freedom becomes an exercise in self-development rather than social responsibility, reducing politics to either the celebration of consumerism or a privileging of a market-based notion of agency and choice that appear quite indifferent to how power, equity, and justice offer the enabling conditions for real individual and collective choices to be both made and acted upon. (p. 197)

Systems of oppression work in convergence and intersectionally to perpetuate a hierarchy that distributes inequitable power, privilege, and status to selective social groups at the expense of marginalization and oppression to others. Therefore, it is necessary to question what is included in the curriculum and how it is (re)presented, just as much as it is important to question what is left out and not (re)presented. This will be an ongoing struggle and a meaningful process as a means to establish a society and understanding of citizenship that prioritizes social justice and equity over national market interests and profit.

9.7 Suggestions for Teaching Citizenship

One of the major new positive additions to the 2013 revised Social Studies curriculum is its pedagogical emphasis on learning through the "inquiry process". The inquiry model "represents a process that students use to investigate events, developments, and issues, solve problems, and reach supportable conclusions" (Ontario Ministry of Education, 2013, p. 7). Similar to the scientific model of doing research, the inquiry process consists of five components which include; formulating questions, gathering and organizing data, interpreting and analysing data, evaluation the data and drawing conclusions, and communicating findings (Ontario Ministry of Education, 2013, p. 10). The push for "inquiry-based" learning is a means of implementing student-centred learning by allowing students' interests and questions to guide the learning process through which curriculum content is taken up to be explored and critically examined. This is a great addition as it allows students to guide the learning process and content, allowing for examination of local spatial power dynamics as well as lived experiences as a form of valuable knowledge.

Another new component of the 2013 revised Social Studies curriculum is the introduction of the Citizenship Education Framework (Ontario Ministry of Education, 2013, p. 10). The Citizenship Education Framework consists of four elements which combine to contribute to understanding and defining what it means to be a "Responsible, Active Citizen";

> *Active Participation* defined as "Work for the common good in local, national and global communities".
> *Identity* defined as "A sense of personal identity as a member of various communities".
> *Attributes* defined as "Character traits, values, habits of mind".
> *Structures* defined as "Power and systems within societies".

Themes and topics suggested under *Active participation* and *Identity* predominantly aligns with emphasizing the *responsible* and *participatory* conceptions of citizenship. They reinforce words such as voting, conflict resolution and peacebuilding, leadership, volunteering, beliefs and values, culture, and community. *Attributes* and *Structures* component presents a unique feature that holds possibilities to develop and reinforce the *justice-oriented citizen*. For *Attributes* and *Structures*, relevant words such as inclusiveness, equity, rights and responsibilities, fairness and justice, democracy, rules and law, institutions, power and authority, and systems are mentioned. Although mentioning of words such as equity and justice is good indication of moving in the right direction, unfortunately the vague and open-ended use of these words does not provide any specific direction for deconstructing the terminology in a manner that facilitates development of the *justice-oriented citizen*. This is an area that further needs to be developed to provide guidance for teachers to engage these words in a manner that promotes critical thinking and critical consciousness (Freire, 1970). For example, although students will learn about the influence of "power and systems within societies", they are simultaneously encouraged to follow rules and laws as a means of being a "good" citizen. The paradoxical nature of the 2013 revised Social Studies curriculum is that although at times it promotes an understanding of the complexities of the world and its social issues through an analysis that considers power of institutions and systems, it consistently reinforces the notion of the responsible, participatory citizen as the ideal prototype of a valuable member of society; a person who respectfully obliges by the rules and laws of the nation even if the outcomes result in marginalization and oppression to certain social groups.

The inquiry process as a tool can be utilized to encourage critical thinking and consciousness in students that goes beyond focusing on individual decisions in relation to acting responsible and following rules and laws. As educators we can strive to utilize various teaching methods such as inquiry-based, student-centred learning to teach towards opening up of new possibilities instead of validating one viewpoint at the expense of disregarding all others. This begins by allowing students to bring their lived experiences into the classroom and acknowledging them as a form of valuable knowledge including the social problems they deal with on a daily basis in their families and communities. The next step would be to interpret the social issues impacting student lives through multiple vantage points, in the process allowing emotions to be expressed and multi-voices and perspectives to be heard to assist and facilitate in finding alternative action-oriented solutions.

Tupper and Cappello (2008) provide a great example of how education, specifically exposure to counter hegemonic narratives, can be used in a way to open up new possibilities. As St. Denis (2011) explains, "normative Canadian history refuses to recognize Aboriginal interpretation of history, and this refusal in turn places limits in understanding Aboriginal sovereignty" (p. 309). Tupper and Cappello (2008) used treaties as counter hegemonic narratives to raise questions about how history is told and interpreted by the dominant gaze and its representations through official curriculum texts. As the authors point out, "mainstream education is an extension of colonization insofar as it has been used to promote a dominant narrative of the past and privilege certain ways of knowing" (p. 563). By conducting qualitative interviews and quantitative surveys, Tupper and Cappello (2008) argue what is said and how it is said is just as important as what is not said or silenced intentionally within the curriculum. Whereas many non-First Nations students began to gain a better understanding of "the mechanisms through which dominance is enacted, privilege secured, and marginalization produced" (p. 570), a more influential micro-level impact included how a First Nations student went from being shameful of her race and heritage to being proud of it.

When considering how to implement different components of the Citizenship Education Framework, it is important to consider whether citizenship education should "nurture loyal law-abiding citizens aware of their duties and responsibilities to state and society, or produce citizens who stand up for their rights, question state authority and are open to other views and cultures" (Janmaat & Piattoeva, 2007, p. 527). Whereas "education for citizenship" emphasizes "responsibility, conformity, national loyalty and service to the community", on the other hand "citizenship education" promotes "democratization, individual autonomy, respect for diversity, and challenging authority and standing up for one's rights" (Janmaat & Piattoeva, 2007, p. 532). This is an important distinction, as the language and objectives of the 2013 revised Social Studies curriculum aligns with neoliberal ideologies of "education for citizenship" with its emphasis on autonomy, objectivity, personal responsibility, and service to the community and the nation. Yet there is potential for deviating from such neoliberal ideologies through constructive use of inquiry-based pedagogy coupled with use of external resources that bring multi-perspectives into the classroom that can inspire and empower students and teachers to work collectively to take action and try to change the world in the name of justice and equity.

9.8 *Youth for Human Rights*: Resources for Development of the Justice-Oriented Global Citizen

Teaching about Human Rights can serve as an alternative framework for teaching citizenship as it deviates from promoting neoliberal ideologies that focuses on personal responsibility and transitions towards promoting a social justice-oriented global citizen based on Human Rights that apply to all regardless of differences. This paradigm shift has occurred in some countries over time due to changes in their sociopolitical sphere and its consequential policy and curriculum reforms. Comparing Civic education through examination of textbooks and policy documents in Costa Rica and Argentina, Suárez (2008) points out that in both countries over time "discussion of rights increase....and the discussion of citizenship as responsibility diminishes" (p. 495).

Another important factor to consider beyond whether or not Human Rights are used to teach citizenship is how Human Rights are discussed in class. Suárez (2008) points out that textbooks in the earlier period in Costa Rica and Argentina avoided discussions of gender and other forms of institutionalized inequality, even if economic, social, and cultural rights were addressed. In the more recent period, textbooks in both countries begin to apply general discussions of human rights to particular groups. From this perspective, silenced groups who historically have been marginalized and struggled for liberation against state authority are affirmed and validated as having an important role in establishing certain Human Rights within the nation through activism and various forms of resistance. Within this paradigm, to be a "good" citizen requires one to oppose, challenge, resist, and act against injustice, which at times involves opposing the state's and nation's policies and practices.

Human Rights as a conceptual framework is not explicitly outlined to be used as a tool to teach about citizenship education within the 2013 revised Social Studies curriculum. Although the open-ended nature of overall and specific curriculum expectations provides flexibility for teachers to utilize their choice of resources to teach citizenship education, one of the downfalls of this vague language is it can omit discussions about Human Rights. This could be done intentionally due to avoidance of controversial topics (Mundy and Manion, 2008) or unintentionally due to lack of tangible resources or lack of support to feel comfortable enough to teach about Human Rights. As Mundy and Manion (2008) point out, "many [educators] view global education activities as an optional rather than a mandatory activity" (p. 956), and where activities took place, it was in the form of one-time fund-raising for charities at the expense of other aspects of global citizenship such as awareness of Human Rights and their violations locally, nationally, and internationally. Mundy and Manion (2008) express,

> The frequency of.... comments in our school-level interviews suggests that much of what is understood as global education in Canadian schools continue to foster a "them/us" mentality that is not in keeping with the themes of global interdependence and social justice that appears as ideals in the global education literature. (p. 960)

Youth for Human Rights as a tangible educational toolkit can be used by any grade level teacher to teach about social justice-oriented citizenship through the framework of Human Rights. *Youth for Human Rights* (www.youthforhumanrights.org) is a non-profit organization founded in 2001 by Dr. Mary Shuttleworth, an educator born and raised in apartheid South Africa, where she witnessed and experienced the devastating effects of discrimination and the lack of basic Human Rights. *Youth for Human Rights* invests in education as a primary tool in addressing root causes of many social issues that are prevalent across the world related to the violation of the thirty universal Human Rights contained in United Nations Universal Declaration of Human Rights. Over time, *Youth for Human Rights* has grown internationally to provide relevant and educational content to educators in more than 190 countries to teach about Human Rights in classrooms and non-traditional settings within a social justice-oriented framework.

Youth for Human Right's website (2018) outlines its purpose as inspiring youth "to become valuable advocates for tolerance and peace". It further states,

> Children are the future. They need to know their human rights and know that they must take responsibility to protect themselves and their peers. As they become aware and active in this cause, the message travels far and wide, and someday universal human rights will be a fact, not just an idealistic dream.

Within this vision, not only is personal "responsibility" and being an "active" citizen emphasized, similar to the current vision of the 2013 revised Social Studies curriculum, but more importantly social justice is reinforced through notions of "protecting themselves and their peers". This vision includes knowing one's human rights rather than responsibilities, and being able to name injustice and inequity, and more importantly, feel obligated to challenge various forms of injustice through personal and collective actions, even if it means opposing, resisting, and challenging state-sanctioned authority and its unfair policies and practices regardless of one's social location.

Youth for Human Rights has made its educational toolkit package content available online as a digital curriculum. This is significant as it makes the material accessible, since anyone with access to Internet can download the resources. Teachers can access the content by signing up free of charge and all lesson plans include a step-by-step breakdown with subsections titled "Primary Question", "Learning Objectives", "Section Content", "Discussion Questions", and "Application". One of the great features of the Human Rights digital curriculum is it can be accessed by students similar to an online course. Students also have the opportunity to discuss and share ideas in the online forums at any time at their own pace. Overall, by incorporating *Youth for Human Rights* educational materials into the Grade 6 Social Studies curriculum and beyond, teachers in Ontario, Canada will be able to better assist students in learning about citizenship through a Human Rights lens. This difference in vantage point places priority on social justice and equity instead of economic and market-driven needs of the nation.

9.9 Conclusion

In 2013, the Ontario Ministry of Education made new revisions to the Social Studies curriculum. It included many new additions including a common vision statement aligning the purpose of the elementary and secondary curriculum, a set of unified goals that students work towards thematically through Grades 1 to 6, an emphasis on inquiry-based student-centred learning, and the introduction of a Citizenship Education Framework as a guide to teach about citizenship. An analysis of the language in the 2013 revised curriculum, specifically the language describing the vision statement, unified goals, and the Grade 6 overview of overall and specific expectations indicated the promotion of neoliberal ideologies of citizenship by constantly reinforcing themes of personal responsibility and the self-regulating citizen who abides by rules and laws approved by state-sanctioned authorities and its institutions. Within this paradigm, being a responsible, active citizen is equated with being compliant and outspoken only to the extent it does not challenge authority and hegemonic status quo.

It is necessary to question what is included in the curriculum and how it is (re)presented, just as much as what is left out and not (re)presented. The problematic language in the 2013 revised Social Studies curriculum does not encourage critical thinking about how institutions and their practices can work in convergence to produce a social and racial hierarchy that marginalizes certain identities and social groups. The language of the Social Studies curriculum assumes that all social groups are heard and treated equitably at a systemic level. Overall, the curriculum reinforces the personally responsible and participatory conceptions of citizenship (Westheimer & Kahne, 2004). As a result, social justice is placed at the periphery and on the margins instead of being the main lens through which citizenship is taught.

There are new additions to the 2013 revised Social Studies curriculum that holds potential for deviating from neoliberal ideologies and transitioning towards citizenship education that reinforces development and growth of a justice-oriented global citizen. These changes include the introduction of a student-centred, inquiry-based pedagogy and the *Attributes* and *Structures* element of the Citizenship Education Framework. The promotion of inquiry-based learning reinforces student-centred teaching, having to take into consideration identities of learners and their interests and questions with respect to their lived experiences and the local context of the community in which they live. The *Structures* component of the Citizenship Education Framework raises some questions about the "importance of rules and laws", "how political, economic, and social institutions affect lives", "understanding of power and authority", and the "dynamic and complex relationships within and between systems" (Ontario Ministry of Education, 2013, p. 10).

Teaching citizenship through Human Rights instead of responsibilities can lead to development and growth of a justice-oriented, global citizen who views difference not through the vantage point that prioritizes self-interests and complicity but through a lens that emphasizes interconnectedness and justice for all. *Youth for Human Rights* and their educational materials, which include tangible resources and an online digital curriculum, can serve as a great starting point for teachers in all grades to implement teaching citizenship education through the lens of Human Rights.

Although this chapter focused on examining the language of the new 2013 revised Social Studies curriculum specifically the Grade 6 content, further studies should analyse contents of other grades to produce further insight about how citizenship is operationalized and implemented. Further areas for exploration which hold potential for blossoming of new understandings include examining how teachers are supported professionally, both provincially and locally, to implement the content of the revised Social Studies curriculum such as introduction of the inquiry-based pedagogy and the Citizenship Education Framework. As well, future studies can interview students about their experiences in the classroom relating to exposure to the new revised Social Studies curriculum. What remains to be seen in the near future is whether Human Rights as a conceptual framework with a focus on social justice and equity will be implemented systemically in Ontario schools and if so, whether it will be in the form of a learning unit or as a cross-cutting theme across the curriculum in all grades and within teacher training programs.

To conclude, we as educators need to strive to do all we can to assist students in breaking free from physical and psychological shackles of oppression and its ongoing effects of creating feelings of apathy and powerlessness. It is critical to develop justice-oriented, global citizens who feel empowered to oppose, resist, and challenge injustice, and through their individual and collective agency make a difference in their lives, local community, and in the larger context of the world through cooperation, collaboration, solidarity, allyship, and implementation of new ideas. By encouraging and promoting critical thinking and social consciousness (Bourdieu, 1999; Freire, 1970) and working with differences through a Human Rights lens, educators can facilitate and encourage students to rupture, subvert, interrupt, and resist in multiple fronts to make the world a better place one step at a time.

References

Althusser, L. (2006). Ideology and Ideological State Apparatuses (Notes Towards an Investigation). *The Anthropology of the State: A Reader, 9*(1), 86–98.

Andreotti, V. (2006). Soft Versus Critical Global Citizenship Education. *Policy & Practice: A Development Education Review, 3,* 40–51.

Apple, M. W. (2004). *Ideology and Curriculum.* New York: Routledge.

Au, W. (2013). Hiding Behind High-Stakes Testing: Meritocracy, Objectivity and Inequality in U.S. Education. *The International Education Journal: Comparative Perspectives, 12*(2), 7–19.

Basu, R. (2004). The Rationalization of Neoliberalism in Ontario's Public Education System, 1995–2000. *Geoforum, 35,* 621–634.

Block, S., & Galabuzi, G. (2011). *Canada's Colour Coded Labour Market: The Gap for Racialized Workers.* Wellesley Institute. Ottawa, ON: Canadian Centre for Policy Alternatives. Retrieved from http://www.wellesleyinstitute.com/wp-content/uploads/2011/03/Colour_Coded_Labour_MarketFINAL.pdf.

Bourdieu, P. (1999). *The Weight of the World, Social Suffering in Contemporary Society.* Palo Alto, CA: Polity Press.

Education Quality and Accountability Office. (2013). *EQAO: Ontario's Provincial Assessment Program—Its History and Influence 1996–2012.* Toronto: Queen's Printer for Ontario. Retrieved from http://www.eqao.com/en/about_eqao/about_the_agency/communication-docs/EQAO-history-influence.pdf.

Fraser, N. (2004). Recognition, Redistribution and Representation in Capitalist Global Society. *Acta Sociologica, 47*(4), 374–382.

Freire, P. (1970). *Pedagogy of the Oppressed.* New York: Continuum.
Giroux, H. (2003). Spectacles of Race and Pedagogies of Denial: Anti-Black Racist Pedagogy Under the Reign of Neoliberalism. *Communication Education, 52*(3–4), 191–211.
Grosfoguel, R. (2011). Decolonizing Post-colonial Studies and Paradigms of Political-Economy: Transmodernity, Decolonial Thinking, and Global Coloniality. *Transmodernity: Journal of Peripheral Cultural Production of the Luso-Hispanic World, 1*(1), 1–38.
Janmaat, J. G., & Piattoeva, N. (2007, November). Citizenship Education in Ukraine and Russia: Reconciling Nation-Building and Active Citizenship. *Comparative Education, 43*(4), 527–552.
Kennelly, J., & Llewellyn, K. (2011). Educating for Active Compliance: Discursive Constructions in Citizenship Education. *Citizenship Studies, 15*(6–7), 897–914.
Mosley, W. (2000). *Workin' on the Chain Gang: Shaking Off the Dead Hand of History.* Toronto: Random House of Canada Limited.
Mundy, K., & Manion, C. (2008). Global Education in Canadian Elementary Schools: An Exploratory Study. *Canadian Journal of Education, 31*(4), 947–974.
Ontario Ministry of Education. (2004). *The Ontario Curriculum Social Studies Grades 1 to 6, History and Geography Grades 7 and 8.* Retrieved from https://www.uwindsor.ca/education/sites/uwindsor.ca.education/files/curriculum_-_social_studies_1-6_history_geography_7-8.pdf.
Ontario Ministry of Education. (2013). *The Ontario Curriculum Social Studies Grades 1 to 6, History and Geography Grades 7 and 8.* Retrieved from http://www.edu.gov.on.ca/eng/curriculum/elementary/sshg18curr2013.pdf.
Pinto, L. E. (2015). Fear and Loathing in Neoliberalism; School Leader Responses to Policy Layers. *Journal of Educational Administration and History, 47*(2), 140–154.
Portelli, J. P., & Konecny, C. (2013). Neoliberalism, Subversion, and Democracy in Education. *Encounters, 14,* 87–97.
Portelli, J., & Sharma, M. (2014). Uprooting and Settling in: The Invisible Strength of Deficit Thinking. *LEARNing Landscapes, 8*(1), 251–267.
Razack, S. (2004). *Dark Threats & White Knights: The Somali Affair, Peacekeeping, and the New Imperialism.* Toronto: University of Toronto Press.
Suárez, D. (2008). Rewriting Citizenship? Civic Education in Costa Rica and Argentina. *Comparative Education, 44*(4), 485–503.
Tupper, J., & Cappello, M. (2008). Teaching the Treaties as (Un)usual Narratives: Disrupting the Curricular Commonsense. *Curriculum Inquiry, 35*(1), 559–578.
Westheimer, J., & Kahne, J. (2004). What Kind of Citizen? The Politics of Educating for Democracy. *American Educational Research Journal, 41*(2), 237–269.
Youth for Human Rights. (2018). *Our Purpose.* Retrieved from http://www.youthforhumanrights.org/about-us/purpose-of-youth-for-human-rights.html.

CHAPTER 10

"What Can I Do?": A Guide for Academics Who (Want to) Support Palestine

Sabrine Azraq

10.1 Introduction

As a Palestinian in the academy, I witness the ways academic research on my people is deeply embedded in colonialism and often benefits the colonizer at the expense of Palestinian labor and hope. I witness this settler colonial academy pervasively consume pain in what Eve Tuck calls the academy's "consumptive implacability" (Tuck & Yang, 2014b, p. 227). In recognition of this, I deliberately leave out anecdotes of Palestinian pain. Our pain is not for sale. I have been told, sometimes tacitly and sometimes directly, to write Palestinian pain in essays, present Palestinian pain at conferences, and display Palestinian pain at symposiums. I have been pushed by the academy to publish Palestinian pain and build a career out of it. To profit from the fetishism of a deeply complicit academy. This settler colonial academy is heavily influenced by the European Enlightenment's notion that "knowledge, which is power, knows no obstacles" (Adorno & Horkheimer, 1979, p. 3). As stated in an earlier chapter, *Canada's Legacy of Colonialism: Implications in Education*, Eurocentric knowledges dominate schooling in Canada, and has been

S. Azraq (✉)
Toronto, ON, Canada

© The Author(s) 2019
F. J. Villegas and J. Brady (eds.), *Critical Schooling*,
https://doi.org/10.1007/978-3-030-00716-4_10

"superimposed in many - if not most - educational systems" (Benn-John, Chapter 4). With modernity as an underpinning, the academy garners power through penetrating the interiority of the colonized whom are made fully accessible and transparent. Rousseau and Starobinski (1988) add to this by equating obscurity with negativity. As academics, we play a vital role in disrupting these colonial ideologies within the academy. One way, as explained in the previous chapter, *Disrupting Princesses*, is to center multiple histories by "centering learnings' social locations in their own knowledge and education" (Brady & Abawi, Chapter 6). Another way we can refuse colonial ideologies in the academy is by refusing to make our pain accessible and transparent for the academy's consumption. Within the dialectics of visibility, anti-zionist/colonial and anti-racist academics should focus on unveiling injustices and make transparent only that which respects the full humanity of the colonized.

I write within an anti-zionist discursive framework rooted in Indigenous, and specifically Palestinian practices of resistance and self-determination to give anti-zionist/colonial and anti-racist academics the theoretical and pragmatic tools necessary to support Palestinians in our quest for freedom. I use both a politics of refusal (Simpson, 2014; Tuck & Yang, 2014b) and a politics of urgency (Hurtado, 2003) as methods of employing Palestinian practices of resistance within the academy.

Refusal, here, is used as a generative stance, a method, and a framework to counter settler colonial logics. The purpose is to focus on practices that we—as implicated bodies—can employ to center Palestinian liberation. Refusal is grounded in a "critique of settler colonialism, its construction of whiteness, and its regimes of representation" (Tuck & Yang, 2014b, p. 242). Refusal takes on many forms; it can be both method and theory (Tuck & Yang, 2014b) and is actualized fluidly depending on the context. Generally, refusal is expansive (Tuck & Yang, 2014b), theoretically generative (Simpson, 2014), and a "redirection to ideas otherwise unacknowledged or unquestioned" (Simpson, 2014, p. 239). It is anti-colonial and focused on potentialities that surpass colonial logics (Simpson 2014; Tuck & Yang, 2014a). Rooted in Indigenous self-determination, Simpson (2014) describes refusal as "the logic of the present" or "feeling citizenships" as a form of counter or alternative logics that "present space of intra-community recognition, affection and care, outside of the logics of colonial and imperial rule" (p. 76). My aim is to employ refusal as a conceptual framework and as a method of positioning our bodies within the academy in a way that better coincides with Palestinian freedom.

Academics concerned with Palestine must acknowledge that Palestinian conditions are worsening and should thus produce knowledge with a sense of urgency. Borrowing from Hurtado's (2003) notion of a politics of urgency (p. 222), concerned academics should intend to produce work that beneficially changes Palestinian political, material, and social current conditions through any means necessary. As I write this, the zionist regime is imposing racist control measures on Jerusalem, Palestine; effectively shutting down Al Aqsa Mosque compound for the first time since 1969. The 2012 report by the United Nations Country Team that stated that Gaza would be "unliveable" by 2020 is now considered optimistic. A July 2017 new UN report projects an even faster deterioration of living conditions with a decline in real GDP per capita and Gaza's coastal aquifer deemed unusable by the end of 2017. Antizionist/colonial and anti-racist academics must register that zionism's pervasive control over Palestine is worsening with time and thrives off disciplinary jargon, complacency, and indifference to Palestinian realities.

David W. Orr (2011) writes that the academy resembles "a cacophony of different jargons" (p. 275) and states that there is a "growing gap between the real world and the academy" (p. 275). We must close the gap by going deeper than current academic discussions and ask ourselves how the academy facilitates injustices and how we as academics can pragmatically facilitate justice within an unjust academy. Aída Hurtado (2003) proposes an "endarkened epistemology" to revolutionize the academy as a framework of political action to change current conditions (p. 219). She argues that academics should not only describe educational institutions but also "transform them through the process of consciousness raising about the invisibility of educational inequality" (Hurtado, 2003, p. 217). With that said, academics concerned with the situation in Palestine should not only describe injustices, but also work to stop them through political actions that I describe below.

We, concerned academics, should not engage in academic debates void of connection to current injustices because, as Hurtado (2003) puts it, "endless debates within the confines of existing theories run the risk of inaction" (p. 223). We must think carefully about our intentions as well as the impacts of our knowledge production to ensure our work is useful to those we intend to be of use to. Similarly, Linda Smith (1999) writes that research must be "talked about both in terms of its absolute worthlessness to us, the Indigenous world, and its absolute usefulness to those who wielded it as an instrument" (p. 3). In my own attempt at useful research, I focus on advancing the struggle for Palestinian freedom within a politics of urgency by centering pragmatic approaches to support Palestinians in our struggle for liberation and self-determination *in the real world*. Beginning with a brief overview on zionism as a settler colonial project, the article turns to Palestine advocacy in "american" and "canadian" universities and the tactics employed to suppress them. It ends with a response to the question academics often ask me after learning of the situation in Palestine; "What can I do?"

10.2 Zionism as a European Settler Colonial Project

Academics interested in engaging in Palestine advocacy should have a clear understanding of zionism. Zionism is an offspring of European settler colonialism and white supremacy that works to invisibilize (Massad, 2006; Said, 1992), racialize, and vilify Palestinians, thus politicizing us. What represents zionism since its political inception is the refusal to admit, and the consequent denial of a Palestinian presence in Palestine. The zionist racial contract thrives off of white supremacy (Smith, 2012), anti-Muslim bigotry (Davidson, 2011), divine doctrine (Alam, 2009), and orientalism (Said, 1978). It works to construct Palestinians as non-existent and void of history, culture, and (home) land (Said, 1978). The zionist regime—in coming into violent existence in 1948—resulted in the ongoing eradication of Palestine (Said, 1978). Since "settler colonialism destroys to replace" (Wolfe, 2006, p. 388), the zionist colonizer creates "home" on Palestinian land by attempting to destroy "home" for the Indigenous population. The colonizer's sense of "home" is thus legitimated through the delegitimization of "home" for the colonized. Theodor Herzl (1997)—a founding father of zionism—summated this settler colonial logic in *Old-New Land* where he wrote, "If I wish to substitute a new building for an old one, I must demolish before I construct" (p. 38). Zionism thus works to destruct "home" for Indigenous Palestinians in order to replace it with "home" for the zionist colonizer through processes of settler colonialism and white supremacist exclusionary policies.

The zionist decision to possess Palestine for mainly foreign Jews and thus dispossess Palestinians from Palestine is the foundation of the "official"—yet nevertheless interminably illegitimate—zionist regime. This is demonstrated in the prevalent zionist refusal to admit that Palestinians are not merely reducible to an inconvenient and temporary hindrance, but that Palestinians lived in Palestine for centuries as a socially, culturally, politically, and economically distinct people and continue to exist with an indissoluble bond with the land of Palestine (Said, 1978). In attempts to authorize the zionist aspiration for perdurable supremacy, the zionist regime relies on historical fabrications of a Palestinian non-presence in a fallacious attempt to construct and legitimate an ancient zionist presence and connection in Palestine. These fabrications are realized through the material destruction of Palestine infrastructure and the elimination of Palestinian knowledges and narratives in public Euro-zionist discourses.

From Turtle Island to Palestine, Indigenous land is stolen and then "gifted back" in the form of Bantustans, reservations, and reserved pockets (Smith, 1999, p. 51). The Palestinian presence in Palestine was—and continues to be—systematically destroyed to fuel the zionist myth that Palestine was mostly empty and thus, an ideal place for the colonial zionist project to take place. As Israel Shahak, a chemistry professor at Hebrew University spelled out, the truth about the indisputable Palestinian presence that existed in Palestine centuries prior to 1948 is "one of the most guarded secrets" among zionists (cited in Massad, 2006). This is further exemplified in the early zionist slogan produced by Israel Zangwill that declared Palestine was "a land without people, for a people without land" (Said, 1978). Joseph Massad, a Palestinian professor at Columbia University, puts this myth into perspective when he informs us that, for this to be the case, the zionists had to have "expelled the majority of the Palestinians to render their vision a reality" (Massad, 2006, p. 39). Thus, this deliberate erasure of a historical Palestinian presence in Palestine manifested itself in the material obliteration of Palestinian life and infrastructure. Shahak outlined this systematic and brutal zionist erasure when he stated that almost four hundred Palestinian villages were annihilated; "destroyed completely, with their houses, garden walls, and even cemeteries and tombstones, so that literally a stone does not remain standing, and visitors are passing and being told that 'it was all desert'" (cited in Massad, 2006). The extent of the zionist physical erasure of Palestinian society is demonstrated in Mosh Dayan's 1969 account in Ha-Aretz, as quoted by Ralph Schoenman (1988) in *The Hidden History of Zionism*:

We came here to a country that was populated by Arabs, and we are building here a Hebrew, Jewish state. Instead of Arab villages, Jewish villages were established. You do not even know the names of these villages and I do not blame you, because these geography books no longer exist. Not only the books, but also the villages do not exist. Nahalal was established in place of Mahalul, Gevat in place of Jibta, Sarid in the place of Hanifas and Kafr Yehoushua in the place of Tel Shamam. There is not a single settlement that was not established in the place of a former Arab village. (p. 41)

Dayan's words illustrate zionism's pervasive erasure of Palestinian infrastructures and knowledges which Ilan Pappé (2006) refers to as state-organized "memoricide". Dayan's account shows how memoricide on Palestinians is facilitated by physically and ideologically concealing Palestinian histories and knowledges. For example, Pappé (2006) points out that the Jewish National Fund's mission is to conceal the remnants of Palestinian villages by planting trees atop of them. Zionists also conceal Palestinian histories through "the narratives [zionism] has created to deny [Palestinian] existence" (p. 228). Approximately, 780,000 Palestinians were dispossessed and displaced in 1948 in order to facilitate the zionist regime's domination in Palestine (Said, 1978, p. 14). Palestinian society was—and continues to be—erased through the deliberate removal of Palestinian narratives within zionist and European public discourse. As Shahak explained, "no publication, book or pamphlet gives either [the] number [of Arab villages] or their location. This of course is done on purpose, so that the accepted official myth of 'an empty country' can be taught and accepted in the...schools and told to visitors" (cited in Davis & Mezvinsky, 1975, pp. 43–44). The active attempt to contemporarily invisibilize Palestinian society is necessary to falsify an Indigenous connection between the zionist regime and the land. In reality, however, zionist society has no Indigenous connection to Palestine and made itself dominant in the land through a modern and racist settler colonial project. This information is important because it gives academics the knowledge to accurately situate zionism within a settler colonial lens.

10.3 Palestine Advocacy in the Academy

Academics interested in joining the Palestinian struggle for liberation should understand the current Palestine advocacy taking place in the academy. Presently, those engaged in Palestine activism in the academy often mobilize around the Boycott, Divestment and Sanctions movement (BDS) and Israeli Apartheid Week (IAW). The Boycott, Divestment and Sanctions Movement (BDS) is a grassroots movement for self-determination and liberation initiated in 2005 by 171 Palestinian civil society groups. Yasmeen Abu-Laban, a Palestinian woman and Abigail Bakan (2009), a Jewish woman born to parents who survived East European pogroms argue that the BDS movement refuses to normalize zionist settler colonialism and is a method of resistance and "cross-border solidarity [that] is intimately connected with a challenge to the hegemonic place of zionism in western ideology" (p. 29). On a fundamental level, BDS refuses white supremacist hegemonic discourses that portray the zionist regime as legitimate and progressive. It is rooted in an understanding and distancing of our particular complicities and is thus "flexible in its application and adaptation" (Abu-Laban & Bakan, 2009, p. 43). BDS has three demands, an end to the zionist occupation and colonization of all Arab lands and the dismantlement of the apartheid wall; recognition of the fundamental rights of the Arab-Palestinian citizens of "Israel" to full equality; and the respect, protection, and promotion of the rights of Palestinian refugees to return to their homes and properties as stipulated in UN resolution 194. Abu-Laban and Bakan (2009) state that the promotion of the BDS movement can challenge elements of Western elite hegemony in the form of zionism and "contests a post-second world war hegemonic construction of state ideology, in which zionism plays a central role and serves to enforce a racial contract that hides the apartheid-like character of the state of Israel" (p. 16). They continue:

> This [BDS] movement has been hampered, we maintain, by an international racial contract which, since 1948, has assigned a common interest between the state of Israel and powerful international political allies, while absenting the Palestinians as both 'nonwhite' and stateless. (Abu-Laban & Bakan, 2009, pp. 32–33)

This excerpt succinctly describes zionism as a colonial and racial project supported by countries such as "Canada" and the "united states" that turns Palestinians into racialized and stateless bodies. It is vital that academics understand their relation to this racial and violent contract as it is constructed and renewed with the support of various colonial countries.

Although the BDS movement is not exclusive to the academy, academics have been focal to its success (Sarick, 2015). The Palestinian Campaign for the Academic and Cultural Boycott of Israel (PACBI) is a part of the BDS movement and was launched by a group of Palestinian academics in Palestine to manage the segment that concentrates on the academic and cultural boycotts of the zionist colony. This offshoot of the BDS movement calls on the global community to boycott all zionist academic and cultural institutions until the BDS demands have been met. PACBI has since been endorsed by nearly sixty Palestinian academic, cultural, and other civil society unions, organizations and federations, including the Federation of Unions of Palestinian Universities' Professors and Employees and the Palestinian NGO Network in the West Bank. PACBI also has an established advisory committee comprised of well-known public figures and academics. In addition, a scholarly collective in Gaza, Palestine formed the Palestinian Students Campaign for the Academic Boycott of Israel (PSCABI) as a means of working with academics and others outside of Palestine on international BDS campaigns ("USACBI," n.d.).

Since its inception, BDS has seen colossal success. The BDS movement has gained momentum in recent years largely through resolutions endorsed by student unions and academy associations on a global scale (Zahriyeh, 2015). On Turtle Island, the call for BDS has made tremendous strides within the academy and academics continue to play a crucial role in the struggle for Palestinian freedom. In "Canada," at least 12 student unions and associations have endorsed the BDS movement; including Ryerson's Students' Union in 2014, the York Federation of Students in 2013, and Concordia University Student Union in 2014 ("CJPME," n.d.). Recently, the University of Toronto Graduate Students' Union initiated a BDS Ad Hoc Committee in response to BDS and has since created a tri-campus campaign (#UofTDivest) to demand the University of Toronto to divest from companies that are complicit in the zionist settler colonial project ("GSU," n.d.) The current campaign highlights the financial investment from the University of Toronto into three companies that help perpetuate the zionist settler colonial project in Palestine. The "ontario" branch of the Canadian Federation of Students (CFS), representing over 300,000 university students, unanimously endorsed the BDS call in 2014. Also, university workers and academics in the Canadian Union of Public Employees (CUPE) representing 200,000 government and other sector workers joined the BDS movement in 2009. In 2008, the Faculty for Palestine (F4P) was formed in "toronto" as a means for academics to assist in BDS campaigns within the academy. F4P consists of over 500 faculty members of all ranks from over 40 universities and 15 colleges across "Canada" ("CAIA," n.d.).

In the "united states" academics have formed Palestine solidarity groups on almost every major university campus, totaling over 115 groups (Mallett-Outtrim, 2015). Academics are instilling compelling awareness tactics in the academy to encourage collective refusal in the form of the Palestinian call for BDS (Mallet-Outtrim, 2015). In 2013, BDS was the primary focus of roughly 150 events that took place within the confines of the academy (Mallet-Outtrim, 2015). The BDS movement has flourished in many of academe's most significant institutions, including Stanford University, San Jose State University, Princeton University, and seven of the nine undergraduate campuses within the University of California (Mallet-Outtrim, 2015). Even more significant, the National Women's Studies Association (NWSA); the largest feminist organization in Turtle Island, endorsed the BDS movement in 2015 with an overwhelming majority. These successes are continuing to gain momentum in the academy as the BDS movement proves to be a venue for academics to voice their solidarity with Palestinians by joining the Palestinian call in affirming Palestinian self-determination and justice.

"Israeli" Apartheid Week (IAW) is a global phenomenon that takes place in more than 150 universities and cities across the world. Conceived at the University of Toronto in 2005, this annual occurrence is organized on the principle of Palestinian refusal by scholars against zionist settler colonialism and systematic apartheid policies imposed on Palestinians. A wide range of people affiliated with the academy host IAW within their particular locations and in diversified ways. IAW can be implemented through panels, film screenings, building mock checkpoints and apartheid walls, sending mock eviction notices to student residences, and other creative measures to raise awareness of the colonial situation in Palestine and to raise awareness of different methods of refusing zionist colonialism and normalcy. Inspired by the ongoing popular resistance across Palestine, IAW is a powerful tool of refusal that connects Palestinians and scholars in a united struggle for justice. Given that the academy is inherently colonial and highly politicized, scholars can use their affiliation with the academy to form alliances rooted in Palestinian refusal as a means to address complicity and pressure the zionist colony to adhere to the demands of Palestinians. Academics have been at the forefront of a surge in Palestine solidarity organizing efforts and successes, particularly within the academy through both the Boycott, Divestment and Sanctions Movement and "Israeli" Apartheid Week. Collectively, these alliances challenge zionist coloniality and address their complicity in the enabling of the colonial project in Palestine.

10.4 SUPPRESSION OF PALESTINE ADVOCACY IN THE ACADEMY

Very little research has been done on the suppression of Palestine advocacy in "american" campuses and almost no research has been done on the suppression in "canadian" campuses. Palestine Legal was founded in 2012 as an independent organization dedicated to protecting the civil and constitutional rights of people in the "united states" who speak out for Palestinian freedom. In 2014, Palestine Legal responded to 152 incidents of suppression and 68 requests for legal assistance in anticipation of suppression. In the first half of 2015, Palestine Legal responded to 140 incidents of suppression of Palestine advocacy. Eighty-nine percent of these incidents targeted students and scholars as "a reaction to the increasingly central role universities play in the movement for Palestinian rights" (p. 5). Palestine Legal categorizes the forms of suppression as follows:

> False and inflammatory accusations of anti-Semitism and support for terrorism
> Official denunciations
> Bureaucratic barriers
> Administrative sanctions
> Cancellations and alterations of academic and cultural events
> Threats to academic freedom
> Lawsuits and legal threats
> Legislation
> Criminal investigations and prosecutions

These forms of suppression are caused by an apparatus of zionist advocacy groups, public relations firms, and zionist think tanks that aim to suppress all criticisms of zionism. Palestine Legal (2012) writes that,

> Rather than engage such criticism on its merits, these groups leverage their significant resources and lobbying power to pressure universities, government actors, and other institutions to censor or punish advocacy in support of Palestinian rights. In addition, high-level Israeli government figures, led by Prime Minister Benjamin Netanyahu, and wealthy benefactors such as Sheldon Adelson and Haim Saban have reportedly participated in strategic meetings to oppose Palestine activism, particularly boycott, divestment, and sanctions (BDS) campaigns. (p. 4)

Since these tactics often prove successful, Palestine Legal was initiated to document the suppression of Palestine advocacy and to provide legal advice, advocacy, and litigation support to college students, professors, grassroots activists, and affected communities who stand for justice in Palestine. Universities are battlegrounds between those who advocate for a free Palestine and those who aim to delegitimize all criticism of the zionist state. This has caused university administrators to "emerge as key decision makers regarding whether to condemn, limit, or sanction Palestine advocacy" (Palestine Legal, 2012, p. 16). In extension, academics are also key decision makers as we play central roles by what we choose to affiliate with and condone. Academics face severe consequences for supporting Palestine against zionist colonization as we are often targeted by zionist advocacy groups and university administrators;

> university administrations have canceled programs, sanctioned students, fired professors, and scrutinized departments in response to external pressure. In so doing, universities treat students who speak out on Palestine differently than other students, indicating that the viewpoint of the speech, and not the facially neutral explanations often put forward, drives the censorship. (p. 16)

These targeted attacks on academics against zionist colonization aim to tarnish reputations, initiate university investigations, and can even be the grounds for termination of employment (Palestine Legal, 2012). For example, Joseph Massad, a Palestinian professor at Columbia University underwent a university investigation for anti-Semitic bias. Massad noted that, the committee's report was forced to acknowledge that I have been the target of a political campaign by actors inside and outside the university, as well as by registered and unregistered students inside and outside my classroom. It affirms that during the Spring of 2002, I was spied upon by at least one other professor on campus, that my class was disrupted by registered and unregistered auditors, and that individuals and organizations outside the university targeted me, my class, and my teaching. (Palestine Legal, 2012, p. 32)

Steven Salaita was fired from his tenured faculty position at the University of Illinois at Urbana-Champaign because of his personal tweets that condemned the 2014 zionist assault on Gaza. San Francisco State University initiated an investigation of Rabab Abdulhadi after a zionist advocacy group accused her of meeting with "known terrorists" on her research trip to Palestine. A zionist advocacy group titled the AMCHA Initiative issues a blacklist of over 200 professors of Middle East Studies for their Palestine advocacy (Palestine Legal, 2012). These acts of suppression are worsening with zionist advocacy groups successfully enacting anti-BDS legislation in the "united states."

10.5 The Role of the Academic

Anti-racist and anti-zionist/colonial academics should pressure their institutions to uphold their mission to foster an environment that encourages academic freedom. The irony of the concept of academic freedom lies in how it is used to violate the freedoms of those marginalized within the academy. For far too long academics have used the right to freedom of expression to deny Palestinians their right to freedom of expression. As academics, we have a responsibility to interrogate our self-implications in larger systems of injustices. Here I call to question the academy's ideal of academic freedom in relation to Palestinian liberation and consider the adherence of our particular academic responsibilities to adhere to Palestinian self-determination.

Linda Tuhiwai Smith (1999) examines the dangers of academic freedom as it promotes autonomous independence without accountability. She argues that academic freedom "protects a discipline from the 'outside', enabling communities of scholars to distance themselves from others and, in the more extreme forms, to absolve themselves of responsibility for what occurs in other branches of their discipline, in the academy and in the world" (Smith, 1999, p. 67). Within a settler colonial academy, highly competitive individualistic research fosters an environment where objectivity and quantity are prioritized and responsibility and ethical morality are absolved. This is apparent in the ways arguments defending academic freedom are used to silence and refuse others of their academic freedom. George Dei's analysis of academic freedom and his call for academic responsibility is useful here. In his article, "The African Scholar in the Western Academy," Dei (2014) analyzed the notion of claiming rights in academic and colonial settings, stating that these rights are "conceptualized as property of dominant bodies" (p. 169). This is most apparent when we see dominant bodies in the academy use arguments defending the right to freedom of expression and the right to academic freedom as a means to further conceal the unfreedoms and non-freedoms of others. In "Decolonizing the University Curriculum," Dei (2015) calls to question institutionalized definitions of academic freedom that fall short of holding academics responsible for what they do with these freedoms. He asserts that, "there is no [academic] freedom without matching responsibilities and an ethically conscious engagement in this freedom" (Dei, 2015, p. 42). He defines academic responsibility as "the need to make education more relevant to the diverse communities and institutions they serve" (p. 31). Smith's (1999) call for scholars to recognize the effects and limits of their research can be included as a form of academic responsibility. How can notions of academic freedom work against the appeals of Indigenous people and communities?

In this case, I analyze how notions of academic freedom impede on Indigenous Palestinian freedom. When we speak of academic freedom, why is the consistent denial of academic and basic freedoms for Palestinian students and scholars under a violent, settler colonial zionist regime fit routinely ignored? For example, Cary Nelson's "The Problem with Judith Butler: The Political Philosophy of the Movement to Boycott Israel" employs academic freedom to include academic alliances between settler colonial universities while ignoring how these universities impede Palestinian academic freedom and Palestinian educational infrastructure. For Nelson, many legislators' and university administrators' academic freedom is violated when students and scholars refuse to make alliances with settler colonial institutions, but it is not violated when settler colonial regimes detain Palestinian students without charge or trial (Flynn, 2013). Amjad Barham (2009), leader of the Palestinian Federation of Unions of University Professors and Employees (PFUUPE) said in his address to the University and College Union (UCU) Congress:

> Is upholding the academic freedom of Israeli academics a loftier aim than upholding the freedom of an entire people being strangled by an illegal occupation? Do Palestinian universities somehow fall outside the purview of the 'universal' principle of academic freedom? Israeli academics who argue for the protection of their access to international academic networks, grants, visiting professorships, fellowships and other benefits of the academic system, have paid scant attention to the total denial of the most basic freedoms to Palestinians, academics or otherwise.

Here Barham (2009) illustrates the hypocrisy in defending academic freedom while simultaneously denying basic freedoms for Palestinians, effectively making clear the irony in excluding Palestinian academics and Palestinian academic institutions from the "universal" principle of academic freedom.

I employ Dei's (2014, 2015) analysis of academic freedom and academic responsibility within an investigative framework of Palestine solidarity to argue that institutionalized notions of academic freedom prohibit Palestinians from access to schooling, and our right to self-determination, and the very academic freedom proclaimed as a valued as a vital commodity. Furthermore, I demand that as scholars within the academy it is our academic responsibility to adhere to the BDS Movement.

The zionist regime regularly denies Palestinians our basic rights as human beings, including the right to open exchange and academic freedom. Scott (2013) highlights that zionist military impedes on "Palestinians' access to university education, freedom of assembly, and the right to free speech" (p. 2). Palestinian intellectuals are forced to go through humiliating and precarious zionist checkpoints, interrogations, harassment, and border crossings in attempt to get to school. Palestinian students in zionist and Palestinian universities and schools experience racist policies and physical and psychological violence (USACBI.org). George Dei (2015) said that, "there is nothing 'free' about freedom! [Academic] Freedom is fought for and is maintained at the expense of the non-freedoms and the cumulative unfreedom of others" (p. 42). In order to hold the zionist regime accountable and to reclaim Palestinian freedoms, we should consider affirming the BDS movement as one Indigenous Palestinian method of refusal. Joan Scott (2013) reflects on the BDS movement as a "strategic way of exposing the unprincipled and undemocratic behavior of Israeli state institutions" (p. 3). She asserts that, "it is because we believe so strongly in principles of academic freedom that a strategic boycott of the state that so abuses it makes sense right now" (p. 3). As Dei (2014, 2015) makes clear, we cannot speak of academic freedom without speaking of our academic responsibilities. As scholars within a settler colonial academy, we are implicitly and at times directly complicit in perpetuating unending militaristic violence and settler colonial erasure on Indigenous peoples and communities.

Rima Najjar Kapitan (2013), distinguishes between academic freedom and academic entitlement and asserts that the academic freedom to boycott must be included in notions of academic freedom. We are obliged to work together to ensure the freedom of the students and scholars who choose to endorse BDS. We have the right to disassociate ourselves from zionist institutions until Palestinian freedom and self-determination is acknowledged. Since academic freedom is used within powerful and interconnected institutions that are deeply embedded in wider societies, academic freedom must be connected to the implications within the societies they affect. When notions of universal academic freedom are used to hinder academic and non-academic freedoms of others, the academic entitlement of dominant bodies supersede their academic responsibility and the limitations of academic and non-academic freedoms of others. Kapitan (2013) asserts that academic freedom "must be flexible enough to allow professors to use expressive disassociation (example, BDS) to bring about education, social and political change" (p. 2). Kapitan states that,

> It is not a violation of anyone's 'academic freedom' if American institutions freely choose to disassociate from Israeli universities until they cease reinforcing Israeli apartheid...So, with respect to many of the demands of the boycott movement, academic freedom is not implicated at all. (p. 137)

We must give attention to the ways in which the academy is gravely complicit in perpetuating the unfreedoms and non-freedoms of Palestinians and we must consider the political context of our scholarly locations when considering false universal notions of academic freedom. Freedom for whom? Freedom to avoid responsibility? To speak of academic freedom without acknowledging how settler colonial universities from Turtle Island to Palestine work to deny people their right to academic freedom is to speak from a location of privilege within a violent academy. The settler colonial academy is deeply complicit with militarization and racial dispossession in Turtle Island and Palestine, and thus our affiliation within the academy means we are implicated as well. It is our academic responsibility to adhere to BDS on an individual, interpersonal, and institutional level. If we truly believe in the principles of academic freedom for all people and if we are to fulfill our academic responsibility, we must strongly take up BDS in order to pressure the zionist regime to stop denying Palestinians our basic freedoms. As Sunaina Maira (2015), a professor of Asian American Studies at the University of California, Davis, states, this is more than just about passing BDS resolutions, this is about "changing the discourse about Palestine in the academy…a war of position, not just a war of maneuver" (p. 83) or a "war of legitimacy" (p. 86). As scholars within an academy that work to prolong and normalize Palestinian subordination, our solidarity with Palestinians must be stronger than our fear of alienation or discomfort when endorsing BDS. When we recognize the very real violence and alienation Palestinians face under the zionist regime, we will be less likely to succumb to counterarguments that affirming Palestinian freedom will somehow cause divisiveness and alienation. As scholars within this settler colonial academy, we must understand that the academy is on the frontlines in the struggle for Palestinian freedom and self-determination. Ashley Dawson and Bill V. Mullen (2015) state that "it is urgent that scholars and students around the world boycott Israeli universities" (p. 1) and endorse BDS fully and publicly. It is our academic responsibility to push for BDS in our respective institutions and personal lives. And it is a form of liberation to refuse the academy's notions of academic freedom and instead affirm a sense of academic responsibility rooted in justice and solidarity with Indigenous and other oppressed groups affected by the colonial academy.

10.6   Conclusion

The growing BDS movement and the growing affirmation of Palestinian indigeneity are gaining momentum, particularly within the academy. It is important that, as affiliates of this settler colonial academy, we understand our varying responsibilities in cutting complicity in intertwining systems of settler colonialism and white supremacy. Our complicity must be confronted by employing Palestinian modes of refusal in the quest for Palestinian self-determination and freedom. In this moment in time, we are aware that, as Saree Makdisi a professor of English and Comparative Literature at University College London put it, "having lost the actual arguments, Israel's defenders have now declared war on argument itself." Refusals will continue to spread despite pressures to suppress them, and as bodies within academe, we hold a prominent place in affirming Palestinian Indigenity.

In conclusion, academics should focus on normalizing, protecting, and engaging in Palestine advocacy in the academy. Normalization can be done by initiating or engaging in BDS campaigns on campus, initiating or support IAW events on campus, conducting scholarship on Palestine through an anti-zionist/colonial lens, educating and endorsing BDS, and participating in programing focused on Palestine advocacy. Academics in support of Palestine should also protest investigations of academics for Palestine advocacy, rally against any and all punitive action directed toward academics for their Palestine advocacy, dispute the requirement for Palestine advocacy student groups to pay "security fees" and instead allocate funding when security is justifiable, document and report incidents of Palestine advocacy suppression in the form of censorship or discriminatory treatment, call on university administrators to take concrete steps to stop suppressing Palestine advocacy, publicly oppose suppression tactics and support academics who are penalized for their advocacy (Palestine Legal, 2012). Since zionism has turned Palestine into a highly contested concept, Edward Said (1978) demonstrates that the very pronouncement of the word Palestine is seen by Palestinians and those rooted in anti-zionist/colonial thought as a gesture of positive assertion. Academics who utter the word Palestine bring into existence a reality that constrains zionist claims over the land, a reality that the zionist project tries heavily to invalidate. The attempted erasure of the word Palestine is similar to the attempted erasure of Indigenous typology in "north america." Linda Tuhiwai Smith (1999) in *Decolonizing Methodologies: Research and Indigenous Peoples*, recounts the stories of Indigenous children in Turtle Island who were forced to mentally and verbally replace their original names of their land with colonial typology. Colonial typology and taxonomy were, and continue to be legitimated by being used on maps and in textbooks. Eve Tuck and K. Wayne Yang's (2014a) note that this process of erasing Indigenous typology feigns normalcy, permanence, and inevitableness. Thus, even the mere remembrance and pronouncement of Palestine and other Indigenous topology is a political act that academics interested in Palestine and Indigenous advocacy can engage in.

REFERENCES

Adorno, T., & Horkheimer, M. (1979). *The Dialectic of Enlightenment*. New York: Verso.
Alam, M. S. (2009). *Israeli Exceptionalism: The Destabilizing Logic of Zionism*. New York: Palgrave Macmillan.
Bakan, A. B., & Abu-Laban, Y. (2009). Palestinian Resistance and International Solidarity: The BDS Campaign. *Sage Journals, 51*(1), 29–54.
Barham, A. (2009). *PACBI-Address to the UCU Congress by Amjad Barham, President, the Palestinian Federation of Unions of University Professors and Employees* (PFUUPE).
Davidson, L. (2011). Islamophobia, the Israel Lobby and American Paranoia: Letter from America. *Holy Land Studies, 10*(1), 87–95.
Davis, U., & Mezvinsky, N. (1975). *Documents from Israel, 1967–1973: Readings for a Critique of Zionism*. London: Ithaca Press.
Dawson, A., & Mullen, B. V. (2015). *Against Apartheid: The Case for Boycotting Israeli Universities*. Chicago: Haymarket Books.
Dei, G. J. S. (2014). Personal Reflections on Anti-racism Education for a Global Context. *Encounters on Education, 15,* 239–249.
Dei, G. J. S. (2015). Decolonizing the University Curriculum. *Social Studies, 10*(2).
Dei, G. J. S., & Asgharzadeh, A. (2001). The Power of Social Theory: The Anti-colonial Discursive Framework. *Journal of Educational Thought, 35*(3), 297–323.
Flynn, K. (2013). *Shackling the Scholar: Israel's Administrative Detention of Palestinian Students*. http://mondoweiss.net/2013/05/administrative-detention-palestinian/. Accessed 18 November 2016.
Herzl, T., & Levensohn, L. (1997). *Old New Land*. Princeton: Markus Weiner Publishers.
Hurtado, A. (2003). Theory in the Flesh: Toward an Endarkened Epistemology. *Qualitative Studies in Education, 41*(2), 215–225.
Jacobson, W. A. (2014). *University Statements Rejecting Academic Boycott of Israel*. http://legalinsurrection.com/2013/12/indiana-wash-u-st-louis-gwu-northwestern-cornell-reject-academic-boycott-of-israel/. Retrieved 18 November 2016.
Kapitan, R. (2013). On Myths, Straw Men and Academic Freedom: A Response to the "Readers Respond" section of the *AAUP Journal of Academic Freedom, 4*.
Legal, P. (2012). *The Palestine Exception to Free Speech: A Movement Under Attack in the US*.
Mallett-Outtrim, R. (2015). *Israel Backers Accused of 'Stifling Dissent' in US Universities*. http://www.telesurtv.net/english/analysis/Israel-Backers-

Accused-of-Stifling-Dissent-in-US-Universities-20150930-0011.html. Accessed 19 November 2016.

Massad, J. A. (2006). *The Persistence of the Palestinian Question: Essays on Zionism and the Palestinians*. New York, NY: Routledge.

Orr, D. W. (2011). *Hope Is an Imperative: The Essential DAVID Orr*. Washington: Island Press.

PACBI-American Anthropological Association (AAA). (2015). Conference Passes BDS Resolution with a Whopping 88% Majority. http://www.pacbi.org/etemplate.php?id=2765.

Pappé, I. (2006). *The Ethnic Cleansing of Palestine*. Oxford: Oneworld.

Rousseau, J., & Starobinski, J. (1988). *Transparency and Obstruction*. Chicago: University of Chicago Press.

Said, E. W. (1978). *Orientalism*. New York: Pantheon Books.

Said, E. (1992). *The Question of Palestine*. New York: Vintage Books.

Sarick, L. (2015). Has the BDS Movement Been Effective? *The Canadian Jewish News*. http://www.cjnews.com/living-jewish/jewish-learning/feature-bds-movement-effective. Accessed 18 November 2016.

Schoenman, R. (1988). *The Hidden History of Zionism*. Santa Barbara: Veritas Press.

Scott, J. W. (2013). *Changing My Mind About the Boycott*. https://www.aaup.org/sites/default/files/files/JAF/2013JAF/Scott.pdf. Accessed 18 November 2016.

Simpson, A. (2014). *Mohawk Interruptus: Political Life Across the Borders of Settler States*. Durham, NC: Duke University Press.

Smith, L. T. (1999). *Decolonizing Methodologies: Research and Inidigenous Peoples*. London: Zed Books.

Smith, A. (2012). Indigeneity, Settler Colonialism, White Supremacy. In *Racial Formation in the Twenty-First Century* (pp. 66–90). Berkeley: Unversity of California Press.

Tuck, E., & Yang, K. W. (2014a). Unbecoming Claims: Pedagogies of Refusal in Qualitative Research. *Qualitative Inquiry, 20*(6), 811–818.

Tuck, E., & Yang, K. W. (2014b). R-Words: Refusing Research. In D. Paris & M. T. Winn (Eds.), *Humanizing Research: Decolonizing Qualitative Inquiry with Youth and Communities* (pp. 223–247). Los Angeles: Sage.

Wolfe, P. (2006). Settler Colonialism and the Elimination of the Native. *Journal of Genocide Research, 8*(4), 387–409.

Zahriyeh, E. (2015). *Report: Anti-semitism Charges Used to Curb Pro-Palestinian Campus Speech*. http://america.aljazeera.com/articles/2015/9/30/anti-semitism-claims-used-to-crush-pro-palestinian-speech-on-campuses.html. Accessed 18 November 2016.

CHAPTER 11

Bridging Borders: Teaching a Bridging Course with Precarious Status Students Transitioning to the University

Paloma E. Villegas

11.1 Introduction

As an undergraduate student, I enrolled in a Women's Studies[1] course focusing on theorizations by and about women of color. One of the assigned readings was Gloria Anzaldúa's (1999) *Borderlands*. My experience is probably a common way to be introduced to Anzaldúa, and despite it sounding like a cliché, reading *Borderlands* changed my life. Born in Mexico, my family migrated to the US in the early 1990s. I grew up undocumented, and as a young undergraduate in the early 2000s, I was not accustomed to openly hearing about the effects of borders on our bodies, psyches, families, and communities. It was taboo in my family, as in many other undocumented families, to speak about such things (Ledesma, 2015; Perez Huber, 2010).

P. E. Villegas (✉)
California State University, San Bernardino, San Bernardino, CA, USA
e-mail: paloma.villegas@csusb.edu

© The Author(s) 2019
F. J. Villegas and J. Brady (eds.), *Critical Schooling*,
https://doi.org/10.1007/978-3-030-00716-4_11

My search for Women's Studies courses in university was a way to understand and interpret the world around me. However, Anzaldúa did more than that; she highlighted the interlocking of my body, gender, racialization, and immigration status. She spoke to me and about me.

As a teacher, it was initially difficult for me to take those lessons and employ them with students. My formal teaching practice has predominantly occurred in Canada. When we found we would be unable to pursue further studies in the US, my brother and I migrated to Canada to complete our PhDs. Canada is a somewhat different context to the US, with a rather small Latinx population. Furthermore, given my position as a woman of color, I was initially hesitant to share parts of my personal narrative in my teaching. I was worried about looking "unprofessional" and the dreaded student evaluations. It took me a while to feel comfortable and share with students how my life experiences shaped my schooling and employment experiences, as well as their connection to the content I teach: migration and interlocking inequities. Finally, though we often share partial political and experiential affinities (Ang, 2003), I recognize that I grew up in a different situation to the students who take my courses.

In 2017, I had the opportunity to teach a course designed as an academic bridging program to facilitate precarious status[2] students' entry to an Ontario University. The course emerged because of an extended effort from a number of stakeholders. It mirrored other bridging programs that seek to provide equitable pathways to postsecondary education to people who have faced historic and existing forms of marginalization (Antone, 2001; Henry & Tator, 1994; Rehner, 2006). To my knowledge, the course is the first of its kind, given its focus on precarious status students. This chapter reflects on the process of planning and teaching the course. In my reflections, I draw on data from research conducted with course participants. As a previously undocumented person and student, I explore the assumptions I had going in to the course, the role of students as "bridges," the role of storytelling and disclosure, and finally the importance of interdisciplinarity. My reflection is therefore a "situated knowledge" and "partial perspective" (Haraway, 1998): a way to situate my experience and students' reflections in a larger context in which students live and (hopefully) study.

11.2 POSTSECONDARY SCHOOLING AND IMMIGRATION STATUS

Research on the experiences of undocumented undergraduates focuses on barriers to access, experiences and difficulties in university, strategies for success, and the types of support students need. Scholarship in this area began to grow in the mid-2000s, given increased access to universities in some US states. Undocumented students face barriers when thinking about applying for university, which affects their aspirations and material realities (Abrego, 2006). A common term to describe these temporal and affective experiences is living in "limbo" (Abrego, 2006; Villegas, 2014). This limbo is particularly felt given the contradiction that ensues when youth have legal access to K-12 schooling and face legal barriers to enter postsecondary schooling (Gonzales, Heredia, & Negrón-Gonzales, 2015). Gonzales' (2016) longitudinal research with undocumented migrants explores the factors that influenced students' decisions to transition into "college-goers" and "early exiters." These factors included family situation, the schooling system, and aspirations for a future profession.

Barriers follow undocumented students as they transition to postsecondary schooling. When choosing an institution, students consider their immigration status and its interlocking with familial responsibilities, economic situation, and the overall social/political context (McWhorter, 2015; Oliverez, 2006). Once enrolled, they experience barriers related to financing their education (Gonzales, 2016; Gonzales & Chavez, 2012; Perez Huber, 2010), campus climate and the potential for visibility around campus (Villegas, 2010), and continuing on to graduate or professional school (Lara, 2014). For instance, Albrecht (2007) found that participants in her study experienced the following barriers:

> (a) struggling to succeed, (b) feeling the pressure of being a role model, (c) coping with frustration and uncertainty, (d) managing life as a "hidden" member of society, (e) missing out on opportunities, (f) perceptions of self as compared to other students, and (g) complications faced in utilizing campus services. (p. vi)

These barriers produce generalized feelings of isolation that interlock with other factors given students' social locations. For instance, Perez Huber (2010) found that students experienced a gendered and racialized campus context.

Given these barriers, Villegas (2006) found that undocumented undergraduates in his study:

> experienced hopeless moments and periods when the limitations placed on them in higher education and after their graduation caused a great deal of stress, and at times depression. Yet, students also displayed an array of persistent behaviours by utilizing the resources available to them. (p. 86)

Therefore, research also identifies the strategies students utilize for success. Part of this research focuses on familial and network supports (Pérez & Rodríguez, 2012; Villegas, 2006). At the same time, it is important to note that not all students have access to family support, or as Rangel (2001) found, family support can sometimes be limited.

Another strategy used by students to cope is to work with "undocu-friendly" allies (Suárez-Orozco et al., 2015). Collaboration can occur one-on-one, through undocumented or *dreamer* centers (Garcia, 2016), or through specific political projects like the book *Underground Undergrads* from the UCLA Center for Labor Research and Education (Madera, Wong, Monroe, Rivera-Salgado, & Mathay, 2008). The book is an example of advocacy, visibility, and resistance from undocumented students themselves. A Canadian version is the book *Seeds of Hope: Creating a Future in the Shadows* (Aberman, Villegas, & Villegas, 2016). The rationale for these collaborations is to understand undocumented students as "assets" to the university, disrupting criminalizing tropes and identifying the important contributions that those experiencing different forms of legal status can bring to campus and learning communities (Suárez-Orozco et al., 2015).

Other research outlines the institutional limitations of postsecondary institutions' services and/or accommodations for undocumented students (Rangel, 2001). This brings up questions of accessibility, confidentially, and knowledgeable staff. Albrecht (2007) notes that "university administrators, for the most part, knew very little about the undocumented student population on their campus" (p. vii). Recommendations include the implementation of "safe zone" workshops for all staff, pre-college counselors and administrators, information about scholarships, internships, and other resources to which students are eligible, and creating a "one-stop shop" or "Dream Center" on campus (many campuses now have Dreamer centers; however, one concern is the visibility they might bring to students) (Gildersleeve & Ranero, 2010; Person, Gutierrez Keeton, Medina, Gonzalez, & Minero, 2017). Thus, resources and accessibility can only increase if administrators are knowledgeable and sensitive to undocumented student populations on their campuses and communities.

This emerging research demonstrates the interwoven barriers and modes of resilience undocumented university students experience. However, more research is needed in several areas. First, as Cuevas and Cheung (2015) identify, "little is known about the school setting or how teachers and administrators interact with undocumented students" (p. 310). Second, the literature often focuses on students who enter postsecondary studies soon after graduating from high school. This might be because of the nature of entry policies in the US that often require graduating from a state high school (and having had attended one for several years). Finally, it is important to understand barriers and access in other contexts given the fact that undocumented, or precarious status, populations are growing across the globe.

11.3 Undocumented/Precarious Status Migrant Schooling in Canada

In order to address the latter research gap, the Canadian context becomes important. Canada has a significant and growing population of precarious status migrants (Goldring, Berinstein, & Bernhard, 2009; Standing Committee on Citizenship and Immigration, 2009). Some of those migrants arrive as children or youth and yearn to transition from K-12 schooling to university. Others come as adults and may have similar dreams (Aberman et al., 2016).

While research on the intersection of immigration and schooling has been sparse, some exists. For instance, Francisco Villegas (2014; Chapter 8) examines K-12 access in Toronto, and the barriers migrant families experience, despite what has been termed as a Don't Ask Don't Tell policy.[3] Given that some precarious status migrants are admitted (with the exception of tourists who are asked to pay fees), Francisco Villegas (2014) anticipates a growing population of university-ready youth. However, Canadian provinces have not passed policies similar to US states, making access expensive, exclusionary, and uneven. As Hayes (2009) notes, "[n]on-status students are excluded from post-secondary education because the fee structure favours the inclusion of international students for the institution's ability to charge exorbitant amounts and the international students' ability to pay" (p. 104). He discusses the link between the growing number of international students in Canada and neoliberal globalization, which excludes precarious status migrants unable to afford exorbitant fees that some (non-status and refugee claimants) are charged (Hayes, 2009).

Hayes (2009) also notes how access has been piecemeal, using the case of Saintsierra Leonty:

> a 20-year-old who arrived in Canada at age 11 from St. Lucia, and completed her first year at York [University] but had to withdraw due to the cost of international fees...As a result of public pressure, the Minister of Immigration intervened in Leonty's case, and York administrators committed to holding discussions around the feasibility of a DADT [Don't Ask Don't Tell] policy. (Hayes, 2009, p. 105)

Leonty had to take a break from university given that she earned minimum wage and could not afford international fees (Leonty & Villegas, 2008). While university administrators committed to a discussion about the feasibility of making postsecondary education accessible for precarious status migrants was heartening, progress has been slow.

Part of the difficulty in establishing access has been identifying who has the jurisdiction and power to enact policy: the universities or the provincial ministry that oversees them, the Ministry of Advanced Education and Skills Development. Given that it is not a politically expedient topic, both bodies have been slow to accept responsibility.

Another concern is privacy and whether universities will share student information with immigration authorities. Writing about the US, Collier (2017) proposes the use of a "digital sanctuary approach," that is, paying attention to digital data when we discuss sanctuary policies given the possibility of hacking or that the government will subpoena information. She states that we need a process for making data available (and what data should be made available) to law and immigration enforcement. University staff should understand how and when they can say no to inquiries about students, and campuses should investigate the legal limits of their noncompliance with such inquiries (Collier, 2017). These processes are important given precarious status migrants' generalized deportability as well as their vulnerability if immigration authorities or the police appear on campus.

An example outside the university structure also exists: the grassroots FCJ Refugee Centre project titled *Uprooted University* (Aberman et al., 2016). The project emerged from the FCJ Youth Network and their desire to continue to postsecondary education. For several years, students met in a community center classroom and learned from and with local university educators about a variety of topics, despite not receiving university credit for their work. As I discussed above, the network published a book about their experiences, to visibilize the intricacies of precarious status for youth in Toronto (Aberman et al., 2016).

11.4 Methods

Data for this chapter comes from several sources. The first is my reflections teaching the course, which occurred at York University in Toronto after the FCJ Refugee Centre received a grant in 2015 to conduct a pilot project from the City of Toronto. I developed the course syllabus in 2016 and taught the course in winter and early summer of 2017. At peak attendance, I had a total of 28 enrolled students in both courses (20 in the winter and 8 in the summer).

The second data source is interviews, conducted with some course participants after they successfully completed the course. Given my double role as the instructor and researcher, I did not recruit students to participate until they successfully finished the course. The rationale was to assure students that no conflict of interest existed. The recruitment process included a conversation about how and participants' relationship with the bridging course manager, the university, and myself would not be affected by their decision to participate (or not). I interviewed a total of 11 participants. Names used are pseudonyms chosen by participants.

In addition to interviews, I also asked participants for permission to analyze their course assignments as data, the third source. Students had the power to exclude any or all assignments. I anonymized approved assignments and linked them to chosen pseudonyms. To protect confidentiality, I also elected to not refer to students' country of origin and instead focus on regions (Africa, Latin America, the Caribbean). I understand this can conflate intricate histories, but the decision was made as a safeguard for participants.

11.5 THE COURSE

My reflections on the bridging course seek to fill a gap of knowledge for how to think through teaching precarious status students transitioning to and attending university given the intricacies of the Canadian context and how precarious status is organized in relation to education and immigration enforcement.

As a teacher, one of my goals is to connect course ideas and concepts to students' lived experiences, contexts, and realities. I approach this by making sure content comes from diverse sources. This entails the inclusion of a diversity of authors and perspectives with the goal of disrupting hegemonic disciplinary canons that occlude the contributions of women, persons of color, immigrants, persons from the Global South (among others). It also means ensuring the content speaks to students' diverse experiences.

I teach courses that interrogate the reasons, causes, and effects of migration. I also teach courses on the effects of interlocking systems of oppression and inequality, including the effects of precarious status in the lives of im/migrants. Before the bridging course, it was somewhat more difficult to make these connections with students. The context in Toronto means that those who make it to university tend to have secure immigration status, or if international students, may not identify themselves as precarious vis-à-vis status. Exceptions include children of immigrants who often make connections to their parents' experiences and students who have transitioned to secure status themselves.

I came to the course with these pedagogic orientations. However, as I discuss below, I had to think through and adapt my teaching practice given the students' social locations, the tension between sharing stories and a need for privacy, and my own investment in interdisciplinarity.

11.6 MOVING BEYOND ASSUMPTIONS: TOWARD PARTIAL AFFINITIES

The course's focus was critical migration studies. While I have taught a number of migration-focused courses, designing this course felt different given the student makeup and what I imagined would be a different teaching practice. I had two specific assumptions. First, I imagined students who took the course would be recent high school graduates, given my own experience and the research from the US. Second, while

I understood that precarious status meant more than undocumented status, in preparing the course, I imagined an undocumented or non-status population. After teaching the course twice, one of the lessons learned was not to make assumptions. Students varied in age, immigration status, and region of origin much more than I anticipated.

I also had to be careful with not assuming my own experience of being undocumented as a norm or model. To think through this, I found Ang's (2003) discussion of partiality useful. In her intervention to how people associate with essentializing feminisms, she states:

> Feminism must stop conceiving itself as a nation, a 'natural' political designation for all women, no matter how multicultural. Rather than adopting a politics of inclusion (which is always ultimately based on a notion of commonality and community), it will have to develop a self-conscious politics of partiality, and imagine itself as a limited political home, which does not absorb difference within a pre-given and predefined space but leaves room for ambivalence and ambiguity. (Ang, 2003, p. 191)

My social location influenced the FCJ Refugee Centre's choice to hire me to both develop and teach the course. It also influenced how I designed and taught it. However, I cannot claim full commonality with the students who participated in the course. The idea of partiality allows for a coalitional politics without reducing or essentializing forms of identification (in this case immigration status and race/nationality). Partiality therefore allows for a productive tension, with room for reflection and re-negotiation.

11.7 Bridging and "Pedagogies of Migration"

I set out to design a course that questioned foundational understandings for the reasons people move, where they go, and how they incorporate in new societies. I also set out to include texts that spoke to students' specific experiences in terms of status, interlocking social locations, and pathways or approaches to receive secure status.

My course design and teaching approach was influenced by pedagogical understandings of teaching as a political practice or act (Freire & Macedo, 1995; Yosso, 2006). Given that the bridging course was meant to encourage the continuing development of students' critical, writing, and oral presentation skills, I realized that there was also a need to bridge our collective understanding of the Canadian immigration system and its historical underpinnings. My goal was therefore to disrupt assumptions about migrant "illegality" as well as explore how the Canadian state has historically welcomed, managed, and excluded immigrants and other actors depending on factors like race, gender, and nationality (for another example, see Gibson-Taylor & Moore, Chapter 5). It was important for me to make connections to the "Canadian context" given that it was a context in which students were intimately embedded. Another reason was that students' knowledge of such histories varied regardless of age or arrival or exposure to prior Canadian schooling. For this reason, I included discussions of Indigenous histories and ongoing colonial practices during the first iteration of the course and incorporated them more concretely in the syllabus for the second iteration after reflecting on the need for more substantive and deliberate discussion.

Another way to think through the experience of "bridging" is through Henry A. Giroux's (1991) discussion of border pedagogies. He explains that

> [s]tudents must engage knowledge as border-crossers, as persons moving in and out of borders constructed around coordinates of difference and power...These are not only physical borders, they are cultural borders historically constructed and socially organized within rules and regulations that limit and enable particular identities, individual capacities, and social forms. In this case, students cross over into realms of meaning, maps of knowledge, social relations, and values that are increasingly being negotiated and rewritten as the codes and regulations that organize them become destabilized and reshaped. (Giroux, 1991, p. 53)

Students in the course were literal border crosses, given that as migrants, they crossed a number of geographic and immigration status boundaries. Those experiences influenced their ability to attend the course as well as complete it, disrupting the romanticization of crossing borders as a "liberatory" practice. Border crossing is not devoid of power relations. Some students were forced to withdraw from the course because of work or family responsibilities. Others were unable to enroll because of similar concerns. Therefore, students were also border-crossers or bridges within the institution/higher education, learning to navigate it while also critical of its exclusionary logic. They pushed the boundaries of who is expected and welcome in university settings and disrupted assumptions about their positionalities in terms of race, gender, age, and family responsibilities.

In other ways, "bridging" was not necessary. As I mentioned above, oftentimes when I teach about immigration status, I have to explain the specifics to students who have little knowledge of the Canadian immigration system or understand it as *only* welcoming and positive. However, precarious status migrants often become immigration "experts" given their personal cases. In the bridging course, we worked with a type of short hand that allowed the discussion to flow beyond general definitions and debates. This did not mean that we were all on the same page. Disrupting systems of oppression is an ongoing process, which is often impeded by assimilatory frameworks. During debates, students pushed each other to unpack assumptions about migrant deservingness, "legitimate" migrants, and manifestations of white supremacy. In that regard, they acted as bridges for each other. We also had a conversation about using the "*i*" word ("illegal" immigrant) several times and the violence that it produces for differently situated migrants. As a class we agreed to avoid the term, however, it is so internalized in everyday conversations that it reemerged a few times during both iterations of the course.

Thinking through these multiple forms of bridging or border crossing, I draw on Lopez' (2010) concept of "pedagogies of migration," which she defines as "individual, family and community lessons used by immigrant and immigrant-identified individuals to survive and resist multiple forms of subordination. Pedagogies of migration are an (undocumented) immigrant way of teaching and learning, an immigrant epistemology" (p. 63). Lopez focuses on different scales of interaction (the individual, family, and community) and how they are influenced by structural forces like immigration regimes, something I also tried to do in the course. Therefore, while Lopez's research is about Mexican migrants in the US, I propose that "pedagogies of migration" travel to Canada.

If we return to Anzaldúa, who co-edited the foundational woman of color anthology, *This Bridge Called My Back: Writings by Radical Women of Color* (Moraga & Anzaldúa, 1981), we can place "pedagogies of migration" in conversation with the understanding of minoritized individuals as bridges. In this sense, the bridging course was not only a bridge to university, but also a way for students and I to understand how they/we negotiate the boundaries that have historically and currently excluded them/us. And as bridges, we also have to think about precarious status students as "assets" (Suárez-Orozco et al., 2015) and recognize their important knowledges and potential contributions to university and other communities. This means understanding their presence and contributions through a lens of "community cultural wealth" (Yosso, 2006), something that becomes difficult given their invisibilized status within the university and often outside of it.

11.8 Writer's Block, Storytelling, and Disclosure

Following other academic bridging programs, the course sought to work with students to develop their writing, reading, presentation, and other skills necessary to transition to university (Antone, 2001; Henry & Tator, 1994; Rehner, 2006). We also attempted to introduce students to university policies (tuition, policing, academic dishonesty) and the types of resources (Writing Center, Disability Services, Counseling Services) available at the university. These were lofty goals, and as any teacher knows, you cannot foresee how a class will turn out until you teach it a few times. Identifying assignments appropriate for the course and the students was difficult, particularly because of questions of safety and confidentiality in relation to immigration status.

In recent years, there has been a push to have undocumented students "come out" and tell their stories publicly in the US, for instance, through slogans like *Undocumented and Unafraid* (Negrón-Gonzales, 2014). This is a controversial move. On the one hand, disclosing one's immigration status can lead to the creation of community ties among people who might not otherwise know they share similar experiences. It can also have political effects—visibility can lead to social change and put a face on what is often discussed as statistics (11 million undocumented in the US, estimates of 500,000 in Canada). Yet as we know, with visibility comes the possibility of deportation, what De Genova (2002) terms deportability.

In preparing the course, I read Alberto Ledesma's (2015) essay, titled "On the Grammar of Silence: The Structure of My Undocumented Immigrant Writer's Block." In the essay, Ledesma reflects on the effects his undocumented status had on his writing practice, even after receiving secure immigration status. He describes how his family's strategy to avoid detection by never disclosing their immigration status led to a series of "predictable silences and obfuscations" (p. 415). He used what in another context Villegas (2006) refers to as "prepared answers," that is, answers that avoid discussing immigration status or make an audience believe one has status in order to avoid further questions. For Ledesma (2015), "prepared answers" and "predictable silences" meant he experienced writer's block during his schooling career through which he sought to become a professional writer/researcher.

Students in the Bridging program were assigned written reflections about course readings before coming to class. They wrote the following after reading the Ledesma (2015) article:

> What mostly caught my attention was the explanation of the writer's block that the author developed as a result from those years of having to hide his history from everyone else. It reminded me of my own experiences trying to write my "own" story...I remembered how I used to avoid giving away too much. (Joey, 22, Latinx first iteration of the course)

> Going through this article, it just clearly confirms what I personally go through each day of my life as an Undocumented immigrant especially when I have to be asked, or when something reminds me of my status. (Gabriella, 27, African, first iteration of the course)

> I ... completely understand what Ledesma means by saying that he had to train himself to talk in half-truths. Even now, when talking to friends or potential friends, I have to be very careful of what I say. I don't want to lie to them, but giving half-truths never feels like I am being honest. It makes me feel like my situation is something that I should consider as criminal, even though I personally don't want to feel about it in that way. (Barbara, 22, Latinx, second iteration of the course)

The students discussed the feelings of shame and criminalization they experienced as a result of their immigration status. During class discussion, we had a conversation about how to reframe the construction of "prepared answers" as lying. Instead, I proposed conceptualizing them as strategies of survival given the way I have worked through "prepared answers" and "uncomfortable questions" in my own life (Bernhard, Goldring, Young, Berinstein, & Wilson, 2007; Villegas, 2006).

I also linked Ledesma's narrative to storytelling. Storytelling is a powerful tool, and therefore, I told a lot of stories in class. Most stories were about my personal experience, though I also conceptualize academic research as stories and often brought those up as well. I used stories as an entry point to build trust with students (given my own experience) as well as to illustrate different concepts: illegalization, deportability, and precarity. The goal was not to elicit stories from students, although sometimes it did, but to open up a discussion where students knew that I was knowledgeable (albeit partially) of some of their experiences and appreciated their input in the conversation.

Given my interest in storytelling, one of the assignments students worked on in the class was a migration story. For the assignment, students narrated a part of their migration experience and related it to the themes discussed in the class. While I believed the assignment would ease students into a writing practice, which later involved writing an argumentative paper on a topic of their choice, I was also worried that asking students to write about their migration experience might make them uncomfortable, trigger a writer's block, negative memories and experiences, or make them feel they had to disclose their immigration status. As Cuevas and Cheung (2015) state:

> For undocumented youth, finding the words to discuss their documentation status in educational settings can be difficult—not only because of the physical and psychological threats of mass deportation and enhanced immigration enforcement, but also because schools and teachers themselves feel uncomfortable with, and perhaps inept at, speaking plainly or openly about issues of legal status. (p. 313)

In order to counteract negative consequences, I was open with students. From the first day of class, I shared my political motivations for teaching the course. We also agreed upon confidentiality as one of our class rules. For the migration story, students had the choice to speak about their own experiences or to discuss a fictional migration narrative. I was also clear that the stories would not be presented in class or in any way shared with their peers unless they chose to disclose information during class discussions.

I recognized that as an instructor, there was a power differential between myself and students, and this meant telling students they had a choice to write about an alternative story several times and that their choice would not affect their mark. In fact, the assignment objectives highlighted students would be graded on the links they made to course content, how they organized the story, and the quality of their writing. We also talked about the power of storytellers to decide where to begin and end a story, and the power of omission. Finally, as I stated above, not all students who enrolled in the course were immediately deportable, some were awaiting the resolution of refugee claims. This meant allowing students to decide whether to use their story or work on an alternative.

Students also worked on weekly reading reflections. We can think through this assignment using "pedagogies of migration"—lessons migrants use to resist the interlocking forms of oppression they experience (Lopez, 2010)—and "politicized funds of knowledge" (Gallo & Link, 2015). "Politicized funds of knowledge" refer to

> the real-world experiences, knowledges, and skills that young people deploy and develop across contexts of learning that are often positioned as taboo or unsafe to incorporate into classroom learning. These funds of knowledge are developed by students from a range of backgrounds. For Latina/o immigrant students from documented and undocumented immigrant families, these real-world experiences may include the knowledges they learn through navigating citizenship status. (Gallo & Link, 2015, p. 361)

In their reflections (as well as the migration story assignment), students shared lessons learned throughout their travels and border crossings and linked them to course content. They drew from "politicized funds of knowledge" as they reflected on individual and family migration decision-making as well as scaling up to think through how the politics of nation-building, borders, and sovereignty impacted them. This, along with other course readings, opened a discussion about precarious status migrants' visibility and vulnerability in Canada.

For example, Zoe, 32 from the Caribbean, wrote the following reflection in relation to the last set of readings in the course (Negrón-Gonzales, 2014; Rebouillat, 2013),

> What is citizenship? Who is a citizen? Is it the place where you're born, the passport you carry, documentation from a governmental power, a settled inhabitant of a particular town or city? Does one need to have built a life there? Raise children, have a job, a place of residence that they pay for, engage in buying and selling, contribute to the economy? What about social involvement, being a member of a communit[y]? Volunteering time, effort energies, expertise towards helping other in that community. What about the children. Do they need to be in school, get good grades, participate in extracurricular activities, have post-secondary educational goals?

Do you need to speak the language, take on the values, appreciate the culture, have a vested interest in the future of the town, city, or country that you live in? is the documentation the be all and end all, so that without it, one is rendered invisible? Does social inclusion count for anything? How about having hopes and dreams? How about wanting to be an asset and contribute to the betterment of society? Where does growing up in a place fit in there? Finding [sic] onesself, setting down roots? How about not having an attachment emotional or otherwise to anywhere else but that country? How much time needs to pass? How much sacrifice and frustrations, and activism and pleas and cries and civil disobedience is necessary to find out? What does it mean to be a citizen? Undocumented, unapologetic and unafraid!

Zoe discussed the categorization of individuals through citizenship status, a process that leads to the differential allocation of entitlements and social goods. She alluded to the emphasis on "contribution" set out by governments vis-à-vis immigrants, one that disciplines those who do not contribute in stereotypical and hegemonic ways. She also referred to a "right to the city" (Lefebvre, 1991) something she expanded upon in her final paper which evaluated the Sanctuary City policy in Toronto.[4] She ended with a reference to one of the assigned reading's title "Undocumented, unapologetic and unafraid" (Negrón-Gonzales, 2014), which is also a slogan used by some undocumented migrants in the US.

11.9 INTERDISCIPLINARITY

The students who took the course were not all going to be sociology majors—the discipline in which I teach. I knew this coming in, given my experience with *Uprooted University*, and tried to incorporate different disciplinary perspectives in my teaching. However, there were limitations to this practice. While I studied biology as an undergraduate, I do not have the knowledge base to teach it. Nor can I teach engineering, or accounting, or multiple other disciplines that interested students. I was limited to the humanities and social sciences as they related to migration.

My goal was to show students the variety of disciplines from which they could take courses. Students often come to university thinking they will be one of a short list of professions: teacher, doctor, lawyer, etc. After the first iteration of the course, I decided that getting them to think about the breadth of disciplines available and what scholars do with them was an important lesson.

Given my own interdisciplinary background, my goal was also to think about students' different abilities in expressing themselves. While sociology evaluates students mainly through writing or exams, I often have students work on creative projects that supplement writing assignments. Thus, as part of students' migration story, they had the option to work on a body map. Body map storytelling is a qualitative research methodology that asks participants to represent their embodied experiences on tracings of their bodies (Gastaldo, Magalhães, Carrasco & Davy, 2012). Participants can incorporate writing, drawing, and pasted images on the body to illustrate those experiences. The body map includes three components, the illustrated body map, the personal narrative or *testimonio*, and a key of the body map. I altered the research methodology and used it as a pedagogical tool (Villegas, 2016). The body map assignment sought to consider students who were interested in creative arts, or those who were weary of writing a longer 4–5-page assignment (the body map option asked for a 2-page written narrative in addition to the body map and key).

While most students chose the written assignment, a few selected the body map. Figure 11.1 illustrates Joey's body map. Joey chose to use quotes and other references to illustrate her experience in the body map stating:

> Even if [sic] i were to map out every detail that represents who I am, I believe that without these words –the words of someone else—I would not be able to give a better insight of myself, or my story. So therefore, I resource back to music, to messages beats and rhythms to try to communicate what a life time of traveling has taught me and how it has contributed to the person I am today. (Joey's Body Map)

During our interview, Joey identified feeling hesitant to tell her story, and as a result, strategically chose what to disclose. This was a strategy of protection, given that Joey did not want specific information to come out and potentially affect an immigration application. The choice reinforces the fact that precarious status migrants often opt not to disclose their stories to protect themselves. It also demonstrates Joey's agency in selecting what to share, which might also be read as resistance to the call for the sharing of stories of pain (for more on the fetishization of stories of pain see Azraq, Chapter 10). While I worried about this when I designed the assignment, during interviews students

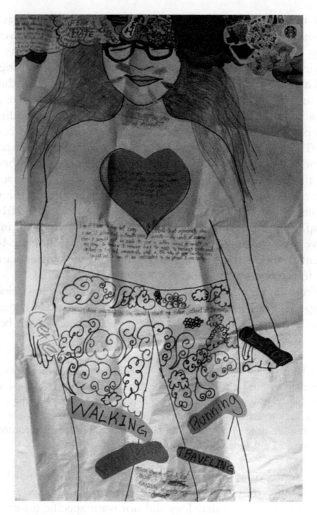

Fig. 11.1 Joey's body map

identified the migration story as their favorite assignment, particularly because they could connect their lived experiences to systemic issues. In this way, students employed "pedagogies of migration" (Lopez, 2010) and "politicized funds of knowledge" (Gallo & Link, 2015).

Joey's focus on music lyrics illustrates the role of cultural processes/artistic expressions in making us feel less isolated. It is also a way to have others explain how we feel, which I read as a way for her to explain her experience without having to undergo the painful process of looking for the words. Referencing lyrics also manifested something emphasized in class: our work, research, and storytelling is a part of an ongoing conversation that requires an ethical responsibility to cite those who have influenced us.

Another example of interdisciplinarity involved the use of visual images to illustrate concepts. This included the use of my own artwork as well as visual representations of migration. I used my artwork when we discussed the production of migrant "illegality" (Coutin, 2003; De Genova, 2005). This was another layer through which students had the opportunity to relate course content to their lived experiences. In addition, sharing my artwork also opened the door for students to share their own. I was happily surprised when, during students' presentations of their final argumentative paper, two students included their own artistic work.

We also did a close reading of a photo-essay that supported the argument for "no borders" (Rebouillat, 2013). We used the photo-essay to discuss migrant justice organizing as well as to problematize "no border" arguments given the struggle for Indigenous sovereignty (Fortier, 2015). Thomas Jefferson, 23, from Africa, and a student from the first iteration of the course, wrote the following reflection about the essay format (photography):

> As I analyzed the pictures it reminded me of how people choose different paths to get to the 'promise[d] land.' I saw those pictures as realities being faced by many people who want to improve their lives. I felt like these pictures told a story of how immigration affects countries, people, laws and etc.

In class, we talked about the power of images using the common phrase "a picture is worth a thousand words." Students felt that the visual representation of borders, and resistance toward those borders, had a powerful effect. We also spoke about the power of representation and how controlling images can influence how people understand migration and im/migrants. Thus, using interdisciplinary perspectives, in terms of assigned readings from different disciplines as well as the use of visual imagery in class and assignments opened up the types of conversations we had in class as well as how differently situated students related to the course and myself.

11.10 Concluding Remarks

Teaching always involves learning. It also always involves a bit of the unknown. Teaching a bridging course for precarious status students transitioning to the university involved both aspects. In this chapter, I discussed some of the assumptions I had going into the class and the lessons I learned through teaching it. I also drew on pedagogical theory to think through the role of students in the course as border-crossers and bridges. I then reflected on assignments I used in class to connect students' lived experience to course content, and the work I did to protect students' confidentiality. Finally, I discussed the importance of interdisciplinarity throughout the process.

There are several implications to my reflections. First, it is imperative to expand access to postsecondary schooling for all precarious status migrants in Canada. Understanding precarious status migrants as "assets" allows for a re-framing of discourses about eligibility and deservingness (Suárez-Orozco et al., 2015). While bridging programs play an important role in preparing students, opening up access would make them less necessary for some students, who might enroll directly. All of this requires further research and reflection in Canada.

Second, opening up access is a community endeavor whereby teachers, students, and administrators become informed about the specific needs of precarious status students. I was only a small part of that process for the bridging course, which could not have been done without the tireless work of community groups, advocates, and the students themselves.

Finally, in teaching a bridging course for precarious status students, it is important to not shy away from difficult conversations, while at the same time being careful to conduct them in a respectful manner. One of the themes that emerged from student evaluations during the first iteration of the course was that students appreciated discussions that made connections between structural forces and lived experience. Students also shared this during interviews. More thought and reflection are necessary to think through how best to include this in all university courses given that we never know, and often do not need to know, the immigration status of students taking them.

Notes

1. Now Women and Gender Studies.
2. Precarious status is an umbrella category that includes undocumented or non-status immigrants as well as other forms of less than full legal status including refugees, refugee claimants, international students, temporary foreign workers, and sponsored spouses (still in the process) (Goldring et al., 2009). Goldring et al. (2009) use the term precarious to point to the instability and flexibility of precarious status, and how it can change across time, as well as its links to other precarious conditions including precarious work. The term is therefore useful to disrupt an undocumented/documented binary.
3. The policy is meant to welcome students to schools, and although frontline staff ask about status, they are not allowed to disclose that information to immigration authorities.
4. The policy was passed in 2013 (Keung, 2013). It provides access to municipal services to anyone regardless of immigration status. Limitations ensue when services are funded by different entities (e.g., provincial and federal governments) that do not have similar policies.

References

Aberman, T., Villegas, F. J., & Villegas, P. E. (Eds.). (2016). *Seeds of Hope: Creating a Future in the Shadows*. Toronto, ON: FCJ Refugee Centre.

Abrego, L. J. (2006). "I Can't Go to College Because I Don't Have Papers": Incorporation Patterns of Latino Undocumented Youth. *Latino Studies, 4*(3), 212–231.

Albrecht, T. J. (2007). *Challenges and Service Needs of Undocumented Mexican Undergraduate Students: Students' Voices and Administrators' Perspectives* (PhD). The University of Texas at Austin (3290814).

Ang, I. (2003). I'm a Feminist but... "Other" Women and Postcolonial Feminism. In R. Lewis & S. Mills (Eds.), *Feminist Postcolonial Theory: A Reader* (pp. 190–206). New York, NY: Routledge.

Antone, E. M. (2001). Adult Social Movement Learning Experience Among First Nations in the Transitional Year Programme at the University of Toronto. *Convergence, 34*(4), 27–40.

Anzaldúa, G. (1999). *Borderlands/ la frontera: The New Mestiza* (2nd ed.). San Francisco, CA: Aunt Lute Books.

Bernhard, J., Goldring, L., Young, J., Berinstein, C., & Wilson, B. (2007). Living with Precarious Legal Status in Canada: Implications for the Well-Being of Children and Families. *Refuge: Canada's Periodical on Refugees, 24*(2), 101–114.

Collier, A. (2017). *"It Should Be Necessary to Start": Critical Digital Pedagogy in Troubled Political Times.* http://redpincushion.us/blog/i-cant-categorize-this/it-should-be-necessary-to-start-critical-digital-pedagogy-in-troubled-political-times/. Accessed 18 August 2017.

Coutin, S. B. (2003). Illegality, Borderlands, and the Space of Nonexistence. In R. W. Perry & B. Maurer (Eds.), *Globalization Under Construction: Governmentality, Law, and Identity* (pp. 171–202). Minneapolis: University of Minnesota Press.

Cuevas, S., & Cheung, A. (2015). Dissolving Boundaries: Understanding Undocumented Students' Educational Experiences. *Harvard Educational Review, 85*(3), 310–317.

De Genova, N. (2002). Migrant 'Illegality' and Deportability in Everyday Life. *Annual Review of Anthropology, 31,* 419–447.

De Genova, N. (2005). *Working the Boundaries: Race, Space, and "Illegality" in Mexican Chicago.* Durham, NC: Duke University Press.

Fortier, C. (2015, September 21). *No One Is Illegal, Canada Is Illegal! Negotiating the Relationships Between Settler Colonialism and Border Imperialism Through Political Slogans.* https://decolonization.wordpress.com/2015/09/21/no-one-is-illegal-Canada-is-illegal-negotiating-the-relationships-between-settler-colonialism-and-border-imperialism-through-political-slogans/. Accessed 18 August 2017.

Freire, P., & Macedo, D. P. (1995). A Dialogue: Culture, Language & Race. *Harvard Educational Review, 65*(3), 377–403.

Gallo, S., & Link, H. (2015). "Diles la verdad": Deportation Policies, Politicized Funds of Knowledge, and Schooling in Middle Childhood. *Harvard Educational Review, 85*(3), 357–382.

Garcia, V. P. (2016). *Exploring a Counter-Space: Recounting Student Experiences During Year One of the AB540 and Undocumented Student Center at the University of California, Davis* (M.A.). University of California Davis, (10194680.).

Gastaldo, D., Magalhães, L., Carrasco, C., & Davy, C. (2012). *Body-Map Storytelling as Research: Methodological Considerations for Telling the Stories of Undocumented Workers Through Body Mapping.* http://www.migrationhealth.ca/undocumented-workers-ontario/body-mapping.

Gildersleeve, R. E., & Ranero, J. J. (2010). Precollege Contexts of Undocumented Students: Implications for Student Affairs Professionals. *New Directions for Student Services, 131,* 19–33.

Giroux, H. A. (1991). Border Pedagogy and the Politics of Postmodernism. *Social Text, 28,* 51–67.

Goldring, L., Berinstein, C., & Bernhard, J. (2009). Institutionalizing Precarious Migratory Status in Canada. *Citizenship Studies, 13*(3), 239–265.

Gonzales, R. G. (2016). *Lives in Limbo: Undocumented and Coming of Age in America.* Oakland: University of California Press.

Gonzales, R. G., & Chavez, L. R. (2012). "Awakening to a Nightmare": Abjectivity and Illegality in the Lives of Undocumented 1.5-Generation Latino Immigrants in the United States. *Current Anthropology, 53*(3), 255–281.

Gonzales, R. G., Heredia, L. L., & Negrón-Gonzales, G. (2015). Untangling Plyler's Legacy: Undocumented Students, Schools, and Citizenship. *Harvard Educational Review, 85*(3), 318–341.

Haraway, D. (1998). Situated Knowledges: The Science Question in Feminism and the Privilege of Partial Perspective. *Feminist Studies, 14,* 575–599.

Hayes, R. (2009). Neoliberal Citizenship: The Case of International and Non-Status Students in Canada. In V. Fynn, P. (Ed.), *Documenting the Undocumented: Redefining Refugee Status, Center for Refugee Studies 2009 Annual Conference Proceedings* (pp. 101–109). Boca Raton, FL: Universal Publishers.

Henry, F., & Tator, C. (1994). Racism and the University. *Canadian Ethnic Studies, 26*(3), 74–90.

Keung, N. (2013, February 22). City Declared a 'Sanctuary'. *The Toronto Star*, p. A1.

Lara, A. (2014). *Navigating Critical Terrain: The Decision Making Process of Undocumented Latina/o Graduate Students* (PhD). UCLA (0249).

Ledesma, A. (2015). On the Grammar of Silence: The Structure of My Undocumented Immigrant Writer's Block. *Harvard Educational Review, 85*(3), 415–426.

Lefebvre, H. (1991). *The Production of Space* (D. Nicholson-Smith, Trans.). Malden, MA: Blackwell.

Leonty, S., & Villegas, P. E. (2008). Between Borders: An Immigrant's Story. *Shameless Magazine,* 12.

Lopez, C. B. (2010). *Las Fronteras de nuestra Education: Documenting the Pedagogies of Migration of Mexican and Chicana/o Undocumented Immigrant Households* (PhD). UCLA.

Madera, G., Wong, K., Monroe, J., Rivera-Salgado, G., & Mathay, A. A. (Eds.). (2008). *Underground Undergrads: UCLA Undocumented Immigrant Students Speak Out*. Los Angeles: UCLA Center for Labor Research and Education.

McWhorter, E. B. (2015). *An Invisible Population Speaks: Exploring College Decision-Making Processes of Undocumented Undergraduates at a California State University Campus* (PhD). Indiana University (3732254).

Moraga, C., & Anzaldúa, G. (1981). *This Bridge Called My Back: Writings by Radical Women of Color* (1st ed.). Watertown, MA: Persephone Press.

Negrón-Gonzales, G. (2014). Undocumented, Unafraid and Unapologetic: Re-Articulatory Practices and Migrant Youth "Illegality". *Latino Studies, 12*(2), 259–278.

Oliverez, P. M. (2006). *Ready but Restricted: An Examination of the Challenges of College Access and Financial Aid for College-Ready Undocumented Students in the U.S.* (PhD). University of Southern California (3257819).

Pérez, P. A., & Rodríguez, J. L. (2012). Access and Opportunity for Latina/o Undocumented College Students: Familial and Institutional Support Factors. *Association of Mexican American Educators Journal, 5*(1), 14–21.

Perez Huber, L. (2010). Using Latina/o Critical Race Theory (Latcrit) and Racist Nativism to Explore Intersectionality in the Educational Experiences of Undocumented Chicana College Students. *Educational Foundations, 24*(1–2), 77–96.

Person, D., Gutierrez Keeton, R., Medina, N., Gonzalez, J., & Minero, L. P. (2017). Effectively Serving AB 540 and Undocumented Students at a Hispanic Serving Institution. *Journal of Hispanic Higher Education, 16*(3), 256–272.

Rangel, Y. T. (2001). *College Immigrant Students: How Undocumented Female Mexican Immigrant Students Transition into Higher Education* (PhD). UCLA (3032926).

Rebouillat, J. (2013). No Border: Photo Essay. *Citizenship Studies, 17*(2), 173–177.

Rehner, J. (2006). Critical Skills Pedagogy: Bridging the Gap. In A. O'Reilly & R. K. Newman (Ed.), *You Can Get There from Here: 25 Years of Bridging Courses for Women at York University* (pp. 61–67). Toronto, ON: York University School of Women Studies.

Standing Committee on Citizenship and Immigration. (2009). *Temporary Foreign Workers and Nonstatus Workers. House of Commons, Ottawa, Canada.* Ottawa: House of Commons. http://www2.parl.gc.ca/HousePublications/Publication.aspx?DocId=3866154&Language=E&Mode=1&Parl=40&Ses=2. Accessed 18 July 2014.

Suárez-Orozco, C., Katsiaficas, D., Birchall, O., Alcantar, C. M., Hernandez, E., Garcia, Y., ..., Teranishi, R. T. (2015). Undocumented Undergraduates on College Campuses: Understanding Their Challenges and Assets and What It Takes to Make an Undocufriendly Campus. *Harvard Educational Review, 85*(3), 427–463.

Villegas, F. J. (2006). *Challenging Educational Barriers: Undocumented Immigrant Student Advocates* (M.A.) San Jose State University.

Villegas, F. J. (2010). Strategic In/Visibility and Undocumented Migrants. In G. J. S. Dei & M. Simmons (Eds.), *Fanon & Education: Thinking Through Pedagogical Possibilities* (pp. 147–170). New York, NY: Peter Lang.

Villegas, F. J. (2014). *The Politics of "Access": Undocumented Students and Enrollment in Toronto Schools* (PhD). University of Toronto, Toronto.

Villegas, P. E. (2014). "I Can't Even Buy a Bed Because I Don't Know If I'll Have to Leave Tomorrow:" Temporal Orientations Among Mexican Precarious Status Migrants in Toronto. *Citizenship Studies,18*(3–4), 277–291.

Villegas, P. E. (2016, May 10). *Body Maps for Teaching Migration.* Paper Presented at the University of Toronto's Teaching & Learning Symposium, Toronto.

Yosso, T. J. (2006). *Critical Race Counterstories Along the Chicana/Chicano Educational Pipeline.* New York, NY: Routledge.

CHAPTER 12

Self-Study of an Indigenous Settler in Ontario Schooling: An Exploration of Living Theory

Umar Umangay

> How a society selects, classifies, distributes, transmits and evaluates the educational knowledge it considers to be public, reflects both the distribution of power and the principles of social control. (Bernstein, 1977, p. 83)

12.1 Introduction

The previous chapter by Paloma Villegas resonates with the power of understanding self, assumptions, learning and how they are complex in their understandings of the needs of students in the schooling process and transitions. Moving our conversations onto the educator, my overall professional practice explores my transformations as an educator through the intersection of anti-racism. I propose to explore the relationship of the self and study beyond action research methodology not as

U. Umangay (✉)
First Nations Technical Institute,
Tyendinaga Mohawk Territory, ON, Canada
e-mail: umaru@fnti.net

© The Author(s) 2019
F. J. Villegas and J. Brady (eds.), *Critical Schooling*,
https://doi.org/10.1007/978-3-030-00716-4_12

an improvement of practice but as an ethical improvement of the settler body. I will engage and critically discuss the question of implementing anti-racist research and methodology through (re)imagining the professional teacher, the action researcher and the educational leader with the complexity of Indigenous and global education practices. I believe that research of the self is not a linear process,[1] especially when racialization, decolonization and ethics intersect and challenge one's thinking of schooling and teacher education. This work documents Living Theory using a reflective, spiralling route with the circumstance of self-study of professional practice being transformed into new understandings of researching the self (Fig. 12.1). My chapter discusses the self-study's context and data, theoretical framework, re-imagining, transformation and future actions.

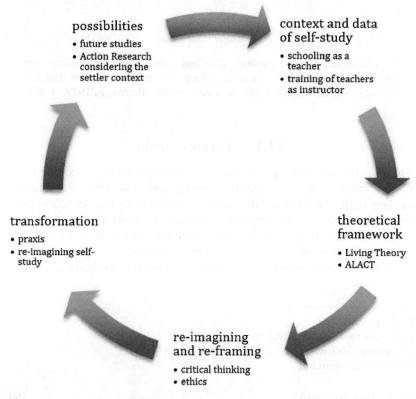

Fig. 12.1 Visual organization of the chapter as Living Theory

My reflection and self-study used data and context that were set in a pre-service teacher education programme that was responding to demands of twenty-first-century schooling and implementing multiple-literacies in Ontario. Korthagen's (2001) ALACT[2] model will be (re)developed with race as the entry point for critical reflection, and for developing critical pedagogy. The intention is to demonstrate the saliency of race and white privilege in our schooling system and in our training of pre-service teacher candidates.

Furthermore, the notion of saliency was brought about by my lived experiences as a professional educator. For instance, my initial awareness of key tensions of schooling came through the content and evaluation on residential schooling for my Grade Four class. Recently, my own experiences in working on reconciliation through exposing how marginalized First Nations were historically left out in their stories, conversations and appearances in schooling were met by scepticism and resistance by colleagues, and later on teacher candidates. This became my introduction to how race became visible in content and interactions. It became my need to understand this conflict, differentiated status of voice and contradiction of teaching ideals within my professional body. With racialization as part of the schooling, this motivated and challenged what I understood as authentic and valid knowledge and pedagogy. I started to appreciate that through material realities, relationships and the complexity of pedagogical practices that learning is neither hierarchical nor linear, and that it is recreated and reproduced in our texts and in our professional practices (Fine, 1994a, pp. 14–17). The specific struggles of colonized peoples embodied through my particular politics, and in my own understanding of Hawaiian, diaspora may be captured in (re)discovering and (re)appreciating *kanaka maoli*[3] identities, languages and histories through my professional and scholarly activities. However, in my context of struggle, the Indigenous in a settler nation state should be mindful of envisioning, reflecting and imagining beyond present realities and engage our future as co-inhabitants of *Mother Earth* with those who are being colonized, with those who are colonizers, and with those who seek a meaningful and peaceful relationship (Battiste, 2008; Corntassel, 2003; Dei, 2008a; St. Denis, 2007). This has become the political tone of my research narrative: "I am a storyteller of the lives of the people that have advised me both here in the now and in my spiritual/dreamtime."

12.2 Contexts for Self-Study

Schooling has been the site of critical thinking and critical pedagogy (Giroux, 1983; McLaren, 1989). My own critical change and transformation in action research in schooling started with engaging with anti-racism in my professional practice (Dei, 1996, 2005). Specifically, this chapter uses the approach of rethinking and decolonizing self-study of teacher education practice (S-STEP) by means of an experience of being Indigenous and being a settler. This version of critical S-STEP engages the intersections of economic materiality, contradictory spaces and the colonizing history of schooling (Cannon & Sunseri, 2011; Corntassel, 2003; Dei, 1994, 1996, 1998, 2008a, 2008b; Fine & Weis, 2003). Furthermore, my reflections, revelations and choosing of experiential data may illustrate the possibility and tensions of an intersectional form S-STEP. In other words, the (re)discovery of the contradictions, impositions and management developed from an interrogation and documentation of one's body, ethics, social economy and place within predominantly white institutions of schooling and teacher education. I chose the data as evidence of the significant and problematic impact, discourse, text and conversations of the surroundings and my relationships.

12.3 Data for Self-Study

Upon reflecting on connections and intersections, I made a judgement that action research had to address the ethical activity of the body/self. My disposition and the questioning of methodology in education were illustrated and informed through the practice of auto-ethnography (Bullough & Pinnegar, 2001; Chang, 2008; Jones, 2005). I used *field notes* from my professional teaching journal to document my thinking and actions. Barkhuizen and Wette (2008) affirmed this approach by stating that "[i]n telling their stories of experience teachers necessarily reflect on those experiences and thus make meaning of them" (p. 374). My notes became an integral part of my lesson planning process. It was my way to capture reactions and memories of my professional practice that set my location and learning context. These field notes are my journal, my resource and my diary. They are textual archives that are part of my body, my memories, my identity and my history of teaching. In this struggle to make sense of myself, they became part of my critical self-study of professional practice.

Besides the field notes, I use the responses from open-ended interviews of teacher candidates in focus group sessions associated with a teacher education programme.[4] The data for this self-reflection were limited to the training and education of pre-service teacher candidates in the subject of science and technology. This approach argues that using voices and stories of the teacher and of their students became a way to gain traction, understanding and authenticity with these reflexive arrangements of anti-racism and in developing the practice of an "activist professional." I hope to share with readers that the imagination and envisioning of an Indigenous anti-racist methodological framework may be co-developed through self-study and the relational experiences from Indigenous and non-Indigenous mentors and students. My own social relations were studied by analysing the effect of the curriculum on my practice and on student engagement. I would consider this action as the ability and skill to articulate the story of one's own thinking. I used this form of interrogation to unpack power relations of injustice and to bear witness on the different ways that I have experienced and addressed these racialized inequalities. When looking back at this entire process of thinking, I found connections with the Living Theory movement in understanding professional practice, and I expand on this movement as a theoretical framework in the next section.

12.4 Theoretical Framework

My self-study of professional practice was based on action research[5] and reflective practice.[6] I consider action research as the thinking of one's own life/self as it intersects with practice and the transformation of one's own knowledge, skills and attitudes. Reflective practice is what I would define as the action/movement of gathering the data for evaluating one's self. Unlike empirical research, there is no determined hypothesis before conducting the study; it is more of a processual, complex and conversational planning of activity that as a researcher you would consider as ethical for the betterment of oneself and of those whom you have contact with. More so, action research is connected to struggle and the intention to understand the situation:

> Action Research does not refer to a methodology that leads to harmonious thought and action but to a problematic practice of coming to know through struggle. My own learning has developed as part of the struggle to understand. (McNiff & Whitehead, 2002, p. 3)

My struggle to understand my professional practice is an intersectional relationship between the theoretical sets of Living Theory and Korthagen's ALACT reflective cycle (Fig. 12.2). I am using Living Theory that has methodological origins from Whitehead's (1989) action research based on lived experiences. The important connection was that through these relational events the interactions between instructor and teacher candidates became relevant, relatable and evidence-based through their co-understanding of their learning and practice.[7] However, I argue and expand the theoretical framework that lived experiences became ethically complex when race was the central factor. Therefore, this ethical complexity may be better understood when thought of as an emergence/alignment in terms of a relational accountability of ethical practice rather than relational recognition of pedagogical practice. To further develop Living Theory, I applied an Indigenous-based principle of uncertainty (Tafoya, 1997). By that I mean, this iteration of complexity from Indigenous scholarship informed my ethics as body/thinking from an Indigenous centre and moved me to (re)introduce an authentic and respectful processing of Indigenous knowledges (IK) (Smith, 1999).

The associated theoretical framework to this chapter is my adaptation of Korthagen's (2001) ALACT reflexive model as the pathway of understanding the social world of schooling. This ALACT framework was transformed within me using Living Theory. My body and professional ethics moved to the Indigenous realm when Indigenous-based thinking, interpretation and complexity were used to re-read, re-write and re-apply my critical reflections of interview transcripts and to re-identify and choose particular teaching journal entries. I arrived at an understanding, interpreting and relating my thinking of racism and colonialism as an underlying, invisible process. I started to develop real and activity-based situations to incorporating IK. This provoked an exploration of other knowledges and pedagogy for the teacher candidates in science. For my professional practice and my ethics as a teacher, the invisibility and power of Western/white supremacy became even more visible, complex and challenging. Perhaps, through this contextual pathway, the complexity of identity of an Indigenous instructor in a settler nation became articulated. It is this through Korthagen's ALACT format that I considered action research facilitated by critical self-study and relational accountability.

This complexity of the Indigenous instructor articulates the world as relational accountability correlates to McTaggart's (1996) representation that "action research is not a 'method' or a 'procedure' for research but a series of commitments to observe and problematize through practice a series of principles for conducting social enquiry" (p. 248). To frame this from an anti-racism lens, the ALACT was the "series of principles" that enhanced relational accountability into Indigenous ways of being, learning and teaching science and technology. So, action research became Living Theory and then became the active, ethical and participatory component that engaged in relational learning. These would be recorded from what I have experienced schooling and educating pre-service teachers and their own resistances—the auto-ethnographic component per se.

12.5 Re-imagining a Critical S-STEP

The development and transformation of the S-STEP methodology came about through the ethical and Indigenous-centred conceptual frameworks of ALACT and Living Theory. The context and data of S-STEP were focused towards the mindfulness of incorporating the traditions, practices and reflections of discourse for consideration of educational change. I was mindful of whether it was appropriate that these voices and viewpoints were being articulated and mediated by biases and settler privilege (Bell, 2003; Borland, 1991; Connolly, 1992; Patai, 1994). That is, was my interpretation a form of settler privilege by using viewpoints as data towards my own end? Could my work as a researcher just perpetuate the colonization of the Indigenous body through social methodology and that as an Indigenous body, I was also complicit in this social behaviour?

In order to advance an anti-racist and decolonizing discourse and challenge the stagnation and parochialism of the field of science and technology, I considered what was most important in the context and evaluation of teaching science and who would understand and listen to anti-racist/ critical stances in professional practice. It was important to critically interrogate the methodology and this version of action research in relation to ALACT modelling, analysis of the focus group sessions and even my own framework around self-reflection. At this point, my particular thinking did not directly connect to Aboriginal schooling issues because I did not want to claim to address, analyse or understand First Nations and Aboriginal epistemologies. The anti-racist and anti-colonial entry point for ALACT was performed with me deconstructing, seeking alignment between pedagogy and social justice and engaging educational change of educators in mainstream, publicly funded school systems in Ontario towards authentic and concrete representations of IK in science and technology. That is, the (re)imagining of educational methodology such as action research became transformed into a critical theorizing of the dominant white supremacy in education culture; however, this may not be done without reference to the effects that teacher education culture has had on educating Aboriginal students and on the training of pre-service teachers. In sum, the theorizing position contested the way that instructors in pre-service teacher education perceive and relate to Indigenous cultures by acknowledging the complexity of using and recording "active" lived experiences from themselves and from their students. I suggest that the conception of decolonization comes through the context, and by reflection on what researchers of Indigenous knowledge perform in the academy/schooling.

12.6   Framing and Context of Practice and of the ALACT

> The school works and in fact makes explicit the links between knowledge production and identity formation. (Dei & McDermott, 2014, p. 46)

The analysis was based on gathering data and observations on knowledge production and identity formation. The context and environment came from the activity of being an instructor at a pre-service teacher education programme in Southern Ontario. The participants were pre-service teachers at the elementary education level who were considered "knowledge generalists" because their curriculum, pedagogy and practice cover subjects of the Arts, Health and Physical Education, Language Arts, Science and Technology, Social Studies and sometimes Catholic religion (Akerson & McDuffie, 2013). Another issue is that white bodies are ubiquitous in terms of the curriculum, policy, administration, faculty, support staff and the teacher candidates (Dei & McDermot, 2014). This became problematic because anti-racism in schooling and professional practice is not a generalist practice and if one acknowledges the saliency of race, then the policies and practice have to consider the invisibility and power of white supremacy. Indeed, the possibilities and praxis of teacher activism emerge to address the racism in the training and education of pre-service teacher candidates and to challenge the ontology of teacher training in Ontario.

The context comes from social justice politics, and specifically, to take on an anti-racist position in my own teaching practice as an instructor of science and technology for the pre-service teacher education programme. I would see the transformation of my body and my thinking with the active disruption of my identity. I began to consciously challenge what was authentic in my professional practice by writing in my journal and on my lesson plans moments of critiques of practice, provocations and contradictions. These notes operated as memory triggers that made my identity troublesome and it became easier for me to see/articulate the consistency of pedagogical challenges when intersecting with race and settler relations. For example, the instruction and pedagogy of science and technology were presented as an exciting subject field with teacher candidates engaged in a dialogue and pedagogy that would open up the possibilities of inquiry, project-based learning and dispositions towards twenty-first-century learning skills (Akerson & McDuffie, 2013). However, I chose the entry point of anti-racism from a form of "literacy of resistance" and to expose knowledge production and identity "when they are operationalized to confer power and/or punishment" (Kempf, 2009, p. 15). Thus, in terms of framing, I argue that when one theorizes one's practice as an instructor through the prism of anti-racism, then the legitimacy and authenticity of science and technology towards promoting discovery and elevated notions of civilizations were but a form of Western cognitive, physical and (non)spiritual imperialism (Cajete, 1994, 1999, 2000). The importance in teacher training is that my experience exposes the possibilities that instructors in the teacher education field and by extension teachers become part of the hegemony of white supremacy. In other words, educators may observe and gather data on settler biases with non-white students by observing the activity of one's own social, management, and emotional practices. For this research context, I gathered information on the professional activity of making invisible the racialization of teaching and learning in the subject of science and technology. These became my observational notes and moments of provocations and contradictions that exposed effects of settler-state hegemony on learners, colleagues and the public discourse.

The framework (re)imagines the trajectory/pathway of Korthagen (2001) ALACT (action, looking back, awareness, creating and trial) model (refer to Fig. 12.2). The chapter will engage and summarize the following:

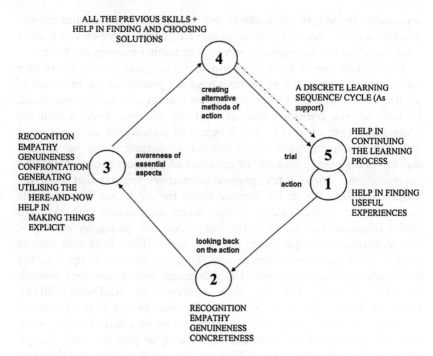

Fig. 12.2 ALACT model adapted from Korthagen (2001, p. 130)

The action (A) phase asked the question of "to what extent is the non-white teacher educator anti-racist?"

The reflection/looking back (L) explored the influence and justification of mainstream education theories on instructional practice. The background of self-study and the authenticity of the action research as a professional teacher were problematized.

The awareness of essential aspects (A) involved confronting the decolonization of the teacher as an academic and professional practice. This was the point of the action research cycle that there was an awareness of trustworthiness of essential aspects of decolonization and anti-racism.

The creating (C) of alternative models happened through praxis where I modified his practice, assessment and worldview that involved Indigenous knowledges and reflective practice to decolonize the thinking of peers, faculty and students.

The trial (T) phase theorized the question "to what extent is the non-white teacher educator transformed through anti-racism?"

12.6.1 Action: To What Extent Is the Non-white Teacher Educator Anti-racist?

The "action" phase started the action inquiry cycle for the ALACT model. I specifically examined the extent of thinking and reflecting about a professional practice that was anti-racist and explored the theoretical underpinnings and the search for authentic, relevant and useful experiences. It gave me a glimpse of the particularity of training and education pre-service teachers, and the larger connections of modernism of settler nations and of the field of science. The imposition of the settler state in training teachers began with John Dewey's democratic education era of the 1920s and transformed and adapted to modernist definition of participatory democracy and inclusive education practices of present times. However, uncovering ideals of democratic education, the themes of the focus group interviews were similar to educational policy-makers adapting concepts from academic discourses, critical theories and business leadership reforms, using terminology such as: needs, empowerment, risk-taking, collaboration, trust, reform, responsibility, standardization, accountability and democracy. For example, learning about democratic grouping without considering race as a factor/intersection was reflected by focus group participant who commented: "More practice is required in doing *tribes* for cooperative learning" (CSU focus group interview, TC1, May 24, 2013).

Reflecting on this event, I captured my thinking in my field notes:

> I found it very difficult to tell the difference between truly beneficial pedagogy and the latest fads and political/corporate agendas. I would attempt with some perplexity to find content, assessments, resources and methods that I thought benefitted my Aboriginal students. I would usually get feedback and understandings from my peers and my self-reflection and collaborations became a naturalized way of professional conduct rather than a policy-driven mandate. In that environment and now looking at the role as a participant observer in the field and in the academy, I would begin to envision the notion of social imagination of our practice and how to capture this data with authenticity and integrity. (January 2008)

I would like to point out that there was no mention of different knowledges and pedagogies used in the science and technology curriculum that influenced my own practice and that were part of workshops in science. The teacher candidates were more interested in developing success criteria by being able to connect science concepts with established definitions and norms of their practicum placement. "We need to be making learning fun and collaborative, but we need standards so that the right definitions are learned in science" (CSU focus group interview, TC3, May 24, 2013). "I'm not sure special education is part of this" (CSU focus group interview, TC1, May 31, 2013).

It seemed the policy and alignment to curriculum and established texts were important to teacher candidates. There was a strong connection with their discussion along Ontario's education system use of a combination of Western-centric liberal multicultural pedagogy, with psychological, morality and performance-based assessments based on Piaget and Kohlberg's stage-development models (Airasian, 1994; Fullan & Hargreaves, 1991; Gibson, 1987; Norris & Boucher, 1980; Parry, 1984; Porter & Taylor, 1972; Schwartz & Pollishuke, 1990). Being an Indigenous body outside of the First Nation identity and carrying the power, privilege and knowledge biases of an instructor schooled in Western and settler nation professional practice, I was able to find alignment through challenging my body and my thinking through IK. This was important to me especially when it was connected to assessment and evaluation of students. I saw this as the professional body using the intersection of race and colonialism redefining what knowledge is important to evaluate as learning and constructing knowledge. There was some embodied activity of using other ways of understanding of the world, used in the science workshops such as creation stories, the importance of the *Kanien'keha*[8] community's concept of the Three Sisters for biodiversity and fertility. But, in my journal and notations made during planning meetings, the concepts of racism and colonialism in terms of social actions of its teachers and administrators were not part of agenda or part of formal discussions. I interpreted this as curriculum implementation, collaborative cultures, pedagogy and day-to-day experiences of schooling pre-service candidates failed to recognize racism and colonialism as part of the discourse of public education. In fact, racism and colonialism were treated as aberrations and psychological disorder of the individual(s) in question and were part of workshop on special education on our campus. The complicity and denial of my own body as an active social agent was further exasperated when I did not account for the racialization and colonizing effect of my own pedagogy, despite doing Indigenous science concepts and practices.

Foster (1998, p. 119) criticized the bureaucracy and elitism in Canadian institutions by noting:

> Once a system of interlocking elites was in place, bridging the gap between executive and bureaucratic decision making, it eliminated the tension between our democratic values and our democratic participation, the tension between our theory and our practice … It relieved us all of the burden of a bad conscience by relieving us of the responsibility of addressing our own principles of nation building.

With this start of the action research cycle, I wanted to understand/uncover the connections between foundational education theories and bureaucracy of teacher education. Expanding on Foster's (1998) critique, a possible complicity and/or silencing of the non-white instructor may be connected to not being ethical/morally responsible (i.e. bad conscience) to our very own thinking and professional practice.

12.6.2 Looking Back: Influence of Mainstream Education Theories in Instructional Practice

The history of education in Ontario and the development of organized schooling during 1960 have used ethnographies and data on minority and marginalized students' performance in schools. There were a number of research studies that have examined factors and their correlation regarding school failure for students (Barman, Hebert, & McCaskill, 1987; Battiste & Barman, 1995; Bernstein, 1977; Bourdieu & Passeron, 1996; Bowles & Gintis, 1976; Glazer & Moynihan, 1963; Jencks et al., 1972; Lareau, 1987; Ogbu, 1987; Olson, 1981; Siggner, 1986; Willis, 1977). The past was influential in determining the idea of excellence and education success. Ontario's public schooling system was to search and examine the factors and themes of why some students fail, and possible changes to the educational structure or to the pedagogical practices of teachers (Dei, 1996, 2008b). By understanding the needs of learners in terms of economics and local cultures, the bureaucracy of training teachers would translate into developing improved educational outcomes through curriculum.

The influence of Marxist frameworks with reflection and teacher education was highlighted through social class and the understanding of economic factors examined in action research. Some research sought to examine and prove that the most important contributor to a student's educational outcome was his or her socio-economic status (SES), usually defined as the combination of occupational and educational status of parents (Jencks et al., 1972; Jones, 1965; Levitas, 1974). Others proposed a "structural correspondence between its social relations and those of production" (Bowles & Gintis, 1976, p. 131). Some researchers have also added that because of a culture of poverty, parents would reproduce negative responses of schooling to their children (Glazer & Moynihan, 1963). These parents did poorly when they were students, and they were unable to transmit the skills needed to allow their children to be successful in the school system. "I wish I could hug all my students" (CSU focus group interview, TC4, May 31, 2013). Lareau (1987) further developed the correlation and reproduction models by suggesting that middle-class parents who have been successful in school understood the nuances of the "hidden curriculum" and knew how to coach their children in the appropriate responses to the system.

Educators and strategic planning used the conceptual framework of a modern community network to address success in the education system. Notions of "raising" students became one of the purviews of teacher training. This was connected to stabilizing the bureaucracy of school boards and the legacy of economics and materialism for school success. "Science class was much better when I had access to smart boards" (CSU focus group interview, TC3, May 24, 2013). I interpreted this as supporting a viewpoint that schools focusing on student success were associated with more technological support, with increased funding in special education and with better availability to learning resources. Besides these materialistic responses, the idea of the "I" as a success criterion of "student-centred" approaches aligned along an ecology of relationships with the individual being central (Bronfenbrenner, 1979).

Looking back, my original conceptual framework and thinking about practice was based on the socially constructed rigor of social reproduction theories and its corresponding correlation analysis of our education system. It was a way for me to make sense and to articulate the question of why educational change seemed gradual and deliberate. "The purpose of such a research perspective should challenge our notion of long term objectives in public and mainstream education" (Field Notes, November 2006). But, if one used the saliency of race as the central pathway of this action research, then the overall methodology comes into question, especially with the historical examination of the economic and social reproduction theories that were devoid of analysis on the dispositions of educators towards race (Dei, 2008b). By looking back and reflecting, the foundation, evolving conceptual framework around the purpose of action research becomes suspect and in need of further investigation and theorization. Teacher education turned out to be a manifestation of "cloning cultures" and developing and desiring norms of the groups and productivity (Essed & Goldberg, 2002, pp. 1075–1076). For this phase of the action research cycle, I understood complicity and rationalized my role as an educator by not interrogating the past and not unpacking the cloning/reproduction of the one-ness/normalization of white identity. I found a connection with Dei (2008b) "[w]e must also challenge the fact that most of our students appear set in their ways of thinking about scholarship because of the school curriculum" (p. xxii). Thus, in order to keep this research cycle progressing, I needed to consciously and actively challenge the continued marginalization of non-white bodies beyond economics, successful group cultures and hidden curriculum.

In regard to a set way of thinking that is heavily influenced by the structures of curriculum and the training of teachers, a pedagogical and ethical change may directly emerge from the teacher. This would allow for the possibilities for the educators to influence themselves, their students and the surrounding communities of practice. For example, the thinking of practice shifted away from structural economies and historical materialism and the teacher became the one to decisively and meaningfully develop opportunities for students. The teacher who claimed non-politics or the absence of race (Dei, 2008b) becomes complicit in the racialization of the students. It would be a methodological progression to connect the politics of how the instructor of teachers could have the role to facilitate emergent pedagogy and knowledge of their teacher candidates. I submit that there is worth and deeper understanding when addressing race as a main factor to learning and the benefit to teacher education comes with reflecting and critiquing around education practices. "I sought to unlearn/deconstruct determined habits of dependency, power, class and privilege via historical colonization" (Field Notes, March 2011).

12.6.3 Awareness: Decolonization and Trustworthiness

Decolonization is a complex process, counter-narrative and project that are transformative to the self, to community, to land and to spirituality (Dei, 2008b; Dei & McDermott, 2014). It becomes in this iteration of ALACT cycle the moment of awareness of schooling practices, and the power and privilege of training teachers. For example, during the spring semester of 2013, I was observing teacher candidates work on their culminating tasks for their science and technology course and noted a connection to an education policy text being used at that time. "Our education system was never designed to deliver the kind of results we now need to equip students for today's world ... we need to think and redesign" (Wagner et al., 2010, p. 1). Decolonization became a meaning-making project towards connections and examining how professional educators may redesign the training of teachers with the framework that Indigenous peoples, communities, families and their children were (un)intentionally left out of the development of pedagogy for teaching science and technology. I noted at the end of the workshop: "What is the unintended communication that may occur through the non-articulation of theories that shape our dialogue and actions as teachers?" (Field Notes, January 2013). This provoked further inquiry into how my body/thinking changed and how my role as an instructor of teacher candidates was read and engaged as a non-white body in their unintentional communication regarding Indigenous issues, histories and epistemologies.

"When I listen and observe teacher candidates in my classes, I see the teacher ed as an example of worlds colliding and mixing" (Field Notes, January 2013). In Ontario, new and improved curriculum and schooling strategies regarding First Nations people were being proposed for Aboriginal and non-Aboriginal teachers (Aboriginal Education Office, 2007, 2009). Specifically, at the campus, graduates were expected at "to engage meaningfully with the culture, experiences, histories and contemporary issues of Indigenous communities."[9] With social justice and reconciliation with Indigenous peoples as one of the key graduate attributes at CSU, the faculty had engaged with an integrated traditional stories, dances and some First Nations language and syllabics as part of the overall teaching practice. The intention was to improve resiliency of the Aboriginal learners by unpacking the hidden curriculum and to have teacher candidates see the world from multiple lenses and fairness (CSU staff meeting notes, August 2012). The question of this decolonization project was "to what extent does our individual worldview hold multiple and negotiated alliances or does it remain mono-cultural?" Worldviews seemed taken for granted and used as academic objects for teacher candidates; however, there were teacher candidates that were influenced and re-evaluated their teaching practices with those they interacted with. Interestingly, these candidates that volunteered for the focus groups had expressed that they had travelled outside of Canada, or taught English in other countries. Of the seven participants, three were visible minorities. This activity of decolonization came through thinking about the practice of teaching being mindful. "I developed and taught a lab class on states of matter, similar to one I did in Taiwan" (CSU focus group interview, TC7, May 24, 2013). Reflecting on this interaction, I believe that teacher candidates that were impressionable and critical of their professional practice easily connected and were involved in their own self-study. Furthermore, I think that their resiliency and their understandings to continue reflecting and to be critical of their pedagogy came through their ownership of action as being meaningful, ethical and just.

The challenge of this non-standard approach to action research, although disruptive of the hegemonic practices of training teachers, involved the production and ethical consideration of the knowledge embodiment of Indigenous and Aboriginal values into a modernist project of teacher training (Borland 1991; Parker & Lynn, 2002). However, the trustworthiness needed to be interrogated through my professional experiences and through the communication with colleagues, peers and students. The decolonization practice articulated by me during our staff meetings at our teacher education programme saw the non-Western approaches at odds or even regarded as dubious pedagogy especially when we discussed curriculum and assessment. Decolonization requires trustworthiness of the practice and data as determined by non-white instructors and researchers. That is, decolonization may create complicity through "anti-praxis" whereby the instructor only articulates the ethics and mindfulness of appropriating Indigenous identity and voices, perpetuating a form of cognitive imperialism and the continued colonization of the Indigenous epistemologies. To put it another way, the decolonization project may ask the instructor to imagine and inform a twenty-first-century classroom on what was different from Western biased and Socratic-style of teaching and learning, but how would it come about through the transformation of the teacher? What would a decolonized classroom be like when framed by the imagination of an instructor from an Indigenous knowledge background? How trustworthy would those results be?

Therefore, to analyse the trustworthiness of decolonizing instructional practice became an uncomfortable ethical journey and it involved taking risks and breaking reliance on Western knowledge practices, so-called colonial expertise and hierarchy of knowledge forms. What was missing from decolonizing process was the possibility that the actual IK practice and activity, as experienced through the personal self was inherently embodied. This may have been previously constructed as an authentic and animated IK learning through learning with other Aboriginal educators and students. So, keeping the nature of the traditional Western academy in mind, I felt and needed to consider how notions of validity and trust of data vis-à-vis reflections on practice/activity actually disrupted this claim of embodied IK. My reflection and the process my body went through kept me unsure of what is authentic knowledge and learning. I decided that for this self-study, there needed a shift to an awareness of the historicized forms of power operating as bureaucracies. Especially, the decolonization process unpacked the learning settings and exposed the extent to which taken-for-granted educational theories solidified and validated these forms of power in my interpretations of classroom interactions especially around Indigenous issues (Dei, 2005; Wilson, 2005). This was especially evident when workshops on science and technology were already framed as one of action research learning IK rather a deficit analysis or social justice workshop. The self as a problematic and embodied discourse used the trustworthiness of critical examinations to expose the nature of what an educator believed/perceived as learning and knowledge (Fine, 1994b). This process of decolonization was through the understanding and experience of the activity of learning about IK rather than relying on "experts" and written forms as panacea to Western knowledge. The movement of instruction posited a direction of using IK in the daily practice of teaching and preparing teachers and their students for the twenty-first-century learning and multiple-literacies.

> ...the more opportunities people have to gain information about racism and the more authority they have by virtue of their social positions, the more responsible they are for the racist implications of their practices. (Essed, 1991, p.viii)

The ethics of trustworthiness and decolonization required that praxis come through social action/activity in understanding the dynamics of differences. Aboriginal Peoples are distinct in their histories, status, notions of power and control, worldviews, social contexts, cultural, linguistic, scholarships, treaty rights, geographies and spiritualities (C. P. Olson, Personal Communication, March 2011). The next phase of the inquiry cycle, creating, argued that the social action of praxis required an understanding of the context and the problematizing of the professional educator.

12.6.4 Creating: Praxis

The ALACT model did not have traction and meaning towards the trial phase, and it required a rethinking by me on the connection between distinctiveness of being Indigenous and being part of mainstream civil society, while living in a settler nation state. This led to evaluating the concept of praxis for an Indigenous framework in the work that I was doing (Field Notes, December 2011). I understand this praxis as the decolonization of the teacher and the activity of teaching.

Freire (1993) added to the concept of praxis by introducing the expression of cultural synthesis:

> Instead of following predetermined plans, leaders and people, mutually identified, together create the guidelines of their action. In this synthesis, leaders and people' are somehow reborn in new knowledge and new action. Knowledge of the alienated culture leads to transforming action resulting in a culture which is being freed from alienation ... In cultural synthesis–and only in cultural synthesis–it is possible to resolve the contradiction between the world view of the leaders and that of the people, to the enrichment of both. (p. 162)

Praxis, in its most generic sense, related to how the action of people, beyond that of a single individual, can transform society. It becomes a co-created guideline of practice. Even by narrowing the focus to within the teacher education system, the importance of praxis is that empowerment was not solely based on the individual student or the individual teacher or the individual administrator. Praxis involved the relationship itself—a complex play between teacher candidates and with instructors so that each one deconstructed and critically examined their own worldview and the worldview that was being presented by teachers and the curriculum (Ronnerman, Furu, & Salo, 2008). It involved the teachers as a community—they have to realize the systemic contradictions, racism, and exploitation that their pedagogy and curriculum presents to those of non-Western worldviews (Dei, 1996; Burns, 1997). Praxis involved administrators—they had to create and stabilize an atmosphere of creativity, risk-taking and change, and they have to accept the fallacy of efficiency and reject the neutrality of the administrative purview (Burns et al., 1994). The students, teachers and administrators were involved in authentic, direct and meaningful action and activities—a cultural synthesis.

However, praxis may be vulnerable to being romanticized, just like the Indigenous body, and it may be overwhelming with such a degree of multiple knowledge forms. With many different knowledges, histories and traditions from the First Nations, Inuit and Metis coupled with concepts of politics and treaty rights, there emerged a complex myriad of data, "faqs," electronic resources, texts, journals and articles and field sites that a teacher in Ontario are and will be exposed to. In terms of praxis, what does the teacher candidate do with the information? Freeman (2010) declared "Today Toronto's Indigenous past is acknowledged only superficially in most quarters and remains largely unknown" (p. 31). The trial or the impact of ALACT cycle would consider the transformation of the teacher educator through praxis and the connection to pedagogy of anti-racism.

12.6.5 Trial: To What Extent Is the Non-white Teacher Educator Transformed Through Anti-racism?

Jones (1965) summarized that

> [A]n educational system is not and cannot be free from influences emanating from the surrounding society; nothing is gained by maintaining the myth of autonomy ... to introduce changes in the educational system, it is essential to recognize and understand the relationship between an educational system and the surrounding society. (p. 1)

The evolution of the teacher education must challenge the ghettoization of Indigenous cultures and alternative educational models based on narratives, spirituality and emotions (Dei, 2008b). However, educational change dealing with IK in science and technology involved factors outside the school system with unpredictable dynamics and challenges along resource allocations and bureaucratic disruptions. But, the constant factor was the concept and saliency of race remaining imperceptible to conversations in teacher education.

I would interpret from a settler and professional point of view, that lifelong learning involves listening and communicating with teachers and instructors and being immersed in professional learning communities (PLCs), school meetings and faculty of education planning sessions. I noted a constant critique of the public elementary education in Ontario as being too conservative and yet, for being too quick with changes and reforms. Changes seemed to be contradictory in terms of action—to critique change and non-change at the same time. Debates regarding bureaucracy of schooling such as class sizes, effective organization of schooling like Bill 160,[10] standardized testing as delivered by EQAO,[11] authentic teachers' assessment, collective agreements and employment contracts moved beyond the classic organization of school boards and provincial governments to include parents, students and local community groups.[12] Despite the surface inclusion of local community, race remained invisible, and white supremacy in terms of bureaucratic control became normalized and unchallenged. My early reflections, inquiry and learning logs noted that my strength, grounding and worldview came from my relations, peers and friends. "I felt constrained by a triple bind of religion, Western epistemology and Indigenous worldview is what the Indigenous educator must challenge" (Field Notes, August 2010).

Instead of organizational or classroom management strategies, I used the activity of teaching at the pre-service level to confront previous liberal multicultural strategies as developed in May (1994) and Nieto (1992). One example of a transformational practice was engaging the teacher candidates in problematizing First Nations peoples as being romanticized as custodians to the land and acknowledged differing ways of analysing the world and developing scientific inquiry. Upon reflection, the practice confronted and provoked the anti-racist and anti-colonial pedagogy, but it did not extend to challenging the Western sociocultural reproduction that claimed aboriginal peoples as "settlers" who travelled across the Bering land bridge and who were also part of the Canadian mosaic. Resistance from candidates came from acknowledging the traditional creation stories as long as the practice accepted that First Nations were part of the multicultural settler societies. The resistance from the instructor came from my internalized struggle with elementary public/separate school educational policy used as a normalized mapping to instruct the delivery of science and technology. The rejection from teacher candidates' bodies and the instructor to conform to liberal and modernist ideals of analysing the natural world supported a silent complicity to reproducing/cloning the setter nation teaching culture and bureaucracy. This would support further inquiry in the next iteration of ALACT by developing Aboriginal identity and knowledges as a counter-pedagogy.

Additionally, my practice was transformed through anti-racist pedagogy and engaging the process of "othering." Although I carried privilege and power as an educator, I was Indigenous through my familial and spiritual connection to Hawaii, through my appearance as a person of colour, and my connections to local First Nations communities when I was a teacher. It has informed my body and my learning of the multiple histories, ethnicities and worldviews that are subject of complexity and variable interpretations. It was at this point for me that the identity and problematic notions of the teaching-self became as wide and as varied as the communities that I had taught in. My field notes captured my thinking:

> When I critically worked towards locating myself in the world around me and in the world of academia, I see myself holding many names, many labels, and many levels of power and control. I am the other and I am a member of the Fourth World because I see family, my relatives, community, and myself as Native Hawaiian. I am a member of the Third World because my ancestors worked as labourers for the sugar cane plantations. I am a member of the First World because I participate in academia and intelligentsia, and I live as a consumer in a modern liberal democratic society. (July 2013)

These labels and codes were all transitory and sometimes contradictory. They had power and meaning through the social context of their usage. However, no matter what label I was given, I was the other.

Again, my thoughts, feelings and the discomfort of my body was captured in my field notes:

> Like the scene at Queen's Park, I am not regarded as a teacher or even activists in the teachers' struggle against an omnibus bill on education control – I am the outsider, a stereotypical Asian newsperson to cover the event, and not an individual involved in a social movement. Yet, when I step into a classroom, I am transformed into an individual with professional status with power and privilege over those that I teach regardless of race, ethnicity, class, and gender. My work as teacher constructs and privileges me as middle-class in terms of status and in terms of relations of production. (November 1997)

12.7 Possibilities for Future Practice

The ALACT model and the process of S-STEP for this chapter were complex, and the intention was that movement of the teaching body, consideration of professional ethics and its thinking were complex and multidirectional. That is, I argue that movement of the process from looking back at the action towards awareness of decolonization (L to A) occurs when the saliency of race and racialized body was central to the action research cycle. When non-white bodies become part of the schooling process, the contradiction of identity and distortion of multiple realities became an explicit process may be labelled as a pathway to decolonization. The process of understanding Indigenous peoples dealt with the difficulties of maintaining cultural identity within a pluralistic education framework and based on white identity as the norm and expectation of excellence. "It was okay to problematize identity and have the students work on activities that searched for their self-identity" (Field Notes, September 2013). Although the pathway of ALACT was articulated as an activity operating at one level, the acknowledging and decolonization process would open the study pathways at many levels due to the complexity of engaging in multiple worldviews. Further research required the triangulation of deep conceptual level factors and themes associated with changes in teachers' knowledge management such as Villegas' research of transitions in schooling (Chapter 11), reflective teaching on place, ethics of the body, mind and spirit, Indigenous knowledges and explorations of biocultural practices by Rostan-Aellen (Chapter 13).

The mainstream/Western academic trend for teacher education has spiralled towards engaging research for the good of society, as Ball (2011) succinctly noted

> that we need to act effectively on what we know ... to be vigilant in ensuring that our research is seen in the language of policy legislation, as well as in the actions of teachers, administrators, school boards, parent groups, community organizers, foundations, and government officials. (p. 198)

Yet, educators and student teachers in mainstream schools were not passive recipients to the uses of Indigenous, Aboriginal and First Nations teachings, and nor should they have blindly accepted the panacea/banners of decolonizing education philosophies, professional development and research practices. Researchers using action research must take risks to authentically and meaningfully engage the nexus of Aboriginal and non-Aboriginal education practices. By using action research and ALACT modelling with a critical anti-racist lens, the understanding and activating a form of research and Indigenous ways of being into a "Living Theory" may be used in non-Indigenous education settings as well as Indigenous community-based settings. For the teacher education field, the transformation of frameworks and personal ethics would come from Indigenous scholars and educators. In general, my reflections and professional experiences became transformative by engaging in the politics of truth, ethics and validity and responding to new evolved forms of colonization of the Indigenous mind, body and spirit. This would offer a basis of self-transformation. However, it is difficult to be an Indigenous educator in a settler and white supremacy school system. The reasoning of authentic relationship through experiences, reflection and the written reflection were intended to interconnect research-based insights to the teacher education community. The relationships were complex despite moments of intentionality and I would submit that future iterations of the ALACT cycle would address the co-construction of narratives and identities from participants, and specifically as a form bounded as a "captivity narrative" of professional practice. When the action research embodied anti-racist and anti-colonial elements, there would be practices/activity for emancipation. This may articulate the education process of self-study and action research as it pertains to the non-white teacher educator, and how one goes about the process towards social justice and articulating Indigenous epistemologies. And perhaps to push the ideas of emancipation further, these explorations and reflective cycles move beyond the mind, but are further manifestations and connections of the body with the world.

Notes

1. It is beyond the scope of this chapter; however, refer to works on the concept of positivism in education such as Peca (2000).
2. ALACT = action, looking back, awareness, creating and trial model developed by Korthagen (2001).
3. Translation: A Hawaiian word meaning human being, used to mean a Hawaiian of Polynesian descent.
4. Focus group data obtained with ethical clearance through Charles Sturt University Human Research Ethics Committee Protocol #2013/067.

5. Action research in education methodology has foundational research with Kurt Lewin (Adelman, 1993).
6. Early published works on reflective practice have been linked with Donald Schon (1983).
7. For more details on the framework, epistemology and framework around Living Theory, please consult the text from Whitehead and McNiff (2006).
8. *Kanien'keha* or "People of the Flint" are the original peoples of Turtle Island that speak the settler-labelled language of "Mohawk." My experiences come from living and teaching in the communities of Tyendinaga and Six Nations.
9. http://www.csu.edu.au/division/landt/sessionalstaff/knowyourstudents/what-are-they-learning.
10. This is the "36:1 Bill 160, Education Quality Improvement Act" (1997). It has importance in that it addressed class sizes and improving student achievement in Ontario schools.
11. The Education Quality and Accountability Office (EQAO, n.d.) as an independent agency in Ontario have a mandate and research capacity regarding the assessment of reading, writing and math.
12. Refer for more details regarding the tensions of schooling with this document: *Public Attitudes Toward Education In Ontario 2015: The 19th OISE Survey of Educational Issues* (Hart & Kemph, 2015).

REFERENCES

36:1 Bill 160, Education Quality Improvement Act. (1997). Retrieved from http://www.ontla.on.ca/web/bills/bills_detail.do?locale=en&BillID=1458&ParlSessionID=36:1&isCurrent=false.
Aboriginal Education Office. (2007). *Ontario First Nation, Metis, and Inuit Education Policy Framework*. Aboriginal Education Office. Ministry of Education. Toronto: Queen's Printer for Ontario.
Aboriginal Education Office. (2009). *Sound Foundations for the Road Ahead: Fall 2009 Progress Report on the Implementation of the Ontario First Nation, Metis, and Inuit Education Policy Framework*. Aboriginal Education Office. Ministry of Education. Toronto: Queen's Printer for Ontario.
Adelman, C. (1993). Kurt Lewin and the Origins of Action Research. *Educational Action Research, 1*(1), 7–24.
Airasian, P. W. (1994). *Classroom Assessment* (2nd ed.). Toronto: McGraw-Hill.
Akerson, V. L., & McDuffie, A. R. (2013). The Elementary Science Teacher as Researcher. In K. Appleton (Ed.), *Elementary Science Teacher Education* (Chapter 14, pp. 1–38, Kobo ebook version). New York: Routledge.

Ball, A. F. (2011). American Educational Research Association 2012 Annual Meeting Call for Submissions. *Educational Researcher, 30*(4), 198–220.

Barkhuizen, G., & Wette, R. (2008). Narrative Frames for Investigating the Experiences of Language Teachers. *System, 36,* 372–387.

Barman, J., Hebert, Y., & McCaskill, D. (1987). *Indian Education in Canada: Volume 2—The Challenge.* Vancouver: UBC Press.

Battiste, M. (2008). Research Ethics for Protecting Indigenous Knowledge and Heritage: Institutional Researcher Responsibilities. In N. Denzin, Y. Lincoln, & L. T. Smith (Eds.), *Handbook of Critical and Indigenous Methodologies* (pp. 497–510). Los Angeles, CA: Sage.

Battiste, M., & Barman, J. (1995). *First Nations Education in Canada: The Circle Unfolds.* Vancouver: UBC Press.

Bell, L. A. (2003). Telling Tales: What Stories Can Teach Us About Racism. *Race, Ethnicity and Education, 6*(1), 3–28.

Bernstein, B. (1977). *Class, Codes and Control* (Vol. 3). London: Routledge & Kegan Paul.

Borland, K. (1991). 'That's Not What I Said': Interpretive Conflict in Oral Narrative Research. In S. B. Gluck & D. Patai (Eds.), *Women's Words.* New York: Routledge.

Bourdieu, P., & Passeron, J. C. (1996). *Reproduction in Education, Society and Culture* (2nd ed., R. Nice, Trans.). London: Sage.

Bowles, S., & Gintis, H. (1976). *Schooling in Capitalist America.* New York: Basic Books.

Bronfenbrenner, U. (1979). *The Ecology of Human Development: Experiments by Nature and Design.* Cambridge, MA: Harvard University Press.

Bullough, R. V., Jr., & Pinnegar, S. (2001, April). Guidelines for Quality in Autobiographical Forms of Self-Study Research. *Educational Researcher, 30*(3), 13–21.

Burns, G. E. (1997, September). *Native Inclusiveness in Education: The Great Canadian Myth.* Paper prepared for the Oxford International Conference on Education and Development, 1997, "Education and Geopolitical Change," New College, Oxford, UK.

Burns, G. E., et al. (1994). *School Boards/First Nations Tuition Agreements Resource Manual.* Toronto: Joint Project of the Ontario Public School Boards' Association, Ontario Separate School Trustees' Association, and the Ontario Ministry of Education and Training.

Cajete, G. (1994). *Look to the Mountain: An Ecology of Indigenous Education.* Skyland, NC: Kivaki Press.

Cajete, G. (1999). *Igniting the Sparkle: An Indigenous Science Education Model.* Skyland, NC: Kivaki Press.

Cajete, G. (2000). *Native Science: Natural Laws of Interdependence.* San Diego, CA: Clear Light Publishers.

Cannon, M. J., & Sunseri, L. (Eds.). (2011). *Racism, Colonialism, and Indigeneity in Canada: A Reader*. Don Mills, ON: Oxford University Press.
Chang, H. (2008). *Auto-Ethnography as Method*. Walnut Creek, CA: Left Coast Press.
Corntassel, J. (2003). An Activist Posing as an Academic? *American Indian Quarterly, 27*(1–2), 160–171.
Connolly, P. (1992). Playing It by the Rules: The Politics of Research in 'Race' and Education. *British Educational Research Journal, 18*(2), 133–148.
Dei, G. J. S. (1994). Reflections of an Anti-racist Pedagogue. In L. Erwin & D. MacLennan (Eds.), *Sociology of Education in Canada: Critical Perspectives on Theory, Research and Practice*. Toronto: Copp Clark Longman.
Dei, G. J. S. (1996). *Anti-racism Education Theory and Practice*. Halifax: Fernwood Publishing.
Dei, G. J. S. (1998). The Politics of Educational Change: Taking Anti-racism Education Seriously. In V. Satzewich (Ed.), *Racism and Social Inequality in Canada*. Toronto: Thompson Educational Publishing.
Dei, G. J. S. (2005). Critical Issues in Anti-racist Research Methodology: An Introduction. In G. J. S. Dei & G. Johal (Eds.), *Critical Issues in Anti-racist Research Methodology* (pp. 1–28). New York: Peter Lang.
Dei, G. J. S. (2008a). *Teaching Africa: Towards a Transgressive Pedagogy* [Adobe PDF ebook version]. New York, NY: Springer.
Dei, G. J. S. (2008b). *Racists Beware: Uncovering Racial Politics in Contemporary Society*. Rotterdam, The Netherlands: Springer.
Dei, G. J. S., & McDermott, M. (Eds.). (2014). *Politics of Anti-racism Education: In Search of Strategies for Transformative Learning* [Apple iBook version]. Dordrecht, The Netherlands: Springer. https://doi.org/10.1007/978-94-007-7627-2.
Essed, P. (1991). *Understanding Everyday Racism*. Newbury Park: Sage.
Essed, P., & Goldberg, D. T. (2002). Cloning Cultures: The Social Injustices of Sameness. *Ethnic and Racial Studies, 25*(6), 1066–1082.
EQAO. (n.d.). *Education Quality and Accountability Office*. Retrieved from http://www.eqao.com/en.
Fine, M. (1994a). Dis-stance and Other Stances: Negotiations of Power Inside Feminist Research. In A. Gitlin (Ed.), *Power and Method: Political Activism and Educational Research*. New York: Routledge.
Fine, M. (1994b). Working the Hyphens: Reinventing Self and Other in Qualitative Research. In N. K. Denzin & Y. S. Lincoln (Eds.), *Handbook of Qualitative Research* (pp. 70–82). Thousand Oaks, CA: Sage.
Fine, M., & Weiss, L. (2003). *Silenced Voices and Extraordinary Conversations: Re-imagining Schools*. New York: Teachers College Press.
Foster, L. (1998). *Turnstile Immigration: Multiculturalism, Social Order and Social Justice in Canada*. Toronto: Thompson Educational Publishing Inc.

Freeman, V. (2010, Spring). "Toronto Has No History!" Indigeneity, Settler Colonialism, and Historical Memory in Canada's Largest City. *Urban History Review, 38*(2), 21–35.
Freire, P. (1993). *Pedagogy of Oppressed.* New York: Continuum.
Fullan, M., & Hargreaves, A. (1991). *What's Worth Fighting for: Working Together for Your School.* Toronto: Ontario Public School Teachers' Federation.
Gibson, A. (1987). *Active Learning. Teaching and Learning in the Junior Division.* North York, ON: North York Board of Education, Curriculum and Staff Development.
Giroux, H. A. (1983). *Theory & Resistance in Education: A Pedagogy for the Opposition.* New York, NY: Bergin & Garvey Publishers Inc.
Glazer, N., & Moynihan, D. (1963). *Beyond the Melting Pot.* Cambridge: MIT Press.
Hart, D., & Kemph, A. (2015). *Public Attitudes Toward Education in Ontario 2015: The 19th OISE Survey of Educational Issues.* Retrieved from http://www.oise.utoronto.ca/oise/UserFiles/Media/Media_Relations/Final_Report_-_19th_OISE_Survey_on_Educational_Issues_2015.pdf?utm_source=Bulletin+and+CEA+Updates+%2F+Bulletin+et+mises+à+jour+de+l%27ACE&utm_campaign=df28449994-Bulletin_ENGLISH_Dec_2015&utm_medium=email&utm_term=0_8ed9356158-df28449994-84846141.
Jencks, C., Smith, M., Acland, H., Bane, M., Cohen, D., Gintis, H., ..., Mickelson, R. (1972). *Inequality.* New York: Harper and Row.
Jones, F. E. (1965). *The Social Bases of Education.* Toronto: Canadian Conference of Children.
Jones, S. H. (2005). Auto-Ethnography. In N. K. Denzin & Y. S. Lincoln (Eds.), *Handbook of Qualitative Methods* (3rd ed.). Thousand Oaks, CA: Sage.
Kempf, A. (Ed.). (2009). *Breaching the Colonial Contract: Anti-colonialism in the US and Canada* [Adobe PDF eBook version]. New York, NY: Springer.
Korthagen, F. (2001). Teacher Education: A Problematic Enterprise. In F. Korthagen, J. Kessels, B. Koster, B. Lagerwerf, & T. Wubbels (Eds.), *Linking Practice and Theory: The Pedagogy of Realistic Teacher Education.* Mahwah, NJ: Lawrence Erlbaum Associates.
Lareau, A. (1987). Social Class Differences in Family-School Relationships: The Importance of Cultural Capital. *Sociology of Education, 60,* 73–85.
Levitas, M. (1974). *Marxist Perspectives in the Sociology of Education.* Boston: Routledge & Kegan Paul.
May, S. (1994). *Making Multicultural Education Work.* Bristol, UK: Londunn Press.
McLaren, P. (1989). *Life in Schools: An Introduction to Critical Pedagogy in the Foundations of Education.* White Plains, NY: Longman.
McNiff, J., & Whitehead, J. (2002). *Action Research: Principles and Practice* (2nd ed.). New York: Routledge Falmer.

McTaggart, R. (1996). Issues for Participatory Action Researchers. In O. Zuber-Skerritt (Ed.), *New Directions in Action Research*. London: Falmer Press.
Nieto, S. (1992). *Affirming Diversity: The Sociopolitical Context of Multicultural Education*. New York: Longman.
Norris, D., & Boucher, J. (1980). *Observing Children Through Their Formative Years*. Toronto: The Board of Education for the City of Toronto.
Ogbu, J. (1987). Variability in Minority School Performance: A Problem in Search of an Explanation. *Anthropology and Education Quarterly, 18*, 312–334.
Olson, P. (1981). Labouring to Learn: How Working Theory Gets Down to Classrooms and Kids. *Interchange, 12*(2–3), 252–269.
Parker, L., & Lynn, M. (2002). What's Race Got to Do with It? Critical Race Theory's Conflicts with and Connections to Qualitative Research Methodology and Epistemology. *Qualitative Inquiry, 8*(1), 7–22.
Parry, C. (1984). *Let's Celebrate! Canada's Special Days*. Toronto: Kids Can Press.
Patai, D. (1994). When Method Becomes Power. In A. Gitlin (Ed.), *Power and Method: Political Activism and Educational Research* (pp. 61–73). New York: Routledge.
Peca, K. (2000). Positivism in Education: Philosophical, Research, and Organizational Assumptions. *ERIC*. Retrieved from https://eric.ed.gov/?id=ED456536.
Porter, N., & Taylor, N. (1972). *How to Assess the Moral Reasoning of Students* (Profiles in Practical Education No. 8). Toronto: OISE Press.
Ronnerman, K., Furu, E. M., & Salo, P. (2008). *Nurturing Praxis: Action Research in Partnership Between School and University in a Nordic Light*. Rotterdam: Sense Publishers.
Schon, D. (1983). *The Reflective Practitioner*. New York: Basic Books.
Schwartz, S., & Pollishuke, M. (1990). *Creating the Child-Centred Classroom*. Toronto: Irwin Publishing.
Siggner, A. J. (1986, Winter). The Socio-Demographic Conditions of Registered Indians. *Canadian Social Trends*, pp. 2–9.
Smith, L. T. (1999). *Decolonizing Methodologies: Research Indigenous Peoples*. New York: Zed Books.
St. Denis, V. (2007). Aboriginal Education and Anti-racist Education: Building Alliances Across Cultural and Racial Identity. *Canadian Journal of Education, 30*(4), 1068–1092.
Tafoya, T. (1997). M. Dragonfly: Two-Spirit and the Tafoya Principle of Uncertainty. In S. Jacobs (Ed.), *Two-Spirit People: Native American Gender Identity, Sexuality, and Spirituality*. Chicago: University of Illinois Press.
Wagner, T., Kegan, R., Lahey, L., Lemons, R., Garnier, J., Helsing, …, Ark, T. (2010). *Change Leadership: A Practical Guide to Transforming Our Schools* [Adobe PDF ebook version]. San Francisco, CA: Jossey-Bass.
Whitehead, J. (1989). Creating a Living Educational Theory from Questions of the Kind, "How Do I Improve My Practice?" *Cambridge Journal of Education, 19*(1), 41–52.

Whitehead, J., & McNiff, J. (2006). *Action Research: Living Theory.* Thousand Oaks, CA: Sage. http://dx.doi.org.proxy.queensu.ca/10.4135/9781849208536.
Willis, P. (1977). *Learning to Labour.* Lexington: D.C. Heath.
Wilson, S. (2005). What Is Indigenous Research Methodology? *Canadian Journal of Native Education, 25*(2), 175–179.

CHAPTER 13

Living Biocultures: A Framework for Building Sustainable Community Well-Being, Resilience and Innovation

Yessica D. Rostan Aellen

13.1 LOCATION AND INTRODUCTION

We live in biocultural Communities and Ecosystems built on relationships with People, Animals, Plants, Land, Water and our environment that come together to form a Living matrix. These ecological and cultural systems to which we are inextricably related are integral parts of being *Humxn*.[1] Despite the vital role of biocultural relationships in our daily Lives and learning, and the large impact Humxns have within these relationships, we see little engagement with these topics in schooling. At this moment, we are in a critical relationship with the Earth and each other, as we experience biological and cultural tensions in our Communities, Ecosystems, economies and local/global political conversations. In order to recognize and change biocultural systems that are destructive, we must create spaces for young People and their Communities to talk about these challenges in

---

Y. D. Rostan Aellen (✉)
Ontario Institute for Studies in Education, University of Toronto,
Toronto, ON, Canada
e-mail: yessi@mindsforhumxnity.com

© The Author(s) 2019
F. J. Villegas and J. Brady (eds.), *Critical Schooling*,
https://doi.org/10.1007/978-3-030-00716-4_13

innovative ways that move towards more healthy and sustainable biocultural solutions. I write this to express my resolution that the components that make up our diverse biocultural Living relationships must be at the centre of education, and that this will lead to more profound understandings of our Selves, the Earth and one another, fostering the type of communication, relationships and resilience necessary for social innovation, Community reorganization and systemic change.

Anti-colonial biocultura is a theory, praxis and/or pedagogical framework that works to create thriving biocultural Communities and Ecosystems. It combines the interdisciplinary perspectives of *anti-colonial theory* and *biocultura-* or Indigenous/ancestral Land- and place-based ethnobiologies, pulling together key concepts to build a framework for Community learning and co-creation. Anti-colonial theory in this text works from the understanding that colonialism, "read as imposition and domination," is ongoing in different forms today and continues to be reproduced in our schools, homes, workplaces and social institutions, resulting in power and privilege for some members of society at the expense of others' Lives (Dei, 2006). The African struggle for independence from Europe was a key site for producing much of the beginnings of anti-colonial literature with the writings of Fanon, Cesaire, Memmi, Bhabha, Mbembe, Gandhi, Guevara and others. Over time, anti-colonial thought has come to encompass and speak to the struggles of cultures in a much broader context and, simultaneously, for particular individual struggles within colonial relations (Kempf, 2009). Colonial oppression always includes the validation and reproduction of certain knowledges along with the erasure or delegitimization of other knowledges, as well as the hierarchical reorganizing of the material world for the benefit of the colonizers (Dei, 2006). Oppressions of race, gender, class, age, ability, sexuality, culture and nation are experienced uniquely by different Communities, depending on a variety of contextual factors.

In Canada, we cannot speak about oppression without also speaking about *settler-colonialism*—the perpetual elimination of Indigenous Peoples, denial of their sovereign right to thrive on the Land, and the persistent impact of colonization and destruction on Indigenous young People and their Communities (Benn-John, Chapter 4; Tuck & Yang, 2012). The aim of anti-colonial theory and praxis is "to subvert dominant thinking that re-inscribes colonial and colonizing relations" "in order to challenge social oppression and consequently subvert domination...acknowledging accountability and power" (Dei, 2006, pp. 3–4).

Through the interrogation of dominant and destructive biological and cultural ideas of Self, each other and Land in the settler-colonial context of "Canada," anti-colonial biocultural frameworks aim to motivate accountability and social change. It begins with asking our Selves about our own relationships to the Land—our own bioculturas. I was born in Paysandu, Uruguay and was brought to Toronto by my parents as a young child in the 90s, seeking medical treatment. My learning and teaching has required me to re-evaluate my biocultural position as a migrant and settler in Canada, as well as my mixed ancestry and settler-colonial relationships in Uruguay. My health has also taught me the deep links between biology and culture, and has led me to seek alternative ways of understanding Life than those offered by Western knowledge.

Biocultura is a term I was introduced to in Chihuahua, Mexico at a conference on critical pedagogies. It refers to the complex Humxn–Nature relationships that cross the imaginary boundaries between biology and culture, as well as the inheritance and creation of Indigenous/ancestral, Land- and place-based biocultural knowledge (Mancera-Valencia, 2015). Within Western academia, biocultura is called "ethnobiology" and is often colonially described as a new and largely undefined field made up of diverse disciplines that looks at "interactions between different components of the ecosystem and dynamic relationships established in time and space" (Albuquerque & Medeiros, 2013, p. 1). Ethnobiology is not new; it is a theoretical field and praxis that Indigenous and rural Communities have for many decades been developing in different places across the globe. It is ancestral and local and arises in connection to Land—the biocultural knowledge of our Abuelas. It is important to differentiate between ethnobiology as a field of study within Western academia, and ethnobiology/biocultura as Indigenous/ancestral biocultural sciences, or ways of knowing.

Taken together, anti-colonial biocultura is the centring of our diverse Humxn–Nature relationships in anti-colonial theory, praxis and pedagogy. It is a framework that creates space for collectively denouncing the destructive biocultural organization that has become normalized in our Communities, asking us to reconsider what we have been taught about being Humxn and reimagine the ways our Communities *could* be organized for sustainable wellness and resilience. Biocultura compliments anti-colonial theory and grounds its praxis because in reimagining our Selves as Humxns we must come to term with our relationships and responsibilities with(in) the time and place/Land we inhabit. Tuck and McKenzie (2015) write that "Theorizations of settler colonialism expose deep behaviors of ignorance toward land, water, environment, and sustainability" (p. 3). They offer that a focus on place and Land "necessitates acknowledgement and reparations based on these histories: of settler colonialism, capitalism, and of separations of mind from body, body from land" (p. 3). Many of us working towards social change within our Communities, even activists who debate most passionately against colonial and capitalist oppressions, are caught in the snares of consumption, financially supporting and ideologically normalizing many destructive, unsustainable, colonial biocultural values hidden behind cunning advertisements, fashionable products and empty promises. At our Community meetings, workplaces and schools, I see few People concerned about waste, for example. By the time we leave the room, we have typically created two or three garbage bags of waste, from plastic bottles, coffee cups, Styrofoam plates, utensils—the list goes on. People will simultaneously speak against capitalism and colonialism while they sip imported coffee from a major corporate chain in a one-time-use cup, or as they chug bottles of Water coming from corporations that are stealing it from Indigenous Lands just a couple hours' drive away. These are simple examples of the small but significant ways we consistently fail on a daily basis to acknowledge Land and our biocultural Humxn relationships with(in) Nature. The inescapability of our Aliveness and connection to the Land is precisely what works to disrupt colonialism and spark innovation—it permeates everything we do; every day and it demands that we get creative to find solutions.

Throughout this chapter, when I use the words Nature and Land I include People, Water, Animals, Plants, Fish, Bodies, Minds, Hearts, Food, Medicine, Moon, Sun and all the interconnected aspects of the Living matrix. I purposefully capitalize these words to honour and remind us of the power of the Land and Living. This calls us to consider "not just the materiality of land, but also its 'spiritual emotional, and intellectual aspects'" as Tuck, McKenzie, and McCoy (2014) describe in their writings on Land, place and environment-based education. Throughout my writing, I use Indigenous names for places as a way to call out settler-colonialism and decentre the Canadian narrative of Eurocentric white nationhood. For Toronto, I use the name Tkaronto which comes from Kanyen'ke:ha, the language of the Kanyen'ke:ha'ka People, or People of the Flint—one of the Six Nations that together make up the

Haudenosaunee.[2] In Tkaronto, Indigenous names for different locations are increasingly used in street signs, popular culture, education and more (Abraham, 2014) as a form of Land education that highlights ongoing Indigenous presence and resistance. My aim is not to appropriate, fetishize or make moves to innocence (Tuck & Yang, 2012), but to actively denaturalize settler-colonialism as the norm and simultaneously locate myself and the reader consciously with(in) it at every possible turn. I also use the names Turtle Island and Abya Yala to refer respectively to the Indigenous Land and cosmologies of the North and Central/South ends of the continent colonially called "America." The name *Turtle Island* comes from the Haudenosaunee Creation Story, "a detailed epic, taking days to tell in its entirety" in which there was only Sky and Water until Sky Woman and the Animals created Land on the Turtle's back (Hill, 2008, p. 24). *Abya Yala*, meaning "Tierra en plena madurez,"[3] is the name given to the continent by the Kuna (Dule or Tule) People located in Panama, Colombia and the San Blas Islands. The name was suggested by Aymara leader Takir Mamani as a unifying term for political mobilization (Tone, 2010). It is important to clarify that Indigenous nations have different biocultures and thus different names for the Land they inhabit, particularly across colonially named "Latin America."

This chapter explores anti-colonial biocultura as a pedagogical framework in the context of settler-colonial schooling in Canada. I make a case for a kind of Learning that looks at our biocultural Natures and prioritizes subjectivity, diversity, Community, co-creativity and change as we learn to Live together. I begin by providing a look into the concept of biopower and describe schooling in Tkaronto as a mechanism that reproduces colonial biocultures, material systems, and ideas about being Alive, including how we interact with the Land, our Selves, and each other. I offer the framework of anti-colonial biocultura; a theory, praxis and pedagogical tool that combines key concepts from anti-colonial theory and biocultura. I make a case for the need to ground learning in the real world and Community in order to build sustainable relationships that lead to solutions, highlighting the importance of Land- and place-based actions. To think about possibilities, I envision what it might look like to build thriving *Schools-as-Biocultural-Community-Learning-Centres*, working with the diverse biocultural knowledges of People in our Communities, honouring the Indigenous biocultures of Turtle Island and building wellness, resilience, and innovation in the Living Communities we take part in.

13.2 BIOPOWER AND THE PROBLEM OF COLONIAL SCHOOLING IN TKARONTO

In his theorizations of power within society, Michel Foucault outlines *biopower* as "a power over *bios* or life," where the Lives of individuals and groups of the population are "managed" (Taylor, 2014). Foucault sees two interconnected levels of disciplinary and regulatory power functioning at the individual Body and population, or species-Body. Taylor (2014) explains that, "While at one level disciplinary institutions such as schools, workshops, prisons and hospitals *target individual bodies as they deviate from norms*, at another level the state is concerned with knowing and *administrating the norms of the population* as a whole" (p. 45, emphasis added). Analysing Foucault's notion of biopower, Mbembe (2003) writes that biopower and sovereignty are "the capacity to define who matters and who does not, who is disposable and who is not" (p. 27). Biopower lies in the intricacies of the state's attempts to "manage" and "administer" Life through "*norms rather than laws...internalized by subjects* rather than exercised from above through acts and threats of violence...*dispersed throughout society* rather than located in a single individual or government body" (Taylor, 2014, pp. 43–46, emphasis added). This managing and administering occurs in the Canadian school system through several means, including curriculum content, representation, accessibility, and discipline. Indigenous, Black, Latinx, Muslim, differently abled, neurodiverse,[4] and LGTBQ2S+ experiences are classified as outside the "norm" of colonial society, and labelled as "inferior," "problems" or "threats" in the state's narrative of nationhood and progress (Madan, Chapter 2).

By teaching only Eurowestern perspectives in curriculums for the sciences, history, philosophy and other ontologically critical topics, students are forced to internalize biocultural "norms" that come from colonial Eurocentric canons rather than their own cultures, creating disconnection in their identity of themselves with(in) Nature. Dei (2012) writes that:

> we need an Indigenous anti-colonial education to challenge the compartmentalization of education into separate social, cultural, spiritual, political and biological dimensions...the split between the social and natural sciences and narrow conceptualizations of what counts as science, intellectuality and critical inquiry...to build liberatory ways of educating our young people and ourselves. (p. 115)

Anti-colonial biocultura frameworks ask us to return to our biocultural roots as sciences so we can question what we have accepted as "obvious" about the Humxn identity and our relationship to Nature, our Selves, our Bodies, the Land, Water and each other. In order to create innovative solutions for biocultural sustainability and wellness in our Communities, we must ask ourselves what underlying assumptions of Humxnness and Living we have internalized that remain unquestioned in our everyday Life-systems and organization. We need to interrogate the culture of consumption we participate in and see the ways it reinforces the biopower of the state to poison Land, Water, Food and Medicine for corporate gains. Understanding how unsustainable relationships of biopower are maintained by colonial schooling is the basis for launching an anti-colonial biocultural method of pedagogy.

Colonial schooling organizes and normalizes oppression because it directly reproduces and transmits the various "norms" of Life that maintain settler-colonial biopower. Consequently, possibilities for epistemological, ontological, biocultural diversity and innovation are suffocated. Celia Haig-Brown (2009) writes that it is important to remember that, "In North America, schooling – or what has been ethnocentrically called formal education – began as a relation between Europeans and Indigenous people" and that schooling "quickly became a major tool for attempted assimilation of First Nations peoples," driven by "the marketplace mentality of the early colonizers" (p. 7). She writes that too often, "these roots of contemporary schooling are conveniently forgotten along with the colonial mentality that continues to inform" schooling today (Haig-Brown, p. 8). This pattern is seen across Turtle Island and Abya Yala, although details are unique and context-specific in each place. Canadian schooling largely denies student heritages and biocultures and can be seen as the systematic inhibition of biocultural diversity, learning and Community wellness. In *Decolonizing Education: Nourishing the Learning Spirit*, Marie Battiste (2013) writes that the legacy of forced assimilative education for Indigenous Peoples, whose "heritage and knowledge [are] rejected and suppressed, and ignored in the education system," "is a subject that every citizen of Canada should know, because every citizen in Canada is connected to it" (p. 23). She explains that educational institutions in Canada serve to create, reproduce and transmit "an imagined culture of nationalism imposed by the state…not reflective of the heritage, knowledge, or culture that the students bring to education, or their skills and shared traditions. It is not reflective of the normal everyday [culture] that they live with their families" (Battiste, 2013, p. 29). Further, "Since there is no agreement about transmitting knowledge, heritage and culture, the resulting curriculum is made normative by a cloak of standards and expectations on all educators and students" (p. 29). We cannot ask students to succeed in school despite the dehumxnizing and demoralizing experience of mental, spiritual and physical un-wellness at the hands and policies of racist, sexist, and ableist colonial educators, frameworks and systems. We must build learning spaces where young People can thrive. We must ask them what it means to succeed.

Schools in Turtle Island today are home to diverse groups of learners that identify in increasingly complex ways to colonialism, depending on their biocultural locations. In Tkaronto and large urban centres especially, many learners are members of diaspora, refugees, and migrants who arrived from countries affected by past and contemporary forms of colonialism (see Azraq, Chapter 10; Calero & Chica, Chapter 7; Gibson-Taylor & Moore, Chapter 5; Villegas, Chapter 11). Cannon (2012) critiques that much of pedagogical literature fails to address ways non-Indigenous Peoples (to Turtle Island) can be engaged to reflect on their identity and take ownership of their participation in ongoing settler-colonialism. Celia Haig-Brown (2009) points out that the "everyday lack of consciousness" in Canada's education "create the conditions that allow them the same possibility of forgetting their pasts and their relation to Indigenous peoples" (p. 12). For members of diaspora and migrants, this may also constitute a lack of consciousness about their relation to Indigenous Peoples and their colonial locations "back home." Haig-Brown (2009) writes that "the simple binary distinctions of colonizer/colonized or Indigenous/ immigrant fail to address the range of ways that people are a part of this country" (p. 14). These binaries do not consider People Indigenous to Abya Yala, Africa, Asia and other places of Earth, or People who through colonization have mixed ancestries, biocultures and intersecting identities that now find themselves in relationship with Indigenous Peoples on Turtle Island. Members of diaspora, refugees, and migrants embody experiences and home Lands directly linked to different forms of ongoing colonialism. How do we engage such diversity of biocultures in moving towards social change and innovation? Battiste (2013) leads us in creating innovative pedagogical frameworks; she writes that,

> The key in designing meaningful education in Canada must begin with confronting the hidden standards of racism, colonialism, and cultural and

linguistic imperialism in the modern curriculum and seeing the theoretical incoherence with a modern theory of society. No theory of Canadian society exists that reflects its order as an eternal pattern of human nature or social harmony. (p. 29)

We cannot continue to allow a singular bioculture, science, and way of knowing to define our Humxn–Nature and Humxn–Humxn relationships, or the learning and success of our Communities. The silencing of diverse biocultures in education has effects on the wellness and resilience of Communities, biocultural knowledge systems and ultimately, People and the Land.

13.3 Building an Anti-colonial Biocultural Framework

Battiste (2013) recommends educators in Canada identify new processes and frameworks that take on the responsibility of "acknowledging excellence through the proper valuing and respectful circulation of Indigenous knowledge across and beyond Eurocentric disciplines" (p. 69). As a form of Land education situated in Turtle Island, anti-colonial biocultural pedagogies strive to centre Indigenous ways of knowing Land and Life, explicitly disrupt settler-colonial normalcy, and to "inspire acts of refusal, reclamation, regeneration, and reimagination" that move towards decolonization and are accountable to Indigenous futurity (Tuck et al., 2014, pp. 18–19). Anti-colonial biocultural frameworks support shifts on all levels of education that will honour diverse knowledge systems, persistently centring First Nations, Metis and Inuit biocultural epistemologies and fostering conversations with the diverse biocultures of settlers, diaspora, refugees and migrants in respective Communities. The goal is to create dialogue about decolonization, and what our roles and responsibilities might look like in the coming decades of biocultural innovation and change. As a social justice theory, praxis and pedagogy, anti-colonial biocultura aims to create healing, nurturing and Life-sustaining learning that has the potential to build new stories, relationships and environments with the collective experiences, biocultural knowledges and imaginaries of learners.

Biocultura asks us to engage our cultural heritages and to see the ways we embody biocultural knowledges. In 2010, the work of Eckart Boege Shmidt, titled "El patrimonio biocultural de los pueblos indigenas de Mexico. Hacia la conservación in situ de la biodiversidad en los territorios indígenas"[5] brought national attention to the framework of bioculturidad, specifically because of his use of context-specific "patrimonio biocultural"[6] connected to Land and time, or the geohistory of the sociocultural, economic, cognitive-episteme and language that implicated a dialectic relationship with the Ecosystems (Mancera-Valencia, 2015, p. 23). Mancera-Valencia explains that the word *patrimonio* in bioculturidad speaks to the cultural heritage or *herencia*[7] of context- and Land-specific and subjective biocultural knowledges that have been passed down by ancestors, families and Communities for thousands of years from generation to generation. He describes biocultural heritage as praxis (reflection/theorizing and action), with properties of dialogical creation, co-construction of knowledge in Community and in dialogue with the territorial Ecosystems, and production for sustenance. Anti-colonial thinking shares these concepts with biocultura in that it "acknowledges and works with the understanding that the self and subjectivity matter in terms of methodological implications/considerations, as well as in the ways we produce, interrogate, and validate knowledge... bodies and identities are linked to the production of knowledge" (Dei, 2009, p. 252). To me, it has made sense to build an anti-colonial biocultura framework for theory, praxis and pedagogy upon the following five concepts shared between anti-colonial thought and bioculturas of Indigenous/ancestral, Land- and place-based ethnobiology. The five concepts are:

1. Individual Biocultural Subjectivity: Identity, Location, Power and Responsibilities.
2. Diversity: Honouring Differences as Possibility.
3. Communion: Interconnection, Communication and Co-creation with(in) Community.
4. Embodied Learning and Growth: Individual and Collective Creativity.
5. Constant Change: Possibilities for Innovation and Reorganization in the Emerging Future.

These five concepts are not discrete categories, but holistic and interconnected. Subjectivity, diversity, communion, learning, co-creation and change occur simultaneously in Life and within Indigenous biocultures and anti-colonial ways of knowing.

Anti-colonial biocultural concepts can be tailored to several curriculum themes and objectives and applied in Tkaronto schools as a way towards co-creating sustainable, anti-colonial futures. In my own work, I use anti-colonial biocultura as a framework for helping students locate themselves within settler-colonialism, connecting questions of location, identity, power, relationship and responsibility through discussions of anti-colonial efforts on Turtle Island and abroad. In order to achieve a spark of consciousness and move towards relationships based on interconnection, anti-colonial biocultural frameworks require locating the subjective Self within learning and Living.

It is essential to recognize subjectivity in learning, in Humxn knowledges, relationships and biocultures. Anti-colonial biocultural pedagogy must engage with the plurality and fluidity of viewpoints in the space, having explicit discussions about how we come to know, the partiality of knowing and thinking about power relations in how knowledge is created, produced and reproduced (Dei, 2012). Our learning spaces must be critical when working with "objective" knowledge, acknowledging that "discursive practices are never neutral or apolitical and that historical accounts and narratives are shaped and socially conditioned" (Dei & Asgharzadeh, 2001, p. 318). Learning spaces must work to value subjectivity, diversity, embodied learning, knowledge co-creation and a reclaiming of roots as important aspects of Living and learning. Centring subjectivity requires us to ask ourselves and our students to locate the Self and envision how individual actions grow into larger social changes in our Communities. It is the first step to co-creation.

Anti-colonial biocultural frameworks also centre the coexistence of multiple subjectivities and the co-creation of knowledge in Community, considering how spaces tell, listen to and honour different stories/histories/perspectives/biocultural knowledges/truths. Currently, Canadian education "engages" with diversity with an "over-riding message of social cohesion and integration into mainstream society, presenting intergroup inequities and frictions as past problems that Canada has resolved" (Joshee, 2004, as cited in Bickmore, 2014, p. 318). This effectively silences oppressive settler-colonial relations within the classroom and the diverse Living experiences of students under the pretence of multiculturalism. Schooling in Tkaronto is not multicultural; curriculums, systems and even teacher education are Eurocentric and deeply colonial. There is little to no biocultural diversity in the content we are teaching and learning, and Indigenous knowledge is only hinted at emptily, if mentioned at all. In a teacher's education course on Democratic Citizenship Education, I was made to read dozens of works by white Canadian scholars about the need to include a diversity of voices in Canadian curriculum, particularly Indigenous voices. Although we had Black, Latinx, Muslim and Asian identities in the room, our perspectives were at best politely nodded at. First Nations, Metis and Inuit perspectives were "suggested," never engaged. Talking about diversity without acting to meaningfully *engage* diverse epistemologies and politics maintains the supremacy of Eurocentric knowledge, simultaneously silencing and devaluing other knowledge systems.

Anti-colonial biocultural pedagogies do not aim for "tolerance," but for a sincere valuing and appreciation of *diversity as possibility* in our learning. This framework sees diversity as a necessity that nurtures both cultural and biological Community wellness and understands that the ways we choose to negotiate differences lead to two general conclusions: (1) the oppression of one party by the other, or (2) learning and growth for all parties involved, which can lead to harmony and conscious co-creation. Anti-colonial biocultural learning and co-creation depends on unoppressive, collective engagement and can be manifested through subjective participation, space and dialogue that honours diversity, empathy, reciprocity, growth and co-operatively finding solutions. This kind of communication and learning requires Self and Community-awareness and an understanding of power dynamics, as well as skills of listening, emotional intelligence and knowing how to hold space, especially during moments of discomfort or disagreement.

Anti-colonial biocultural frameworks centre interdependence in the ways we Live, learn and communicate with the world, and expose the "falsity" in the colonial concept of individualism (Fanon, 1963). Co-operative learning and communication, although major determinants of Humxn Lived experience and culture, are not explicitly taught in schools. This is another way in which the biocultural Humxn identity remains largely uninterrogated and under-explored in colonial schooling. Anti-colonial biocultura engages with subjectivity and diversity while maintaining Community, interconnection and co-creation at the centre, rejecting hierarchical ways of existing and raising questions of responsibility and reciprocity. It works from the understanding that everyone (everything that Lives) is already inherently political and involved in either the harming or nurturing of others within an ecological framework—just by being Alive and Living. To be Alive is to be a political actor in the world. Indigenous epistemologies recognize that biology and culture are made up of relationships and relationality, and "prioritizes the reality that human life is connected to and dependent on other species and the land" (Tuck & McKenzie, 2015, p. 4). Perspectives of "ecological citizenship" understand that individual acts impact the collective, and that public decisions affect the private, and vice versa (Huckle, 2008). This requires thinking about the fact that we "are 'always already' acting on others" and that "such citizenship focuses on horizontal citizen-citizen relations rather than vertical citizen-state relations" (Huckle, 2008, p. 6). Responsibility is thus directly connected to biocultural understandings of participatory and reciprocal co-creation. How can we bring interconnection, conscious coexistence and co-creation into education?

Anti-colonial biocultures understand that learning is achieved through Community relationships, where each Person brings and is given space for their own skills, gifts, needs and perspectives to the whole. It asks us to redefine and reclaim the biocultural relationships we co-create and embody every day, with the Land and with each other. Forward-thinking theories of resistance, futurity and transformation call us to ask ourselves, our students and Communities to reflect on how collective change happens, and our responsibilities on the individual level. Eve Tuck and K. Wayne Yang (2014) write:

> According to the poststructuralist turn, change is always occurring, and within a more cynical critical approach, change is never happening or if it does, it reinscribes relations of power. Within many Indigenous epistemologies, change is always happening (although different from the poststructuralist sense), and it can take on many forms – desirable or otherwise. These varying perspectives on change matter with regard to human agency, and thus matter with regard to resistance. Each perspective is going to have different implications for how humans should spend their time on the planet. (p. 120)

We need to explicitly discuss ideas of co-creation, innovation and change in our learning spaces, locating ourselves and our Communities within historical and current biocultural contexts. We need to create space for critical questions and reflection about how to "transform moral outrage into concrete attempts" of social change (Giroux, 2014).

Young People are expressing individual and collective outrage, co-creating projects and spaces that embody, critically imagine and redefine traditional paradigms, claiming "collective agency in which their voices must be heard as part of a concerted effort to shape the future that they will inherit" (Giroux, 2014). Anti-colonial biocultura builds spaces of Community co-creation, where collective hope and responsibility can be nurtured and mobilized into actions that contribute to innovation. Learning spaces that allow us to fully explore, dream and create are essential in reclamation and embodiment of Humxn biocultural identities of subjectivity, diversity, Community, learning, co-creation and change. Freire (1993) tells us:

> Soñar no es solo un acto político necesario...forma parte de la naturaleza humana que, dentro de la historia, se encuentra en permanente proceso de devenir...No hay cambio sin sueño, como no hay sueño sin esperanza...La comprensión de la historia como *posibilidad* y no *determinismo* seria ininteligible sin el *sueño*, asi como la concepción *determinista* se siente incompatible con el, y por eso lo niega. (pp. 116–117)[8]

Anti-colonial biocultural pedagogies work to create this essential catalytic space for dreaming, exploring, theorizing and creating the Self and Community, looking always to get to know and experience our Humxn identities with(in) Nature. To encourage and enable the creation of culture by young People, we must "welcome diverse cultural identities and recognize the structural inequities these young People encounter, along with their boundless capacity for confronting injustice" (Sutton, 2007, p. 617). In "Methodology of the Oppressed" Chela Sandoval (2000) describes the co-creation of "a deregulating system" that decodes/recodes and produces knowledge/media "by practicing on cultural artifacts of every kind – from film, television, and computer representations to architectural environments, literature, theory, and science" (p. 9). Co-creation and dreaming can take many diverse pedagogical forms in learning spaces, including but not limited to: play, visual arts, music and song creation, dance, slam poetry, writing, film, fashion, theatre, cooking, herbalism, permaculture and Land practices, critical media, research, sciences, architecture and action projects that spark anti-colonial conversations and biocultural innovation.

13.4 Addressing Biocultural Sustainability

We must centre ourselves on the Land and begin with our locations in order to reclaim ourselves as Humxns with(in) Nature. This is imperative for moving towards biocultural-centricity and I have seen the success of centring place/Land first hand in educational spaces. According to students, one of the most memorable and impactful workshops in a sustainability programme I was a part of involved a Live Turtle (rescued) that the youth learned to interact with respectfully. It seems silly, but for young People from the city especially, sharing space and connecting with a Live Turtle was the highlight of the programme and made their learning about sustainability that much more important to them. The experience placed them back on the Land and invited them to interrogate their Humxn identity, along with questions of sustainability and the ways we could do more to protect Life on Turtle Island. How can we creatively find ways to persistently build relationships with the Land, Water, Plants, Animals, our Bodies and one another? We do not heal simply by talking about healing; we heal by actively sharing and co-creating strong Community connections between one another, seeing the ways in which we are connected. Rebuilding biocultural Humxn relationships depends on the understanding that Community sustainability leads to more possibilities of well-being, resilience and innovation. Thus, anti-colonial biocultural pedagogies must take a serious look at how we are implicated in the destruction of Lives, cultures and Land, here in Turtle Island and abroad. This means reflecting and acting on where we Live, what we consume, the waste we create, what our money is funding and how our Lifeviews and Lifestyles perpetuate colonial biopower and violence. If we can slowly organize our Communities to grow and harvest more Food, build relationships with neighbours and local farmers, create and harness energy, build more sustainable homes, reorganize to share resources, and create strong local or alternate economies in our Communities, we will no longer need to rely on the biopower of colonial systems that destroy us, we will have reclaimed Individual and Community biopower.

These concepts of Community biocultural reorganization are not new. Amilcar Cabral (1970), a Guinea-Bissauan and Cape Verdean anti-colonial thinker and agricultural engineer, tells us that there are "strong, dependent and reciprocal relationships existing between the cultural situation and the economic (and political) situation in the behavior of human societies," and that:

culture is always in the life of a society, the more or less conscious result of the economic and political activities of that society, the more or less dynamic expression of the kinds of relationships which prevail in that society, on the one hand between man (considered individually or collectively) and nature, and, on the other hand, among individuals, groups of individuals, social strata or classes. (p. 2)

In other words, a society's culture is made up of the everyday interactions of "Life"—the conscious and the unconscious (or learned and unquestioned) patterns of activity and Living relationships between People, and between Nature and People. Cabral embodied this understanding through his concerns with material or "practical things" and "real improvement" in People's Lives, seen in his insistence and teaching of agricultural and economic independence (Lopes, 2006). Cabral knew that change towards liberation was an act of culture and that cultural possibilities emerged through "a continued process of social and structural revolution, capable of drawing whole peoples into an arena of active participation" (Lopes, 2006, pp. 2–3). This is one of the strengths of anti-colonial biocultura; it implicates you personally and draws you in with the concept that we can and must all participate in reorganizing our daily Humxn–Nature relationships.

Exciting examples of this biocultural reorganizing can be seen increasingly in local and global contexts. In February 2016, I witnessed a completely self-sustainable public school built in Jaureguiberry, Uruguay from mostly recyclable materials (tires, bottles, sand, etc.). This school is "off grid" and yet located right off the main highway to Montevideo. It has over a hundred children re-learning and reimagining their roles as Humxns with(in) Nature on a daily basis, year round. The children and surrounding Community learn how the building works to heat itself (using solar power and recycled tires as heat batteries), collect Water and grow Food, and a large part of their curriculum consists of reconnecting with the Land through action and embodied learning. I know of similar spaces being built in Argentina, in Six Nations and across Turtle Island. Increasingly we are seeing Community gardens, repair cafes, trade systems, upcycling and sharing trends, as well as a gradual rise in green energy and sustainability initiatives brought about by Community organizing and changes to policy. Biocultural change is already happening, and the possibilities are vast. The potential for transformation that comes from this kind of Community sustainability is crucial to anti-colonial biocultura, the reclamation of biopower, and the building of thriving biocultural Communities. It begins in relationships that respect Land and Indigenous Nations through action projects that slowly work to reorganize Community spaces and schools. Anti-colonial biocultura needs to make spaces for students to come to term with and experiment new ways of honouring our relationships and responsibilities within the time and place/Land we inhabit.

Collaborating in programmes of Community sustainability and co-creating youth action projects has allowed me to have conversations with hundreds of Tkaronto youth about what sustainability means to them. In the words of the youth I have met, sustainability is "managing our things better" and "learning to share." It is recognizing that "the government is not helping" and that we need to "do it ourselves." It is acknowledging that "society is not fair to everybody" and that we have to prioritize our "needs over wants" and "not use so much pointless stuff" or "more than we need when others have nothing." In the words of a grade eight student: "It's our garbage, so it's our responsibility." Young People and children are able to connect questions of social, cultural, economic, political and environmental sustainability to real situations in their worlds and Communities, helping to spark in-depth conversations on location, power, privilege and responsibilities. Perhaps most importantly, looking at current, local projects working towards change nurtures hope, collaboration and imagination in what can otherwise seem like a very scary future for a kid growing up in seemingly apocalyptic times. Creating hope for young People is critical in the climate of increasing mental health crises seen across Canada. The conclusion students often reached together is that sustainability is not an unattainable thing—it is simply the reorganization of how we get things done in our economies, Communities and daily Lives. It is the rebuilding of Living relationships right where we are.

Usually, there is a mix of emotion in the groups as we discuss sustainability, with most pessimism becoming a little more hopeful by the end of the workshops. Students often describe themselves as feeling "uncomfortable" and "afraid" of what they hear on the news and see on social media about the world. Many admit that they feel they have nobody to talk to about "these things" in their families or their Communities. This indicates a need for guardians, elders, teachers, family members and Community leaders to find ways to address the valid questions, concerns, emotions and fears young People are facing today. During one workshop, a student grew exasperated and shouted: "It's impossible! Nobody cares." When I asked if he wanted to share why he felt that way, he said, "...that's just human nature, people are greedy and if they haven't change till now after all these years, they are never going to change!" The class fell silent and heavy. Before I could find the right words, countless others in the class raised their voices at once, saying: "That's not true, I care," and "YEAH! it *is* possible," and "People need to wake up and stop being selfish!" and "We just need to learn to work together!" I was so grateful for the courage of the young People in that room. Learning moments like these allow the dialogue to hit a level of emotion and realness that is necessary for healing, growth and mobilization. It is important to talk about what it is like to maintain hope throughout daily attacks on Life, People and Land. It is important because the young People in our Communities experience these attacks. They Live, see and feel what is happening as much as adults do. Our classrooms and Communities must provide spaces to have these conversations, discuss wellness, debrief, process emotions involved, heal together, reorganize and act together.

The ultimate goal of anti-colonial biocultura is to co-create Community action projects that tackle local challenges to economic, cultural, social and/or environmental sustainability in a way that addresses responsibilities and relationships within settler-colonial contexts. Community education and action that begins with the sustainability of Life, Peoples and Land, in past and present, local and global contexts, can help us to collectively imagine new ways of organizing and being that centre interdependence, responsibility and solidarity. The growing questions of sustainability and biopower on the planet require us to think about these relationships and to be accountable for our pasts and futures. In the words of Fanon (1963), we are facing a "colossal task, which consists of reintroducing man into the world, man in his totality" (p. 62). To do this, he writes, we must "confess" our different modes of participation in colonialism, "decide to wake up, put on [our] thinking caps and stop playing the irresponsible game of Sleeping Beauty" (p. 62). Biocultural wellness and sustainability are entry points that offer a place- and Land-based sense of urgency in which we may bring home and call to question our colonial implications and responsibilities in building biocultural wellness, resilience and innovation.

13.5 Grounding Learning in Community Spaces and the Real World

Schooling often disconnects learning from the Lived experiences of young People in their Communities, but anti-colonial biocultura does just the opposite, focusing on place and the real everyday Lives of learners in order to spark innovation. Tuck and McKenzie (2015) write that "it is the specificity, the rootedness of place that makes it so important in (post) human imagination" (p. 5). They ask whether we are capable of addressing the challenges of our time and suggest that "theorizing and practicing place more deeply is at least a step in the direction of such a path" (p. 3). I have experienced this myself first hand in my teaching. Every time I invite open dialogue to tackle current real-world questions, young People surprise me with how much they already know and how much they care about the state of the world and their Communities. I have heard 6-year-olds discuss politics and local challenges more competently than some adults who have the right to vote. I have also seen how much young People worry. These conversations are especially crucial to racialized, marginalized and criminalized youth—Indigenous, Black, Brown, Latin American, Muslim, diversely-abled, neurodivergent, LGTBQ2S+, migrant, refugee and undocumented youth. I have been called into schools with the so-called toughest kids and heard dialogues so critical and creative that some adults in the room (sometimes myself) were not able to keep up. Young People know more than we give them credit and they have dreams and ideas for changing the spaces around them for the better. In their paper on co-developing Youthtopias with youth of colour, Akom, Ginwright and Cammarota (2008) tell us that "youth need new kinds of spaces where resistance and resiliency can be developed through formal (and informal) processes, pedagogical structures, and youth cultural practices" (p. 2). Yet too often in Tkaronto schools and youth programs I have been told by program directors that discussions about oppression, power, social justice and colonialism are "too political," or that the youth are "not old enough," or "uninterested."

At a sustainability conference last year, after I led a workshop on pipelines in which we discussed ongoing resistance to Canadian oil companies led by First Nations youth, I was told by the conference director, "Advocacy is great, but you should really focus more on the program objectives." I fail to see how opening respectful honest dialogue about real sustainability and Land concerns does not meet program objectives of increasing awareness and agency, and empowering young People to be Community sustainability leaders. However, refusing to speak to real issues upholds a settler-colonial and oppressive educational space. Dei (2009) asks us: "who (or what agenda) is best served by the maintenance of the discursive divide between teaching and activism? Who benefits from teachers' collective refusal to engage as activists, citing professionalism and objectivity?" (p. 255). We cannot be afraid to include present-day local struggles for change and reorganization in our teaching—it is our responsibility as educators to create spaces for these conversations. Why would I not mention the work of Black Lives Matter, the BLM Freedom School and the Black Liberation Collective in Tkaronto? Why omit mentioning the youth-led Standing Rock movement and its global Humxn influence, Unist'ot'en in British Colombia, or the young People protesting the Line 9 pipeline in Ontario, the expansion of Kinder Morgan on the west coast, or the superfluity of Canada 150 celebrations? Why not highlight the Earth Guardians, an international sustainability movement led by Indigenous youth? Why not tell them that young People just like them are acting in innovative ways?... speaking at the United Nations, creating revolutionary art and music, and demanding accountability from their local governments for not taking significant action on issues that matter to them and affect their Lives. As a teacher, I want to create space for young People to learn about things that affect their Lives on a daily basis, their Livelihood and dreams for the future, their families and Communities. Conversations about current, local issues and how they are already being tackled are not only effective for engaging even the most "unengaged" students, they are crucial to our learning, wellness and sense of hope and Community resilience. Anti-colonial biocultura addresses and engages with the diverse identities, needs and questions of young People today in a way that is empowering, action-focused, and hopeful rather than disempowering and silencing. We can no longer remain silent in education about issues that are so obviously impacting youth's wellbeing. Bringing examples of current resistance and solidarity into the classroom can help bring settler-colonialism "home" in a way that empowers students to hope and to envision the ways they can be a part of social biocultural innovation and change. Young People have the right, as Living participants in the world, to be informed, ask questions and co-create the world around them. The challenges our Communities face in the world are real and should be a regular part of conversations in schooling so that we can work together to imagine and create real solutions.

I have found that teachers and Community workers often do not feel equipped or prepared to handle certain real-world conversations, particularly in vastly diverse spaces. There is an opportunity here. Grounding learning in Community and the real world means building connections and relationships in Community so that we may learn together and from each other. Working in Tkaronto schools, organizations and Communities I have seen that there are dedicated, compassionate, well-prepared and knowledgeable People ready to take the lead. They reorganize Communities and schools every day, lead dialogue and change, create anti-racist and anti-oppressive frameworks and policies, redefine reconciliation and solidarity, fine tune peacebuilding methods, rethink mental, physical, emotional and spiritual health, build Community wellness, sustainability and more. We need to think about what more grounded, accessible and extensive Community–school partnerships could look like. We can increase the roles of bioculturally revelvant, knowledgeable Community members, artists, elders and young leaders in schools. We can build capacity building programs directly from these Community-centred frameworks and support the funding of these initiatives and Community leaders in schools. We can engage teachers as participants or co-facilitators during these programs, while simultaneously creating space for Community members to share knowledge and build relationships with students. Taking this idea further, what could the reorganization of *Schools-as-Biocultural-Community-Learning-Centres* look like in Tkaronto? I envision connecting place- and culturally specific Community workers, resources, methods and services to schools, creating Community-learning centres that build wellness and sustainability within Tkaronto's Communities. This type of reorganization can help disrupt the normalization of Eurocentric knowledge and organization as all-encompassing, making space for the knowledges in the Community to come forward, tackling place-specific challenges and building biocultural resilience. We must work to build these connections.

Anti-colonial biocultura aims to focus our attention away from the prescribed "norms" and systems within colonial Lifeviews so that we may refocus on bioculturally redefining ourselves and our relationships in Community. Education *for Communities* must be brought back *to Communities*, meaning Community members and students should be leading the learning with their embodied knowledges and questions. Anti-colonial biocultura interrogates our Humxn–Nature relationships by asking us, as teachers and learners, how and why we learn while placing a critical lens on schooling and learning itself. We must ask: What are our ideas of Living and being Humxn and where have they come from? How do we think learning happens? What is learning/school for? What do we want it to be for, or what *could* it be for? And what do learners need in that space for it to become a place where they can learn and grow into what they envision for themselves and their Communities?

13.6 Possibilities for Biocultural Innovation

We have seen that anti-colonial biocultural frameworks must be rooted in Land, Community and the real world, or the biocultural experiences of the People in the space. All People on this Land are part of the colonial biocultural reality of Canada and are both implicated in and impacted by cultural and ecological destruction, as well as movements of Land and sustainability. The urgent complexity of our current historical moment in Turtle Island and around the world requires a comprehensive approach to education that encompasses our individual and collective stories and imaginaries about what it means to be Alive. Anti-colonial biocultura as a pedagogical framework asks us to focus on our Living Humxn relationships to Self, Land and one another. Any education that attempts to control and silence diverse ways of knowing instead of encouraging communication and co-creation is inhibiting the capacity of learners to change the world around them for the better. We must recognize that we are at a necessary and critical point of social change and that this will require new, creative forms of learning and Living on the planet. Education should invite us to learn, strategize, reorganize and co-create sustainable biocultures in our Communities.

Anti-colonial biocultura means creating Community spaces that engage both the biological and cultural lived realities of Community members, purposefully challenging the dominant Life narratives and power structures that are presented by Eurocentrism, allowing plurality of biocultures and innovative ways of being with(in) Nature to flourish. It means reclaiming a biocultural Humxn identity and growing together. Living Communities are resilient, finding the means to organize and create constructive system changes for their own wellness. Community discussion and innovation in educational programs is spearheaded by

Community members who notice urgent needs and seek to increase representation and dialogue within the school system. Groups creating change are self-forming forces in Tkaronto, with sustainable networks of solidarity among skilled, passionate educators, artists, young People and Community workers taking on projects that are driving the forefront of innovation in our schools and Communities.

Anti-colonial biocultural frameworks are a critical tool for thinking about how we can build thriving schools and Communities. Subjectivity, diversity, interconnectedness/Community, learning and change are grounded in conversations of current, real-world challenges in specific places and look to possibilities in the emerging future. Within formal and informal learning spaces, biocultura can be used for discussing how we co-create our worlds, and for understanding diverse biocultural Humxn identities and possibilities. It requires that we ground learning on the Land and in our Bodies and talk about components of economic, cultural, social and environmental sustainability. Anti-colonial biocultura creates space for dreaming up innovative solutions and responsibly co-creating projects that reorganize our Communities towards manifestations of Humxn–Nature relationships that are nurturing and sustainable.

It is a time of revival, reimagining and co-creation. It is a time of survival and reclamation. The call is for us to denounce disconnection, to seek the interconnections between our cultural and biological histories, presents and futures, and to Live differently, breaking the patterns that continue our destruction to build new ones that are Life-sustaining and relevant to today's challenges. The invitation is for us to move beyond talk and ideas to seriously consider our ideological and material biocultural organization as Communities, and to have the courage to breathe innovation, love and creativity into what is no longer of use. The answers already exist in our diverse ancestral heritages and relationships to our Bodies, Nature and the Land; biocultura is largely a matter of taking accountability and action in our re-learning, relating and reorganization of ourselves. Co-creating resilient biocultural Communities means learning and creating *as* Communities. This requires looking with an open Mind and Heart at the colonial wounds in our Humxn identities so that we may reorganize into Life-nourishing relationships and systems. We must remember our Selves and our ancestors, who and what we are, our locations both socially and biologically on the Land. We must take up the responsibilities that come with those identities, honouring the

Land we Live with(in) and its Indigenous People and biocultures. We Live together in diversity and impact each other bioculturally in more ways than we realize. It is up to us to learn to thrive together, building Community wellness, resilience and innovation.

Notes

1. I use the word *Humxn* to highlight: (1) the common X chromosome among People regardless of gender or sexual identity; (2) the biocultural understanding that everything that is Alive exists on a spectrum of diversity rather than within narrow categories or binaries; (3) ethnobiological approaches, and our current lack of these approaches in education and politics; (4) the bringing forth of old–new Humxn relationships with(in) Nature such as those described by Fanon's concept of "sociogeny" (1967) and Wynter's hybrid nature-culture (2001).
2. This knowledge is not cited because I learned it orally and through Living relationships in Community.
3. Land in full maturity or ripeness.
4. "Neurodiversity" was coined by autism advocates to describe neurological differences in Humxns (such as autism, ADHD, Tourette's, anxiety and others) and to move away from the violence of "normalcy" politics (Armstrong, 2012; Blume, 1998; Singer, 1999).
5. "*The biocultural heritage of Indigenous Communities of Mexico. Towards the in situ conservation of biodiversity in Indigenous territories/lands.*"
6. *Biocultural heritage.*
7. *Inheritance.*
8. "*Dreaming is not only a necessary political act...it forms part of human nature which, within history, finds itself in a permanent process of becoming....There is no change without dreams just as there are no dreams without hope....The understanding of history as* possibility *rather than* determinism...*would be unintelligible without* dreams, *just as a* deterministic view *feels incompatible with them and, therefore, negates them*".

References

Abraham, P. (2014). Toronto vs Everybody Gets Indigenous T-Shirt Translation. *Humber College News.* http://humbernews.ca/toronto-vs-everybody-gets-Indigenous-t-shirt-translation/. Accessed February 2016.

Akom, A. A., Ginwright, S., & Cammarota, J. (2008). Youthtopias: Towards a New Paradigm of Critical Youth Studies. *Youth Media Reporter: The Profession Journal of the Youth Media Field, 2*(4), 1–30.

Albuquerque, P. U., & Medeiros, P. M. (2013). What is Evolutionary Ethnobiology? *Ethnobiology and Conservation, 2*(6), 1–4.

Armstrong, T. (2012). First Discover Their Strengths: A Neurodiversity Perspective Can Help Educators Create Learning Environments in Which All Students Flourish. *Educational Leadership, 70*(2), 10–16. Alexandria: Association for Supervision & Curriculum Development.

Battiste, M. (2013). *Decolonizing Education: Nourishing the Learning Spirit.* Saskatoon: Purich Publishing Ltd.

Bickmore, K. (2014). Citizenship Education in Canada: 'Democratic' Engagement with Differences, Conflicts and Equity Issues? *Citizenship Teaching & Learning, 9*(3), 257–278.

Blume, H. (1998, September 30). Neurodiversity: On the Neurological Underpinnings of Geekdom. *The Atlantic.* www.theatlantic.com/magazine/archive/1998/09/neurodiversity/5909. Accessed August 2017.

Cabezas, A. (2013). De cuerpos abyectos y violencias de genero contra las personas LGTBIQ. *Politica y Sociedad, 50*(3), 763–770.

Cabral, A. (1970). National Liberation and Culture. *The Journal of Pan African Studies, 3*(5), 1–8.

Cajete, G. (2004). Philosophy of Native Science. In A. Waters (Ed.), *American Indian Thought: Philosophical Essays* (pp. 45–57). Cambridge: Wiley-Blackwell.

Calderon, D. (2014). Anticolonial Methodologies in Education: Embodying Land and Indigeneity in Chicana Feminisms. *Journal of Latino/Latin American Studies, 6*(2), 81–96.

Cannon, M. J. (2012). Changing the Subject in Teacher Education: Centering Indigenous, Diasporic, and Settler Colonial Relations. *Cultural and Pedagogical Inquiry, 4*(2), 21–37.

Dei, G. J. S. (2006). Introduction: Mapping the Terrain—Towards a New Politics of Resistance. In G. J. S. Dei & A. Kempf (Eds.), *Anticolonialism and Education: The Politics of Resistance* (pp. 1–23). Rotterdam: Sense Publishers.

Dei, G. J. S. (2009). The Anticolonial Theory and the Question of Survival and Responsibility. In A. Kempf (Ed.), *Breaching the Colonial Contract: Anti-colonialism in the US and Canada* (pp. 251–257). New York: Springer.

Dei, G. J. S., & Asgharzadeh, A. (2001). The Power of Social Theory: The Anti-colonial Discursive Framework. *The Journal of Educational Thought, 35*(3), 297–323.

Dei, G. J. S. (2012). Indigenous Anti-colonial Knowledge as 'Heritage Knowledge' for Promoting Black/African Education in Diasporic Contexts. *Decolonization: Indigeneity, Education and Society, 1*(1), 102–119.

Fanon, F. (1963). *The Wretched of the Earth*. New York: Grove Press.

Fanon, F. (1967). *Black Skin, White Masks*. New York: Grove Press.

Freire, P. (1993). *Pedagogia de la esperanza: un reencuentro con la pedagogia del oprimido*. Mexico: Siglo Veintiuno Editores.

Giroux, H. A. (2014). Youth in Revolt: The Battle Against Neoliberal Authoritarianism. *Critical Arts, 28*, 103–110.

Haig-Brown, C. (2009). Decolonizing Diaspora: Whose Traditional Land Are We On? *Cultural & Pedagogical Inquiry, 1*(1), 73–90.

Hill, S. M. (2008). 'Travelling Down the River of Life Together in Peace and Friendship Forever': Haudenosaunee Land Ethics and Treaty Arrangements as the Basis for Restructuring the Relationship with the British Crown. In L. Simpson (Ed.), *Lighting the Eighth Fire: The Liberation, Resurgence, and Protection of Indigenous Nations*. Winnipeg: Arbeiter Ring Publishing.

Huckle, J. (2008). Sustainable Development. In J. Arthur, I. Davies, & C. Hahn (Eds.), *The SAGE Handbook of Education for Citizenship and Democracy* (pp. 342–355). London: Sage.

Joshee, R. (2004). Citizenship and Multicultural Education in Canada: From Assimilation to Social Cohesion. In J. A. Banks (Ed.), *Diversity and Citizenship Education: Global Perspectives* (pp. 127–156). San Francisco: Jossey-Bass.

Kempf, A. (2009). Contemporary Colonialism: A Transhistorical Perspective. In A. Kempf (Ed.), *Breaching the Colonial Contract: Anti-colonialism in the US and Canada* (pp. 13–34). New York: Springer.

Khalfa, J. (2005). My Body, This Skin, This Fire: Fanon on Flesh. *Wasafiri, 20*(44), 42–50.

Lavallee, L. F., & Poole, J. M. (2010). Beyond Recovery: Colonization, Health and Healing for Indigenous People in Canada. *International Journal Mental Health Addiction, 8*, 271–281.

Lopes, C. (2006). Amilcar Cabral: A Contemporary Inspiration. *African Identities, 4*(1), 1–5.

Mancera-Valencia, F. J. (2015). Introduccion: La descolonización del saber y conocimiento tradicional. In F. J. Mancera-Valencia (Ed.), *Patrimonio biocultural de Chihuahua* (pp. 117–146). Chihuahua: Instituto Chihuahuense de la Cultura.

Mbembe, A. (2003). Necropolitics. *Public Culture, 15*(1), 11–40.

Sandoval, C. (2000). *Methodology of the Oppressed*. Minneapolis: University of Minnesota Press.

Singer, J. (1999). Why Can't You Be Normal for Once in Your Life? In M. Corker & S. French (Eds.), *Disability Discourse* (pp. 59–64). Buckingham: Open University Press.

Sutton, S. E. (2007). A Social Justice Perspective on Youth and Community Development: Theorizing the Processes and Outcomes of Participation. *Children, Youth and Environments, 17*(2), 616–645.
Taylor, C. (2014). Biopower. In D. Taylor (Ed.), *Michel Foucault: Key Concepts* (pp. 41–54). New York: Routledge.
Tone, E. F. M. (2010). La Chakana como elemento posibilitador de la integración latinoamericana. *Pensamiento y Cultura en Colombia y en America Latina, 31*(102), 17–24.
Tuck, E., & McKenzie, M. (2015). Relational Validity and the "Where" of Inquiry: Place and Land in Qualitative Research. *Qualitative Inquiry, 21*(7), 633–638.
Tuck, E., McKenzie, M., & McCoy, K. (2014). Land Education: Indigenous, Post-colonial, and Decolonizing Perspectives on Place and Environmental Education Research. *Environmental Education Research, 20*(1), 1–23.
Tuck, E., & Yang, K. W. (2012). Decolonization Is Not a Metaphor. *Decolonization: Indigeneity, Education & Society, 1*(1), 1–40.
Tuck, E., & Yang, K. W. (Eds.). (2014). *Youth Resistance Research and Theories of Change*. New York: Routledge.
Wane, N. N. (2011). Reclaiming Our Spirituality: A Pedagogical Tool for Feminism and Activism. *Canadian Women's Studies, 29*(1/2), 159–170.
Wynter, S. (2001). Towards the Sociogenic Principle: Fanon, Identity, the Puzzle of Conscious Experience, and What It Is Like to Be "Black". In M. F. Duran-Cogan & A. Gomez-Moriana (Eds.), *National Identities and Sociopolitical Changes in Latin America* (pp. 30–66). New York: Routledge.

CHAPTER 14

Community, Schooling, and the Education of Racialized Students: A Postscript

Carl E. James

In his essay, "Be a good citizen or else! Neoliberal citizenship and the Grade Six 2013 revised Ontario Social Studies Curriculum," Ardavan Eizadirad (Chapter 9) explores both the personal and the State's conceptualization of citizenship noting the "socio-culturally constructed boundaries and psychological shackles that indoctrinate our minds" primarily through institutions such as schools. Utilizing the lens of neo-liberalism, with its emphasis on individualism, neutrality, merit, colour-blindness, personal responsibility, and self-regulation, he shows how the Ontario Social Studies curriculum inscribes a notion of citizenship that excludes those who are not "old stock Canadians"—to use former Prime Minister Stephen Harper's term (see Gollom, *CBC News*, 2015). For even as Canada boasts of its carefully curated multi-cultural image—which is premised on neo-liberalism and promulgated through school programs and educational curricula—the presence and experiences of Indigenous and racialized people and communities continue to be discounted (see Benn-John, Chapter 4). Indeed, as Eizadirad

C. E. James (✉)
Jean Augustine Chair in Education, Community & Diaspora,
York University, Toronto, ON, Canada
e-mail: cjames@yorku.ca

© The Author(s) 2019
F. J. Villegas and J. Brady (eds.), *Critical Schooling*,
https://doi.org/10.1007/978-3-030-00716-4_14

suggests, school curricula are not student-centred, which make the need for the "important conversation(s)" in which contributors to this volume engage us.

In contributing to this conversation, I highlight the usefulness of a student-centred approach noting how community—as a geographic space (e.g. place of residence) and social grouping (e.g. ethnic, immigrant, and/or social identification)—mediates school participation and education performance of students. Indeed, Villegas and Brady (Chapter 1) raise a number of questions related to community observing the interlocking relationship of communities, their members, and the schooling and education of young people (see also Chapter 7, Calero and Chica). It is helpful to recognize, as Villegas and Brady (Chapter 1) signal, the distinction between schooling and education. For while they are overlapping processes; as Shujaa (1993) points out, "You can have one without the other" (p. 328).

My interest here is with the schooling and education of marginalized and racialized students for whom race and socio-economic status operate as barriers to their educational outcomes. And consistent with critical theories such as anti-colonialism, anti-racism, Black feminism, Queer Theory and others, which inform the essays in this volume, I draw on Critical Race Theory (CRT) to explore the place of race in the experiences, circumstances, and life trajectories of students (see Anderson & McCormack, 2010; Gillborn, 2015; Howard, 2008; James, 2011; Milner, 2008). CRT points out that

- inequity exists in society and is sustained by such structures as racism, classism, sexism, homophobia, xenophobia;
- race operates as a central component in the identification of members of society, and simultaneously intersects with gender, class, ethnicity, language, sexuality, and other demographic factors;
- racialization operates to essentialize racialized people, thereby ignoring intragroup differences and diversity;
- the dominant Eurocentric perspective or discourse obviates others and must be challenged;
- the work of critical theorists is to expose and challenge the myth of multiculturalism as advancing policies and programs that serve to foster harmony among the culturally and racially diverse population;
- racism is manifested largely by pointing to cultural differences as intractable and not merely through biological differences;

- context, and how it informs contemporary social, political, economic, cultural situations, and issues, is important to any analyses of the situations and experiences of individuals. These situations and experiences must necessarily be historicized;
- the specificity of the experiences of various racialized groups must be acknowledged, in order to address their racialization experiences;
- equity—giving attention to individual differences; and not equality—treating individuals the *same*—must be the foundation to serving individuals;
- counter-narratives or counter storytelling are central to presentation of the voices and experiences of racialized people;
- the positionality of researchers, authors, teachers, etc. must be made explicit for it informs the ideas expressed.

Inherent tensions (see Villegas & Brady, Chapter 1) notwithstanding, CRT is a useful framework for examining (and exposing) racial inequities that structure the schooling opportunities, educational performance, and academic achievements of racialized students with attention to how notions of fairness, equity, meritocracy, colour blindness, and neutrality operate in the lives and educational trajectory of students.

Space is important in any analyses of how racial inequity operates in the schooling and education of students—for as Shabazz (2015) writes, "physical space and where one is located within it tell us much about [them]" (p. 1). In other words, the residential area, community, or neighbourhood in which students and parents reside plays a consequential role in the construction of their identities and the meanings that they make of themselves and others of them—all of which serve to explain their world and highlight what is particular and/or different about them (Shabazz, 2015, p. 46). The fact is, communities or neighbourhoods are "often a more tangible manifestation of systemic racial inequalities" (Neely & Samura, 2011, p. 1940). And as Knowles (2003) asserts:

> Space is an active archive of the social processes and social relationships composing racial orders. Active because it is not just a monument, accumulated through a racial past and present – although it is also that – it is active in the sense that it interacts with people and their activities as an ongoing set of possibilities in which race is fabricated. (p. 80)

Insofar as communities are not neutral spaces (Shabazz, 2015), but with their accorded meaning and reputation—based on, among other characteristics, location (inner city, urban area), history, who resides there, how residents' bodies are read, and media representation—they play a significant role in the life trajectory of individuals.

Therefore, in serving communities, institutions, like schools, either help to maintain the meanings and reputation of the neighbourhoods where they are located or help to construct a counter-narrative and identity of the community. This is done in middle-class neighbourhoods where teachers and school administrators work to support the reputation of the community/neighbourhood, as well as the needs, interests, and aspirations of students in ways that ensure their educational success. Ultimately, awareness of the communities and its residents is critical if teachers are to create an educational program and curriculum that is relevant and responsive to the expectations of students and parents. Doing so, necessarily must be from the perspective of their students, and listening to how their perspectives are informed by the community in which they reside, the reputation of the school, and the messages from and relationship with individuals around them—parents, peers, teachers, and significant others (e.g. coaches, extended family members, fictive kin).

Here is how Sam Tecle, a former Toronto teacher, explained how his student-centred approach to his teaching and the knowledge gained from hearing directly from his students, shifted his conception of how pedagogy—the exercise of teaching and learning—is conceptualized when attempting to work meaningfully and deeply with students. In what follows, Sam cogently describes how his own pedagogical orientation and teaching philosophy shifted when he "got out of the way." By making space for students' expertise in their own community to come to the fore, the learning and education that occurred was made bidirectional. Sam's account demonstrates how teachers, while having the best of intentions, can sometimes "get in the way" of their students' learning, growth, and development by not creating the space for students to step into the role of teacher, educator, and student simultaneously.

> I tried to design an educational program with an array of cultural resources that I thought would speak to the diverse needs and interests of the students. But my attempts at being a critical and reflexive educator were having no effect on them, and so very little learning was occurring. The ways in which the students reacted to my lessons were all over the place. This continued for a few weeks, until we engaged in a community

walk. I told the students that the assignment was for them to teach me about their community, about their lives, about their individual reality. And with a class of eight students, each student was able to take a turn being the tour guide and explaining significant and meaningful sites in their community. They showed me routes they took walking to school, where they played, which areas they were not to venture into late at night. Many of the students also invited me into their homes. This experience, for me, was informative and paradigm changing. It radically altered the ways I have come to construct, direct, and articulate my pedagogy, as well as altered my perception and orientation toward teaching and learning. And from this experience, a deeper relationship was forged between myself and the students.

While not captured in the above epigraph, Sam grew up, was working, and continues to live in the same community in which these students were living. His visit to the community with his students highlights the point that still, while quite familiar with the community and its history, the students when positioned as expert and educator still had very much to teach Sam about the community, how they saw it, and how they moved, lived, and made a life there. This type of openness and willingness to learn provided Sam and his students a deeper and more meaningful schooling and educational experience.

Another point that should not be missed in Sam's coming to "know" his students is the way in which he gets them to educate him about the context in which they were living their lives, formulating their interests, and finding resources to which they had access—in short, as Sam terms it, "their individual reality." That reality is mediated by the people and issues to which our students are exposed, and hence will vary in relation to economic, social, cultural, and political context, generational differences and parental aspirations. With this information about the students, Sam was well-positioned to create a curriculum and employ a pedagogical approach that was relevant and responsive to his students' interests and learning desires. This is important for it is useful for teachers to know or understand the extent to which students avail themselves of information or comprehend what is being taught at that time is consistent with aims and objective of students (or parents). For instance, in her research of the "social justice pedagogy with suburban and urban elite," Swalwell (2013) observes that in a lesson in which a high school teacher introduced the concept of hegemony, as the teacher paused to write the word on the board and explain, Jennifer [a student] grabbed her notebook and exclaimed, 'Oh! Hegemony – that's a great SAT word. I should write that down!' Rather than expressing curiosity about hegemony as a concept useful for understanding oppressive forms, her interest in learning the word ... stemmed from a desire to enhance her performance on high-stakes tests. (p. 83)

In addition to the insights into the realities of the students that purposeful community visits can provide teachers, can also come to know their students by having them become acquainted with and participate in research projects.[1] For instance, not long ago, I worked in a suburban community school for a school year with Grade 12 students in an *Introduction to Anthropology, Psychology, and Sociology, Grade 11, University Preparation* (HSP3U) course. The teacher and I worked collaboratively to develop a course that provided students with experience in conducting community-based research that was relevant to them. In the first class, students were asked to tell us about their community, thus providing their individual perspective that enabled us as a class to develop a collective narrative of the community. And using a version of the community visit I usually assign to students in the Urban Education class I teach at the university, we asked the Grade 12 students to use the cameras we provided them to capture an element of the community that had a particular appeal or meaning for them. This was taken up in class. A second assignment was for the students to interview their parents (and if they wished, other family members) about the community, their schooling experiences, their interactions with the school, teachers, and administrators, and the education and career aspirations they have or had for them (their children).

These assignments and class discussions provided education about life in the suburb for racialized second-generation Canadian youth—especially for someone like me who has never lived in the suburbs and wanted to make informed contributions to the students' educational process. I was persuaded by the fact that the suburbs had become, and continue to be, the area of choice for both recent and more established immigrant families aspiring for a "heathier life," better opportunities, and upward social mobility for their children. To this end, the growing outer suburban communities surrounding Toronto are places to which families migrate with the belief that these safe and peaceful communities have "good" schools that will provide their children with the necessary education for them to attain their ambitions (James, 2018).[2] So, given the opportunity to get to know one of these suburban neighbourhood schools northwest of Toronto meant studying the educational, social, and familial lives of students. The students who attending the 4-year-old high school at that time were largely second-generation Canadians of South Asian (70%), Black (20%, African and Caribbean) origins. The others were of European and other descent.

The grade twelve students who participated in our study over a two-year period hoped to attain a university (rather than college) education mostly in business, engineering, law, and pharmacy. These areas of study were encouraged by their parents who maintained, as one participant declared: "For Indians, your choices are lawyer, doctor or engineer." But their parents' aspirations were not accompanied by involvement in their children's schooling in ways that teachers expected. In fact, apart from attending parent–teacher meetings and university information sessions, parents did not get involved in routine school activities (such as parent council). Neither did parents call the school for information about their children. One participant explained: "It all goes back to time.... [and with] both parents working late night shift, they are tired at the end of the day." Another cited cultural differences and their parents' limited knowledge of schooling in Canada.

These suburban students generally shared their parents' belief in the possibilities that education affords, as well as their optimism and hope for a "better life" in Canada. They felt that they had a responsibility to their parents who have "sacrificed" to provide for them. One student explained: "Back in India my dad was an engineer, but here he drives a truck...." Therefore, the perception that the large two-car garage houses are occupied by middle-income families belies the vulnerable regrettable economic situation of many students' families—a situation which serves to inspire the students to do well in school.

As indicated above, many parents migrate to the suburbs thinking that these new communities are enough distance from the racialized, "stigmatized" (Wacquant, 2008), and "troubled" (James, 2012) neighbourhoods in urban areas where "disenfranchised immigrants" (Wacquant, p. 1) are believed to reside. It is in some of these "immigrant reception areas" that so-called illegal immigrants are able to find homes. And coupled with the stigma of the residential area and their racialization, those who seek to find refuge in what they might have thought to be a "sanctuary city" are likely to be disillusioned.[3] For seen as "illegals," they are deemed *not* to be honest, socially responsible, and intellectually capable people who would have been favourably screened and approved for residency by "old stock" bureaucrats. And to have children of "undocumented immigrants" in schools that are designed to socialize young people into the existing norms and values of the society and thereby maintain the status quo would be antithetical the mission of schools. Hence, to further Villegas' (Chapter 8) discussion, schools are loathed—and often unwilling—to be seen as sheltering undocumented youth and by extension, their families, hence the policy of "Don't Ask, Don't Tell" (DADT).

Further, as institutions which are structured to advance the values, norms, and aspirations established by European setters—or "old stock Canadians"—at the expense of Indigenous People, schools often operate to maintain the status quo, and do so through their disciplinary measures. In this regard, as Madan (Chapter 2) explains, School Resource Officers (SRO, a euphemism for police officer), over the years have seemingly become part of the school staff. The idea being: that the presence of police officers in schools will help to curb the anti-social, disruptive, and unlawful behaviours of students—especially males who are believed to be gang members or suspected to be "at risk" of becoming gang members.[4] The ethics of punishment through which these schools seek to administer, maintain, and "restore" discipline in students serve to re-enforce inequities and much concern among parents and students. This was made clear in recent (fall, 2016/winter, 2017) research consultations we conducted with community members, parents, educators, youth workers, and school administrators about the schooling of Black students in the Greater Toronto Area (Toronto, and the regions of Peel, York, and Durham) (James, Turner, Tecle, & George, 2017). We heard from participants that the presence of police in schools was having

> a 'devastating effect' on Black students, in that it was contributing to their criminalization and "the entrenchment of the school to prison pipeline." There was a concern that school boards were more likely to place police officers in schools with large Black populations because of the stereotypes of Black students. (p. 57)

In a region outside of Toronto, an educator shared with me that because of the school's large Black student population, there was a nickname that signals it to be a school in which criminal activities were common. And students reported that it is these schools that "school administrators and police were vigilant in seeking out drugs." Yet in schools with predominantly White students, where there was "higher rates of drug use, school administrators were not as vigilant and, as one student reported, 'ignored evidence' of drug use" (p. 58). In the schools where police were present, students reported that "they felt more unsafe than safe, and they minimized their involvement in school activities in order to limit contact with officers." Commenting on this situation, one student claimed that: "Students don't trust the police. They make you feel like a criminal before you even do anything. They instill fear in the school and change the culture" (p. 58).

In the same consultations (James et al., 2017), after presenting disaggregated data on the schooling experiences and educational outcomes of Black students in the Toronto District School Board, participants told us that it was the first time they were shown such quantitative data. Those participants connected to the other school boards, including Catholic school boards, expressed concerns that these school boards were not collecting similar data, and in so doing, were allowing the problems of Black students in their boards to go unacknowledged, unchallenged, and unaddressed. Befittingly, they asked: "What do these other boards not want to know?" Some participants went further to suggest that it is highly likely that the situation of Black students "may even be worse" in these other regions—especially in the marginalized communities—"because of lack of attention to ensuring equitable outcomes for Black students and addressing the racism that they experience" (p. 38). Community advocates argued that the lack of data has allowed school boards to continue to ignore their tireless and incessant calls for systemic change on the basis that the negative experiences and outcomes of Black students are isolated incidents and the result of individual cases (p. 38). Indeed, without data—definitely disaggregated—how will educational officials and practitioners be able to fully understand the particular needs of students based on their race, ethnicity, area of resident, etc.? How will they be able to provide programs, curriculum activities, and pedagogical approaches that are relevant and responsive to the education of students, and thereby make education cost-effective? And with regard to Calero and Cica's work (Chapter 7), how else will parents and community members ascertain equitable educational outcomes for Latinx students? Undeniably, race, class, and religion, like gender, are demographic characteristics that must be taken into account in data collection and analyses.

14.1 IN CONCLUSION

By way of concluding, I offer what I refer to as Community-Referenced Approach to Education (CRAE) which places students and their communities at the centre of their schooling and education. I am reminded here of a question posed by a youth worker during a discussion of the educational problems of students residing in marginalized communities. She asked: How is it that in many cases, extra funding is provided to schools to address the educational issues of students in these communities, yet nothing changes? The answer: Were students, their parents, and community members ever consulted about their programs that should be put in place? Truly, we would struggle to find teachers, educators, school administrators, and funders who talk to students about a schooling program that would be appropriate or satisfactory to them. The point is, education for students, should be about them and should involve consulting them. To this end, CRAE

- begins with an understanding that students exist in relation to their communities and in turn the larger economic, political, and social structure of society;
- recognizes that the cultures of the communities that help to shape students' behaviours, and frame their perceptions of needs, interests, potentials, expectations, and aspirations;
- engages with students' families and community-informed social and cultural capital in making learning relevant to students;
- Encourages the integration of knowledge from *and* of the community in building teacher–learner relationships;
- utilizes the backgrounds and experiences of the students to develop curricula resources, pedagogical tools, and schooling programs to meet their needs, interests, and aspirations;
- ensures that the lessons, curricula, pedagogy, resources, and programs help students to make sense of their community, their social circumstances, and the relationships with others;
- works with students to develop the relevant skills, talents, and capacities to effectively learn, live, play, and work in their communities and society in general;
- promotes critical reading of the media thereby encouraging deconstructing the reports and representations of their communities to show the inherent biases structured in all reporting;

– participates in the collection and use of data to understand the gaps in the schooling and education of students in relation to the structured opportunities and possibilities afforded them.

Acknowledgements Thanks to Sam Tecle for telling me about his experiences with students as he endeavoured to create an educational program that was meaningful to them.

Notes

1. Indeed, research, and Youth Participatory Action Research (Fine, 2012) is an important advocacy tool for not only does it provide evidence of the issues/problem that youth find important, it is something that is conducted "with" and/or "by" youth as opposed to "on" youth.
2. But in the Urban Education classes, there are often discussions about "urban-like" schools with similar problems as those in Toronto's disenfranchised communities, and where the police presence in schools is evident.
3. This postscript was written at a time when many Torontonians were expressing concern with gangs and gun-violence, particularly among racialized youth (and Black youth in particular), which were resulting in a significant number of civilian deaths including children. This concern with gangs was also occurring at a period when Ontario politicians—including the premier—were calling for the Federal Government to step in to control the flow of "illegal immigrants" into Toronto.
4. The number of shooting incidents in Toronto over the past seven months (January–July 2018)—many believed to be gang related involving racialized young men—have Torontonians calling for the re-instatement of the SROs in those schools boards where they have been removed from the schools; and in boards where this continues to be the practice, there are calls for the these "disciplinary agents" to remain in schools.

References

Anderson, E., & McCormack, M. (2010). Intersectionality, Critical Race Theory, and American Sporting Oppression: Examining Black and Gay Male Athletes. *Journal of Homosexuality, 57,* 949–967.

Fine, M. (2012). Youth Participatory Action Research. In N. Lesko & S. Talburt (Eds.), *Keywords in Youth Studies: Tracing Affects Movements Knowledges* (pp. 318–324). New York: Routledge.

Gillborn, D. (2015). Intersectionality, Critical Race Theory, and the Primacy of Racism: Race, Class, Gender, and Disability in Education. *Qualitative Inquiry, 21*(3), 277–287.

Gollom, M. (2015, September 19). Stephen Harper's 'Old-Stock Canadians': Politics of Division or Simple Slip? *CBC News.* http://www.cbc.ca/news/politics/old-stock-canadians-stephen-harper-identity-politics-1.3234386.

Howard, T. C. (2008). Who Really Cares? The Disenfranchisement of African American Males in Prek-12 Schools: A Critical Race Theory Perspective. *Teachers College Record, 110*(5), 954–985.

James, C. E. (2011). Students "At Risk": Stereotyping and the Schooling of Black Boys. *Urban Education, 47*(2), 464–494.

James, C. E. (2012). *Life at the Intersection: Community, Class and Schooling.* Halifax: Fernwood Educational Publishing.

James, C. E. (2018). "Singled Out": Being a Black Youth in the Suburbs. In L. Foster, L. Jacobs, & B. Siu (Eds.), *Racial Profiling and Human Rights in Canada: The New Legal Landscape* (pp. 133–151). Toronto: Irwin Law.

James, C. E., Turner, T., Tecle, S., & George, R. (2017, April). *Towards Race Equity in Education: The Schooling of Black Students in the GTA.* The Jean Augustine Chair in Education, Community & Diaspora, Faculty of Education, York University. http://edu.yorku.ca/files/2017/04/Towards-Race-Equity-in-Education-April-2017.pdf.

Knowles, C. (2003). *Race and Social Analysis.* London: Sage.

Milner, H. R. (2008). Critical Race Theory and Interest Convergence as Analytic Tools in Teacher Education Policies and Practices. *Journal of Teacher Education, 59*(4), 332–346.

Neely, B., & Samura, M. (2011). Social Geographies of Race: Connecting Race and Space. *Ethnic and Racial Studies, 34*(11), 1933–1952.

Shabazz, R. (2015). *Spatializing Blackness: Architectures of Confinement and Black Masculinity in Chicago.* Urbana and Chicago: University of Illinois Press.

Shujaa, M. J. (1993). Education and Schooling: You Can Have One Without the Other. *Urban Education, 27*(4), 328–351.

Swalwell, K. M. (2013). *Educating Activist Allies: Social Justice Pedagogy with Suburban and Urban Elite.* New York: Routledge.

Wacquant, L. (2008). *Urban Outcasts: A Comparative Sociology of Advanced Marginality.* Cambridge, MA: Polity.

Index

A

Abya Yala, 11, 40, 147, 164, 165, 303, 305, 306
Academics, 1, 13, 85, 100, 226–228, 230, 232–238, 241, 242
Activist, 11, 90, 92, 107, 165, 180, 192, 194, 235, 273, 290, 302, 318
Advocate, 11, 115, 154, 158, 159, 161, 188, 220, 235, 264, 322, 335
African feminism, 10, 76–78
Afro-Caribbean, 10, 100, 101, 104–107, 109–111, 115, 116, 119, 120
Agency, 1, 3, 5, 35, 77, 105, 109, 118, 119, 133, 156, 162, 165, 175, 194, 196, 215, 223, 261, 293, 311, 312, 318
Ancestors, 10, 90–93, 108, 128, 141, 290, 308, 321
Anti-Blackness, 10, 76, 110, 114, 127, 150, 156
Anti-colonial, 7, 8, 10, 15, 77, 78, 90, 94, 107, 126, 130, 131, 133, 135, 136, 139, 142, 144, 226, 276, 289, 292, 300, 301, 303–305, 307–321
Anti-colonial theory, 7, 11, 126, 128, 132, 143, 300, 301
Anti-Indigenous, 10, 16, 76, 131, 139, 150, 162
Anti-racist, 2, 7, 10, 14, 76–78, 94, 107, 139, 148, 226, 227, 236, 269, 272, 273, 275–279, 288–290, 292, 319, 328
Art, 11, 90, 126–128, 130, 132–137, 139, 140, 142–144, 318

B

Banking on education, 14
Belonging, 6, 9, 11, 15, 16, 110, 179
Biocultura, 15, 16, 291, 299–322
Black, 8–10, 16, 22–24, 28, 29, 36, 37, 40, 48–51, 58, 59, 69, 80, 99–101, 106–117, 119, 120, 125, 126, 128, 129, 131, 132, 134, 135, 137–141, 144, 181, 209, 304, 310, 317, 318
Black feminist, 7, 100, 128, 132, 328
Black feminist thought, 7

Border, 12, 13, 35, 129, 143, 175, 177–179, 190–192, 194, 195, 231, 238, 245, 254, 255, 259, 263
Border-crossers, 15, 254, 264
Bourdieu, P., 9, 55–58, 60, 69, 204, 223, 281
Bridging, 14, 118, 246, 251–257, 264, 281

C

Canada, 1, 4–8, 10, 12–15, 27–29, 35, 41, 66, 110, 112, 116, 119, 140, 176, 179, 181, 182, 188, 189, 194, 196, 197, 201, 209–214, 221, 225, 232, 233, 246, 249, 250, 255, 256, 259, 264, 285, 300, 301, 303, 305–307, 309, 318, 320
Citizen, 2, 3, 11–13, 16, 30, 111, 116, 176, 188, 189, 201–208, 211, 213–223, 226, 231, 249, 259, 260, 305, 310, 311
Civic engagement, 12, 157, 207
Classist, 7, 12, 16
Co-creation, 11, 88, 143, 300, 308–312, 320, 321
Colonial, 3, 5, 6, 8–10, 15, 16, 76–79, 81–87, 89–91, 94, 101, 108–110, 112, 125–128, 130–144, 150, 163, 164, 214, 225–234, 236, 237, 239–241, 254, 274, 280, 286, 300–307, 309, 310, 313, 316–321
Communities, 1, 3–6, 8–12, 14–16, 22, 23, 26–33, 35, 38, 40, 41, 51, 62, 63, 66, 68, 76–78, 80, 82, 83, 87, 88, 90, 91, 102–105, 107, 108, 110, 112, 114–120, 127, 132, 134, 136, 137, 139, 142, 147–166, 175, 177, 179, 181, 185, 188, 190, 192, 194–196, 201–209, 216–218, 222, 223, 226, 232, 235–237, 239, 245, 248, 249, 251, 253, 255, 256, 259, 264, 280, 282–284, 287, 289–293, 299–303, 305, 307–322, 327, 329–337
Criminalizing, 8, 176, 196, 248
Critical pedagogy, 14, 16, 130, 152, 153, 271, 272
Curriculum, 6, 13, 48, 49, 51, 61, 62, 70, 76, 78, 81, 83, 86, 87, 89, 91, 93, 100, 112, 113, 121, 126, 136, 151, 152, 155, 156, 186, 187, 202, 205–209, 211–215, 217–222, 237, 273, 276, 279–285, 287, 306, 307, 309, 310, 314, 327, 330, 331, 335

D

Decolonization, 14, 77, 90, 91, 93, 103, 130, 133, 135, 137, 138, 142, 143, 165, 270, 276, 278, 284–287, 291, 307
Dominant, 3, 4, 11, 25, 26, 39, 57, 69, 77, 81, 86, 87, 90, 92, 125, 126, 133, 134, 136, 144, 152, 156, 160–162, 166, 188, 195, 202, 203, 212–214, 217, 230, 237, 239, 276, 300, 301, 320, 328
Don't Ask Don't Tell, 15, 182, 192, 249, 250

E

Education, 2–5, 13, 14, 16, 22–24, 28, 31, 32, 40, 51–54, 58, 61, 67, 68, 75, 76, 78, 81–83, 85, 86, 88–91, 94, 100, 108, 109, 111, 113–117, 119, 126, 127,

130, 142, 148, 149, 151–158, 161, 162, 164–167, 187, 189, 190, 196, 204–206, 209, 211, 212, 217–222, 226, 237–239, 246–252, 254, 270–273, 276–285, 287–293, 300, 302–307, 309–311, 316, 320, 322, 328–330, 332, 333, 335–337

Educator, 4, 8, 13, 14, 16, 22, 26, 28, 31, 37, 40, 54, 55, 57, 58, 65–67, 70, 81, 83, 92, 121, 126, 131, 142–144, 154, 188, 217, 219, 220, 223, 251, 269, 271, 276–278, 282–284, 286–292, 306, 307, 318, 321, 330, 331, 334, 336

Equity, 5, 11, 23, 49, 57, 62, 69, 119–121, 148, 150, 153–156, 161–163, 165, 166, 177, 185–188, 196, 202, 204, 206, 213, 215, 216, 218, 221, 222, 329

F
Freedom of speech, 3
Freire, P., 14, 113, 115, 135, 204, 216, 223, 253, 287, 312
Futurity, 3, 307, 311

G
Gender, 3, 7, 9, 11, 12, 29, 57, 58, 62, 78, 80, 82, 85, 100, 101, 104, 106, 109, 113, 120, 128, 129, 132, 136, 137, 139, 140, 144, 149, 154, 164, 180, 182, 214, 218, 246, 247, 254, 265, 290, 300, 322, 328, 335

H
Hawaii, 14, 271, 290, 292

I
Identity, 2, 9, 11, 15, 57, 79–81, 87, 101, 109, 112, 116, 117, 119–121, 126, 127, 133, 136, 137, 139, 143, 148, 150, 153, 154, 159–163, 165, 209–211, 216, 272, 274, 276, 277, 280, 283, 285, 290, 291, 304–306, 308–310, 313, 320, 322, 330

Indigenous, 5, 10, 14, 15, 23, 24, 77–79, 81–83, 86–94, 126, 127, 129, 131–135, 137, 139, 142–144, 150, 152, 156, 162, 164, 209, 226–230, 237, 239–242, 254, 263, 270–276, 278, 280, 284–292, 300–311, 315, 317, 318, 322, 327, 334

Intersectionality, 11, 104, 111, 159
Invisibility, 10, 76, 79, 81, 89, 109, 227, 274, 276

L
Land, 14, 15, 127, 228, 299–303, 305–308, 311–316, 318, 320–322
Latinx, 11, 24, 40, 147–149, 151–157, 159, 161, 163–167, 246, 257, 304, 310, 335
Liberation, 7, 92, 219, 226, 228, 231, 236, 240, 314, 318

M
Multiculturalism Act, 5

N
Nation, 2, 3, 5, 7, 12, 66, 77, 79, 81, 82, 100, 110, 116, 120, 127, 132, 143, 150, 176–179, 202, 205, 207–209, 211–214,

216–221, 227, 233, 253, 259, 271, 274, 276, 279–281, 284, 287–291, 293, 300, 302–305, 307, 308, 310, 314, 315, 317, 318
Neoliberal, 5, 13, 31, 39, 180, 202, 203, 206, 213, 214, 218, 221, 250, 327

O
Oppression, 2, 7, 12, 77, 80, 84, 85, 92–94, 100, 111–113, 130–132, 144, 149, 150, 155, 163, 165, 166, 187, 196, 203, 210, 215, 217, 223, 252, 255, 259, 300, 302, 305, 310, 317
Other, 12, 79, 81, 290

P
Palestine, 13, 227–236, 238, 240–242
Patriarchy, 3, 80, 83, 106, 107, 112, 132
Pedagogy, 2, 6, 7, 11, 23, 28, 47, 49, 61, 113, 115, 120, 126, 127, 129, 131, 132, 140–143, 152, 202, 215, 218, 222, 253–255, 261, 262, 264, 271, 274, 276, 277, 279–281, 283–285, 287–290, 300, 301, 303, 305–310, 312, 313, 317, 320, 330, 331, 335, 336
Police brutality, 4, 25
Policy, 4, 6, 8, 10, 12, 13, 15, 16, 23, 24, 35, 36, 39, 49, 50, 53, 110, 111, 152, 156, 175–183, 185, 187–190, 192–197, 203, 206, 207, 209, 213, 218, 220, 228, 233, 238, 249, 250, 256, 260, 265, 276, 279, 280, 284, 289, 291, 306, 319, 328, 334

Politics of refusal, 13, 226
Politics of urgency, 2, 13, 226–228
Power, 2, 7, 13, 25, 26, 32, 37–39, 41, 48, 57–60, 62, 67, 69, 76, 78, 79, 92, 94, 100, 103, 120, 130, 131, 137, 144, 155, 160, 183–187, 201–204, 206, 207, 209–212, 215–217, 222, 223, 225, 226, 235, 250, 251, 254, 258, 259, 263, 269, 273, 274, 276, 277, 280, 283, 284, 286, 290, 300, 302, 304, 308–311, 315, 317, 320
Praxis, 2, 8, 14, 16, 92, 126, 127, 132, 144, 277, 278, 286–288, 300, 301, 303, 307, 308
Punish, 8, 9, 37, 48, 53, 64, 202, 206, 235, 277, 334
Push out, 4, 150

R
Racism, 3, 4, 6, 7, 9, 10, 22, 25, 26, 39, 49–51, 58, 59, 69, 76–78, 85, 100, 108, 109, 111, 112, 116, 120, 143, 151, 152, 160, 163, 201, 203, 211, 274, 277, 280, 286, 287, 306, 328, 335
Reclaiming, 15, 132, 133, 309, 320
Re-envision schooling, 6
Representation, 11, 50, 62, 83, 125–128, 130, 131, 133, 135, 136, 142–144, 155, 156, 163, 166, 168, 210–212, 217, 226, 263, 275, 276, 312, 321, 330, 336
Resistance, 3, 6–8, 10, 11, 13, 15, 16, 39, 40, 76–78, 84, 89–94, 100, 102–111, 115, 120, 130, 143, 148, 161, 162, 164, 178, 186, 195, 219, 226, 231, 234, 248, 261, 263, 271, 275, 289, 303, 311, 317, 318

S

Saliency of race, 11, 271, 276, 282, 288, 291
Schooling, 1–10, 12, 14–16, 28, 39, 66, 76, 82, 88, 100, 112, 119–121, 126, 140, 148–150, 152, 155, 157, 177, 178, 180–182, 184–196, 201, 202, 225, 238, 246, 247, 249, 254, 257, 264, 269–272, 274–276, 280–282, 284, 289, 291, 293, 299, 303, 305, 309, 310, 317, 319, 320, 328, 329, 331–337
School Resource Officers (SROs), 8, 15, 21–38, 50, 51, 156, 334
Sexism, 9, 10, 76–78, 107, 108, 328
Social location, 1, 11, 16, 67, 78, 85, 104, 126, 127, 133, 135–137, 143, 144, 220, 226, 247, 252, 253
Solidarity, 3, 120, 166, 179, 207, 223, 231, 233, 234, 238, 240, 316, 318, 321
Spirit, 82, 92, 103, 108, 114, 132, 271, 277, 284, 287, 288, 290–292, 302, 304, 306, 319
Spiritual harm, 3, 83
Standards of beauty, 11, 137
Systemic violence, 1, 9

T

Teacher, 3, 4, 8, 14, 22, 25, 31, 36, 48, 49, 52, 54, 59–65, 67–69, 112, 113, 136, 180, 192, 201, 202, 209, 216, 218–222, 246, 249, 252, 256, 258, 260, 264, 270–292, 309, 310, 315, 318–320
Tkaronto, 15, 302, 303, 306, 309, 315, 317–319, 321
The 2013 revised Social Studies curriculum, 13, 208, 211, 213–216, 218–222

U

Undocument, 6, 12, 23, 36, 175–196, 245–249, 253, 255–260, 265, 317, 334

W

White, 5–7, 9, 10, 16, 29, 38, 50, 76, 78–81, 83–86, 89, 90, 105, 129–132, 134, 135, 137–141, 176, 204, 209, 214, 231, 271, 272, 276, 283, 291, 302, 310
White supremacy, 3, 4, 6, 10, 83, 85, 106, 109, 112, 113, 136, 138, 139, 150, 209, 228, 241, 255, 274, 276, 277, 289, 292

Z

Zero-tolerance, 8, 24, 39

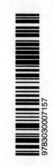